Conversion to Christianity

Conversion to Christianity

Historical and Anthropological Perspectives on a Great Transformation

EDITED AND WITH AN INTRODUCTION BY

Robert W. Hefner

UNIVERSITY OF CALIFORNIA PRESS

Berkeley Los Angeles Oxford

University of California Press
Berkeley and Los Angeles, California

University of California Press, Ltd.
Oxford, England

Library of Congress Cataloging-in-Publication Data

Conversion to Christianity : historical and anthropological perspectives on a great transformation / edited and with an introduction by Robert W. Hefner.
p. cm.
Includes bibliographical references and index.
Contents: World building and the rationality of conversion / Robert W. Hefner—From the Jesus movement toward institutional church / Howard Clark Kee—The local and the global in southern African religious history / Terence Ranger—Of faith and commitment, Christian conversion in Muslim Java / Robert W. Hefner—Conversion and colonialism in northern Mexico / William L. Merrill —Conversion and community in Amazonia / Donald K. Pollock—We are Ekelesia [sic] / John Barker—Religion, morality, and prophetic traditions / Aram A. Yengoyan—Why the Thai are not Christians / Charles F. Keyes—The glyphomancy factor / David K. Jordan.
ISBN 0-520-07835-7 (cloth : alk. paper).—ISBN 0-520-07836-5 (pbk. : alk. paper)
1. Conversion. 2. Converts. 3. Missions—Anthropological aspects. 4. Religion and politics. 5. Region and culture. I. Hefner, Robert W., 1952– .
BV4916.C67 1993
248.2′4—dc20
92-3113
CIP

Printed in the United States of America
9 8 7 6 5 4 3 2 1

The paper used in this publication meets the minimum requirements of American National Standard for Information Sciences—Permanence of Paper for Printed Library Materials, ANSI Z39.48-1984. ♾

CONTENTS

PREFACE

Recently the topic of religious conversion has been at the center of discussion in several academic disciplines. From the start of our dialogue, therefore, the contributors to this volume sought to speak across disciplinary boundaries and address colleagues in anthropology, sociology, history, theology, and religious studies. Early versions of some of the chapters in this book were presented at a conference on "Conversion to World Religions: Historical and Ethnographic Interpretations," held at Boston University, April 14–15, 1988. Over the next two years many of the participants continued the dialogue begun at that meeting, which has resulted in the present volume.

I wish to express my thanks to the officers of Boston University and, in particular, its Humanities Foundation for their generous support of the original conference. Two scholars presented important papers at that meeting but, in the end, were unable for personal reasons to contribute their essays to this book: Michele Salzman of the Classics Department at Boston University and Jean Comaroff of the Department of Anthropology at the University of Chicago. I wish to express my special gratitude to Dr. Comaroff, whose critical insight greatly influenced the subsequent revision of several of the papers.

Jacob K. Olupuna of Amherst College, Dana Robert of Boston University, and Stanley J. Tambiah of Harvard University also participated in the conference. I owe special thanks to Dr. Tambiah, whose comments and scholarship influenced my own analysis of religious rationality, and to Dr. Robert, whose expertise as a Christian missiologist helped many of the anthropologists at the conference to see Christian missionizing "from the other side." I should also thank Michael Lambeck, Michael Peletz,

Nancy J. Smith-Hefner, Robert Weller, Peter Wood, and, especially, Rita Smith Kipp for their patient help in reading and commenting on the introduction to this volume. Responsibility for its argument is, of course, my own. I also wish to thank Peter L. Berger, director of the Institute for the Study of Economic Culture at Boston University. Though not directly involved in this volume, through his example and urging Peter has shown me the importance of dialogue like that attempted here between anthropology, sociology, religion, and history. Finally, at the University of California Press, I am grateful to my editor, Sheila Levine, for once again showing great patience and good humor with me.

The purpose of this volume was to address a phenomenon of broad historical and cross-cultural importance and to do so in a way that contributed to the growing awareness that most important intellectual issues are best dealt with across conventional disciplinary boundaries. Those of us who contributed to this volume came to feel that the effort ultimately revises one's understanding of that phenomenon and the place of one's discipline in the larger horizon of intellectual life. Something of the catholic nature of our own "conversion experience" will, we hope, be apparent to the readers of this book.

R. Hefner

NOTES ON CONTRIBUTORS

John Barker, the editor of *Christianity in Oceania* (1990), is assistant professor of anthropology at the University of British Columbia.

Robert W. Hefner, associate professor of anthropology and associate director of the Institute for the Study of Economic Culture at Boston University, writes on religion, politics, and economic change and is currently preparing a book on Islam and modernity in Southeast Asia.

David K. Jordan is professor of anthropology at the University of California, San Diego, and the author of numerous works on Chinese religion and culture.

Howard Clark Kee is professor of New Testament, emeritus, at Boston University and the author of many works on early Christianity and the New Testament, including the widely read *Understanding the New Testament* and *Christian Origins in Sociological Perspective*.

Charles F. Keyes is professor of anthropology and Southeast Asian studies at the University of Washington. His most recent book is *Reshaping Local Worlds: Education and Cultural Change in Rural Southeast Asia* (New Haven: Yale University Southeast Asian Studies).

William L. Merrill is curator of western North American ethnology in the Department of Anthropology, National Museum of Natural History, Smithsonian Institution. He has conducted research on the culture and history of the Rarámuri Indians of Chihuahua, Mexico, since 1977 and is currently completing a cultural and social history of northern Mexico.

Donald K. Pollock teaches anthropology at the State University of New York at Buffalo, and conducts research on the culture and social organization of medicine, including indigenous ethnomedicine in Brazil, Western biomedicine, and cultural dimensions of psychiatric illness.

Terence Ranger is Rhodes Professor of Race Relations at St. Antony's College, Oxford, and the author of many books on African history and Christianity.

Peter Wood, assistant provost and adjunct assistant professor in the Department of Anthropology at Boston University, studies Catholic sectarianism and American religious movements.

Aram A. Yengoyan is professor of anthropology at the University of California, Davis, and the author of numerous studies on the culture and history of Aboriginal Australia, the Philippines, and the Pacific region.

PART ONE

Introduction

CHAPTER ONE

Introduction: World Building and the Rationality of Conversion

Robert W. Hefner

The conventional wisdom in the historiography of the ancient world is that the emergence of what we call civilization was marked by the rise of the state, government bureaucracy, writing, and a complex division of labor. Less widely noted, but of equal import, was the conversion of tribal and nonstate peoples to more socially expansive and doctrinally formalized religions, including those today identified as "historic" or "world" religions. For many peoples, it would appear, incorporation into a broader social order brought not just technological and political transformations of traditional lifeways but far-reaching adjustments in the canons of divinity, identity, and social ethics as well.[1] Here is a development at the origins of the world we call civilized, but one about which there is surprisingly little intellectual consensus.

What makes this phenomenon all the more intriguing is that conversion to more inclusive or world religions is not just a distant event in an unknowable past but a process that continues in the backlands and barrios of the developing world today. Indeed, though empires and economic orders have come and gone, the world religions have survived. They are, we might say, the longest lasting of civilization's primary institutions. Just why this is so is an important question: it challenges our understanding of "traditional" and "world" religions, forces us to reflect on how people become converted from one form of religion to another, and shows how deeply religious reformation is implicated in the making of the modern world.

This world-building aspect of religious conversion is the focus of the essays in this volume. All examine the twin phenomena of Christian conversion and Christianization—the reformulation of social relations, cultural meanings, and personal experience in terms of putatively Christian ideals. Though studies of conversion have traditionally privileged its psychology (or, all too often, a reification of that psychology),[2] the authors of these essays explore Christian conversion in its full complexity —sociological and historical, cultural and psychological. Rather than elevate the individual experience of conversion above the social world, they examine how social and individual processes interact over time. The studies reveal that conversion takes many forms. Not always an exclusivistic change of religious affiliation requiring the repudiation of previously held beliefs (Nock 1933), conversion assumes a variety of forms because it is influenced by a larger interplay of identity, politics, and morality.

A second characteristic of these studies is that they explore Christianity as a world religion rather than as a uniquely Eurocentric one.[3] This cross-cultural focus speaks to the reality of Christianity in the premodern and modern eras and to how it has shaped our world. It highlights what is distinctive about Christian conversion and how it relates to the more general reformation of religion and moral authority that marks human history. Why do people convert? Why are some cultures so resistant to Christian appeals while others eagerly embrace the faith? Does the widespread incidence of conversion to Christianity and other world religions suggest convergence in the development of religion, ethics, and authority across cultures?

A comparative understanding of these questions promises to be of interest not only for anthropology and sociology but also for comparative politics, ethical history, and, indeed, our understanding of the civilized world. My intent in the present chapter is to outline something of this broader context. I will emphasize two points from the start. First, though most of the discussion in these essays centers on Christianity, my remarks here are necessarily broader. For the sake of comparison, I speak of Christianity as a species of world religion and seek to explore the differences between world religions and the other great family of religions referred to, much too generally, as traditional.

When used in too bipolar a fashion, the categories of traditional and world religion are simplistic and reinforce certain prejudices of the putative rationality of the modern world and the irrational traditionalism of the premodern. Most such modernist generalities are of little analytic value. But one distinction made between traditional and world religions points to something quite real: only a few religions have shown great success in propagating themselves over time and space. This seemingly obvious aspect of their sociohistorical distribution, we shall see, has had some not-so-obvious influences on the ideals and social organization of the faiths we call world religions.

Situating Christianity in history and in relation to other world religions, the discussion which follows departs somewhat from anthropological research on Christianity and indeed from the focus of some of the other essays in this volume. Recent anthropological work has emphasized that Christianity in a cross-cultural context is far less socially and ideologically monolithic than the "salvationist orthodoxy" (Schneider and Lindenbaum 1987:4) often attributed to it. Contrary to essentialist characterizations of its meaning, Christianity has demonstrated a remarkable ability to take on different cultural shadings in local settings (Badone 1990; Boutilier et al. 1978; Saunders 1988; Schneider and Lindenbaum 1987). The Christian message of individual salvation, for example, has often been marginalized or recast to meet communal needs; elsewhere, believers have been inclined to seek blessing not simply for otherworldly ends but also for "the fulfillment of needs and desires in the here and now" (French Smith 1988:42; cf. Schneider and Lindenbaum 1987:2).

Having refuted the myth of the Christian monolith, however, we must not fall into the converse error of extreme cultural particularism, so thoroughly deconstructing Christianity as to conclude that it is really no more than a congeries of local traditions. Though, in absolute terms, all religions and all cultures are unique, the faiths we know as world religions show striking continuities over time and space. This simple fact indicates their social and moral distinctiveness.

The second point I should stress is that my discussion of the social science commentary on conversion is inevitably selective, designed less to provide an exhaustive history of ideas than to highlight a few recurring themes. Central among these are the nature of the world religions and the source of their remarkable social power. Wherein originates the capacity of these religions to challenge the received lifeways and moral imagination of people incorporating into the civilized social order? Is it a function of the association of these religions with imperial or hegemonic powers? Is conversion, then, first and foremost a colonization of consciousness? Alternately, or in addition, do Christianity and the other world religions embody a cultural logic uniquely adapted to the challenge of the civilized macrocosm?

Whatever our answers to these questions, this much is clear: human history bears witness to the enormous, and sometimes tragic, power of the world religions. Originating in ancient times and thriving still today, they are among the deepest and most enduring of the great transformations that have given us our world. An understanding of these religions and of how people are converted to them must be at the center of any truly comparative study of religion.

CONVERSION TO WORLD RELIGIONS

Though conversion to world religions seems to recur in the civilizing process, understanding it has challenged students of religion and social theory for well over a century. In part this difficulty reflects a chronic lack of agreement on what, if anything, distinguishes traditional and world religions. Does their difference lie, as is often suggested, in the intellectual rigor and social complexity of the world religions? How do we explain the peculiar origins of the world religions in ancient empires and their expansion through to modern times? As these questions indicate, theoretical accounts of conversion have long been entangled in debates concerning the nature of cultural evolution and the rationality of different types of religion.

In the late nineteenth and early twentieth centuries Western scholars had ready answers to all these questions. In their view world religions could be distinguished by their greater intellectual coherence and moral rigor. Primitive religions, by contrast, were regarded as murky amalgams of magical delusion and fetishist taboo. They lack any real system of ethics, it was said, and develop their doctrines opportunistically as the needs of their practitioners require. As a society's intellectual and technical equipment evolves, however, the need for such traditionalist placebos diminishes. Conversely, the need for a more systematic and ethical cosmology increases, predisposing people to the higher truth of the world faiths (Frazer 1922; Tylor 1913; cf. Douglas 1966; Tambiah 1990).

According to this late–nineteenth-century view, then, both the development of the world religions and, by implication, the decision of an individual or a community to convert are part of an inevitable march toward human enlightenment. Like all of culture the history of religion is one of upward evolution, toward greater reason and deeper ethical awareness. Herein, too, lay the impetus for conversion to world religions.[4]

Although this view of religious evolution reflected assumptions once widespread in the West, it failed to provide a convincing account of religion's cross-cultural reality. Premised as it was on a unilinear view of cultural evolution, the model was unable to explain variation in ritual and ethics among societies that seemed, by other measures, to be at the same "stage" of social development. As anthropological research into small-scale societies intensified during the twentieth century, it became increasingly apparent that though some "primitives" were practical-minded and indifferent toward matters of religion others subscribed to richly elaborate and deeply ethical cosmologies (Douglas 1970; Evans-

Pritchard 1956; Horton 1967; Lienhardt 1961). This anthropological research succeeded in abolishing the myth of the monochrome primitive. In so doing it also cast doubt on unilinear models of religious evolution and the theory of conversion they sustained.

Impressive as it was, however, anthropology's antievolutionist critique left unresolved whether global patterns are evident in religious conversion or broad commonalities exist among the civilization-based faiths we call world religions. In the heady triumph of their critique social anthropologists preferred to describe particular societies in detail rather than address comparative concerns. They argued that before sustained historical or cross-cultural comparisons are possible we would need more comprehensive accounts of the range of human communities and the types of religion they support.

During the 1940s and 1950s, then, anthropology developed a richer understanding of small-scale societies than previously available and resisted efforts to reincorporate its insights into a comparative model of cultural development. Other disciplines and other schools within anthropology, however, were less reluctant to take on the topic of religious evolution. In the 1950s and early 1960s, in particular, social theory in the United States saw renewed interest in comparative history and social change. In part this was related to the postwar preoccupation with political-economic development, a concern given theoretical expression in the modernization theories of the era (Hoben and Hefner 1991). Scholars influenced by this approach were not at all averse to presenting their views on the role of religion in history, because, for them, the changing nature of religion illustrated general principles of social development.

WEBER AND WORLD RELIGION

Some of the most influential American social theorists of that postwar period—Talcott Parsons, Edward Shils, Clifford Geertz, and Robert Bellah, among others—looked to the German sociologist Max Weber for their understanding of the reality of religion and the forces for its change. Building on ideas of the nature of magic, science, and religion widespread in the late nineteenth century,[5] Weber had argued that the key feature distinguishing traditional and world religions was the superior rationalization of the latter (Weber 1956; Bendix 1977:87). Traditional religions are piecemeal in their approach to problems of meaning, he believed, but world religions formulate comprehensive responses to the ethical, emotional, and intellectual challenges of human life.

For Weber the ideal-typical representative of traditional religion was the magician, and his portrayal of that role illustrates his view of the cultural divide between traditional and world-historical religions. Rather than develop a sustained ethical relationship with spiritual beings as, Weber believed, later prophetic religions do, the magician seeks to achieve a "coercive" and essentially mechanistic control over the supernatural. The spirit who is the object of such magical coercion, Weber suggested, is only weakly personified; he is more a force to be manipulated than a deity to be dignified with worship (Weber 1956:28, 44; cf. Whimster and Lash 1987:6). Such simpleminded magicality has serious consequences, Weber believed, because it requires little systematic reflection and inspires only "ad hoc" answers to problems of life's meaning (Weber 1956:38). In other words, as the American sociologist Talcott Parsons later put it, Weber saw traditional religion as overwhelmingly instrumental, wielded "in the interest of mundane, worldly concerns: health, long life, defeat of enemies, good relations with one's own people, and the like" (Parsons 1963:xxviii; cf. Bendix 1977:88; Weber 1946:277).

One of the most influential works in the sociology of religion during and after the 1960s is Robert Bellah's (1964) "Religious Evolution." Bellah drew heavily on Weber's insights to provide a comprehensive typology of religious change. Though he spoke of five stages in the development of religion (1964:361), Bellah's evolutionary sequence was still constructed around Weber's basic contrast between primitive and world religions. He observed, for example, that the former are more "compact" in their approach to problems of meaning (1964:359, 363–64). Citing Levy-Bruhl's (now discredited) model of the "primitive mentality,"[6] Bellah argued that traditional religions invade the self "to such an extent that the symbolizations of self and world are only very partially separate" (1964:373). In a similar fashion, he observed, the institutions of primitive religion are poorly differentiated from the rest of society. As a result they provide little intellectual leverage with which to evaluate or criticize received arrangements. In other words, primitive religions are so thoroughly this-worldly in orientation as to be incapable of challenging the status quo (1964:360). Providing little independent or rationalized doctrine, they are essentially conformist toward social conventions.

By contrast, Bellah believed, world religions present an entirely different social mien. Judaism, Christianity, Buddhism, and Islam are all characterized by dualistic cosmologies of "world rejection" (Bellah 1964: 359, 366). Whatever their theological disagreements, these religions agree in proclaiming the existence of a transcendental realm vastly superior to that of everyday reality. In so doing they legitimate salvation quests designed to link humans to that higher realm. Like Weber, Bellah argued that the possibility of redemption is world-shaking in its consequences.

The recognition of a transcendent reality "dualizes" believers' cosmologies in such a way that, at least at times, the received world is evaluated in light of higher ideals and found wanting. Echoing a theme first developed by Weber (1956:58), Bellah observed that this transcendental tension creates pressures for societal reform. The result is nothing less than revolutionary: The mute traditionalism of primitive society, at least as Weber and Bellah saw it, is shattered. Driven by a redemptive vision, world religions have the capacity to remake the world rather than passively accept it.

Bellah's account was subtler than Weber's in its treatment of traditional religion and more balanced in its assessment of the varieties of modern religion. It nonetheless echoed Weber in its stark characterization of traditional society as unreflectively conformist and historic religion as an agent of dynamic reform. As a number of essays in the present volume demonstrate, recent historical and ethnographic research makes such a simple polarity hard to sustain. The model overlooks the tensions and developmental vitality internal to many traditional societies and the organic potentialities of local variants of world religions.[7] Kenelm Burridge (1969), for example, has demonstrated the widespread incidence of prophetic movements of redemptive renewal in Oceania. In a similar fashion Terence Ranger in this volume shows that traditional African religions were sometimes used to challenge extant hierarchies and promote reform rather than, as Bellah's model assumes, blindly legitimate the status quo. Though focused on quite different societies, the essays of David Jordan, Donald Pollock, and Aram Yengoyan in this volume provide similar evidence of the ability of traditional religions to challenge received lifeways and adapt to new social horizons.

Bellah also argued that, over time, religious ideas tend to evolve toward "more differentiated, comprehensive, and in Weber's sense, more rationalized formulations" (Bellah 1964:360). Here again, Bellah regarded rationalization as an event with dramatic consequences for the individual: "For the individual, the historic religions provide the possibility of personal thought and action independent of the traditional social nexus" (Bellah 1965:177). Echoing Emile Durkheim's ideas on mechanical solidarity, Bellah implied that by smothering independent reflection traditional religion impedes individual creativity. Loosening the grip of tradition on the individual, the world religions lay the foundation for human freedom.

In the 1960s and 1970s this vision of religious rationalization was popular in historical sociology and religious studies. More surprising, perhaps, given the cultural relativism that predominates in the field today, the model also had its adherents in American cultural anthropology. There it was associated with no less a figure than Clifford Geertz.[8] Though he balked at embracing a fully evolutionary model and explicitly rejected any variant of unilinear evolutionism, Geertz (1973) described traditional and world religions in essentially the same terms as Bellah. He observed, for example, that the primary difference between traditional and world religions is that the former are organized around a "rigidly stereotyped . . . cluttered arsenal of myth and magic," but the latter "are more abstract, more logically coherent, and more generally phrased." In other words, world religions show "greater conceptual generalization, tighter formal integration, and a more explicit sense of doctrine" (Geertz 1973:171–72). Like Weber and Bellah before him Geertz held that the driving force behind world religions, and the source of their appeal for believers, was religious rationalization. A number of questions remained unresolved by Geertz, however, especially what rationalization means for believers and when and why it occurs.

PROPHECY AND TRANSCENDENCE

Even though they uniformly emphasize that rationalization is fundamental to world religions, scholars in the Weberian tradition disagree on what promotes such systematic cultural reformulation. Is rationalization primarily the product of a cognitive "break-through" (Parsons 1963:xxxiii), in which prophets, priests, or other influential intellectuals formulate new and more comprehensive answers to life's challenges? Can one speak, as some Weberians do, of whole Occidental, Asian, or Muslim rationalities, which permeate entire societies? Or does rationalization proceed unevenly or tentatively, more the consequence of environmental influences than of an underlying ethos or worldview?

No clear consensus on these issues has yet emerged among Weberian social theorists. The confusion that surrounds these topics goes back to Weber himself, who presented several different accounts of the historic causes of rationalization. Weber's early writings were influenced by the Hegelian ethos of late–nineteenth-century German social thought and held that rationalization was intrinsic to social development. As the German historian Wolfgang Mommsen has emphasized, Weber's view implied that social evolution was a "directional and irreversible process in which the principle of rationalization . . . triumphed out of inner necessity" (Mommsen 1987:38). Though consistent with nineteenth-century evolutionary ideas, this view says little about the social arrangements through which this putative principle is realized and substitutes a dubious thesis for a true sociology of knowledge.

In his mature writings, however, Weber pulled back from this rationalist vision of history in favor of a more conditional or circumstantial historiography, in which the social realization of religious (or other) values depends upon their formulation and implementation by different social "carriers." In this sense, as Parsons (1956:xxix) has emphasized, Weber's later writings portray rationalization as a complex process shaped by the interplay of material conditions, social groupings, and value commitments.

Weber's most sustained comments on this interplay appear in his *Economy and Society*, the most relevant portion of which for religious topics was translated into English as *The Sociology of Religion*. In this work Weber observes that a critical influence on the systematization and codification of the world religions was a "closing of their canon" early in their development. By this Weber means that a core body of scripture and dogma was enunciated and then elevated above the rest as sacred and inalterable. In explaining why this took place, Weber makes no reference to the teleological principles of his early work. Instead he cites three influences on the closing of the canon, all of which are related to the sociopolitical conditions in which world religions take shape.

The first cause of doctrinal canonization, Weber observes, is the "struggle between various competing groups and prophecies for the control of the community. Wherever such a struggle failed to occur or wherever it did not threaten the content of the tradition, the formal canonization of the scriptures took place very slowly" (Weber 1956:68). Here, then, Weber sees rationalization as the result of *intra*denominational contests to control doctrines implicated in the organization and leadership of a religious community. The process is motivated in the first instance not by some generalized cultural ethos but by a social contest between different status groups to win followers and institutionalize religious ideals.

A second influence, Weber remarks, is "the struggles of priests against indifference" (1956:71) among the laity. Here too Weber's discussion recognizes a complex interplay of circumstances and ideals in the rationalizing process. He recognizes, of course, that social action is influenced by both material and ideal interests and emphasizes that different status groups are disposed to different ethical styles (Bendix 1977:270). But he implies here that the struggle to promote orthodoxy among the laity may be motivated as much by the priests' desires to defend status privileges as by their commitment to the abstract truth of religious ideals.

Third, Weber writes that the elevation and codification of religious doctrines can occur through the efforts of religious communities to distinguish themselves from rivals. They do so to "make difficult the transference of membership to another denomination" (Weber 1956:71). In this instance, in other words, *inter*denominational competition for followers and, beyond that, for the realization of a certain ideal of human community provides an additional impetus for doctrinal rationalization.

In these, his most succinct comments on the social forces that promote doctrinal rationalization, Weber demonstrates that though he believed in the ability of religious ideas to motivate actors independently he by no means regarded religious rationalization as a self-actualizing historical principle. On the contrary, his explanation is much closer to what contemporary scholars sometimes refer to as a "political economy of meaning" (Eickelman 1979), which emphasizes the interplay of political rivalries, economic interests, and competing visions of moral community in the creation and reformation of cultural meanings.

In Weber's view, however, there was another, more critical dimension to rationalization, one that was less directly determined by the influences governing the closing of the canon. This was doctrinal revelation itself—that is, the initial creation, or revivalist reformulation, of religious truths by prophet-intellectuals working under charismatic inspiration (cf. Bendix 1977:258). Not surprisingly, Weber regarded revelation of doctrine as more idiosyncratic than the institutionalization of canon. The latter is a public process, he observed, shaped by clerical struggles and community rivalries. The revelation of canon, by contrast, depends strongly on the personal brilliance and visionary fervor of a charismatic prophet. As a result it is subject to social-psychological influences more obscure in their geneses than the forces involved in the closing of canon.

As numerous commentators have observed (Bendix 1977:89; Parsons 1963:xxxiii), this discussion of prophecy is one of the most interesting aspects of Weber's analysis of religious rationalization; it is also among the most problematic. It provides the analytic linchpin for his classification of religions into the two great categories of traditional and modern. The overall argument is, in fact, rather simple. The prophet is the voice of antitraditionalism. Since, for Weber traditionalism involves "unthinking acquiescence in customary ways" (Weber 1978:30), he presents the prophet as someone who repudiates custom and denounces the privileged class of religious specialists who have heretofore benefited from the unquestioning traditionalism of the masses. In place of blind conformity the prophet promulgates a higher and more deliberate religious ideal. His challenge is driven by new answers to the problems of meaning and new norms for the regulation of social life:

> Prophetic revelation involves for both the prophet himself and for his followers a unified view of the world derived from a consciously integrated and meaningful attitude toward life. To the prophet, both the life of man and the world, both social and cosmic events, have a certain systematic and coherent meaning. To this meaning the conduct of mankind must be

> oriented if it is to bring salvation, for only in relation to this meaning does life obtain a unified and significant pattern. (Weber 1956:58)

In other words, the prophet is an intellectual who, as Weber says of all intellectuals, "transforms the concept of the world into the problem of meaning" (Weber 1956:125). He does so in a peculiarly comprehensive way, forging a system of meaning organized around "an ultimate and integrated value position" (Weber 1956:69). Then he demands that other people bring their lives into conformity with its urgent, world-building truth. Inasmuch as this value system rejects the world as given, it affirms a transcendent ideal, establishing new standards for the meaning and organization of life. In so doing it also denies the authority of traditional ways and becomes the clarion call for the redemptive transformation of the social world.

Whether this bold appeal is realized is, of course, an issue more complex than the phenomenon of prophetic rationalization alone. If it is to be successfully propagated, revelation has to be further clarified and systematized by a class of literate clerics, and the prophet's followers have to be transformed from a loosely organized charismatic community into a routinized church. But the basic point here is that Weber believed that where embraced by an effectively organized community of followers prophetic ideals can become a force for world transformation as powerful as any in human history. He emphasized this, clearly signaling his central disagreement with Karl Marx concerning the role of (socially organized) ideas in history.[9] The transcendental tension prophetic ideals create—between social reality as it is and as revelation insists it should be—is for Weber the prophet s crowning achievement. It is also the hallmark of the world religions and, ultimately, the source of their remarkable power to transform the world.

Several elements are notable in this account of religious rationalization. Weber's recognition of the role of intellectuals in religious change, first of all, is a useful corrective to the more romantically collective models of historical change typical of much social theory, especially that associated with the variants of Marxism and Durkheimism that influenced sociology and anthropology in the 1960s and 1970s. To this day Weberian sociology is distinguished by its recognition of the formative role of intellectuals in social change.

Weber's model has less felicitous aspects, however. First, as noted earlier, Weber's emphasis on prophecy overlooks the fact that prophets do arise in otherwise traditional societies (Burridge 1969; Evans-Pritchard 1956; Lienhardt 1961). Though, as I will suggest below, prophetic revelation in the world religions has a distinctive content and is subject to a peculiar social management, the occurrence of prophecy and the aspiration for redemptive renewal are by no means confined to the world religions.

Another weakness of Weber's model of prophecy is that at times his portrayal emphasizes charisma so strongly that it implies that this personality trait is the real key to a prophet's success. As numerous scholars have observed (Bourdieu 1987; Burridge 1969), without a broader account of the intellectual and political circumstances in which the prophet's message takes shape this line of reasoning invites a naively heroistic explanation of historical change.[10] Studies of early Christianity (Kee 1980; MacMullen 1966) have consistently demonstrated that more prophecies were "available" prior to and during Jesus' life than were accepted and transformed into sustainable religious movements. The challenge for an interpretive history of prophecy and conversion, then, is to illuminate the broader circumstances that make a prophet's message compellingly real at a given time and place. This is to say that charisma must be understood relationally, with reference not only to the prophet's personality but also to the historical climate that disposes people to respond to it.

Clifford Geertz and Robert Bellah follow Weber in identifying doctrinal rationalization as the distinctive feature of the world religions (see Bellah 1964, 1965; Geertz 1973). Although Geertz shies away from overemphasizing the role of the charismatic prophet, nonetheless, like Weber, he attributes to intellectuals a central role in religious change. He observes, for example, that the "disenchantment" of traditional religion often results from intellectuals' success at suppressing belief in magic and local spirits (cf. Weber 1956:125). This creates a spiritual gap, Geertz says, because "the divine can no longer be apprehended *en passant* through the numberless concrete, almost reflexive ritual gestures strategically interspersed through the more general round of life" (Geertz 1973:174). By implication, to satisfy this spiritual need, people are thus drawn to more rationalized religious forms. This phenomenon, Geertz suggests, is occurring even today in many parts of the developing world.

RATIONALITY VERSUS RATIONALIZATION

What insights remain from the Weberian model of traditionalism and rationalization, and what are their implications for understanding conversion to world religions? In one sense historical and ethnographic studies confirm that most of the "successful" faiths we identify as world religions do tend to be more consistently rationalized than traditional ones—*if* we limit rationalization to mean the formal systematization and codification of rite, doctrine, and authority. With their literate technologies, regularized clerisies, uniform rites, and sacred scriptures, world religions show a strong preoccupation with standardizing religious ideas and actions. But such generalizations about cultural form do not yet say much about its influence on the life-world or understanding of believers. Can we really be sure, for example, that for followers of the world religions "problems of meaning . . . get inclusive formulations and evoke comprehensive attitudes" (Geertz 1973:172)? On this point we must distinguish cultural rationalization—the enunciation, systematization, and formalization of cultural truths in light of a particular value or ideal, a quality of sociocultural *systems*—from the broader concept of rationality, or the effectiveness of certain ideas at making sense of an individual or group's life-world, again with reference to some underlying value complex.

Many religious scholars assume that a more or less unproblematic equivalence holds between cultural rationalization and experiential rationality at the level of the individual. Weber himself tended to speak this way, moving uncritically from the detail of religious doctrines to assumptions about their effective internalization by believers (see Bendix 1977:273–76). With such an approach it is easy to conclude that religions with more rationalized doctrines must also rationalize their believers' worldviews and behavior. But a well-established heritage in anthropology questions this unproblematic equivalence and the model of cultural internalization it implies. It disputes the automatic attribution of comprehensive rationality to the world religions and its denial to the traditional religions. For example, anthropologists as diverse as Bronislaw Malinowski (1948), E. E. Evans-Pritchard (1937), Claude Lévi-Strauss (1966), and Stanley J. Tambiah (1990) have succeeded in demonstrating that traditional modes of thought can be more flexible and systematic than Weberian characterizations of traditionalism would allow. Their studies and the work of others suggest that it is highly misleading to claim, as some Weberian sociologists still do, that traditional religions are "unable to go beyond the world as it is immediately experienced" (Whimster and Lash 1987:6).

In a similar vein, historical and ethnographic essays like those of Ranger, Jordan, and Yengoyan in this book have convincingly demonstrated that traditional religions are, in fact, quite diverse and often well differentiated from local social structures (see Shapiro 1987). Religious tradition need not be a timeless institution mechanically reproduced by unreflective adherents; at times it may be critically reformed and used to challenge social arrangements. The dynamic and potentially reflexive nature of "tradition" has been a recurring theme in the modern anthropology of religion (Burridge 1969; de Craemer et al. 1976; Evans-Pritchard 1956; Hefner 1985; Lienhardt 1961). These studies suggest that the category of traditional religion, if it is to be useful at all, must not imply social organicism or uncritical conformism.

Anthropologists have raised a related point that further underscores the importance of distinguishing rationalization at the level of doctrine from life-world rationality at the level of the individual. Scholars have observed that the systematization and canonization of doctrine seen in world religions (or any other highly formalized system of knowledge, such as political ideology) can rigidify knowledge and impede the open inquiry that is the hallmark of genuine rational reflection (Bloch 1974; Gellner 1983:21; Goody 1986:8–22). In other words, whatever its internal rigor, the practical constraints that limit access to and utilization of religious canon may preclude its appropriation by believers in a coherence-enhancing, "rational" way (see also Bloch 1989; Harris and Heelas 1979; Hefner 1985).

Similarly, the doctrines and meanings formalized in religious canons may, in fact, have little to do with believers' motives for embracing them. This appears to have been the case, for example, among Merrill's Tarahumara and Yengoyan's Aboriginal Australians. Both at times endorsed elements of Christian cosmology, but they did so more for reasons of protection and access to resources, than from intellectual commitment. All this makes the putative rationality of religious doctrine a shaky ground on which to build a theory of world religions or a general model of conversion. In an early essay Robert Bellah attempted to speak to this problem, arguing that canonization need not undermine the rationalizing effect of cultural knowledge:

> Of course, it is also true that, in every case, the great systematizers and commentators themselves came to be accepted as final and unchallengeable authorities, and in this way inhibited further cultural rationalization. And indeed some of them may be viewed as sanctified cultural dead ends. But unless we are to buy the specious argument that Aristotle, for example, simply because he was often blindly followed, did not himself make any important contribution to the development of cultural capacity in the West, then the significance of the great religious thinkers should not be minimized. (Bellah 1965:1809)

Bellah's argument overlooks some of Weber's earlier insights into the closing of the canon, specifically the importance of understanding rationalization in relation to doctrinal canons *and* the sociopolitical institutions through which they are propagated. From this sociology-of-knowledge perspective it is clear that the arrangements through which

Aristotle's truths were elevated to prominence in Western culture were quite different from those that canonized Christian doctrines. The cultural products may look similar, inasmuch as both bodies of knowledge came to occupy prestigious positions in Western culture. But Aristotle's truths were never sanctified as dogma, defended by vigilant clerics, or imposed through the brutalizing of heretics, as was at times the case with Christian dogma. The social regime that supported each truth system was different and so too was the impact of each on rational inquiry. Thus we must be careful not to equate the formal systematization seen in religious doctrines, that is, "rationalization," with the coherent reordering of cognition and action at the level of the individual, or enhanced "rationality." Clearly, the possibility of a powerful linkage of public doctrine and personal experience exists, and where this potential is realized religion can have a profound effect on believers' worldviews.

Contrary to some psychological accounts of conversion (James 1982; Nock 1933), however, we must *not* assume that such a deeply systematic rationalization is necessary or intrinsic to religious conversion. To make such an assumption is to project an interiorist bias onto a phenomenon that comes in a wide array of psychocultural forms. The essays in this volume illustrate the variability of the phenomenology of conversion. On their evidence interpretations of conversion must begin by acknowledging its experiential variation and then go on to explore its genesis in different social and intellectual milieus.

Such a comparative exercise yields one additional insight. The most necessary feature of religious conversion, it turns out, is not a deeply systematic reorganization of personal meanings but an adjustment in self-identification through the at least nominal acceptance of religious actions or beliefs deemed more fitting, useful, or true. In other words, at the very least—an analytic minimum—conversion implies the acceptance of a new locus of self-definition, a new, though not necessarily exclusive, reference point for one's identity. To draw on terms from David Jordan's essay, conversion is a matter of belief and social structure, of faith and affiliation. More particularly, as William Merrill and Charles Keyes emphasize, conversion need not reformulate one's understanding of the ultimate conditions of existence, but it always involves commitment to a new kind of moral authority and a new or reconceptualized social identity.

Whether with the new beliefs to which they say they subscribe, individuals or groups actually go on to rationalize their experience is a more complex question. Is the religious community organized so that believers have access to sacred doctrines, or is a detailed understanding of their truth restricted to clerical specialists? If there is public access, or if popularized variants of high doctrines are readily available, are there cultural media that promote this religious knowledge so that it becomes an integral force in people's lives? Finally, do believers interpret and apply the rationalized doctrines in ways consistent with their formal truth? Anthropological studies (Badone 1990; Farriss 1984; Hefner 1985; Schneider and Lindenbaum 1987) have repeatedly demonstrated that certain religions can work well enough without a comprehensive correspondence between high doctrine and popular belief. Alternately, a religion's central doctrines may remain latent for long periods, only to be taken up when conditions favor their revivalist application to new historical circumstances. In modern times the egalitarian appeal of both scripturalist Islam and evangelical Christianity provides telling examples of just such a process of doctrinal rediscovery (Gellner 1981; Martin 1990; Munson 1988).

We know too that some individuals engage the truths of their religion only long after their general identification with the tenets of the faith. In a certain sense, as I suggest in my case study in this collection, religious conversion always involves such authoritative acceptance of as yet unknown or unknowable truths.

RELIGIOUS REGIMES

Casual references to rationalization thus hide what are, in fact, several different processes, each subject to different organizations and controls. Religious rationalization includes (1) the creation and clarification of doctrines by intellectual systematizers, (2) the canonization and institutionalization of these doctrines by certain social carriers, and (3) the effective socialization of these cultural principles into the ideas and actions of believers. In addition, doctrines may not always be directly appropriated by believers but may be made indirectly available to them, usually through a clerisy-supported scriptural or ritual tradition, as a familiar and readily accessible reservoir of meanings to be drawn upon in moments of personal or social crisis.

This more complex understanding of rationalization encourages us to recognize the pluralistic nature of religious knowledge and culture itself. No cultural tradition is "the undivided property of the whole society" (Bourdieu 1977:73), and the relation of an individual to his or her culture is never simply a matter of internalizing prefigured truths (Bloch 1989; Hefner 1985; Schwartz 1978). Rationalization may occur in one religious sphere without occurring in all others. It may display its effects unevenly: for example, church doctrines may become the esoteric concern of a clerical elite or, as with Keyes's new Buddhists, new converts may have not yet learned all there is to know about the faith. Alternately, religious dogmas may be applied in ways that have little to do with their formal truth. This happened, for example, when the Spanish crown used Catholic doctrines to justify policies designed to transform people in northern Mexico into a docile labor force (see Merrill's essay). These and other examples show that it is misleading to assume that the formal truths embedded in religious doctrines directly reflect or inform believers' ideas or actions.

Having qualified it so thoroughly, what have we left of Weber's model of the rationality of world religions? The answer, I believe, is that the heart of his analysis still provides a powerful insight. As Weber claimed, the doctrines of the world religions (or, again, their most successful institutional carriers) *do* seem to be organized around a unified view of the world derived from a consciously systematized attitude toward life. And these same dogmas do tend to agree in demanding that men and women conduct themselves according to this unified and significant pattern. This thesis goes too far if it is interpreted to mean that such doctrinal systematization is sufficient to guarantee the rationality of all believers' worldviews. It also errs if it implies that traditional religions lack all such systematization, or if it is used to assert that religious tradition involves unquestioning conformity to received social ways (cf. Burridge 1969; Hefner 1985; Hobsbawm and Ranger 1983; Laitin 1986).[11]

Weber's views on the world religions retain keener insight, however, on one important point: the severity of the transcendentalism he correctly identifies at the core of their doctrines. It is not just that the doctrines of these religions put a greater distance between the mundane and spiritual worlds or that they "reject this world" by redefining it in relation to another. At least in doctrinal principle they do all this—but then so do a number of religions that have shown markedly less success at winning followers. The real force of the world religions lies in their linkage of these strict transcendental imperatives to institutions for the propagation and control of religious knowledge and identity over time and space.

In other words, the most distinctive feature of the world religions or of, again, their most institutionally successful variants is something both doctrinal and social-organizational. These religions regularize clerical roles, standardize ritual, formalize doctrine, and otherwise work to create an authoritative culture and cohesive religious structure. At times this cultural impetus may be subverted or challenged, giving rise to heterodox or localized variants of the faith that challenge its transregional integrity. Such a process seems to have regularly occurred, for example, in Sufi and folk variants of Islam, in Gnostic and folk Christianity, and, as Keyes's essay aptly illustrates, in popular Theravāda Buddhism. In instances such as these it may not be useful to identify localized or sectarian variants of the faith as world religions at all, except in a loose genealogical sense. This implies, of course, that the concept of world religion suffers from much of the same analytic overextension as does that of traditional religion. Not all of the communities said to be part of a world religion really partake of the world-building qualities mentioned above. But the schisms, localization, and segmentation that take place in world religions only illustrate the remarkable achievement of those communities that can sustain their faith and knowledge over time and space.

The development of institutions capable of standardizing knowledge and identity across history and culture has allowed the religions we know as world faiths to take advantage of the conditions that have accompanied the emergence of multiethnic, state-based societies. Indeed, from this perspective the world religions appear to be complex responses to the challenge of identity and moral community in a plural world. In such a context, the world religions' message of a Truth and a redemptive identity incumbent upon all people and their introduction of a social organization for the propagation of that message have proved to be revolutionary forces in their own right, well suited to the challenge of life in a new kind of social macrocosm.

FROM MICROCOSM TO MACROCOSM

The debate sparked by Robin Horton's stimulating essays (1971, 1975a, 1975b) on African conversion provides an alternative vantage point for evaluating the rationality of religion and the forces promoting conversion to world religions. While preserving Weber's emphasis on meaning as the key to religious change, Horton insists that traditional religions are not necessarily less rational than world religions, just narrower in focus. The difference, he implies, is quantitative rather than qualitative, a matter of scope or range, not superior rationalization per se. Rather than address topics of universal relevance, traditional religions concentrate on a smaller, more local array of problems. This is not surprising, Horton remarks, because people in traditional societies live in smaller, more territorially restricted communities. The spirits most commonly invoked in traditional religions—ancestors, territorial guardians, nature spirits—are similarly drawn from familiar terrains. This does not mean that traditional beliefs are either irrational or even less rational than more encompassing canons. They can be entirely rational in relation to the circumstances they engage. Indeed, in a restricted social context the more universalistic dogmas of the world religions might well be meaningless.

Horton cites numerous African studies that indicate, contra Weber, that the multiplicity of spirits in traditional religions does not indicate intellectual opportunism or deep-seated irrationality. "The spiritual beings of the traditional cosmologies are generally thought of as operating in a more or less regular manner, and [the] multiplicity of spiritual agencies is by no means synonymous with confusion, inconsistency, or incoherence" (Horton 1971:99).

Horton also observes that most peoples in sub-Saharan Africa already had a concept of a supreme deity before their contact with Christianity or Islam. He explains that their religious cosmologies often had two tiers, a lower level of local spirits and a higher one of a supreme god or gods. The lesser spirits were "in the main concerned with the affairs of the local community and environment—i.e., with the microcosm," and the supreme being was "concerned with the world as a whole—i.e., with the macrocosm" (Horton 1971:101). In the premodern era most people lived "within the microcosm of the local community . . . to a considerable extent insulated from the macrocosm of the wider world" (Horton 1971:101). As a result their religious ideas focused on lesser spirits, and they devoted only marginal attention to the cult of the supreme being.

Horton's model can be faulted for overemphasizing the boundedness of traditional communities. In this volume, Yengoyan, Jordan, Pollock, and Ranger demonstrate the error of automatically identifying traditional religions with closed, microcosmic worlds. Much as Kopytoff (1987) has argued for African institutions in general, Ranger shows that in premodern Africa many religions were not uniquely microcosmic but bridged ethnic and territorial boundaries. Criticizing our myth of "secure corporate identities" grounded on "immobilized societies," he notes that even before colonial times southern Africans in different locales drew on a common pool of mythic symbols and were widely involved in transregional cults. Jordan's essay on Chinese religion in this volume brilliantly demonstrates a similar truth.[12]

Horton's model, then, conflates two concepts that are better kept distinct: the contrast between traditional and world religions and that between localized and transregional religions. In reality these contrasts need not neatly overlap. As the essays by Kee, Ranger, Barker, Merrill, and Pollock illustrate, the tension between the local and global can be played out within both indigenous and world religions (see also Badone 1990; Eickelman 1982; Schneider and Lindenbaum 1987).

This much said, Horton's model retains much relevance for our clarification of the phenomenon of conversion and, in particular, Christianization. It quite properly draws our attention to how incorporation into a larger social order acts as a catalyst for both conversion and the reformulation of indigenous religion. Horton is right to emphasize that this event is a powerful impetus for the reconstruction of religion. As long as we do not assume that traditional religion knows nothing of such broader involvements, the model is useful and provides another perspective on the sociology of religious change.

Having emphasized that an individual's or community's involvement in the macrocosm will influence the choice of cosmology, Horton concludes that it is the dissolution of microcosmic boundaries that propels people toward more universalistic doctrines. Conversely, those who remain within microcosmic worlds are more likely to devote their attention to lesser spirits and more restricted religious idioms. This leads Horton to a startling conclusion. Even in the absence of Christianity or Islam, he asserts, most African peoples would have developed a cult of the supreme being and a more overarching cosmology as they made their way into the "macrocosm" (Horton 1971:102–3). Drawing again on Ranger's revisionist reading of the African data, we could add here that in precontact times many Africans had apparently already begun to do just that.

Horton's argument challenges conventional analyses of conversion. For Horton the "crucial" variables affecting religious change among indigenous peoples "are not the external influences (Islam, Christianity) but the pre-existing thought-patterns and values, and the pre-existing socioeconomic matrix" (Horton 1975a:221). In other words, "acceptance of Islam and Christianity is due as much to the development of the traditional cosmology in response to other features of the modern situation as it is to the activities of missionaries" (Horton 1971:103). Religious change is first and foremost "dictated by the postulates of the 'basic' cosmology" and the "dissolution of microcosmic boundaries" (Horton 1975b:381). Islam and Christianity, then, are little more than "catalysts—stimulators and accelerators of changes which were 'in the air' anyway" (Horton 1971:104).[13]

POLITICS AND INTELLECTUALISM

At first many scholars welcomed Horton's analysis of conversion because it portrayed Africans as active players in religious change rather than as passive consumers or victims. The model also challenges the Weberian characterization of traditional religions as intellectually piecemeal or nonrational, replacing it with what we might call an ecological appreciation of their logic. Horton's model is flawed, however, by several shortcomings in addition to those mentioned above.

The most vexing aspect of Horton's model is its neglect of political and structural influences on conversion. Originally, Horton referred to his model as a "thought experiment" in which he invited us to reflect on the likely course of religious change in a hypothetical Africa to which Islam and Christianity had never come, but into which political and economic institutions of increasing social scope were introduced. In his subsequent discussion, however, Horton unwittingly transformed this imaginative exercise into a hidden analytic premise. One can argue, as he does, that a shift to the higher end of the cosmological spectrum would have occurred even in the absence of Islam and Christianity. But one cannot logically conclude from this that the institutions of Islam and Christianity were insignificant in the cosmological changes that actually took place. Influences other than intellectualist ones were at work in the transformation of native cosmologies. Horton may be right to insist, then, that Africans exposed to the macrocosm would have adjusted their cosmological horizons even without the catalyst of Christianity or Islam. We must add, however, that the timing and content of actual change were profoundly affected by the European presence and the crisis of identity and authority that presence provoked.

Jean Comaroff (1985), Humphrey Fisher (1973), and Caroline Ifeka-Moller (1974:59) all criticize Horton on this point. They show that many African societies were incorporated into broader polities without developing the monolatrous (single-divinity-focused) emphasis that Horton predicts. Emefie Ikenga-Metuh (1987:26) observes that the more common indigenous response has been not monolatry or monotheism but the incorporation of new forms of worship into an already existing pantheon. Nancy Farriss (1984:302) and William Merrill (this volume) note the same tendency in the Maya and Tarahumara religions of Mesoamerica before and after the Spanish conquest. David Jordan's essay demonstrates that a similarly inclusive, "additive" quality has long characterized traditional Chinese religion—and is a reason why Christian exclusivity has not been well received by Chinese (see also Fried 1987:102).

Fisher (1985:165) underscores the broader issue here: "One fundamental novelty introduced, in the long run, by Islam [and Christianity] has been the idea of an exclusive religious allegiance." For this and other reasons, he argues, Islam and Christianity are more than catalysts for changes "already in the air." Once implanted in local environments, they create a "juggernaut" that "advances under its own momentum" (Fisher 1985:153) rather than, as Horton would have it, under the dictates of indigenous cosmology.

For students of religious conversion the challenge in this controversy is to strike a balance between the two extremes of intellectualist voluntarism and structural determinism. Even if politically imbalanced, conversion encounters are always two-sided, and the social and intellectual dynamics of each camp affect the outcome. Rather than overemphasize intrinsic or extrinsic variables in conversion, then, we should explore the way in which the two interact and expect that the relative importance of each may vary in different settings. Such an approach would clarify why some indigenous peoples eagerly embrace Christianity (Barker's Maisin, Kee's early Christians, as well as numerous examples from Oceania, see White 1988; Boutilier et al. 1978), but others tend to appropriate its meanings selectively (Tarahumara, Aboriginal Australia, Taiwan) or reject them outright (Amazon, Thailand).

This same insight is related to the earlier discussion of religious rationalization. As Weber argued, the intellectual formulation of doctrines is just one element in their effective institutionalization. Another is the development of authoritative organizations for the propagation and control of religious knowledge and identity: here traditional religions are often at a severe disadvantage relative to their world-religious rivals. As Jack Goody (1986; cf. Tapp 1989) has noted, many traditional religions are illiterate and thereby encounter serious technical obstacles to the codification and dissemination of their doctrines. Equally important, these religions often lack institutions for coordinating membership and authority over large social expanses. By contrast, their rivals can be characterized as "world" religions precisely because—even if locally they are deeply embedded in parochial social arrangements (see, e.g., Badone 1990)—they have developed something that the other type of religious community lacks: transregional organizations for the indoctrination of the faith and the regularization of community.

Not coincidentally, these same world religions sometimes accompany political agents with their own designs on local lives and resources. Whether government policies explicitly support missionizing (as in the examples from colonial New Guinea, Mesoamerica, and Brazil in this book) or provide no such direct assistance (as in colonial Java,[14] modern Australia, and Thailand), the impact of foreign expansion may severely challenge indigenous social structures and the religious identities they sustain. Even in the absence of missionary initiatives, therefore, social dislocation may encourage people to look elsewhere than the canons of tradition for an understanding of who they are and how they should live (cf. White 1988).

The neglect of politics and sociological features in religious conversion justifies, then, criticisms that approaches like Horton's are, as I. M. Lewis (1980:vii–viii) has put it, too "mentalistic" and thus unable to recognize how religions like Christianity and Islam provide "an identity as well as a religious faith" and a "set of rules for life" in addition to instruments for the intellectual control of space-time events. Recognition of the broader influences at work in conversion encounters, however, need not imply repudiation of Horton's admirable effort to see religious change, as he puts it, through believers' eyes. The changing social environment in which conversion so often unfolds is not simply a product of material forces. Its effects register not only in actors' material well-being but also in their sense of self-worth and community and in their efforts to create institutions for the sustenance of both. This problem of dignity and self-identification in a pluralized and politically imbalanced world lies at the heart of many conversion histories.

THE MORAL ECONOMY OF SELF-IDENTIFICATION

We can now see that conversion is related to a process of identity development often referred to as "reference group" formation. Bridging social psychology and the sociology of knowledge, reference group theory emphasizes that self-identification is implicated in all choice, in all matters of self-interest, and in the myriad conflicts and solidarities of human life (Merton 1968; Sherif and Sherif 1969; Shweder et al. 1987; Hefner 1990).[15] More specifically, reference group theory stresses that in the course of their lives individuals develop a real or imagined reference group—an anchor for their sense of self and other and for the entitlements and obligations thought to characterize relationships—and refer to that reference group when evaluating people, situations, and life projects. As the philosopher Lawrence Blum (1987:331) has observed, such a viewpoint challenges the "too-sharp separation between self and other" characteristic of utilitarian models of the human actor; it emphasizes instead that "our connection to others and our capacities for responsiveness are a central part of our identities, rather than being mere sentiments or voluntary commitments." Acknowledging this powerful truth, we are thus challenged in all social inquiry to explore how societies affect the development of personal identity and commitments and to compare how different social orders influence the foundation of personal morality (cf. Douglas 1970).

Though sometimes described as unitary, actors' reference group orientations can actually be plural or contradictory. One's ethnic allegiances, for example, may at some point conflict with those of nation, race, gender, religion, political affiliation, or any other of the host of allegiances available for self-identification in a plural society. Much of the poignancy of life in a modern society originates in that sobering fact, which suggests a practical as well as a moral dimension to the dynamic of self-identification. It may be only in the course of quotidian life, with its ongoing commitments, pain, and rewards, that the entailments of one allegiance quite unexpectedly contradict those of another, forcing reflection on what one values in others and what of oneself one holds dear.

The dynamic of reference group orientation involves an ongoing, "reflexive monitoring" (Giddens 1984:6) of one's self-image and goals in social action. Though one's identity *is* abstract and deeply psychological, it is not *just* an abstraction held in some inaccessible psychological reserve. One's self-identification is implicated in all social interactions. Events in the world, new opportunities and dilemmas, feed back on this guiding sensibility, forcing adjustments to one's image of self and other. Social groups are themselves shaped by this economy of values and commitment. Personal commitments are in turn influenced by the ability of different social groupings to inspire or enforce allegiance to their ideals of self, status, and community.

By training our attention on this moral economy of self-identification, reference group theory encourages us to recognize that human identity is not innate or wholly socially determined but develops from ongoing and deeply contingent social-psychological interactions. Self-identification must be at the heart of our efforts to understand individual life-worlds and the creative agency of human beings. Though culture is implicated in the creation of self, its precise effects are mediated by the dispositions of the individuals it engages, their positions in a particular social world, and their ongoing efforts—never themselves fully culturally programmed—to assess the meaning and value of all that goes on around them. Little of this interaction can be reduced to the status of sociological fact or considered the passive internalization of cultural symbols, religious or otherwise.

One important insight follows from this more dynamic view of human development. Contrary to many approaches in the social sciences, reference group theory denies that we can assume that an individual's membership group—the world he or she inhabits day to day—is always the source for reference group identification (Merton 1968; Hefner 1990). Not everyone need subscribe to the canons of his or her community. Alienation occurs even in small-scale societies. Some individuals retreat to personal fantasies or, where intercultural contacts allow, look elsewhere than to their community of origin for alternative notions of self and self-worth.[16]

This last point is important in understanding the logic of religious change in intercultural encounters. As a society is thrust, sometimes against its members' wills, into a larger or reorganized macrocosm, new lifestyles and ethical options appear. Missionaries or other proselytizers may lead in this challenge to tradition (Beidelman 1982; Burridge 1978;

Farriss 1984). But even in their absence the threat to received ways may be severe. As a society is brought into contact with a larger politico-economic order, institutions once vital for the sustenance of indigenous identities may be abolished or subverted, bringing new circuits of status, investment, and self-validation into existence (Comaroff 1985; Hefner 1985; Volkman 1985). In such a context a religion that promises a new measure of dignity and access to the values and rewards of the larger society may find a ready following among peoples previously committed to local ways. As Kenelm Burridge (1969:133) has observed of millenarian movements, this crisis of self-identification is as much moral as it is material, because "the politico-economic conflict . . . is also a conflict between two different kinds of prestige system," two different ways of affirming human value.

If their lifeways are to survive, an indigenous people will need to maintain institutions capable of inspiring or imposing a sense of identification with those ways. This too is as much a political as a moral achievement, and it may be especially difficult in the face of powerfully intrusive polities or mission proselytizers promoting ideas that deny the truth of local ways. Where, as among Keyes's Thai, Pollock's Culina, or Jordan's Taiwanese, however, the institutions that support indigenous solidarities remain resilient, or where missionizing is not intensive or sustained (Brown and Bick 1987; Wedenoja 1988), the effective appeal of the incoming religion may be quite limited. Alternately, where a tribal minority is threatened with cultural extinction at the hands of fast-encroaching neighbors, it may adopt a world religion other than that of its proximate rivals, maintaining its larger ethnic identity by giving up its traditional religion (see Keyes and Pollock below and Kammerer 1990; Stearman 1987; Tapp 1989). The survival of local lifeways depends on how or to what extent people can integrate their indigenous institutions into a now more inclusive social world.

What all this means is that our accounts of conversion must be "multi-causal rather than mono-causal," as Emefie Ikenga-Metuh (1987:25) has put it. But we must recognize that multicausality is itself a consequence of a more general fact, widely recognized in contemporary social theory (see Berger 1967; Bourdieu 1977; Comaroff 1985; Eickelman 1985; Giddens 1984; Hefner 1985). As a social phenomenon religion is, to use Anthony Giddens's phrase, "dually constructed"—emerging both from the ideas and intentions of individuals and from the institutions and circumstances that constrain and routinize the world in which people act, often outside their full awareness.

This simple insight into what Peter Berger (1967:4) once called the "dialectic process of world building" is a useful reminder of a methodological issue raised again and again by the essays in this volume. Accounts of conversion that emphasize its putative psychological reality —such as the classic essays by Nock (1933) and James (1982) or a surprising number of studies in contemporary American sociology (Snow and Machalek 1984)—remain incomplete if they neglect the broader context that informs the self- and situational-evaluation of the converted. Politics and social ethics are *intrinsic* to the psychocultural reality of conversion, informing an agent's commitment to an identity and the moral authority that commitment implies. From this perspective, rather than oppose psychological models of conversion against sociopolitical ones, we should insist on and explore their interpenetration.

FROM BABBLE TO WORD

The incorporation of indigenous communities into a new or larger macrocosm, then, has been one of the most pervasive supports for conversion to world religions thoughout human history. This is not to imply, of course, that the politico-moral crises that accompany incorporation are *always* the catalysts for conversion. Sometimes they may be of little import, as, for example, when an individual in Taiwan (see Jordan's essay), northern Thailand (see Keyes's), Central Australia (see Yengoyan's), or northern Mexico (see Merrill's) converts to a new faith because it provides better relief from affliction than traditional therapies did. Nonetheless, the incorporation of small-scale societies into new or more expansive polities has been a powerful, though by no means unilinear, current of world history since ancient times. As the Yengoyan and Merrill essays demonstrate, some traditional religions may dig in, reorganize, and survive this integrative revolution. But the world religions often enjoy a competitive advantage over their rivals in that they are ideologically and organizationally preadapted to the macrocosm. Catalysts of moral crisis, they stand ready to provide, or impose, prefigured ideals for a posttraditional world.

All the world religions emerged after the formation of the supraethnic, state-based societies we identify with civilization. Weber (1956:48) notes this fact when he says that both the world religions and prophecy had something to do with the spread of the great world empires. Having originated *in* empire, however, the world religions have not always been religions *of* empire. Sometimes, of course, they directly supported imperial policies. In fact, however, attitudes toward state power vary among the world religions and even within the same religion, as Howard Kee shows in his study of early Christianity. The essays by Merrill, Barker, Pollock, Yengoyan, and Hefner make a similar point, showing that in modern times the relationship between Christian missionaries and state authorities has varied widely (see also Beidelman 1982; Huber 1987; Kipp 1990).

Whatever their relationship to official power, the world religions arrive with the most remarkable of appeals. They proclaim a Truth that stands above others and assert that its recognition is essential for a meaningful life. Their redemptive message seeks to relativize the taken-for-granted status of traditional ways and may create great excitement or confusion. The message may be used to justify attacks on received social values and their elite custodians. It may also be used to mandate conformity to new rituals and to establish circuits of value and investment different from those of the previous social regime. In so doing the message may also create new opportunities for social mobility and prestige. Where, as among outcastes in modern India (Forrester 1977) or women in the early Jesus movement (Kee 1989:92) and some areas of the developing world (Bond 1987:64), the new religion opens opportunities to individuals previously excluded from prestigious positions, it may bring about important changes in gender roles, class, and status.

Such influences may be especially effective when the Word is proclaimed at the same time that politics, commerce, and communications force or allow growing numbers of people into a larger or reorganized macrocosm, deepening the crisis of received social ways. Burdened with a sense of oppression and powerlessness, an indigenous people may by themselves come to feel that they are in need of, and moving toward, social redemption, that is, a state that provides relief from an intolerable situation through new morality and social relations. In some cases their efforts at revitalization may be millenarian, drawing on only partially detraditionalized idioms (Burridge 1969). Where native society is already in disarray or where its cosmology is more malleable (cf. Sahlins 1985, White 1988:11), however, Christianity or other exogeneous religions may present an appealingly ready-made formula for a revitalized social community.

Through a conceptual legerdemain that is their hallmark, world religions respond to this crisis of tradition in a most unusual way. They declare their rejection of human community in its everyday form. The new life they promise is not just of this world, they say, but based on a transcendent truth and divinity. In practice, of course, this message of salvation may attract less attention than the practical benefits of membership in the new religious community. This may be especially true where traditional religion is associated with the collapsing structures of local society and the new faith is perceived to be tied to a larger and more bountiful political economy (see Comaroff 1985; Hefner 1987). From this perspective the message of radical "world rejection" may in fact carry less weight than the new religion's perceived worldly benefits.

But the intellectual logic of the world religions is not reducible to a broader economic struggle. The world religions *do* have distinctive cosmologies, the logic of which is best illustrated in their attitudes toward the traditional cults they seek to abolish or subsume. The hallmark of the world religions—or, again, of their most successfully institutionalized core variants—is their subordination of local spirits, dialects, customs, and territory to a higher spiritual cosmology. They declare the superiority of God or gods over low spirits, scriptural Word over local babble, transregional clerics over local curers, and a Holy Land or lands over local territory (Hefner 1987). Their world rejection, then, is of worldly consequence. It relativizes everyday reality by proclaiming that the new religion stands above local custom or community. For at least some believers, as Weber stated, this claim creates a passionate imperative for the reevaluation of local ways.

But the success of a world religion may also present it with a dilemma. The transregional community it creates cannot assume the same depth of shared experience as local faiths, nor the same intimate mechanisms of social control. Left to itself the Word dissolves into local babble, jeopardizing its urgent truth. The most successful variants of the world religions, however, seem adapted to meet just this challenge. They support institutions for the dissemination and standardization of sacred truths. Alongside their scripture and high doctrines they develop simplified rites and beliefs, neatly packaged for mass consumption. Not coincidentally, this standardized material also provides an accessible body of symbolism for the creation of a broadly cast religious identity.

The perceived need to stave off babble and disseminate the Word in an enduring fashion also inspires prophets and clerical intellectuals to emphasize ecumenical unity and develop doctrines that are "more abstract, more logically coherent, and more generally phrased" (Geertz 1973:172). Specifically, the universalization in the doctrines of the world religions is motivated not just by the search for more "comprehensive answers to problems of meaning," as conventional Weberian accounts would have it, but also by the interest of religious intellectuals in assisting the elaboration and regularization of the faith.[17] In so doing, as Weber observed, these clerics also help to legitimate the community to which their own status and identity are tied.

From a sociology-of-knowledge perspective all these arrangements testify to the emergence of a new kind of religion, characterized by a powerful organization for shaping ethics, knowledge, and identity. Originating as it did in a crisis of multicultural community, the regimen is uniquely adapted to the world-building possibilities of the civilized macrocosm and the problems of identity and moral differentiation at its core.

THE CHRISTIAN MACROCOSM

Born in a plural social milieu, each of the world religions has survived by responding effectively to three issues: defining the boundaries and membership of religious community; establishing the relationship of religion to political power; and controlling belief among a laity ignorant of or uninterested in official doctrine. What is unique about Christianity's response to these problems?

As Howard Kee (1980, 1989, and this volume) observes, Christianity originated in an era in which Roman conquest had generalized a sense of marginality and forced detraditionalism among the peoples of the Mediterranean. Rome did so without managing to win most of these people to the high Hellenistic culture it sought to promote (Kee 1980:75). The empire, then, was an unusually effective catalyst of macrocosmic crisis. In the years before Christ's mission the Roman cults had fallen into decline, and new cults of oriental divinities found "appeal across barriers of family, ethnic origin, and social status" and "aroused the hopes of the alienated as well as the privileged" (Kee 1980:84). The shift toward a higher cosmology was already in the air.

In this uneasy macrocosm a movement emerged proclaiming a new interpretation of the Jewish covenant. Paul—apostle of the macrocosmic universe par excellence—above all committed himself to the formulation of a more inclusive concept of the covenant. New Testament accounts show Jesus making vague pronouncements on the issue; Peter, similarly, seems to have been uncertain about the precise nature of the covenant revision. After Christ's death there were several Christian communities other than the "structured city congregations" which recognized Paul's authority (Kee 1980:94). Over the long run, however, Paul's vision won out, defining the covenant inclusively, so that it spanned a broad range of social and ethnic strata.

With its initially urban, mobile, and multiethnic social base, early Christianity was little inclined to emphasize traditional forms of kinship or ascribed social status. Jesus is said to have appealed to his followers to commit themselves to the family of God rather than to the social and biological family. Though, as the essays in this volume demonstrate, Christianity can be adjusted to a variety of social and kinship organizations, its scripture can and has been used to promote the simplification of kinship relations and even the individualization of social ties. Weber (1956) and, in a recent essay, Jane Schneider (1990) have argued that such an individualizing message gave Christianity an elective affinity with one of the modern era's key structural dispositions, social individualization. Drawing on Burridge's (1978) account of Christian individualism, Yengoyan illustrates the converse. Where, as among Central Australian peoples, the autonomy of the individual is downplayed in favor of a view of the actor as socially embedded, the Christian message may seem unappealingly foreign or subversive of extant social relations (cf., for China, Fried 1987:103). Where that same social order is in decline, however, the individualism of the Christian message may be powerfully appealing, legitimating nonconformism and the organization of new forms of social relationship (cf. Martin 1990; White 1988).

Having emerged in a state-based society, Christianity, like all the world religions, was also obliged to develop a policy toward the powers that be. Here again the New Testament writers display quite varied attitudes. With his apocalyptic view of history Mark was inclined to urge "noninvolvement, in view of the expectation that all worldly powers were soon to be brought to an end by direct divine action." In contrast, Paul took the view that "the mission could be fulfilled only if political and civil order were maintained throughout the empire" (Kee 1980:120).

Even in early times, then, Christian policies on church-state relations were considerably more varied than the familiar "give-unto-Caesar" image would suggest. Despite this variability, however, Christianity's carriers have shown a general tendency toward what Ernest Gellner (1981:2) has called "political modesty." Even when, as during the European Middle Ages, church and state were interwoven, the clergy hesitated to formulate a systematic politico-legal corpus. The legacy of Christ and Paul's segregation of religious and political realms, as recorded in scripture, haunted Christian scholarship.

In this respect, of course, Christianity differs markedly from the core tradition within Islam. Within this mainline tradition, Islam can be interpreted to make a more sustained claim to power. Its scriptures and commentaries provide an explicit, if still incomplete, program for what is to be done once power is won. In this, as Gellner (1981:5) has noted, one sees the difference between Christian and Muslim origins. Christianity originated at the margins of empire, indeed, originally at the margins of Judaism; Islam arose at the heart of an expansionist imperium. Reacting against the "legalistic erudition" of Pharisaic Judaism (Weber 1956:131, 270), early Christianity seemed little inclined to enunciate policies for the management of an empire to which, some time later, it would become a reluctant heir. Drawn into empire, eventually its clerical officers did help to develop the bureaucratic and legalistic machinery required for congregational management and political rule. But at its scriptural core remained the message of its origins, proclaiming itself for the poor in spirit. Here too was a latent reservoir of meaning to be revived by later generations of Christian evangelicals (see Martin 1990).

The mainline Christian response to the third and final problem of the world religions—the problem of lay heterodoxy—is equally distinctive. Like Islam (though Muslims insist their monotheism is purer than Christian trinitarianism), Christianity inherited Judaism's commitment to one God, and the monotheism it promoted had exclusivistic pretensions. Rather than incorporate extant spirits into a larger cosmological framework, as Hinduism and, in a somewhat different fashion (see Keyes's essay), Buddhism do, orthodox Christianity and Islam demand the recognition of a single godhead and the repudiation or, at the very least, cosmological demotion of lesser world spirits.

In the course of their histories both medieval Christianity and Islam relaxed their monotheism and incorporated a cult of the saints into their pantheons; the relaxation of monotheistic principles was taken even further in Gnostic and folk variants of Christianity (Badone 1990; Taylor 1987) and in some forms of folk Islam and Sufism (Lewis 1980; Nadel 1954). But the similarities between these two faiths hide an important difference in their clerical management. Lacking a centralized church structure, mainline Sunni Islam has tended to take an ecumenical stance toward indigenous clergy, allowing native clerics (who are, of course, not priests but specialists of religious and legal knowledge) to rise from popular ranks. In modern times, as I. M. Lewis (1980:82) has noted, this has allowed recent converts in places like West Africa and Southeast Asia to quickly identify the faith as indigenous and to use it as a rallying cry against foreigners and colonialism. At times, though by no means universally, it has also allowed for a more gradual accommodation of local cosmology to high doctrine.

By contrast, with its centralized hierarchy, the pre-Reformation church was less inclined to allow open admissions to the clergy. As Beidelman's (1982) East African study illustrates, even modern Protestant missions have been reluctant to allow such open access where the mission-pagan divide coincides with marked political and ethnic inequalities (see also Comaroff 1985; Farriss 1984). Such centralized control has created an organizational environment conducive to the strict management of doctrine and regular campaigns against heterodoxy. Merrill's essay in the present volume illustrates the complex relationship between administrative hierarchy and the suppression of heterodoxy in colonial Mexico; Farriss (1984) discusses a tragic example among the nearby Maya. Attitudes on clerical recruitment and doctrinal control vary among contemporary Christian denominations, of course. Modern evangelical Christianity, in particular, has adopted a new and more open pattern of clerical recruitment (see Hefner, below, and Martin 1990). For much of its history, however, the looming presence of a well-organized church has disposed Christianity to regular campaigns against heresies that are themselves product, in part, of the great divide between clerical and popular cultures.

CONCLUSION: WORLD BUILDING AND TRANSCENDENCE

Like all the world religions Christianity represents a unique response to the problems of a plural world. Having originated in macrocosmic crisis, Christianity and the other world religions have developed distinctive institutions for controlling ethics, knowledge, and identity over time and space. For scholars accustomed to thinking of religion in purely theological terms, this conclusion may seem disappointingly thin. In fact, however, rather than diminishing the accomplishment of Christianity or other world religions, this perspective underscores their world-transforming achievement.

All the world faiths relativize received social ways by announcing a Truth without which, they claim, human existence has no real meaning. This foundational belief legitimates doctrines and rites to which, in principle, all people are to be drawn. It may also mandate the organization of institutions for the propagation of the faith and the sustenance of "imagined communities" (Anderson 1983) unlike any previously seen. For a social science that recognizes that problems of morality and self-identification are central to all social life (Blum 1987; Gadamer 1975; Hefner 1990, Shweder et al. 1987), this aspect of the world religions places them among the most remarkable achievements of human culture.

Indeed, these religions are without parallel in human history. Political empires and economic systems have come and gone, but the world religions have survived. *They are the longest lasting of civilization's primary institutions.* Their genius lies in their curious ability to renounce this world and announce another, more compelling and true. They relocate the divisive solidarities of language, custom, and region within a broader community and higher Truth. They do so ideally, of course, and it goes without saying that the ideal may be, and routinely is, ignored or violated by those who would use the Truth for other ends. At times, of course, redemptive ideals may lose their appeal. History is not linear, and communities once thrust into expansive world orders may suddenly turn inward. Alternately, as in the modern West, secular idioms may provide a non-spiritual alternative to the ideals of religious transcendence, or the give and take of self-interested exchange may narrow moral vision and erode popular interest in projects of ethical transcendence.

But history suggests that the ideal of transcendence will endure. The message carries well in a world of expansive horizons and ethical challenge. In such contexts the world religions offer the promise of community recast according to a divine plan. It goes without saying that the promise is never fully realized. But the ideal survives. The very generality of its ethic allows this ideal to exert powerful influence on the most diverse human affairs and provides living testimony to one of the most enduring responses to the challenges of identity and morality in our complex world.

NOTES

1. It should be emphasized, however, that the reformulation of identity and morality that takes place in intercultural contacts can be mediated by other sociocultural arrangements as well. Ethnicity, nationalism, and political ideology, among others, can play just such a role. Pollock's essay in the present volume shows that intercultural contact in the Brazilian Amazon has given rise to a secular pan-Indianist ideology known as *comunidade*. Jordan's essay indicates that the elaborate constellation of ideas and practices surrounding Chinese ethnicity has served to provide a similar canopy for translocal identity. Like Comaroff's (1985) study of southern African Christianity, Ranger's examples from modern Africa demonstrate that religious, ethnic, and regionalist idioms are often interwoven in the same social movements. The present essay should not be interpreted, therefore, as attributing primacy to religious idioms in the reconstruction of macrocosmic identities. Rather, it seeks to place religion alongside other cultural media involved in the elaboration of translocal community. See Anderson (1983), Gellner (1983), and Hefner (1990, 1991).

2. Among the most influential in the early study of conversion, the works of A. D. Nock (1933) and William James (1980:89) both display such a subjectivist bias, influenced no doubt by Protestant ideas as to what constitutes proper conversion. For James, conversion is "the process . . . by which a self, hitherto divided, and consciously wrong inferior and unhappy, becomes unified and consciously right superior and happy, in consequence of its firmer hold upon religious realities." It is not that such a deeply subjective reorientation never characterizes conversion, but that it is only one variety of conversion experience and one that provides an inadequate understanding of the conditions of its own possibility at that.

3. For reasons that will become clearer presently, my definition of world religion is a minimalist one, referring simply to those religions that, as Weber put it, "have known how to gather multitudes of confessors around them" (Weber 1946:267). This definition shifts attention from the difficult question whether these religions possess similar cosmologies (I suggest that on several key points

they do) to the simpler and more important feature of their success at "gathering multitudes"; I am primarily concerned with the logic of this success. I am less interested in determining which religions in which periods can properly be called world religions. Many religions—Hinduism being the most dramatic example—vacillate between the ideal-typical extremes of traditional and world religions; the purpose of classification here is not to pigeonhole the varieties of religion but to highlight certain ideological and organizational features the underlie the "success" of a few.

4. My characterization here is broad. It overlooks how in the nineteenth century evolutionary themes were more prominent among scholars (e.g., Tylor and Frazer) explicitly concerned with cross-cultural comparisons than among those (e.g., William James) who used the other approach to the study of religion popular at the time, psychologism. Not surprisingly, however, even among the latter, evolutionary biases often lie just below the surface. Though James (1982:29), for example, insists that he is not concerned with "the institutional branch" of religion but instead focuses on "personal religion, pure and simple," he makes blatant evolutionary assumptions throughout his text. He observes, for example, that "religion does in fact perpetuate the traditions of the most primeval thought" (1982:495), the qualities of which were an inability to distinguish fact from fantasy and a "coercive" attitude toward divinity. Nock (1933:2–3) characterizes conversion in similarly psychologistic terms, though his historical discussion is more subtle. To illuminate the distinctiveness of prophetic religions (his primary object of inquiry), however, Nock is obliged to invent a category of "religions of tradition" that, once again, reproduces the most simplistic evolutionist dichotomies.

5. Stanley Tambiah's recent essay (1990) provides a penetrating analysis of the origins and development of this modernist understanding of magic, science, and religion. Tambiah's essay allows one to place Weber in a Western genealogy broader than the one I can provide in the present discussion.

6. For excellent overviews of the Levy-Bruhl controversy, see Cole and Scribner (1974:19–24) and Tambiah (1990:84–110).

7. This tension between the local and global in world religions is a useful reminder that, viewed sociologically, no world religion has in fact ever been free from parochial associations. Rita Smith Kipp (1990:15) has expressed this point aptly, remarking that the contradiction between "Christianity as a Western attribute and a transcendent faith" has been a recurrent feature of missionary histories. In an excellent study of Christian symbolism in colonial Mexico, William Taylor (1987:11) remarks that the Christianity brought by Cortés to the New World contained many elements from Spanish "little tradition," but Aztec religion displayed many of the features commonly associated with "great traditions." For other examples of the way in which world religions can be thoroughly "localized," see, for Christianity, Barker (1983), Christian (1981), and three outstanding edited collections, Badone (1990), Schneider and Lindenbaum (1987), and Saunders (1988). For a similar perspective on Buddhism in local context see, among others, Gombrich and Obeyesekere (1988), Ortner (1989), Smith (1978),

and Tambiah (1970). For several of many examples from Islam see Bowen (1991), Eickelman (1976), Lewis (1980), and Roff (1987). However, Roff (1987), Eickelman (1982, 1987), and Tambiah (1970) all provide cogent cautionary reminders of just why, as we explore world religions in local context, we must not lose sight of their transregional and transtemporal capacities.

8. Geertz's interest in evolutionary issues at this time showed the influence of his mentors, Talcott Parsons and Edward Shils. His recent work displays an entirely different cultural particularism, which avoids causal analysis and cross-cultural comparison in favor of a descriptivistic "appraisal" of cultural meanings (see Geertz 1983).

9. As Gianfranco Poggi (1983) has argued, it is best *not* to locate Weber's critique of Marx in the exhausted paradigm of "idealism" versus "materialism." Weber's mature views on the role of ideas in history steer clear of genuine idealism by insisting that ideas have historical significance inasmuch as they are institutionally embedded and borne by distinct social "carriers."

10. Pierre Bourdieu (1987:119) has aptly characterized this weakness in Weber's sociology of religion: "In his persistent efforts to make out a case for the historical efficacy of religious beliefs against the most reductionist forms of Marxist theory, Max Weber is sometimes led to privilege the notion of charisma in a manner that, as some writers have noted, is not without resonance of a Carlylean, 'heroic' philosophy of history." Arguing from a similar perspective, Kenelm Burridge provides an eloquent alternative to Weber on the social reality of prophetic charisma:

> Yet a prophet who asserted his lone singularity would not find himself welcome or wanted. He must fulfill his uniqueness not as singular merely, but as a particularly intense expression of those qualities which his audience regards as specifically fitting the nature of man. Not singular in a way that will make him an outcast, a prophet sees in himself all those to whom he speaks, and they see themselves in him—a communion from which charisma is surely born. (Burridge 1969:162)

11. A similar conceptual shift has recently occurred with the concept of culture in anthropology. The earlier image of culture as a "text" or unified corpus of symbols and meanings has given way to a new emphasis on its "distributional," pluralistic, and sometimes contested nature (Bourdieu 1977; Clifford 1986:19; Hefner 1990:239; Marcus and Fischer 1986; Ortner 1984; Schwartz 1978).

12. George Bond (1987) and Judith Shapiro (1987) present similar examples of traditional religions that are by no means immobile or inflexibly wed to local social structures.

13. On this point Horton's account resembles the widely influential "conjunctural" model Marshall Sahlins (1985) has developed for the analysis of cultural history. Like Horton, Sahlins emphasizes that structural dispositions within indigenous cosmologies are critical in mediating native perceptions of external forces.

14. The situation in the Dutch Indies as a whole was more complex than this simple statement might imply. Rita Smith Kipp (personal communication) has reminded me that outside Java the mission schools in the Dutch East Indies were

eligible for government subsidies after 1905, and the government also supported mission polyclinics and hospitals. She adds, "The government itself was not in the business of teaching Christianity or evangelizing, but it supported some of the 'social organizational' features that so often empower Christianity." Kipp's (1990) study of Dutch missionaries in the Karo lands of Sumatra provides additional detail on this complex relationship as well as an insightful anthropological account of the missionary project in general.

15. As I have discussed elsewhere (Hefner 1990:5, 239–44), this effort to bring self-identification into the center of theoretical discussion is related to the larger task of criticizing, and bridging, the opposition between meaning-centered or "interpretive" approaches in the human sciences, on one hand, and decision-making or "rational-actor" methodologies, on the other. A thoroughly revised concept of "self"-interest is pivotal in this effort. Rather than draw on the hollow shell of selfhood presented in economic models of human actors, such an alternative would replace the abstract *Homo economicus* with real people, situated in particular histories and cultures. Then it would listen carefully to learn who they are and who they wish to be. The "self" implicated in self-interest thus moves to the fore, forcing us to attend to the moral quality of social ties and their impact on a person's self-image and aspirations.

16. This point is discussed with great sensitivity by Gananath Obeyesekere (1981). Obeyesekere demonstrates that cultural meanings are not finished mental constructs but symbols that must be integrated through additional psychic "work" into the mind and practice of the individual.

17. This implies that we must qualify yet another feature of the orthodox-Weberian model of rationalization. The impulse for doctrinal universalization originates not so much in spiritual "disenchantment," as Weber (and Geertz [1973]) claimed, as in the commitment of key religious carriers to these absolute truths and the model of inclusive community they imply. Numerous ethnographic studies have demonstrated that "enchantment" (belief in magic and local spirits) is entirely compatible with adherence to a world faith. This is as true in traditional Islam and Christianity, whose official doctrines seem less tolerant of low-cosmological beliefs, as in Buddhism (see Keyes's and Jordan's essays, and Tambiah [1970]) and Hinduism, which tend to be more accommodating.

REFERENCES

Anderson, Benedict. 1983. *Imagined Communities: Reflections on the Origin and Spread of Nationalism*. London: Verso Editions.

Badone, Ellen, ed. 1990. *Religious Orthodoxy and Popular Faith in European Society*. Princeton: Princeton University Press.

Barker, John. 1983. "Missionaries and Mourning: Continuity and Change in the Death Ceremonies of a Melanesian People." In Darrell L. Whiteman, ed., *Missionaries, Anthropologists, and Cultural Change*, pp. 263–94. Williamsburg, Va.: Studies in Third World Societies.

Beidelman, T. O. 1982. *Colonial Evangelism: A Sociohistorical Study of an East African Mission at the Grassroots*. Bloomington: Indiana University Press.

Bellah, Robert N. 1964. "Religious Evolution." *American Sociological Review* 29(3): 358–74.

———. 1965. "Epilogue: Religion and Progress in Modern Asia." In Robert N. Bellah, ed., *Religion and Progress in Modern Asia*, pp. 168–229. New York: Free Press.

Bendix, Reinhard. 1977 (1960). *Max Weber: An Intellectual Portrait*. Berkeley and Los Angeles: University of California Press.

Berger, Peter L. 1967. *The Sacred Canopy: Elements of a Sociological Theory of Religion*. New York: Doubleday.

Bloch, Maurice. 1974. "Symbols, Song, Dance, and Features of Articulation: Is Religion an Extreme Form of Traditional Authority?" *European Journal of Sociology* 15:55–81.

———. 1989. "From Cognition to Ideology." In Maurice Bloch, *Ritual, History, and Power: Selected Papers in Anthropology*, pp. 106–36. London: Athlone Press.

Blum, Lawrence. 1987. "Particularity and Responsiveness." In Jerome Kagan and Sharon Lamb, eds., *The Emergence of Morality in Young Children*, pp. 306–37. Chicago: University of Chicago Press.

Bond, George C. 1987. "Ancestors and Protestants: Religious Coexistence in the Social Field of a Zambian Community." *American Ethnologist* 14(1):55–72.

Bourdieu, Pierre. 1977. *Outline of a Theory of Practice*. Translated by Richard Nice. Cambridge: Cambridge University Press.

———. 1987. "Legitimation and Structured Interests in Weber's Sociology of Religion." In Sam Whimster and Scott Lash, eds., *Max Weber, Rationality, and Modernity*, pp. 119–36. London: Allen and Unwin.

Boutilier, James A., Daniel T. Hughes, and Sharon W. Tiffany, eds. 1978. *Mission, Church, and Sect in Oceania*. ASAO Monograph No. 6. Lanham, Md.: University Press of America.

Bowen, John R. 1991. *Sumatran Politics and Poetics: Gayo History, 1900–1989*. New Haven: Yale University Press.

Brown, Diana De G., and Mario Bick. 1987. "Religion, Class, and Context: Continuities and Discontinuities in Brazilian Umbanda." *American Ethnologist* 14(1):73–93.

Burridge, Kenelm. 1969. *New Heaven, New Earth: A Study of Millenarian Activities*. New York: Schocken Books.

———. 1978. "Introduction: Missionary Occasions." In J. Boutilier et al., pp. 1–30.

Christian, William A., Jr. 1981. *Local Religion in Sixteenth-Century Spain*. Princeton: Princeton University Press.

Clifford, James. 1986. "Introduction: Partial Truths." In James Clifford and George E. Marcus, eds., *Writing Culture: The Poetics and Politics of Ethnography*, pp. 1–26. Berkeley: University of California Press.

Cole, Michael, and Sylvia Scribner. 1974. *Culture and Thought: A Psychological Introduction*. New York: John Wiley and Sons.

Comaroff, Jean. 1985. *Body of Power, Spirit of Resistance: The Culture and History of a South African People*. Chicago: University of Chicago Press.

De Craemer, W., R. Fox, and Jan Vansina. 1976. "Religious Movements in Central Africa: A Theoretical Study." *Comparative Studies in Society and History* 18(4):332–56.

Douglas, Mary. 1966. *Purity and Danger*. Harmondsworth: Penguin.

———. 1970. *Natural Symbols: Explorations in Cosmology*. New York: Pantheon Books.

Eickelman, Dale P. 1976. *Moroccan Islam: Tradition and Society in a Pilgrimage Center*. Austin: University of Texas Press.

———. 1979. "The Political Economy of Meaning." *American Ethnologist* 6:386–93.

———. 1982. "The Study of Islam in Local Contexts." *Contributions to Asian Studies* 17:1–16.

———. 1985. *Knowledge and Power in Morocco: The Education of a Twentieth-Century Notable*. Princeton: Princeton University Press.

———. 1987. "Changing Interpretations of Islamic Movements." In William R. Roff, ed., *Islam and the Political Economy of Meaning*, pp. 11–30. London: Croom Helm.

Evans-Pritchard, E. E. 1937. *Witchcraft, Oracles, and Magic among the Azande*. Oxford: Clarendon Press.

———. 1956. *Nuer Religion*. Oxford: Clarendon Press.

Farriss, Nancy M. 1984. *Maya Society under Colonial Rule: The Collective Enterprise of Survival*. Princeton: Princeton University Press.

Fernandez, James. 1978. "African Religious Movements." *Annual Review of Anthropology* 7:195–234.

Fisher, Humphrey J. 1973. "Conversion Reconsidered: Some Historical Aspects of Religious Conversions in Black Africa." *Africa* 43:27–40.

———. 1985. "The Juggernaut's Apologia: Conversion to Islam in Black Africa." *Africa* 55(2):153–73.

Forrester, Duncan B. 1977. "The Depressed Classes and Conversion to Christianity, 1860–1960." In G. A. Oddie, ed., *Religion in South Asia: Religious Conversion and Revival Movements in South Asia in Medieval and Modern Times*, pp. 35–66. Delhi: Manohar Press.

Frazer, J. G. 1922. *The Golden Bough*. London: Macmillan.

French Smith, Michael. 1988. "From Heathen to Atheist on Kairiru Island." In G. Saunders, pp. 33–46.

Fried, Morton H. 1987. "Reflections on Christianity in China." *American Ethnologist* 14(1):94–106.

Gadamer, Hans-Georg. 1975. *Philosophical Hermeneutics*. Berkeley and Los Angeles: University of California Press.

Geertz, Clifford. 1973. "'Internal Conversion' in Contemporary Bali." In Clifford Geertz, *The Interpretation of Cultures*, pp. 170–89. New York: Basic Books.

———. 1983. "Blurred Genres: The Refiguration of Social Thought." In Clifford Geertz, *Local Knowledge: Further Essays in Interpretive Anthropology*, pp. 19–35. New York: Basic Books.

Gellner, Ernest. 1981. "Flux and Reflux in the Faith of Men." In Ernest Gellner, *Muslim Society*, pp. 1–85. Cambridge: Cambridge University Press.

———. 1983. *Nations and Nationalism*. Ithaca: Cornell University Press.

Giddens, Anthony. 1984. *The Constitution of Society: Outline of a Theory of Structuration*. Berkeley: University of California Press.

Gombrich, Richard, and Gananath Obeyesekere. 1988. *Buddhism Transformed: Religious Change in Sri Lanka*. Princeton: Princeton University Press.

Goody, Jack. 1986. *The Logic of Writing and the Organization of Society*. Cambridge: Cambridge University Press.

Harris, Paul, and Paul Heelas. 1979. "Cognitive Processes and Collective Representations." *European Journal of Sociology* 20:211–41.

Hefner, Robert W. 1985. *Hindu Javanese: Tengger Tradition and Islam*. Princeton: Princeton University Press.

———. 1987. "The Political Economy of Islamic Conversion in Modern East Java." In William R. Roff, ed., *Islam and the Political Economy of Meaning*, pp. 53–78. London: Croom Helm.

———. 1990. *The Political Economy of Mountain Java: An Interpretive History*. Berkeley and Los Angeles: University of California Press.

———. 1991. "State, Nation, and Ethnicity in Modern Indonesia." In Uri Ra'anan, ed., *State and Nation in Multiethnic Societies: The Breakup of Multinational States*, pp. 198–220. Manchester: University of Manchester Press.

Hoben, Allen, and Robert W. Hefner. 1991. "The Integrative Revolution Revisited." *World Development* 19(1):17–30.

Hobsbawm, Eric, and Terence Ranger, eds. 1983. *The Invention of Tradition*. Cambridge: Cambridge University Press.

Horton, Robin. 1967. "African Traditional Thought and Western Science." *Africa* 37:50–71.

———. 1971. "African Conversion." *Africa* 41:85–108.

———. 1975a. "On the Rationality of Conversion: Part One." *Africa* 45:219–35.

———. 1975b. "On the Rationality of Conversion: Part Two." *Africa* 45:373–99.

Huber, Mary Taylor. 1987. "Constituting the Church: Catholic Missionaries on the Sepik Frontier." *American Ethnologist* 14(1):107–25.

Ifeka-Moller, Caroline. 1974. "White Power: Social-Structural Factors in Conversion to Christianity, Eastern Nigeria, 1921–1966." *Canadian Journal of African Studies* 8:55–72.

Ikenga-Metuh, Emefie. 1987. "The Shattered Microcosm: A Critical Survey of Explanations of Conversion in Africa." In K. Holst Petersen, ed., *Religion, Development, and African Identity*, pp. 11–27. Uppsala: Scandinavian Institute of African Studies.

James, William. 1982 (1902). *The Varieties of Religious Experience: A Study in Human Nature*. New York: Penguin Books.

Kammerer, Cornelia Ann. 1990. "Customs and Christian Conversion among Akha Highlanders of Burma and Thailand." *American Ethnologist* 17(2):277–91.

Kee, Howard Clark. 1980. *Christian Origins in Sociological Perspective*. Philadelphia: Westminster Press.

———. 1989. *Knowing the Truth: A Sociological Approach to New Testament Interpretation*. Minneapolis: Fortress Press.

Kipp, Rita Smith. 1990. *The Early Years of a Dutch Colonial Mission: The Karo Field*. Ann Arbor: University of Michigan Press.

Kopytoff, Igor. 1987. "The Internal African Frontier: The Making of African Political Culture." In Igor Kopytoff, *The African Frontier: The Reproduction of Traditional African Societies*, pp. 3–84. Bloomington: Indiana University Press.

Laitin, David D. 1986. *Hegemony and Culture: Politics and Religious Change among the Yoruba*. Chicago: University of Chicago Press.

Lévi-Strauss, Claude. 1966. *The Savage Mind*. Chicago: University of Chicago Press.

Lewis, I. M. 1980. "Introduction." In I. M. Lewis, ed., *Islam in Tropical Africa*, pp. 1–98. 2d ed. Bloomington: Indiana University Press.

Lienhardt, Godfrey. 1961. *Divinity and Experience: The Religion of the Dinka*. Oxford: Clarendon Press.

MacMullen, Ramsay. 1966. *Enemies of the Roman Order: Treason, Unrest, and Alienation in the Empire*. Cambridge: Harvard University Press.

Malinowski, Bronislaw. 1948. *Magic, Science, and Religion*. New York: Free Press.

Marcus, George E., and Michael M. J. Fischer. 1986. *Anthropology as Cultural Critique: An Experimental Moment in the Human Sciences*. Chicago: University of Chicago Press.

Martin, David. 1990. *Tongues of Fire: The Explosion of Protestantism in Latin America*. Oxford: Basil Blackwell.

Merton, Robert K. 1968. *Social Theory and Social Structure*. New York: Free Press.

Mommsen, Wolfgang. 1987. "Personal Conduct and Societal Change." In Sam Whimster and Scott Lash, eds., *Max Weber, Rationality, and Modernity*, pp. 35–51. London: Allen and Unwin.

Munson, Henry Jr. 1988. *Islam and Revolution in the Middle East*. New Haven: Yale University Press.

Nadel, S. F. 1954. *Nupe Religion: Traditional Beliefs and the Influence of Islam in a West African Chiefdom*. New York: Schocken Books.

Nock, A. D. 1933. *Conversion: The Old and the New in Religion from Alexander the Great to Augustine of Hippo*. Oxford: Oxford University Press.

Obeyesekere, Gananath. 1981. *Medusa's Hair: An Essay on Personal Symbols and Religious Experience*. Chicago: University of Chicago Press.

Ortner, Sherry. 1984. "Theory in Anthropology Since the Sixties." *Comparative Studies in Society and History* 26(1):126–66.

———. 1989. *High Religion: A Cultural and Political History of Sherpa Buddhism*. Princeton: Princeton University Press.

Parsons, Talcott. 1963. "Introduction." In Max Weber, *The Sociology of Religion*, pp. ix–lxvii. Boston: Beacon Press.

Poggi, Gianfranco. 1983. *Calvinism and the Capitalist Spirit: Max Weber's Protestant Ethic*. Amherst: University of Massachusetts Press.

Roff, William R. 1987. "Islamic Movements: One or Many?" In William R. Roff, ed., *Islam and the Political Economy of Meaning*, pp. 31–52. London: Croom Helm.

Sahlins, Marshall. 1985. *Islands of History*. Chicago: University of Chicago Press.

Saunders, George R., ed. 1988. *Culture and Christianity: The Dialectics of Transformation*. Westport, Conn.: Greenwood Press.

Schneider, Jane. 1990. "Spirits and the Spirit of Capitalism." In Badone, pp. 24–53.

Schneider, Jane, and Shirley Lindenbaum, eds. 1987. *Frontiers of Christian Evangelism. American Ethnologist* (Special Issue) 14:1.

Schwartz, Theodore. 1978. "Where Is the Culture? Personality as the Distributive Locus of Culture." In George D. Spindler, ed., *The Making of Psychological Anthropology*, pp. 419–41. Berkeley: University of California Press.

Shapiro, Judith. 1987. "From Tupa to the Land without Evil: The Christianization of Tupi-Guarani Cosmology." *American Ethnologist* 14(1):126–39.

Sherif, Muzafer, and Carolyn W. Sherif. 1969. "Reference Groups: Anchor Groups for the Person's Ego-Involvements." In Muzafer Sherif and Carolyn W. Sherif, *Social Psychology*, pp. 417–37. New York: Harper and Row.

Shweder, Richard A., Manamohan Mahapatra, and Joan G. Miller. 1987. "Culture and Moral Development." In Jerome Kagan and Sharon Lamb, eds., *The Emergence of Morality in Young Children*, pp. 1–83. Chicago: University of Chicago Press.

Smith, Bardwell L., ed. 1978. *Religion and Legitimation of Power in Thailand, Laos, and Burma*. Chambersburg, Penn.: Anima Books.

Snow, D. A., and R. Machalek. 1984. "The Sociology of Conversion." *Annual Review of Sociology* 10:167–90.

Stearman, A. M. 1987. *No Longer Nomads: The Sirionó Revisited*. Lanham, Md.: Hamilton Press.

Tambiah, Stanley J. 1970. *Buddhism and the Spirit Cults in Northeast Thailand*. Cambridge: Cambridge University Press.

———. 1990. *Magic, Science, Religion, and the Scope of Rationality*. Cambridge: Cambridge University Press.

Tapp, Nicholas. 1989. "The Impact of Missionary Christianity upon Marginalized Ethnic Minorities: The Case of the Hmong." *Journal of Southeast Asian Studies* 27:70–90.

Taylor, William B. 1987. "The Virgin of Guadalupe in New Spain: An Inquiry into the Social History of Marian Devotion." *American Ethnologist* 14(1):9–33.

Tylor, E. B. 1913 (1871). *Primitive Culture*. London: Murray.

Volkman, Toby Alice. 1985. *Feasts of Honor: Ritual and Change in the Toraja Highlands*. Illinois Studies in Anthropology No. 16. Urbana: University of Illinois Press.

Weber, Max. 1946. "The Social Psychology of the World Religions." In H. H. Gerth and C. Wright Mills, eds., *From Max Weber: Essays in Sociology*, pp. 267–301. New York: Oxford University Press.

———. 1956. *The Sociology of Religion*. Translated by Ephraim Fischoff. Boston: Beacon Press.

———. 1978. *Economy and Society: An Outline of Interpretive Sociology*. Edited by Guenther Roth and Claus Wittich. Berkeley: University of California Press.

Wedenoja, William. 1988. "The Origins of Revival, a Creole Religion in Jamaica." In Saunders, pp. 91–116.

Whimster, Sam, and Scott Lash. 1987. "Introduction." In Sam Whimster and Scott Lash, eds., *Max Weber, Rationality, and Modernity*, pp. 1–31. London: Allen and Unwin.

White, Geoffrey M. 1988. "Symbols of Solidarity in the Christianization of Santa Isabel, Solomon Islands." In Saunders, pp. 11–32.

PART TWO

Community Recast:
The Form and Meanings of Christian Conversion

CHAPTER TWO

From the Jesus Movement toward Institutional Church

Howard Clark Kee

THE JEWISH CRISIS OF SOCIAL IDENTITY AT THE OPENING OF THE COMMON ERA

With the seemingly irreparable loss of political autonomy for the Jews in their Palestinian homeland in 63 B.C.E. as a result of the Roman invasion under Pompey, the options for social identity of this ancient people were many.[1] Culturally, tens of thousands of Jews living in urban areas across the Middle East and the Mediterranean world, in various ways and to widely different degrees, assimilated to the dominant Greco-Roman culture. The successors of Alexander the Great had established Hellenistic-style cities in Palestine, Syria, and east of the Jordan, where all the features of Hellenistic culture were present and inviting participation: theaters, hippodromes, gymnasia, temples. Especially in Alexandria, in cities along the Mediterranean coast of Palestine, and on the shores of the Sea of Galilee, many Jews were—in varying degrees—assimilated to the dominant culture. They adopted Greek as their basic language and sought to perceive the underlying commonalities between their ancient scriptural traditions and the philosophical insights of the Greeks, especially the ontology of Plato and Stoic ethics. The Law of Moses and the law of nature were seen as basically compatible, especially when allegorical modes of interpretation were employed to get behind the literal meaning of the narratives and legal prescriptions. One of the chief centers of this Hellenizing influence was Sepphoris, which lay just a few miles from Nazareth, the hometown of Jesus.

For Jesus, however, and for the majority of his Jewish contemporaries the impulse was not to assimilate but to define anew what it meant to regard oneself as a member of the covenant people of God, and to seek to discern how God was still at work to bring to fruition his purpose for his chosen people. We must examine both the subsequent development of Judaism and the rise of Christianity as a breakaway movement from Judaism in the light of the social and conceptual solutions that developed in response to this crisis of social identity. The closely linked issues of covenantal definition and divine agency must be looked at in some detail.

The conviction basic to the whole of the Jewish scriptural tradition was that down through the centuries God had chosen certain patriarchal figures to be the progenitors and leaders of a people who stood in direct relation to the creator and through whom the divine purposes were to be achieved in the world. The details of that corporate relationship changed over the centuries, reaching what was to remain the norm in the reworked historical and legal traditions of Israel. These traditions were given final form by the Jewish leaders who reorganized and reconstituted the Jewish people following their return to Palestine in the sixth century at the instigation of the Persians and under the subsequent leadership of Ezra and Nehemiah. Although the latter were priests, their cultural role was to propagate their edited version of the scriptural traditions of Israel and instruct Israel in its teachings.

That program seems to have continued effectively under the benign and cooperative rule of the Persians, but after Alexander, their Hellenistic successors sought aggressively to convert to Greek cultural and conceptual modes all peoples subject to them, including the Jews. The resistance of the latter to this enterprise led to the Maccabean revolt in 168 B.C.E. and to the establishment of an independent Jewish state, which survived in increasingly secular and conflict-ridden form until the coming of Pompey in 63. From this time on the basic issues for Jewish group identity were: What are the requirements for admission to the covenant people? and How is status to be maintained within this people? Ironically, the seriousness of this identity problem was compounded by the fact that through the writings of culturally assimilated Jews, and the availability of a Greek version of the Jewish Bible (evidently prepared in the second century B.C.E.), many thoughtful non-Jews were attracted to the strict monotheism and the high ethical standards of the Jewish biblical tradition. Some of these Gentiles merely associated loosely with the Jewish communities, but some of the men accepted circumcision and sought to become full participants in the covenantal life. The question was pressing, therefore: How were the boundaries of Jewish covenantal existence to be drawn?

The Nationalistic Option

For some the main issue was political autonomy for the Jewish people, although as the sole criterion this was seriously undermined by the growing secularization of the Maccabean rulers in the later second and early first centuries B.C.E. Not until the mid-sixties C.E. and then again in 132–135 were broad-based nationalistic movements formed. Both attempts went down to resounding, catastrophic defeat, as is attested by the ruins of Masada, the nationalists' last stronghold overlooking the southern Dead Sea, and by the reports of their group suicide.

The Priestly Option

The alternative options for Jewish group identity were, from the first century until modern times, to be of paramount significance for both Judaism and nascent Christianity. One option took the point of view that because God had decreed the establishment of the central shrine in Jerusalem and had given detailed instructions on how his people were to deal with him there, and because he was thought to dwell invisibly in the innermost shrine, the major task for the maintenance of Jewish existence was to preserve the temple and to perform the appropriate ceremonies there. The priestly establishment, therefore, was the central agency for carrying foward the special relationship that God had chosen to establish with his people. A group of aristocratic Jews, who by a combination of convictions and politico-economic connections stood to benefit from the perdurance of the temple and its priesthood, supported this point of view. Known as the Sadducees, they had the strong backing of the Roman authorities, who recognized the symbolic value for Jews of this splendid structure in Jerusalem as well as its central economic function in the region. Jewish pilgrims came by the thousands, as did sightseeing Gentiles. Their expenditures for food and lodging and for the appropriate sacrifices for participation in the temple cult provided the chief source of income in the land. Nothing could be allowed to threaten this religio-economic establishment.

The Separatist Option

With the growing secularization of the Maccabees, however, many Jews had sought an additional instrument of religious identity that would not replace the temple but which would provide a sense of direct and steady involvement in the life of God's people. This thrust toward group piety was expressed by two major groups during the period under investigation, the Essenes and the Pharisees. The origins of the Essene movement were illuminated by the discovery in the mid-1940s of a library of documents, apparently stored by the Essenes in caves on a barren bluff overlooking the northern end of the Dead Sea when, in the mid-sixties of the first century, the Roman army under Titus invaded Palestine to put down the revolt of the Jewish nationalists. After archaeologists studied the documents, the nearby site of the community headquarters was excavated, and other documents were found as well.

The documents reveal that a dissident priest had become convinced that the priestly establishment no longer served the God of Israel and that the temple was no longer the locus for the true and pure worship of God. Rallying a group of followers, the One Who Teaches It Right (as he dubbed himself) withdrew to this desert retreat. There the members of his community devoted themselves to the study of the Jewish scriptures, which they interpreted as indicating that they were the divinely chosen heirs of the tradition. They alone defined and obeyed the pure law of God for his people and would survive a final battle with the forces of evil (human and angelic), whereupon God would establish them as the true and pure priesthood in a radically rebuilt Jerusalem temple. Into that city and into the renewed temple could come only those who were pure according to their most rigid standards. Thus, for example, the blind, lame, lepers, demoniacs, menstruating women, and any who had contacted a corpse were denied entry. Only members of the twelve Jewish tribes could enter the temple, and converts to Judaism who had gone through years of probation.

The Essenes lived in the towns and cities of Palestine, although they were expected to maintain a high degree of ritual purity even there, and multiple copies of what seems to have been a basic set of rules for them were found at the Dead Sea site. They were obligated to visit the community center annually. The leaders of the sect lived according to another, more demanding, constitutional document, the Scroll of the Rule, which included extremely strict rules of purity, violation of which could result in penalties ranging from temporary to total expulsion from the group. In addition to the reading, study, and exposition of the scriptures and their own sacred legal and hymnic writings, the group's rituals seem to have included periodic ceremonial washings. The excavators found pools for this near the community center. From the documents it is also evident that their central corporate act was eating a meal of bread and wine, in anticipation of the day when God would send into their midst the two anointed agents who would lead them into the New Age of righteousness: the anointed (messiah) king and the anointed (messiah) priest. With the destruction of their community center and the subsequent reorganization of Jews by the Romans after 70, this group disappeared, its definition of covenant identity and divine agents unknown until the chance discovery of the Dead Sea Scrolls.

The Pietistic Option

Apparently disillusioned by their vain efforts to combat the growing secularism and ruthless internal struggles for power among the Maccabean rulers and their descendants, a group calling themselves Pharisees (which probably means "purists") turned from politics to personal piety.[2] They transferred the rules for purity from their original application to the priesthood and the operations within the central sanctuary to the realm of the home and of the voluntary community gathered there. The "community" might have been an extended family or a larger gathering of people who met in a home. There the group studied the Jewish scriptures, perhaps supplementing these improvised expositions with hymns and prayers. Table fellowship, for which the purity regulations of the scriptural tradition were freshly interpreted and applied, was also central to their group life.

Although the Pharisees seem to have continued to visit the temple on the appropriate or required occasions, the major focus of their common religious life was the voluntary gathering, which in Greek is *synagoge*. All the oldest archaeological evidence suggests that, until the late second or early third century, these groups met in homes or in informal settings. Their mode of study and worship seems to have been unstructured and as ad hoc as their meeting places.

Only after the destruction of the temple and with the encouragement of the Roman authorities did the Pharisees begin the long process of designating which of their biblical traditions were to be considered authoritative and of developing the elaborate interpretations of those traditions to demonstrate their relevance for their own time. The results of this process were the Jewish canon of scripture and the beginning of the literary enterprise that produced the Mishnah and the Talmud in the period from the second to the sixth century. The patterns of leadership, worship, and instruction that became rabbinic Judaism also emerged. Through these developments the Pharisees were able to live within the pagan-dominated culture, and yet through the regular retreats to the communal piety of the gathered group they were able to maintain their identity as God's people. In later centuries they claimed that these modes of community identity went back to the time of Moses and the first giving of the Law, providing an example of the process of legitimation that sociologists of knowledge have taught us to observe.[3]

Divine Agents of Community Renewal

Obviously, there is a direct correlation between any of these visions of the new community and the agent of God through whom they are to be realized. For the nationalists the king was the obvious figure, and in Jewish tradition the king was believed to stand in a special relationship to God. Thus in Psalm 2, the king is addressed as the Son of God. One image of this royal figure for the renewal of Israel was a star, descended from Jacob, the progenitor of the twelve tribes of Israel (Nm 24:17). It is not surprising that in the year 132 the last claimant to this royal role, Bar Kozibah, gave himself a new name, Bar Kochbah (Son of the Star). We have already noted that in the Dead Sea community, one of the two messiahs was apparently to be a king, although his role was secondary to that of the anointed priest.

The Dead Sea writings refer to the coming of a prophet at the end of the present age, as predicted by Moses in Deuteronomy (18:15). In Deuteronomy, Moses laments that his contemporaries did not fully heed his counsel and decrees and says that one day another prophet would come in their midst to whom they would give full obedience. Josephus in his *Wars of the Jews* foretells the role of that prophet. He describes those who called people to gather around them east of the Jordan so that they might reenact—with divine support—the entrance into the Promised Land, recalling the Israelites under Joshua twelve hundred years earlier. The miraculous signs that accomplished the work of prophets in the Jewish biblical tradition were said to have been evident among these latter-day prophets as well.

Among the Essenes and the Pharisees the teacher, the interpreter of the biblical tradition, had the primary role in preparing the covenant people for their final and ultimate renewal under God. This teacher set the standards for their individual and group behavior, and through him God would disclose to this body of the elect his purposes for the creation and for his people within it. The common meal of fellowship was central to this awaited time of fulfillment, because in sharing the sacred bread and wine the members anticipated the accomplishment of the divine purpose in and through them.

THE JESUS MOVEMENT IN ITS ORIGINS

The oldest sources we have for the origins of what we are calling the Jesus movement are: (1) a few traces of tradition about Jesus preserved in the letters of Paul, written in the fifties; (2) a source used by the writers of the Gospel of Matthew and the Gospel of Luke, consisting mostly of sayings of Jesus (called Q by scholars, from the German word *Quelle* [source]); (3) the Gospel of Mark, which was also used as a major source by Matthew and Luke, and which provided the basic framework for the other gospels. In all these sources Jesus is pictured as one through whose words and actions his followers perceive God at work, preparing for the renewal of his covenant people and, through them, for the overcoming of the powers of evil and the renewal of the creation.

The radical nature of this promise of divine renewal is apparent throughout the teachings of Jesus. In Mark 4:30–32 he compares what

God is doing for his new people with a seed that is growing unobserved but which will produce astonishingly abundant fruit. Using the familiar metaphor of guests invited to a supper (Lk 13:16–23), he makes the point that those to whom the invitation was first extended are too preoccupied with their routine affairs to accept. As a result the invitation then goes to those whom society shuns as socially, physically, or ritually marginal. Similarly, in response to questions from John the Baptist, whose follower Jesus had been, Jesus describes and justifies his activities as follows: "Go and tell John what you have seen and heard: the lame walk, the blind see, the deaf hear, and the poor have the good news preached to them" (Lk 6:20–23). These phrases are all drawn directly from the Jewish prophetic tradition (Is 29:18–19; 35:5–6; 61:1). The designations are precisely those used in the Parable of the Supper (Lk 14:15–29): those who are outsiders by traditional, ritual, and ethnic standards become included in the people of the new age.

To engage in the activities that are attributed to Jesus and to which he calls his followers (Mk 3:13–14; 6:7–12), involved them inevitably in a break with their families and the normal pattern of social performance and responsibility (Lk 9:57–62). That this was indeed the result is apparent when, in the midst of Jesus' exorcisms, his mother and brothers and sister come to take him home, assuming that he has gone mad (Mk 3:21, 31). His response is to redefine the family as those who do the will of God—thereby setting aside the basic patriarchal, hereditary structure of social identity in the Jewish tradition.

Intensifying the radicalness of his definition of God's people, he even depicts God as one who takes the initiative in bringing into right relationship with himself those who have been regarded as lost. Building on the familiar image of Israel as the flock of God (Ps 23; Ps 80; Jer 23; Ez 34), Jesus compares God's seeking the alienated and estranged of humanity to a shepherd leaving the conformist flock to seek and restore his lost sheep (Lk 15:3–7).

In the Gospel of Mark, Jesus focuses his healing and exorcisms on those who by ritual standards of the time would have been excluded from full membership in the covenant people: lepers, demoniacs, pagans, and those polluted by contact with the dead or by bodily emission. Jesus is seen as justifying these activities not only by linking them with the Jewish prophetic tradition, as we noted above, but also by explicitly claiming that the "finger of God," which was at work in the ancient history of Israel, delivering the people from slavery in Egypt (Ex 4), is now at work through him to liberate the creation from the powers of evil and to establish God's rule on earth (Lk 11:20).

The symbolism of covenantal renewal is evident in the familiar stories of Jesus' miraculous feeding of thousands in a desert-like area in Galilee (Mk 6:30–44). The parallels with the Old Testament story of God's feeding Israel under Moses in the desert of Sinai are obvious. To ensure that the reader does not miss the point that the renewal of the covenant people is of paramount interest here, Mark employs a symbolic phrase depicting Israel as a shepherdless flock, a term that appears on two occasions in the biblical tradition: Numbers 27:17, where Israel in the wilderness seems to be leaderless, and 1 Kings 22:17, where the Israelite monarchy is about to go into decline. Jesus' activity—whatever the historical origins of these narratives may have been—is here pictured as the work of God's agent in renewing his people in their time of anguished transition and despair.

In sharp contrast to the more or less triumphant expectations of covenantal renewal that we have been examining, in the Markan tradition Jesus announces that he and his followers will suffer and die, not in spite of their role in the divine purpose but because of it. The nearest precedents to this in the Jewish tradition appear in Isaiah 53, where the nation is pictured as a servant who suffers in the course of obedience to God, and in the Book of Daniel, where those who refuse to conform to the decrees of the pagan ruler are threatened with death but then miraculously delivered. In both the later Jewish prophetic tradition and here in the older gospel tradition, apocalypticists believe that the faithful must endure suffering and even martyrdom, but that they do so in the assurance that God will intervene in their behalf and ultimately vindicate them and the divine plan.[4] Not surprisingly, therefore, in Mark the disciples repeatedly reject the notion that Jesus' role under God involves his suffering and death or that they abandon him in the hour of his execution. Yet they, too, are called to suffer: "If anyone would come after me, let him deny himself and take up his cross and follow me. For whoever would save his life will lose it, and whoever loses his life for my sake and that of the message of Good News will save it" (Mk 8:34–35).

Converging lines of evidence—from Paul, Q, and Mark—point to Jesus' final meal as the occasion of his explanation to his followers that his impending death is the sacrifice which will ratify the new covenant of God and that he and they would be vindicated in the new age and have authority over the new covenant community. The pouring of the wine and the breaking of the loaf symbolize his death (Mk 14:24–25; 1 Cor 11:23–25). In the Q variant of this tradition Jesus addresses those who have stayed with him during this time of testing and tells them that just as God has covenanted a kingdom for him so has he covenanted for them that they will share the table fellowship with him in the new age. Their fidelity will be rewarded by God in that they will "sit on thrones judging the twelve tribes of Israel" (Lk 22:28–30).

Meanwhile, however, his followers need to carry on the work of propagandizing (Mk 6:6–11). There are instructions to them for the ongoing life of the community, covering issues ranging from divorce and marriage to attitudes toward wealth and relationships among the members. Yet these guidelines are not given institutional support, because the end of the age is expected to occur within the generation of Jesus' followers (Mk 9:1; see also Paul's expectation in 1 Cor 15:51; 1 Thes 4:15). And no provision is made for authority or leadership roles among the followers. Their main objective is to spread as widely and quickly as possible the message of the new age and the signs of its coming, which appear as healings and exorcisms. Jesus' followers need no credentials or support system: that they have been commissioned by him suffices for the effective carrying out of their work.

We have here a prime example of the charismatic origins of a religious movement becoming differentiated from the tradition in which it initially took its rise. Already within the Gospel of Mark, however, the signs of the formalization and definition of responsibility over against the Jewish matrix appear. Thus in Mark 7 distinction is made between purity as perceived by—or attributed to—Jesus and those principles of purity that were being developed by the Pharisaic-rabbinic movement by the last third of the first century. As I note in my detailed study of Mark, *The Community of the New Age*, the latter half of the Gospel of Mark takes the form of what might be called a foundation document, which outlines not only the origins of the religious movement but also the moral and community obligations of its adherents. Here the analogy with the Scroll of the Rule in the Dead Sea community is quite exact, even though the specifics of the purity laws differ so sharply. In Mark only the structure of the inner circle is defined: there are no signs of hierarchy or authority figures within the community.

Mark depicts the gatherings of Jesus' followers as taking place in homes or in public settings. Judging by the importance of justifying Jesus' interpretation of the divine will by appeal to the Jewish scriptures, and by the implications that central to their existence was table fellowship, one must conclude that to the external observer the Christians' gatherings would have looked very much like those of the Pharisees. The crucial differences were in the criteria for participation and for maintenance of membership.

THE PAULINE MOVEMENT IN ITS ORIGINS

Careful analysis of the career of Paul, based on his fairly frequent autobiographical remarks and asides as well as on our knowledge of events and rulers of the early empire, makes possible a dependable chronology of his life. His conversion apparently took place within one or two years of the death of Jesus, and his execution occurred under Nero in the sixties. The early Christian movement associated with Paul developed concurrently with that of the Jesus movement proper, which derived its tradition and its leadership from those associated with Jesus during his public career. As one can infer from Paul's fluent Greek, his literary facility, and his knowing use of such technical philosophical terms as conscience and natural law, he was profoundly influenced by the aggressive Hellenistic culture of the northeastern quadrant of the Mediterranean where he lived during the early years of his career. Although the (later) book of Acts links him with Tarsus, which was a major center for Stoic thought in this period, Paul mentions as the locus of his earlier activities the thoroughly Hellenized cities of Antioch-on-the-Orontes in Syria and Damascus, the largest of the cities of the Decapolis, which successors of Alexander had built or rebuilt in Syria and Palestine to foster the Hellenization of the region. It should not be surprising, therefore, that Hellenistic thought and literary culture strongly affected Paul's perception of Jesus and his significance.

Yet when Paul offers autobiographical information, as he does in his letter to the Galatians, he speaks only of his Jewish heritage, training, and activity. He identifies himself as a Jew by birthright, emphasizing his Hebrew heritage, and as one deeply committed to the Pharisaic understanding of that tradition. He first encountered the Jesus movement through a gathering of its devotees in Damascus. That he made every effort to destroy the movement is understandable on the grounds that, in contradiction to the Pharisaic requirements for participation, its membership standards were wholly open, and the group very likely included many who would have been totally objectionable by Pharisaic norms. Mingling boasts and confession, he depicts himself as having exceeded all his contemporaries in his zeal to stamp out this revolutionary mode of covenantal identity deriving from Jesus.

He gives no details about the nature of the mystical experience through which God "revealed his son to [or in] me" (Gal 1:16). He came to understand this as a vision of Jesus whom God had raised from the dead and as a commissioning act on the part of Jesus, calling Paul to the special task of announcing primarily to Gentiles the good news of what God had done to renew the covenant people. Whatever the basis of his experience, it came to be equated with the appearances of the risen Christ to his own disciples, as the argument of Paul in 1 Corinthians (9:9; 15:3–9) makes clear and as seems to have been acknowledged by the Jerusalem disciples in accepting Paul's divine authorization for his special task. The motif of an inclusive community, which is implicit in the gospel tradition and which seems to have been a major source of the hostility that Jesus encountered from his contemporaries, became the central focus of Paul's outlook and career.

There seems to have been no precedent for a systematic outreach to the Gentiles, although as we have seen, the gospel tradition included several examples of Gentile participation in the new community, and ethnic inclusiveness was implicit in what Jesus said and did. Because Paul's strategy was to move from city to city around the eastern Mediterranean, it was essential that he have coworkers in those cities as his work prospered, not only to assist him as he developed new communities but also to carry on after his departure. In his letters he refers to men and women who aided him in his work (Rom 16:3, 9) and who provided their homes as meeting places for the emergent and growing communities (Rom 16:5; 1 Cor 16:19). He says explicitly that instead of establishing uniform rules and procedures for all these new groups, he adopts the strategies and norms that seem to be appropriate to the local situation (1 Cor 9:19–23). Although he gives many specific ethical injunctions, he considers mutual love to be the binding force within the group and the guiding principle of common action (1 Cor 13). Yet on certain issues, such as a member of the Corinthian community living in an incestuous relationship, he flatly decrees that the community gather and solemnly expel the offending member (1 Cor 5:1–8). His major goal is to cover the entire Roman world with his message (Rom 15:19–20, 24), and he promotes the adoption of new strategies and standards to achieve this vast and urgent goal.

The basic principle for acceptance within the new covenant community is trust in the reconciling action of God in having sent Jesus, and in allowing him to die and be raised again to atone for the world's sins. In one of Paul's central statements (2 Cor 5:9) he declares that "in Christ God was reconciling the world to himself . . . and has committed to us [Paul, the other apostles, and their converts] the work of reconciliation." He denies that divine acceptance is in any way conditional on human ritual or ethical behavior or that divine rejection is the consequence of violation of either Jewish law or the law of nature. Paul's major task is the call for universal reconciliation, and it requires the services of fellow workers, men and women. But in light of his expectation that the work will be done and the new age will come within his own lifetime (1 Thes 4:13), he has no interest in setting up rules or leadership structures. What is called for is a dedicated pragmatism that can assure that the vast task of world mission will be speedily achieved.

THE JESUS MOVEMENT BECOMES THE CHURCH

The ancient decision to position the Gospel of Matthew at the beginning of the collection of early Christian writings known as the New Testament was, from the standpoint of those who made it, wise and fully justified. This gospel works to achieve simultaneously two goals: to show that the enterprise that Jesus launched was the divinely intended culmination of the laws and promises made to Israel of old, and to demonstrate that Jesus arranged for institutional patterns of authority and behavior for the membership of the new community. Not surprisingly, the term "church" is used only in Matthew among the gospels. The Greek original, *ekklesia*, meaning a group called together, sharply and intentionally contrasts with *synagoge*, the current Jewish term for community gathering.

As we have noted in connection with the rise of rabbinic Judaism in the later first century C.E., legitimation is a major concern. To achieve this, the claim is made that everything that happened from the birth to the death of Jesus is verified in Matthew by his constant repetition of phrases such as, "This was done in order that it might be fulfilled which was spoken by . . . ," followed by a reference to Moses or one of the prophets or psalmists and then usually the relevant quotation. Each detail of the story of Jesus' birth is linked with scriptural prophecy or precedent, from its location in Bethlehem to Joseph's retreat to Egypt to escape Herod's slaughter of the children. Matthew even justifies the holy family's move to Nazareth by an apparent reference to scripture, even though no explicit mention of this village is made in the Old Testament (Mt 2:23). The aim of this appeal to ancient documentation is to prove to the readers of Matthew, and especially to the members of his community, that Jesus is the true heir of the promises to Israel and that his calling into being this new covenant people therefore consummates the divine purpose.

The contrast between the leader of the old covenant people, Moses, and Jesus is implicit throughout Matthew. Matthew frequently depicts Jesus as instructing or feeding his people on a mountain (4:8; 5:1; 8:1; 14:23; 15:29; 17:1; 21:1; 28:16), recalling Moses on Mount Sinai. The basic literary structure of Matthew is marked by a five-times recurring phrase (7:28; 11:1; 13:53; 19:1; 26:1): "When Jesus had finished . . ." These words appear following each of the five major discourses into which Matthew has arranged his report of the teachings of Jesus. The first is the Sermon on the Mount (Mt 5–7); the second is Jesus' commissioning of the Twelve to carry forward his work, greatly expanded from the Markan version (Mt 10); the third is Matthew's greatly expanded collection of the parables of Jesus (Mt 13); the fourth is a set of instructions to the church about settling disputes among its members (Mt 18); and the fifth is Matthew's expanded edition of Jesus' disclosure to his followers of the events of catastrophe and judgment that will occur at the end of the age and from which they will be miraculously delivered (Mt 24–25). (We comment below about the other extended discourse section, Matthew 23, which consists of a direct, bitter attack on the Pharisees.) A more general collection of material, which includes narratives about Jesus and scattered reports of his teachings, precedes each discourse. Considering the narrative section of Matthew as introduction and the story of Jesus' trial and death as conclusion, the central section of Matthew (Mt 3–25) falls into five sections—apparently an intentional parallel to the fivefold Torah of Israel, or Law of Moses, which makes up the first five books of the Bible.

Matthew assures us throughout his account of Jesus' giving of the new law that modern interpreters have not imposed this contrast with Moses on the writing; Matthew has Jesus observe that "you have heard it said of old [i.e., by Moses, since he is in each case quoted], but I say to you" (5:21; 5:27, 31, 33, 38, 43). Jesus' primary concerns in Matthew are defining the community in contrast to the other Jewish options of the period (especially Pharisaism) and regularizing life within the community. Jesus is obviously fulfilling for Matthew this assignment as the New Moses, and the requirements of the new community are more stringent than those of the old: the righteousness of its members must exceed those of the scribes and Pharisees (5:17–20).

The negative quality of this community in opposition to Judaism is how Matthew forcefully assigns the primary blame for Jesus' death to the Jewish leaders. Their bitter hostility toward Jesus is underscored throughout the gospel and culminates in the events leading up to his trials and condemnation in Jerusalem. Only in Matthew does Pilate want to release Jesus as innocent, and only there do the leaders cry out, "His blood be upon us and our children" (27:25). Only in Matthew is the guard placed at the tomb to prevent the followers of Jesus from stealing his body in order to claim that he had been raised from the dead, and only in this version of the story is the implicit charge of fraud made by them in connection with the resurrection tradition.

Matthew is undoubtedly writing his gospel when hostility and competition between the leaders of the two groups is mounting. Each claims to be the true heir of the biblical hopes, to have the true interpretation of the scriptures, and to be developing the divinely ordained institution that will carry forward this understanding of the tradition. As we have noted, one of these hostile groups calls its gatherings *synagoge*, and the other uses a comparable term for a meeting, *ekklesia*. Although in Mark there are references to the Jewish groups under the designation of "their synagogues" (Mk 1:23, 29), that term is greatly expanded in Matthew (Mt 4:23; 9:35; 10:17; 12:9; 13:54; 23:34).

By the time Matthew is writing—probably at the end of the first century—the Pharisaic movement has been transformed into the beginnings of rabbinic Judaism, with growing attention to regularizing membership in the gathered groups, to specifying how the ancient laws should be applied in the present situation, and, negatively, to defining what modes of thought and action are unacceptable for the membership. The most dramatic evidence of this from the Jewish side appears in the so-called Eighteen Benedictions, one of which refers to heretics—almost certainly the early Christians—whose teachings and claims regarding biblical tradition are to be denounced. In Matthew 23 we have the bitter denunciation of the Pharisees as hypocrites and religious frauds, in language that goes far beyond that of the other gospels in its hostile, irreconcilable tone and substance. The conflict with emergent rabbinic Judaism is not theoretical but probably in process. This vitriolic chapter was probably added to the original gospel as the competition became fiercer.

In the rabbinic materials, keys are one of the recurrent images for the terms of admission to the covenant community. As instruments of inclusion and exclusion, their import is clear. What is significant is that keys are used to refer to the specifics of the terms under which participation is or is not appropriate. In one of the best-known passages of Matthew—one which is unique to this gospel (16:19)—Jesus gives the twelve apostles the keys of the kingdom, with the instruction that they are to determine admissibility.

Matthew 18, as we noted, is concerned with similar decision making about which disobedient members of the community are to be forgiven and restored and which are to be excluded. Even the process of evaluation is briefly described, involving solemn meetings of the members for that purpose. The final court of appeal is to the group (*ekklesia*) as a whole (Mt 18:17).

The last chapter of Matthew (Mt 28), in which Jesus commissions his followers to carry on his work, fits precisely the pattern of emergent institutionalization. It refers to ritual initiations (baptism), to liturgical formulations (the trinitarian mode), and to a pattern of instruction—rather than merely conversion—that the disciples are to carry out. The potential membership is all the nations of the world, in sharp contrast to the explicit instruction at the outset that the twelve disciples are to limit their evangelizing to "the lost sheep of the house of Israel" (Mt 10:5). Indeed, Matthew has reworked the tradition to show that the church will be a new entity, replacing the ethnic origins of traditional Israel. In his version of the Parable of the Wicked Vineyard Workers (Mt 21:33–46), which builds on the prophetic image of Israel as God's vineyard (Is 5), Matthew has Jesus say that the vineyard will be taken from Israel and given to a "new people" (in Greek, *ethne*). Matthew's transformation of the Jesus tradition from its charismatic, improvisatory origins is quite complete.

ECCLESIASTICAL STRUCTURING IN THE PAULINE TRADITION

More than a third of the writings attributed to Paul in the New Testament are widely recognized on linguistic and conceptual grounds to be pseudonymous, that is, written in Paul's name by those of a later generation who regarded themselves as standing in the Pauline tradition. These deutero-Pauline writings, as scholars have come to call them, include the letters to the churches of the Colossians and the Ephesians and the ostensibly personal communications, two to Timothy and one to Titus. In these documents we can observe the significant changes that have occurred within the early Christian communities with regard to the attitudes toward fellow members within households and the emergence of a clearly demarcated leadership structure.

In these letters we find lists of members of the households—wives, husbands, children, slaves, masters—together with specifics about relationships and assignment of responsibilities. The Roman and earlier Jewish paternalism, which was challenged by Jesus and by the older gospel tradition, has now become the norm within Christian households as well. Women are to be submissive to their husbands. Their most significant function is childbearing. They are to avoid ostentation in dress or jewelry and are to be models of humility and decorum. No role within the church organization is assigned to them, except that widows are to be the special concern and beneficiaries of the common funds of the churches. Children are instructed to obey their parents, but no special welcome is indicated for them in the community, in contrast to the implication of Jesus' welcoming of children into the kingdom of God (Mk 9:37; 10:15). Slaves must obey their masters; there is no hint of change in their social status.

Operationally, there are three levels of leadership in the churches: deacons, elders, and bishops. The etymology of the first category, which derives from a Greek word for serving or attending to someone's needs, fits the job description: to meet the ongoing requirements of the community for basic necessities for the common life. Presumably these would entail preparing food for common meals and taking care of the collection and distribution of funds. In the authentic letters of Paul women served as deacons (Rom 16:1), but in the later Pauline tradition the office seems to be exclusively male. The elders were the honored leaders of the community and seem to have met as a committee or board to establish rules and to ensure orderly routines within the life of the church. Bishop derives from *episkopos*, or "overseer." Hence, the bishop is the one who presides over the church, standing at the peak of the hierarchy with everyone subject to his authority. This basic pattern was to become normative for all the churches by the early years of the second century, as the church moved increasingly away from its charismatic origins to its developed institutional forms, dominated in each area by a monarchic episcopacy.

Although the churches presumably continued to engage in evangelism, their continued existence depended in considerable measure on the procreation of the members, whose offspring could then carry on and accept responsibilities within the institution. Timothy, for example, took on a leadership role in a tradition of Christian identity that went back to his mother's and his grandmother's generations (2 Tm 1:5). The economic spread of the church membership is considerable, and so the rich are warned not to show off or to dominate the poor among the members. The clear implication is that the wealthy have power within the group.

A basic shift in the self-definition of the community is also revealed in the different connotations of "faith." In the writings of Paul faith is primarily trust, reliance, and confidence in God's words and deeds. A prime example is Abraham's trust that God would provide him a son, so that the covenant promises might extend to his posterity. Paul, in his letters to the Galatians and the Romans (Gal 3; Rom 4), saw that confidence in the divine promise as the basis of one's relationship to God and participation in his covenant people. In the deutero-Pauline materials, in contrast, faith means right belief or true doctrine. A direct and sharp attack on false doctrine and on heresy is promulgated within the church (1 Tm 6:11–16; Ti 2:1). This emphasis on faith as correct belief does not eliminate the need for members to trust God and his word, but it indicates a consolidation of the group's beliefs and a careful delineation of acceptable religious concepts and of those that could lead to expulsion. Socially, conceptually, and structurally, the churches in the Pauline tradition had become by the turn of the second century unmistakably institutional.

CONCLUSION

The developing structures of the community were not limited to the Matthean and Pauline strands of the early Christian tradition. In the Johannine tradition, for example, the community addressed in the Gospel of John has no leadership structure. All members are equal, and their only ethical norm is to love one another. In the last of the Epistles of John (3 Jn), in contrast, one Diotrophes is sternly rebuked for failing to accept the authority of the elder and is charged with disrupting the programs of the bishop. In the Christian writings of the first half of the second century known as the Apostolic Fathers, the consistent pattern is one of male domination, of service provided by the deacons, and of authority exercised by the bishop. All of this is justified by appeal to the example and words of Jesus. But beyond doubt, the factors that led to this basic change in self-understanding of the covenant people include the spontaneous shift from charismatic origins to institutional structures, driven by the need to protect a movement launched with the expectation of a speedy end to the present age, and the necessity to adjust to a movement that had spread with such astonishing rapidity by the opening years of the second century. Although the tradition looks back to Jesus and his message in the Jewish prophetic and apocalyptic tradition, the patterns that it adopts and adapts are those of the wider Roman world: two centuries later it would provide the emperor Constantine a centralizing and coordinating system.

NOTES

1. The historical survey offered here is given in fuller form in chapters 1 and 2 of my *Understanding the New Testament*. The epistemological and hermeneutical approach used is described in detail in my *Knowing the Truth: A Sociological Approach to New Testament Interpretation*.

2. The phrase comes from the title of Jacob Neusner's (1979) study of the origins of Pharisaism, *From Politics to Piety*.

3. See, for example, Berger and Luckmann (1967).

4. See my *Community of the New Age*, pp. 50–100; see also Gager (1977).

REFERENCES

Berger, Peter, and Thomas Luckmann. 1967. *The Social Construction of Reality: A Treatise in the Sociology of Knowledge*. New York: Doubleday.

Gager, John. 1977. *Kingdom and Community*. Englewood Cliffs: Prentice-Hall.

Kee, Howard Clark. 1977. *Community of the New Age*. Macon, Ga.: Mercer University Press.

———. 1983. *Understanding the New Testament*. 4th ed. Englewood Cliffs: Prentice-Hall.

———. 1989. *Knowing the Truth: A Sociological Approach to New Testament Interpretation*. Minneapolis: Fortress Press.

Neusner, Jacob. 1979. *From Politics to Piety*. Englewood Cliffs: Prentice-Hall.

CHAPTER THREE

The Local and the Global in Southern African Religious History

Terence Ranger

The most recent review of interpretations of conversion in Africa bears the significant title "The Shattered Microcosm." Its author, E. Ikenga-Metuh, finds that most of the dominant analyses depend upon the idea of smallness of scale of traditional African religion and the consequent redundancy of local religion in the face of wide-ranging social change. Ikenga-Metuh himself criticizes the overgenerality of any explanation of conversion that depends merely on this notion of the shattered microcosm. Nonetheless he writes:

> No one can dispute the fact that the rapid social change that came in the wake of colonialism shattered the structures of traditional societies, which had previously sustained traditional religion. Nor can anyone contest the fact that traditional world-views needed to change considerably in order to cope with the much enlarged world to which they were now exposed. Adherents of African religions turned to Islam and Christianity as a convenient means of coping with the changed situation. (Ikenga-Metuh 1987:13)

I propose to take this passage as a text, because I am attracted by its challenge. *No one*, it says, can dispute its premises of microcosmic African religion and of the relevance of Islam and Christianity to macrocosmic change. Perverse as I am, I cannot read such a challenge without immediately thinking, "Well, we'll see about that—I shall contest it." So in this chapter I want to make a (no doubt unbalanced) case for the defense and look at everything that can be argued *against* the identification of African religion with the microcosmic and of mission Christianity with the macrocosmic.

I begin by stating the need to penetrate appearances, illustrating this banal injunction with a particularly striking example. I then go on to argue that microcosmic African religion is just such a deceptive appearance—or an invention of the colonial twentieth century. In place of this illusion I seek to establish the genuine range and dynamism of much of precolonial southern African religion. I argue, moreover, that even though administrators and chiefs and African organic intellectuals colluded to localize African religion in the twentieth century many mass movements of African religion escaped from their control and operated over ever wider areas. I then turn to the key question of literacy, arguing that there was no *necessary* connection between its introduction into much of southern Africa in the nineteenth and twentieth centuries and conversion to Christianity, even though there was, of course, an actual connection. Beginning as the monopoly of mission Christianity, literacy became available first to movements of African independent Christianity and at last to leaders of movements of African traditional religion. What these have done and are doing with it challenge some of the old generalizations.

Next I turn to mission Christianity itself. Here I argue that mission Christianity needed "to take hold of the land" to find local and rooted symbolic expression. Such symbolic localization often combined with missionary enthusiasm for stable peasant societies to produce remarkably microcosmic "village Christianities"—the village itself being a twentieth-century invention in many parts of southern Africa. Movements of African independent Christianity and movements of African traditional religion ranged over much wider territories.

Having conjured up a striking contrast between the macrocosmic potentialities of much of African religion and the microcosmic realities of much mission Christianity, I then abandon the advocate's role. Merely inverting the terms of a false contrast makes little sense. It makes much more sense to realize that the tension between the local and the global has played itself out both within African religion and within mission Christianity. The topic remains central to African religious history but in restated terms.

PENETRATING THE APPEARANCES

The journal *Cultures et Développement* has consistently shown interest in religious change and conversion. Especially stimulating is V. Neckebrouck's "Inculturation et Identité." This takes as its problem the apparent "total" conversion of many Kikuyu in the early days of mission Christianity. Such converts appeared to turn their backs completely on the "local" and to have aspired to all the lifestyles of the colonial macrocosm—in dress, diet, housing, and conduct. A conversion such as this, as Neckebrouck remarks, would be a scandal to adaptationist missionaries today. And yet, he argues, beneath the appearances lies remarkable continuity. The convert, who seemed to be abandoning everything local, was in fact acting within an intensely local idiom.

Neckebrouck argues that in the region in which the Kikuyu lived lifestyles and religious conduct were determined by the choice of particular patterns of economic activity. Hunters were "Ndorobo"; cultivators were "Kikuyu"; pastoralists were "Maasai." Each identity, apparently ethnic and primordial, could be abandoned or assumed or reassumed. People ceased to be Kikuyu to become Maasai or vice versa. Neckebrouck remarks: "Such changes of ethnic identity involved real religious changes, since a Kikuyu who became Maasai also quite naturally adopted the religion of his new ethnicity. This change, in which one can see a type of conversion, was confirmed by a public ceremony. The term for this 'traditional conversion' was *Guciaruo*" (Neckebrouck 1984:257). Neckebrouck holds that *Guciaruo* was a ceremony of rebirth, having much in common with "the phenomenon of conversion as it was introduced by the missionaries." The new Kikuyu converts to Christianity were preeminently adopting a new economic role and embracing the lifestyle that went with it. For them baptism was the equivalent of *Guciaruo*: "Converts abandoned their traditional religion for Christianity on an existing traditional model. . . . All those changes today vilified by critics who espouse tradition were in fact admirably adapted to the most local and traditional models of behaviour" (Neckebrouck 1984:265).

One cannot hope for many such spectacular reinterpretations, and the case of *Guciaruo* is hardly typical. But it may usefully stand as a warning that in the history of African religion things are rarely what they seem.

INVENTING TRADITIONAL LOCALISM

At least one hundred years now separate us from the realities of precolonial religion. A century is quite long enough to have given an apparently immemorial legitimacy to a model of African religion that most of us have come to take for granted. We think of African religion as restricted to the tribe and as functioning conservatively to maintain tradition and to validate the authority of the king or the chief or the elders. We think of African rural society as intensely religious and ritualistic and of authority within it as deriving more from supernatural sanctions than from economic power or military force. Religion in this model controlled and limited the exploitation of the environment; religious sanctions (often expressed in the form of witchcraft accusations) prevented the entrepreneurial acquisition of wealth. This model will be instantly recognizable.

And yet its picture of intensely local, communitarian, and hierarchical religion is itself a construct.

Construction began in classification. Early missionaries had classified much of African tradition *out* of the religious sphere, maintaining that Africans had no religious sense. Thereafter, however, both missionary and administrative classifications served to separate and define a distinct "religious" sphere of life. This happened both negatively and positively. Negatively, colonial ordinances defined many local activities as antireligious and antisocial. These activities included many of the great movements of African religion: movements aimed at the eradication of the possibility of witchcraft; prophetic movements of regeneration, which were now seen as mere fanaticism and as subversive of chiefly authority; and movements of possession by spirits from outside the local society. It was no accident that most of these penalized antireligious activities were geographically wide-ranging.

By contrast, colonial administrations came to favor local institutional religion, especially where it lent support to kings or chiefs or elders. Karen Fields (1985) illustrates this process in her study of Northern Rhodesian Indirect Rule and its interactions with religious history. Fields argues that in precolonial times political status was achieved rather than prescribed, gained by military or economic strength rather than by normative procedures or succession. Ideological legitimacy and normative rulers became much more significant under colonialism, when the autonomous deployment of material force by African rulers became impossible. In Bembaland, for example, the bloody rivalries of precolonial adventurers gave way in the colonial mind to the stately rhythms of tradition. The Chitimukulu paramount came to be seen as a miniature version of a British king; the Shimwalule priest was archbishop of Canterbury and anointer of kings.

Administrative religion in effect amounted to a set of new rules and rites, designed to rule out political-economic and ideological struggles in "a world of norms, rules, and overarching values. . . . Customary order is encapsulated in ritual and supernatural belief, in traditionally legitimated norms, in flamboyant ceremonial and magic incantation." It was, says Fields, "the plan of colonial rule that reoutfitted the customary order to look this way." African rulers were transformed from authoritarian politicians to "mere repositories of custom." Fields concludes that "paradoxically, the role of the 'supernatural' increased as Africa's history joined that of secularized modern society" (Fields 1985:65–66).

At the same time, however, certain kinds of supernatural challenges to kings and chiefs were ruled out. Movements to reconstitute society and reprove corrupt rulers—whether led by prophets or millenarian witchcraft eradicators—were frowned upon and their leaders prosecuted. In this way the balance within African religion was distorted. In this way, too, African religion was miniaturized. There were further localizations not only in Northern Rhodesia but in many other parts of eastern and southern Africa.

Thus, Indirect Rule ethnography privileged the "tribe" and "tribal religion." Tribes were ideally defined as uniting language, culture, self-identity, polity, *and* religion. Where religious rituals involved people from many different language and culture groups—as with the initiation rites of southern Tanzania—ethnographers strove to disentangle the "mixed elements" in such "impure" ceremonies so as notionally to reconstruct the original ethnic religion. The interaction within one cult of people of different ethnicities was thought a product of tribal breakdown and thus deplored.

Religious movements, which spread rapidly across tribal boundaries, were suspect to colonial administrations for many reasons. They confused categories; they suggested the frightening possibility of pantribal alliances against colonialism. Such movements were closely watched, and the historian can find plenty of documentation about them in the colonial administrative archives. But one can rarely find there any sense that such movements had been and were part of the total balance and dynamic of African religion. They were seen as something new, as subversive of "traditional society" as of colonial order (Vail 1989; Ranger 1986).

As they began to concede that Africans possessed "religion," missionaries also defined its local manifestations and functions as valuable and positive, while setting their faces against wider-ranging movements. Leading proponents of adaptation theology, such as Vincent Lucas, bishop of Masasi in southeastern Tanzania, strongly supported Indirect Rule assumptions, seeking to reconstruct or invent small-scale units of "pure" Makua culture and politics and to destroy so-called polyglot chiefdoms (Ranger 1979). Lucas sought to Christianize local initiation ceremonies and to use them to restore rural stability (Ranger 1972a). He and his clergy denounced witchcraft eradicators to the administration, excommunicating any of their flock who participated in the cleansing (Ranger 1972b). In his composite theology Lucas saw the great strength and gift of traditional religion in its capacity to sacralize local relations of hierarchy between the sexes, the generations, and the classes. Adapted Christianity had to learn from African religion how to do this, while itself contributing through its schools all that was necessary for those interactions with the outside world that could not be avoided.

Nor was this process of defining African religion and of privileging its local manifestations a matter only for Europeans. Many recent studies have emphasized the crucial role of African "organic intellectuals" in the creation of tribal identity and ideology. Using the new, written vernaculars of mission literacy, in what MacGaffey and Janzen call the "ethnographic" mode, such African Christian intellectuals produced an account of local traditional culture; they wrote the histories of "tribes"; they offered their alliance to chiefs. Since they were themselves converts, men of religion, they placed particular emphasis on the supposed organic solidarities of local traditional religion to which they themselves claimed to be heir (Janzen 1985; MacGaffey 1986b; Roberts 1989). John Iliffe has sketched this process most succinctly:

> Just as later nationalists sought to create a national culture, so those who built modern tribes emphasized tribal cultures. In each case educated men took the lead. . . . One area of rethinking was an interest among African Christians in the indigenous religions against which early converts had often reacted violently. . . . It was not until the missionaries studied African religions carefully during the 1920s that most Africans dared to reconsider their attitudes publicly. Michael Kikurwe, a Zigua teacher and cultural tribalist, envisaged a golden age of traditional African society: "In each district men and women were busy to help each other, they taught their children the same laws and traditions. Every Chief tried as much as he could to please his people and likewise his people did the same in turn, they all knew what was lawful and unlawful, and they knew that there is a powerful God in heaven, and they had many ways of worshipping him." (Iliffe 1979:334–35)

There could hardly be a clearer expression of the assumptions and values of the cult of localist traditionalism.

So far I have been writing about Indirect Rule contexts. In a country like Southern Rhodesia anything like Indirect Rule ethnography was delayed until the late 1960s and the 1970s, when the Rhodesia Front regime sought belatedly to stem the advance of radical nationalism by fostering local culture and, in particular, local religious culture (Ranger 1983). Nevertheless, Shona organic intellectuals had long been engaged in the same invention as Kikurwe. Although privileged tribal authorities may not have emerged in Southern Rhodesia, intensely local popular Christianities certainly did, as a result of the missionary zoning policy of the Rhodesian government. African catechists, preachers, and teachers stated their claims to a legitimacy greater than that of the white missionaries in terms of the continuities between their roles and those of the famous local religious leaders of the pre-Christian past. Scattered about in the Zimbabwean Christian literature, we find a black Salvation Army officer telling an oral historian how the local spirit medium blessed a new church building by sitting cross-legged and entranced on a table at the opening ceremony and invoking the blessing of the ancestors (Mashingaidze 1976). We find elsewhere an Anglican priest stressing the mediumship of his father as an analogy to his own priesthood (Madziyere 1975). We find black American Methodist teachers and preachers in eastern Zimbabwe—heavily involved in the creation of a regional language, *chi-manyika*—creating also an oral tradition of the origins of their church that differed greatly from the written chronicles of the missionaries. The missionaries saw the rise of the church as the result of the introduction of transatlantic enlightenment into societies of petty illiteracy and ignorance. The black preachers and teachers saw the descent of the Holy Spirit on a dignified local tradition of politics, war, and religion (Ranger forthcoming).

Many modern African theologians, such as John Mbiti, whose *African Religions and Philosophy* has sold so widely and influenced so many blacks in Africa and America, stand in this line of localizing organic African intellectuals. In many ways, far from revealing fresh realities, Mbiti is the Indirect Rule inventor of the tribe writ large: "Traditional religions are not universal: they are tribal. . . . One traditional religion cannot be propagated in another tribal group. . . . Each people has its own distinct language, . . . its own geographical area, common culture, common history, common customs, morals, ethics, social behaviour. . . . Each people has its own religious system" (Mbiti 1969:1, 2, 5, 131, 134). The latest stage in localization is the involvement of self-proclaimed spokespersons of African religion itself. In Zimbabwe the shrewd spirit mediums who both informed and manipulated Dr. Michael Gelfand emphasized that Shona religion produced stability, order, and communalism (Gelfand 1959; Ranger 1982). In South Africa today the best-known spokesperson for "traditional" religion is Credo Vusamazula Mutwa. Mutwa's extraordinary books are sometimes taken seriously by those who should know better. For me the last word on Mutwa comes from Joseph Lelyveld, who visited his shrine in the townships and found him to be a client of the South African regime. Lelyveld offered a religious insight that defined Africans as people of the instinctive microcosm:

> I don't mean to imply that Credo Mutwa occasionally pandered to white prejudice. I mean to say that had become his essential business, so that finally the Africa he portrayed was an almost perfect reflection of the Africa the white wanted to see. . . . He teaches that blacks are universally great fatalists, that they lose their soul in cities, have no appetite for any thing mechanical, . . . that any black who speaks of democratic values, Christianity, the modern world . . . is an imitation white, a fraud, a lost soul. (Lelyveld 1985:251)

Yet even though it is tempting to dismiss Mutwa, or the Bantustan organic intellectuals who are manipulating religious traditions to invent convincing local identities, as mere puppets, the range of interests involved in creating this localized model of traditional religion and the increasing reality of that model make it impossible to regard it just as a distorting fraud. I will argue that African religion was different in its precolonial totality from this limited vision of it. But one has to accept that colonialism not only *imagined* localized religions and communities but also *created* them. As Marcia Wright has written of the region between Lake Nyasa and Lake Tanganyika, "the second half of the nineteenth century was a fluid world of economic change, social dislocation and regrouping, armed conflict and striving for security." Men and women characteristically traveled long distances and interacted with many different societies and cults. This fluidity climaxed in economic, military, ecological, and conceptual crisis, into which the colonialists entered. As Wright concludes: "The terms of reconstruction were dictated by the colonial authorities in the years after 1895, when pacification came to mean immobilization of populations, reinforcement of ethnicity, and greater rigidity of social definition" (Wright 1984:58). Ideas of "custom" derived from this newly and artificially immobilized society were wildly off the mark, but immobilization itself became a reality, especially for women. Hence, part of the religious history of twentieth-century southern Africa is made up of the functioning and development of local institutional religion in such immobilized societies.

PRECOLONIAL FLUIDITY AND AFRICAN RELIGIOUS MOVEMENTS

If I am going to argue that this model of a tribally homogeneous, intrinsically stable, ritualized, traditional, local religious world has been the invention of administrators, missionaries, African organic intellectuals, and African "religious leaders" themselves, I have an obligation to present an alternative model of precolonial religion in southern Africa. In fact I have been seeking to provide such an alternative since at least the publication of *The Historical Study of African Religion* (Ranger and Kimambo 1972). In this section I summarize the arguments of my most recent attempts (Ranger 1986, 1987a).

First, precolonial east and southern Africans did *not* live in immobilized societies. For most of them, as for Marcia Wright's peoples of the lake corridor, their world was one of "economic change, social dislocation, and regrouping." Only in a few instances was self-identity conceived in terms of ethnicity; in most cases it was politically defined, so that people were primarily members of polities, whose boundaries could and did shift. But they were not exclusively members of polities. Men interacted with others outside their polity as traders, as hunters, as pilgrims. Relationships were not exclusively small-scale or face-to-face, nor even exclusively with other citizens in a single polity. Relationships had to be and were established with caravan leaders and porters and shrine priests and gun hunters, with emigrants and immigrants, with traveling craftspeople and diviners. People constantly moved out of their microcosmic homesteads or villages, and other people as constantly passed into and through them.

All this necessarily had an impact upon religious forms. Since, among much else, African religions were symbolic of relationships, and cults were often a means of articulating such relationships, the complex patterns of society and economics were matched by equally complex religious patterns. As I have stated elsewhere (Ranger 1987a:151), one can see that African religions were multilayered and dynamic, with a history of contradiction, contestation, and innovation. From this perspective one might replace the model of the total organic collectivity with something else—a model of creative and resilient pluralism. Such a model helps to explain the remarkable adaptability of African societies and individuals during the changes of colonial capitalism.

Of course, what I have been calling local religion *was* important. Religious observances, usually directed toward the ancestors, certainly did underlie and correspond to the relationships of men and women within the family and the strategies of heirship. Often, though by no means always, these ancestral observances *were* focused on the homestead or the village. Equally, those religious ideas and practices that sustained polities were important. But even at this level religion did not take a single, monolithic form. There were counterideologies and symbolic resources of criticism and authority. In patrilineal homesteads and villages, with wives marrying in from outside, forms of female religion existed alongside the dominant cult of the male ancestors. In chiefdoms and kingdoms there were often the barely submerged shapes of religious institutions that had preexisted the state or that overlapped with it, and there were traditions of symbolic criticism and censure that could result in movements of prophetic renewal. Moreover, even at the most local, microcosmic level people were conscious that their religious observances and ideas were linked with those of others across wide areas of eastern and southern Africa. As Igor Kopytoff and his contributors have shown, much of African history consisted in settlers moving out of "metropoles" into "frontier" zones where settlers constructed new societies by following culturally valued social models more faithfully than they could ever have been followed in the metropoles (Kopytoff 1987).

Over and above local religion, whether of the homestead or of the polity, existed regional structures of relationship and interaction. One such network was made up of linked territorial cult centers. The crucial need for rain and for the fertility of land directed people's imaginations toward spirits of the land and waters, to whom offerings were made at specifically located shrines. These could be—and perhaps originally generally were—sited locally, in a grove or on a stream near the village. But in many parts of central and southern Africa centralization had long been taking place, through which particularly striking and efficacious shrines had emerged to dominate extensive cultic networks. Pilgrims came to these shrines, and local communities sent representatives to them over hundreds of miles (Hilton 1985; Schoffeleers 1978a; Werbner 1977).

Another network consisted of hunters' cults or guilds. Once again, hunting and hunting cultic observations may well once have been localized, but by the nineteenth century, at least, organized hunting of elephant and other big game had arisen that took men over long distances and involved them with "strangers" from other societies. African hunters sought permission to hunt from territorial shrines, were initiated into hunting guilds, and competed for the most powerful hunting medicines (MacKenzie 1988). Yet another network concerned long-distance trade, as caravan or trading parties, bearing ivory, metals, slaves, and cereals, moved from the interior to the coast or to regional entrepôts. Traders needed to establish relationships with peoples all along their routes and often did so through the medium of cults of possession by spirits external to any localized society, so that both traders and hosts became initiated into cults that claimed members over hundreds or even thousands of square miles. Sometimes, in a region where trade had replaced agriculture or hunting as the major economic activity and where control of trade had slipped from the hands of chiefs or kings, such possession cults became the central and dominant religious mode (Janzen 1979, 1982).

A hypothetical man in precolonial southern Africa could belong successively, or even simultaneously, to all these overlapping networks of religious relationship: for example, he could express his control of his household through a localized ancestral cult, carry tribute to a distant territorial shrine, belong to a gun-hunter's guild, and be an initiate of a spirit possession cult that linked him to the men and women who lived along a trading route. The various cultic layers to which my hypothetical man belonged did not fit neatly together to form a single collective religion coexistent with one polity or society. All this is quite different from the organic model of the identity of society, state, collectivity, and religion. The local community was, of course, tremendously important, but it was situated in these various networks of symbolic and practical recourse.

This revised model has further implications, some of which I have discussed elsewhere (Ranger 1987a:151–53). If this *is* a more accurate picture of precolonial Africa, then the impact of Christianity and colonialism is different from the notion of a fatal smashing of secure corporate identity. If I am right, then African religions were already adept at reflecting and expressing multiple identities, and African "believers" were already experienced in responding to new religious ideas. People were also familiar with the balance of tensions *within* African religions and between those religions and the state. They were already familiar with sweeping economic, political, *and* religious change. Hence, they were not nearly so defenseless against the impact of capitalism and "individualistic" Christianity as we often imagine.

Students of comparative religion may find this discussion too closely linked to society and economics, too reductionist of religious symbol and experience. But the point is that the locus of symbolic innovation and myth creation was the macrocosmic region rather than the microcosmic village or chiefdom. As Christopher Wrigley has recently remarked, "African priests and poets worked with more interesting ideas than those relating to ancestor spirits." He goes on to argue for a common pool of myth and symbol stretching from interlacustrine East Africa to the Shire Valley of southern Malawi, from the savanna of Zaire to the plateau of Zimbabwe (Wrigley 1988:380).

Now, this idea of broad regions of societal, individual, and symbolic interaction helps us to situate my earlier emphasis in this chapter on *movements* of African religion. Movements, as contrasted to institutions, could and often did arise within the local polity, as prophets challenged corrupt chiefs or as witchcraft eradicators strove to reduce acute local tensions by the establishment of a golden age of harmony. But the messages proclaimed by particular prophets or the rituals instituted by particular witchcraft eradication movements could and often did spread across the boundaries of one polity. Such movements flowed readily through regions that already shared many religious interactions, symbols, and practices. When they reached a symbolic border zone, they sometimes ran out of energy and relevance, but they also sometimes paused, allowing creative ideological entrepreneurs to restate their message in terms that allowed them to spread across a new region (de Craemer, Fox, and Vansina 1976).

As I have elsewhere observed (Ranger 1986:41–47), African traditional religion has not often been thought of in terms of movements. Rather, African religious ideas and institutions have been seen as constitutive of an overall authoritative model of the society as a whole. In such a perspective it is not really until the colonial incursion, when new ideologies of leadership and new divisions of labor were established, that African religions can be seen to shift from the center and thus become available to inspire religious movements. Significantly, other scholars have begun to break down such a model and to stress the way in which traditional religious movements could respond to and create counter-presentations other than those of the community or the state. Movements have become more frequent and have spread over wider areas during the twentieth century. Nevertheless, they clearly have not been merely a reaction to colonialism; many of them have been concerned with internal cultural or political tensions that existed before colonialism (and exist after it). Insofar as they have been responses to colonialism or to the postcolonial state, they have been developing a symbolic language already available.

These general propositions allow me now to relate the specific realities of precolonial southern African religion more directly to my argument about the colonial invention of localism. It will have become clear, I hope, that I do not dispute the importance of localized religion in precolonial southern Africa. Nor do I dispute that *sometimes* processes of religious consolidation, similar to those aimed at and often effected by colonial administrators and African organic intellectuals, took place in precolonial southern Africa. The manipulation of religion to legitimate ethnic identity or stronger central political authority *did* happen in precolonial times. Thus one could argue that the Zulu state in the nineteenth century used cultural and religious "markers" to evolve a sense of ethnic prestige and self-identification. It is a sign of the complexity of this whole discussion, indeed, that the process of Zulu self-consciousness can be seen as an enlargement of scale—creating a Zulu nationality out of dispersed Nguni-speaking groups—*and* as a reduction of scale because of the erection of boundaries in a hitherto unbounded culture zone.

Moreover, even though Fields is certainly right to emphasize the military and economic bases of political power in precolonial southern Africa, undoubtedly in many cases chiefs and kings *did* capture and reconstitute cults. As Matthew Schoffeleers writes in an introduction to his collection on the territorial cults of Central Africa:

> Control of cults is one of the issues central to the historical process. Whenever new political elites arise or invasions take place, the resulting arrangements of power distribution are likely to be reflected in cult organizations. . . . The emergence of centralized states affected the autochthonous cults indirectly by the transformation of political structure, and directly by the tendency on the part of the rulers to obtain control or part

> control of territorial religion above the local level. . . . One obvious change was the introduction of royal cults, which were concomitant with the introduction of mystical concepts about the ruler himself as being able of affecting climate and fertility. (Schoffeleers 1978a:13, 27, 30)

Indeed, some of the most stimulating work on African religious history concerns the drama of the capture of cults by chiefs and kings, whether in Jan Vansina's account of how Kuba kings seized the *Ngesh* nature spirit cult by becoming *Ngesh* themselves (Vansina 1978), or in Schoffeleers's own reconstructions of the martyrdom of the Mbona prophet by Chief Lundu and the subsequent emergence of the Mbona cult as the ideological mainstay of the Lundu state (Schoffeleers 1972, 1978b). These too were processes of *political* enlargement but at the same time broke up what had been a wider network of religious interaction.

Hence, there certainly were some precolonial examples of local patriarchal authority being sustained by ancestral cults, or of ethnic religion or of political institutional religion, or, indeed, of the use of initiation ceremonies to achieve social solidarity. The point rather is that the colonial concentration on these as alone legitimate disturbed the balance between them and quite different processes in precolonial Africa. I have implied that African religious institutions were limiting and stabilizing but African religious movements were radical and wide-ranging—hence colonialism backed the first and repressed the second. And by so acting, colonial agents, black and white, distorted the structures and dynamics of African religion. Yet this dichotomy between institutions and movements is in itself misleading. Institutions often gave rise to movements; movements often aimed to reconstitute and revalidate institutions. The dynamism of the system was not in the strength of one part or the other but in the interaction of the parts.

Thus, Schoffeleers shows that chiefs and kings never gained control of cults so completely that they could exploit them entirely for their own hegemonic purposes. As he writes: "Territorial cults . . . constitute a different source of authority which on occasion may be identifiable with secular political institutions but which remain in principle different from them" (Schoffeleers 1978a:6). He emphasizes that "control of cults can be effected in a variety of ways"; "rituals may be controlled by an autonomous priesthood, by secular rulers or by a combination of priests and rulers." He then observes: "The main question which historians have to ask themselves in this context is which factors in the formation of state systems lead to one arrangement rather than another. The answers . . . are not nearly as easy as is sometimes thought. . . . Often it is not even clear which party in a conquest situation is religiously dominant" (Schoffeleers 1978a: 14–15). In short, political-institutional religion in precolonial Africa rarely operated as it was supposed to do in Indirect Rule Northern Rhodesia.

Moreover, even where cults seem most like political institutions, as with the Lundu-dominated Mbona cult, appearances are deceptive. Schoffeleers himself has suggested a threefold model for the historical operation of the Mbona cult, in which at varying times the chiefs, the priests, or the people exercise a dominant influence. In its "normal" operation the priests run the cult under the direction of the chiefs, keeping the possessed mediums of Mbona's spirit silenced and controlled. In periods when chiefs are weak but there is little public protest, the priests build up their own influence, keep all the tribute offered to the shrines, and make claims that their office should be inherited by their sons or nephews. But the Mbona cult is based on the myth of a martyr-prophet. It can always generate resistance. When the people distrust their chiefs and fear witchcraft or epidemics, pressure springs up from below. The people demand that one or other of the Mbona mediums take on the prophetic role and head a movement of religious *and* political purification.

Within the cult, then, there has been a regular oscillation from established religious institutions to protest movements, and back again as legitimacy is reestablished. Such movements arose in precolonial times when there were oppressive chiefs; they have arisen in the twentieth century against wealthy cattle owners whose beasts have invaded the fields of poorer men (Schoffeleers 1974, 1978b; Ranger 1986). If the crisis that precipitates the prophetic protest movements is regional or general, then the cult can spread to areas far outside the Lundu chiefdom. John Janzen and Wyatt MacGaffey constructed a similar model of prophetic movements of "renewal" for the Bakongo state and subsequent Kongo chiefdoms (Janzen 1977; MacGaffey 1977). Thus, if religion was one of the ways in which kings and chiefs could most effectively express their legitimacy and the identity of their subjects, it was also one of the most difficult cultural features to incorporate or to subdue fully.

In addition to this dynamic of protest and renewal within state cults, in precolonial southern Africa territorial cult networks remained which were so widely influential that they were never contained within any single polity. The most striking example here is the High God cult of the Zimbabwean southwest, with its ramifications in what are now Botswana, the Transvaal, and southern Mozambique (Werbner 1977, 1989). The High God (Mwari) cult had to interact with a succession of powerful precolonial states, but it maintained its own regional politics of competitive shrine hierarchies, flows of tribute, expansion into new areas, and so on. This suprastate network and capacity for rapid expansion meant that the High God cult could respond to ecological, epidemiological, or other emergencies over a wide area. As one powerful state fell and was succeeded by another—the Torwa, the Rozwi, the Ndebele, the whites—so the High God cult elaborated its myth of divine continuity and secular transition. This myth has provided the ideological context for cult prophecies in southwestern Zimbabwe to the present day (Ranger 1979). Another set of myths concerns the rise and fall of corrupt priestly families at the main cult shrines: within the cult itself there has been constant prophetic challenge to instituted authority.

Having said this much about the institutions and prophets in precolonial Africa, I need in conclusion to turn to movements of other kinds. As will already have become clear, I believe that missionaries and administrators in the twentieth century were mistaken to regard witchcraft eradication movements and spirit possession cults as something new or as indications in themselves of the collapse of proper African traditional religions. Such movements were certainly important in the nineteenth century and probably far earlier. We have known since Mary Douglas's (1963) study of the Lele that certain African cosmologies exist in which the strains and costs of routine witchcraft belief and accusation demand the regular eruption of utopian movements designed to eradicate the very possibility of witchcraft. We now know that from such societies this type of movement can spread into others at times of general crisis.

As for cults of affliction and mass spirit possession, John Janzen's remarkable study of Lemba shows that the history of such cults can be traced back to the seventeenth century (Janzen 1979, 1982). Indeed, Janzen's work is relevant to discussion of the macrocosmic potential of African traditional religion. The Lemba cult came to prominence precisely because the scale of economic relations north of the Loango River became too extensive and diffuse for the king of Loango to control them. The ancestral and earth cults that had provided legitimacy to the Loango kingdom dwindled into relative insignificance. In their place, and extending over a much wider area in which concepts of kin or territory would have been unpersuasive, arose what Janzen calls a "corporate" cult of affliction and possession. Its members were brought together by a consciousness of shared suffering—the suffering of being rich and hence of attracting the envy of the poor. They dealt with this sickness by propitiating the spirit that was held to cause it, Lemba. The Lemba cult knitted together the traders and caravan leaders and controllers of markets in a new religious expression of identity. Then, in the later nineteenth century, as trading networks came under European domination, Lemba ceased to be a corporate cult of governance and developed into something much more like the classical twentieth-century cult of affliction. Nobody has made the same sort of study for the eastern African trading zone, but no doubt a similar demonstration could be made there.

AFRICAN RELIGIOUS DYNAMISM IN THE TWENTIETH CENTURY

I have already made a number of points about changes induced in African religion by the economic, political, and ideological consequences of colonialism that I may usefully summarize here. Corporate cults of possession broke down, moving from the center to the periphery and becoming movements rather than institutions. Witchcraft eradication movements ceased to be an accepted part of the dynamics of political-religious systems; the idiom of "revival," like that of mass possession, was likewise thrust from the center to the periphery. Such peripheral movements of possession and eradication were feared by missionaries and administrators, and usually by chiefs and African Christian leaders, as a challenge to the authority structures of colonial localism. Meanwhile, as I have suggested, localized interactions of political and ritual power developed that have their own twentieth-century history.

The temptation is once again to polarize. One could say that African religious institutions, encapsulated in the new localism, genuinely became more microcosmic in their significance and range. By contrast, one could say that African religious movements, however distrusted and repressed, were positively *freed* from political control and left able to respond to change over wide regions and at the macrocosmic level. There would indeed be some truth in this. The twentieth century has been the century par excellence of possession cults and witchcraft eradication movements. They have occurred more frequently and in much larger scale and scope; they have entered many societies hitherto unfamiliar with their idioms; and they have been able to respond to crises of epidemics or of economic depression. Wim van Binsbergen has persuasively argued that there has been an overall pattern of development in the modern history of such movements, with their increasing scale and their increasing abstraction of spiritual principles reflecting their engagement with the macrocosmic (Binsbergen 1976, 1981). With other scholars I have myself sought to show the trajectory and significance of twentieth-century religious movements (Cross 1972; Fields 1982; Ranger 1972b; Vansina 1971, 1973), which undoubtedly retain their relevance. Witchcraft eradication and cleansing have been important in postindependence Zimbabwe, in the Zambian rural areas of today, and in the Tanzania of the *ujamaa* (cooperative) village (Brain 1964; Westerlund 1980; Lan 1985; Ranger 1989b). Cults of possession flourish in the towns of

Zaire, East Africa, and South Africa. John Janzen argues that the very discorporate character of these cults, their open syncretism, allows them to form, even without knowing it, a vast regional network that responds to that most macrocosmic of all problems—the dislocations and traumas of modern urban society (Janzen forthcoming).

But to place all my macrocosmic emphasis upon movements would be to understate the advocate's case. One can also show that apparent localisms retain or develop a macrocosmic pertinence, for example, even in the "immobilized" societies of northeastern Zambia. One can show that religious institutions, however manipulated by various colonial ideologues of localism, retained autonomous capacities of growth and change.

The most dramatic example of localism reinterpreted comes from George Bond's work on the Yombe of northern Zambia. In 1978 Bond published an analysis in which he drew a sharp contrast between Yombe traditional religion, particularly the ancestor cult, and "the fundamentalist, mission Christianity of the Free Church of Scotland," which had many adherents among the Yombe. The two religions coexisted, thought Bond, because Yombe society remained poised between microcosmic and macrocosmic concerns. Bond had no doubt that the ancestral cult pertained to the microcosmic and Scottish Protestantism to the macrocosmic:

> The specific argument of this article may be stated quite simply: it is that the Yombe ancestor cult, anchored as it is in relations of status, has provided an ideological framework appropriate to a confined local community, the "microcosm," dependent upon hoe cultivation. . . . The fundamentalist mission . . . based as it is in relations of contract, has been more suited than the ancestor cult to the complex, variegated changes of urbanization and industrialization and their effects on rural communities. The ancestor cult's cluster of beliefs and practices seeks to explain and is part of social and economic processes that stem from the internal modes of production, hoe agriculture, whereas the cluster of Christian beliefs provides for relations based on a wage economy and contractual arrangements involving the individual. (Bond 1978:24)

One could hardly imagine a text more contrary to the case I am seeking to argue, and Bond's article has indeed become a classic statement of the macrocosmic-microcosmic divide. In his mind, as expressed in 1978, conversion to Christianity *has* been a business of shattering the microcosm:

> I have not attempted to analyze [Yombe Christian beliefs] as a system of symbols, statements about Yombe social order, simply because I feel it is more useful to view Yombe Christian beliefs as contributing to the process of transforming subsistence cultivators into wage labourers. Thus these

> beliefs provide an explanation for those space-time events that transcend the "microcosm" and at the same time they supply an ideological framework for integrating the Yombe into an expanding urban-industrial complex. (Bond 1978:34)

In 1987, however, Bond returned to the problem and emerged with different results. This time he emphasized that the "domestic [ancestral] cults of commoners are not restricted to locality. The Yombe believe that the ancestors deal with conduct, relationships, and misfortunes of their agnates, no matter where they live. At this level the ancestors transcend local territory." Drawing upon this new perception, Bond now asserts:

> The kin-based cults were highly suited to the types of changes brought about under colonial rule and capitalism. They had developed under a productive mode, the swidden cultivation of millet, that required movement. Since ancestors were not tied to a particular location, but were easily moved, labour migration and wage-earning were integrated into the pattern of cult beliefs. . . . A bridge had been established between the capitalist and domestic economy. The pull was not, however, unidirectional, as it is sometimes portrayed. Through money the capitalist order appropriated the labour of the Yombe migrant, and through the ancestor cult the Yombe sought to appropriate money, thus restoring a modicum of their worth and customary social persona. Labour migration did not extinguish the ancestor cult nor the dominant role of men within it. (Bond 1987:61)

Bond goes on to show that "the Yombe constantly attempt to bring new items of technology, such as maize-grinding mills, plows, and tractors, into the cult's domain" (Bond 1987:63). If *this* is true, or has become true by means of innovations within the ancestor cult, what constitute the crucial differences between the cult and Scottish Protestantism? Both now seem like ways of relating to the macrocosm.

Bond's analysis is now different: "The differential standing of women and men is a key point of difference between the two religions." The ancestral cult continues to be dominated by men. By contrast, there has been "a gradual predominance of women in the ranks of the Free Church." Hence, "women tend to be concentrated in the Free Church and men in the ancestor cult" (Bond 1987:64–65). These findings plainly vary from the polarization of ten years earlier.

In light of that earlier article, indeed, it is astonishing to find the Free Church mainly concerned precisely with those who have the least rather than the most involvement with the macrocosmic urban and industrial economy. Bond's conclusions make an implicit critique of his earlier views:

> Many anthropologists have assumed that the parochial religions of local African communities would be rapidly displaced or thoroughly trans-

> formed by the penetration of Christianity, the colonial state, and capitalism. And yet in Unyombe and in other local African communities, the ancestor cult persists. . . . Its religious ideology provides the context for obscuring the gradual expansion of commercial relationships based on exchange value. To advance in the domain of commercial transactions, successful entrepreneurs have employed the ideology, symbols, and practices of the ancestor cult and the customary order, thereby masking the consequences of commercial hybrid maize farming and other entrepreneurial activities, and allowing these emergent capitalist enterprises to take root and expand. (Bond 1987:70–71)

The most dramatic examples of institutional vitality in the twentieth century come from Zimbabwe. I can deal with them briefly because the literature is recent and has caused something of a stir. I argued above that the High God cult of the Zimbabwean southwest had never been encapsulated within any precolonial state. Under colonialism it continued to overlap several colonial boundaries, continued to pursue its own political dynamic, and continued to show its ability to expand rapidly at times of crisis. In 1915, for example, it produced a classic example of how an institution could generate a movement. That year drought, famine, and disease swept across the whole region from southwestern Zimbabwe to southern Mozambique. In its Zimbabwean heartland the High God cult generated a healing and cleansing movement whereby dancing women removed "the sickness of Mwari" from their own kraal and carried it on to the next, where the process was repeated. At the same time doctored seed or tobacco from the High God shrines was distributed to guarantee a good crop.

As the movement spread further east and south into Mozambique, its character changed, taking on the nature of a witchcraft eradication movement. The tobacco snuff brought from the shrines to the southeastern peoples was distributed to protect fields from thieves and to ensure fertility. At the same time it was believed that it would kill the evil but be harmless to the innocent. Those who practiced witchcraft after taking it would split open and die. These areas were outside the historic zone of influence of the Mwari cult and were more familiar with the idiom of witchcraft eradication than with the idea of a powerful Creator God of the Earth. Nevertheless, the so-called Murimi movement in Mozambique did introduce a momentary notion of God Himself as in charge of good and evil, drought and plenty. Murimi was a response to a crisis of subsistence that was perceived as new, because it largely had to be faced by women in areas of wide-scale labor migration. Murimi constituted a new order empowering chiefs and women; returning migrant laborers had to be purified before they were allowed to enter a Murimi village (Rennie 1973).

Yet more interesting, in this context, is that the Mwari cult itself, in its ongoing institutional form, also adapted to the changing realities of the colonial economy. Cult priests and messengers showed themselves hostile to African rural entrepreneurs, but they accepted the necessity under colonialism for tribal cultivators to turn themselves into small peasant producers. Cult messages coordinated small peasant responses to the vagaries of the colonial political economy. When grain prices fell or a local trader sought to establish a monopoly so that he could drive down prices, Mwari representatives organized a boycott by peasant producers. When prices rose the priests allowed renewed sales (Ranger 1985b). The cult retained its sense of a divinely ordained history in which regimes rose and fell as they served or flouted the High God. When, in the 1950s, African politicians and trade unionists consulted the shrines, the cult was able to fit the nationalist struggle into this history and to promise another transition, this time to an African state. Guerrillas had recourse to the shrine in the war of the 1970s. Since 1980 the shrines have been important in the politics of Matabeleland, as leaders of the Zimbabwe African People's Union (ZAPU) have sought to compensate for electoral defeat in the country as a whole by developing the shrines into an international pilgrimage center and by secretly using one shrine as a source of political and military advice (Ranger 1989a).

Those other survivors of Shona institutional religion—the spirit mediums of central and eastern Zimbabwe—seem to have related even more spectacularly to revolutionary change. At any rate, in David Lan's brilliant analysis, these "makers of history" proved able during the liberation war of the 1970s to draw on the symbols of oral-historical discourse to integrate young, alien guerrillas into the supreme legitimacy of being "sons of the soil." Though they too had adapted to peasantization and to missionary education, the spirit mediums nevertheless continued to represent a claim to the lost lands in the name of the ancestors, an ideology of conservation and relationship to the earth that ran counter to government-imposed agricultural rules, and a mastery of the living and changing past that easily captured "tradition" for the guerrilla revolution rather than for the antiquarian Rhodesia Front. In Zimbabwe in the 1970s spirit mediums proved relevant to a territory-wide war (Lan 1985; Ranger 1985a).

In short, I do not believe the argument for the inevitable redundancy and archaism of African religions in modern times. Wherever one looks, whether at movements or institutions, the reality seems different. Old dynamics remain vital; new principles of generalization have been developed or have become available. And in recent times the generalizing potentialities of literacy, so long the monopoly of Christianity or Islam, have become available to the spokespersons of African religion.

LITERACY AND RELIGION

A crucial dimension of religious transition from the microcosmic to the macrocosmic is held to be the accompanying transition from oracy to literacy. Literacy enables the African Christian to capture tradition and also to revolutionize it. Kevin Maxwell's *Bemba Myth and Ritual: The Impact of Literacy on an Oral Culture* (1983) is an unusually full statement of this idea. Writing again of that Zambian northeast where we have seen the establishment of colonial immobilization, and where George Bond has changed his mind about the macrocosmic potentialities of the Yombe ancestor cult, Maxwell makes another case for the "shattered microcosm." By means of literacy, he writes: "Christianity began almost immediately to wrest control of the Bemba religious tradition from its oral authorities by writing it down and making the written version 'standard.' . . . The Christian missionaries turned over the new literate means of communication to the new breed of Bemba elite. . . . The written word, not the oral word, was true. Literacy short-circuited seniority." Literacy also changed the content of the religious experience: "For the oral religion, the encounter leads to the disjoining of the sacred symbiotic relationship of the cosmic continuum between human culture, nature, and the realm of the spirits. Writing makes the world knowable. . . . Its analytic, perspectival mode dehumanises, devocalises, and depopulates the natural cosmos. The oral synthesis of the Bemba universe is broken down" (Maxwell 1983:xvii–xviii, 33). Literacy enabled the forging of connection with Christian ideas and congregations far outside Bembaland and provided the analytical tools to operate in the new, enlarged world.

Maxwell raises the possibility of literacy coming to Bemba religion without the mediation of mission Christianity only at once to dismiss it:

> Bemba Traditional Religion remains tied to its oral origins and closed to the raised consciousness of Bemba literates. It might have developed along literate lines itself had literacy not come to the Bemba world firmly allied to the new religion. . . . Bemba oral religion can live a new kind of life in its written form [only] in alliance with the usurper. . . . The cultural advantages of writing will not be exploited for the benefit of traditional religion, not even by literate Bemba. Over 72% of the tribal population has already converted to Christianity. It is clearly too late for a literate revision of oral religion as a whole.

It is necessary, he concludes, that "Bemba religion die itself and be buried" in Christian texts, "in order to be transformed by a later resurrected life in the Christian economy" (Maxwell 1983:162–63, 166).

Maxwell's case seems to be a strong one, but two things are chiefly wrong with it. One is that he polarizes literal and oral communication completely. For him religious literacy is all analytical and linear. There is no room for gnomic literacy, though many studies are beginning to show us how important this has been in recent African religious history. The other error is that Maxwell is wrong about the ways in which Africans in northeast Zambia have used literacy for religious purposes. The work of Clive Dillon-Malone on the Mutumwa "churches" (discussed below) reveals a different sort of process.

John Janzen's 1985 review of the consequences of literacy in African religion shows how often literacy can solidify oracy; how dreams and visions rendered into writing were first a major genre of mission Christian conversion and then a major instrument of African prophetic expansion; how literacy can give form to such oral expressions as songs, narratives, and glossolalias. In this way "a potential religious literature is born." Janzen notes:

> Many African religious traditions—regional Islamic communities, independent Christian churches, nationalizing mission churches, and renewed historic traditions of African religion—are involved in one or another stage of this transition to literacy. The consequences of such a transition to literacy are far-reaching. Literacy, as such, permits a greater degree of uniformity in a religious order; it certainly permits the existence of such an order on a larger social scale; it permits the renewal of cultural and spiritual traditions to occur with reference to the past-in-the-present; it permits a greater participation in the central issues of religious order. (Janzen 1985:248–49)

For my purposes the key phrase here is Janzen's inclusion of "renewed historic traditions of African religion" among those religious traditions making the transition to literacy. Much more work needs to be done on this belated, but highly significant, stage in African religious history.

Literacy has certainly come to rituals of kingship, with the recording of what were formerly purely oral texts, not for ethnographic but for functional purposes. It has equally certainly come to territorial cults of ecology and cleansing. There has been, for instance, an attempt to bureaucratize the High God cult in both Botswana and Zimbabwe with written constitutions and manifestos. As we have seen, the High God cult has shown in its purely oral form a remarkable capacity to expand its influence over wide regions, but the use now being made of literacy by some of its adherents is clearly designed to appeal to a "national," if not an "international," constituency. As the Hosanna Religious Traditional Association of Botswana puts it, "the worship of MWALI through the traditional ceremonies . . . is an important aspect of Black Culture and is a contribution to the cultural and moral fiber of a nation" (Last and Chavunduka 1986).

But literacy has come to African religious movements as well as to institutions, and sometimes the use of literacy by the leaders of movements has served to institutionalize them. Witchcraft eradicators, such as Chikanga of Malawi, now keep extensive written case records. And Dillon-Malone has shown how the use of literacy in Zambia transformed witchcraft eradication movements into structured organizations of exorcism and healing.

What Dillon-Malone calls the Mutumwa movement—a crossethnic movement for the prevention of witchcraft and for healing—originated in northeastern Zambia in the 1930s. It drew its inspiration equally from the prophetic Mchape witchcraft eradication movement and from some of the texts of Christianity. At its core was the revitalizing role of the *nchimi* diviner, and Mutumwa leaders were in personal contact with "the famous Malawian *nchimi*, Chikanga, whose influence and reputation were so widespread in the 1960s." Mutumwa leaders, however, say that Chikanga's work never "developed into the formation of churches as theirs had done" (Dillon-Malone 1983:167). Chikanga might use literacy to keep case records, but Mutumwa leaders went beyond that, using literacy bureaucratically to achieve "church" organization. The Mutumwa movement thus developed into two streams, one calling itself the Mutumwa Nchimi Church of Herbalists, the other merely the Mutumwa Church. The first sounds more "traditional," and the second more "Christian." But to divide them in this way is a sterile exercise. Both have been influenced by witchcraft eradication *and* by Biblical healing texts; both invoke the Holy Spirit, exorcise, and recruit by means of the affliction and sickness of their converts. The whole movement could be regarded as "syncretic" or as a Christian heresy. I argue that it can validly be regarded as an instance of what can happen when African traditional religious movements become structured by literacy. As Dillon-Malone writes: "The Mutumwa churches of Zambia . . . succeed in supplying the positive functions of traditional medico-religious specialists in a more durable, because literate, belief system (although interpreted in accordance with traditional religious beliefs)" (Dillon-Malone 1983: 167). With forty-three branches on the urbanized Copperbelt, the Mutumwa churches have certainly related to macrocosmic change.

Of course, because literacy is now available to African religious movements does not liberate them from confrontation with the prestige of the prior texts of mission Christianity, particularly the Bible. The Mutumwa leaders drew heavily on the Book of Acts to legitimate their healing. And if their reaction to biblical Christianity does not seem to have been limiting, Schoffeleers (1985) has given us an example of a much more "reactionary" development. He describes the rapidly growing influence in southern Malawi in the 1970s of the Church of the Black Ancestors. This self-consciously Africanist and nationalist movement called upon Africans to return to their traditional religion. It published a brief counter-text to the Bible: *The Truth about Jesus: The Saviour of the Israelites and the Whites*. As Schoffeleers comments, the Bible itself provides the movement with its unifying symbol. Lapsed Christians make indispensable officers of the movement because of their familiarity with the Bible and their capacity to criticize it.

In order to oppose to mission Christianity a "religion" equally exclusive and dogmatic, the Church of the Black Ancestors sought to possess all the traditional religious resources of southern Malawi and then to generalize them into what amounted to a party ideology. The lay bureaucracy of the church was paralleled, in theory, by a ritual hierarchy made up of all traditional chiefs, headmen, shrine priests, and territorial mediums. As it spread through southern Malawi, the Church of the Black Ancestors tried to capture the shrines of the Mbona territorial cult. Outside the Mbona zone it sought to generalize village ancestral cults. Schoffeleers shows that many shrine priests and mediums, as well as many chiefs and headmen, bitterly opposed the imposition of this new generalizing and politicizing creed. These religious leaders still stood by a layered, ambiguous, and plural system. But the leaders of the Black Ancestors succeeded in polarizing the religious field into the confrontation of the two books, the Bible and *The Truth about Jesus*. According to Schoffeleers (1985), by the end of the 1970s the centuries-old Mbona cult had virtually disappeared. Meanwhile, however, the name of Mbona, released from the shrines, was on the lips of the followers of the Black Ancestors, who spoke of Mbona as a Black Christ. Priests and mediums of the old cult had often also been baptized Christians as they lived out overlapping interactions. Now frenzied mobs of Black Ancestor followers disrupted the celebration of the Mass, shouting that Christ was for the whites but that Mbona was the Savior of Blacks.

Schoffeleers obviously deplores the polarization of southern Malawi, the collapse of the Mbona cult, and the starkly drawn lines of hostility between neotradition and Christian ideologies. The Church of the Black Ancestors may not have a secure future in view of the disapproval of the Malawi government. Nevertheless, it is a fascinating example of the capacity to generalize traditional religion by means of literacy.

MISSION CHRISTIANITY AND THE LOCAL CHURCH

I have been arguing for the capacity of African religion to engage with the widening scale of modern African life. Next I discuss briefly the ways in which mission Christianity was much *less* macrocosmic than the conventional model supposes. The problem is that the best-known missionaries and missions are the ones that were most committed to the transformation of small-scale Africa. Early nineteenth-century Protestant missionaries in South Africa were undoubtedly committed to the ideals of the Scottish Enlightenment and to the emergence of a liberal capitalism that would replace both Boer feudalism and African tribal society. They would bring an evangelized South Africa into conversion and communication with the enlightened world. David Livingstone's slogan "Christianity, Commerce, and Civilization" is probably the one thing a non-Africanist knows about mission history in Africa. Other nineteenth-century missionaries believed in the essential benevolence of expanding British imperialism. The devotedly modernizing Livingstonia Mission of the Free Church of Scotland sent out the African elites of Malawi and Zambia to assist in the building of the Southern African industrial system: all these missionaries were undoubtedly men of the macrocosm. (This has been the subject of the best modern missionary histories; see, e.g., Crehan [1978], Ross [1986], McCracken [1977]).

These men remained the focus of attention when African nationalist historiography developed, partly because they provided the most convincing examples of European arrogance and partly because their African converts provided the most convincing link between the African past and the founders of the new African nations. Yet it has long been clear that there are serious difficulties in treating this little cluster of missionaries and missions as typical of the microcosm-shattering effect of Christianity. For one thing considerable tensions exist between the aims and the effects of missionaries of this sort. George Bond's Scottish missionaries in Unyombe were certainly part of the radical Protestant tradition, and yet we have already seen how paradoxical were the local consequences of their evangelism. Then there are problems of chronology. Confidence that capitalist, urban, and industrial development was a totally benevolent part of the divine plan was easier to sustain in the first half of the nineteenth century than it was at the end of it, and easier even then than it had become by the end of the First World War. Most twentieth-century missionaries were anticapitalists, hostile to urban life, anxious to rebuild rural solidarities. Finally, there are problems of denomination. The views of the radical Protestants were not shared, even in the nineteenth century, by Roman Catholic missionaries nor by High Church Anglicans. A majority of missionaries were always and everywhere concerned mainly with building local communities.

These points have been most effectively made in the mission historiography of Malawi. Reacting against a linear nation-building history, with its emphasis on the modernizing nationalist elites produced by the Scottish mission schools, Martin Chanock proposed a new problematic as long ago as 1972:

> Our understanding of recent Malawi history is out of focus. We focus on the role of the educated elite in a peasant dominated country; on the influence of urbanization in a country with no cities; on the influence of industrialization in the most rural part of Central Africa. . . . The belief that Christianity and Commerce were roads to progress still runs through the writing of the history of the colonial era. The present general scenario of Malawian history is one of innovating precolonial societies forming states, engaging in long-distance trade, set back a little by colonial conquest which, however, planted the seeds of its undoing because missionaries and migrant labour gave rise to a new forward-looking class which sired Malawi nationalism. (Chanock 1972:434)

Chanock called instead for a historiography that would "demodernize the Christians" so that "we would then be able to regard the nationalist movement for what it was—a mass movement in a peasant country" (Chanock 1972:434).

Chanock found that historians were still victims of the image that the missions had of themselves and accepted the missionary assumption that Christianity was a modernizing religion. He points out that for Malawi such a view requires an exclusive focus on the Scottish missions, ignoring "the Catholics and the Dutch Reformed missions which did not play this role." He also observes that, even for those Christian converts whose ambitions had been fired by the teaching of the Scots, actual experience was one of progressive promises betrayed: "A brief and intermittent acquaintance with a rural mission school and a puzzling and bruising contact with Christian hypocrisy did not produce men objectively capable of 'taking the process of betterment' into their own hands" (Chanock 1972:436–38).

Two years later, in 1974, Ian Linden published a treatment of Malawi's missionary history that came close to realizing Chanock's program. Linden set out his revisionist intentions in his preface. In the dominant Protestant historiography of Malawi:

> The history [of the country] is the story of a generation of African leaders, fostered in the Scots missions where they received their education, who finally swept the country into an era of mass nationalism. Behind every pew there seems to lurk a protonationalist. Roman Catholic missionaries in Nyasaland did not produce leaders of modernizing movements. . . . Not surprisingly, they have been ignored. Yet there are over three-quarters of a million Catholics amongst Malawi's four million people, mainly peasant subsistence farmers. A historian studying the Catholic missions is obliged

> to concentrate on a peasant church, whose essential conservatism calls in question, or at least balances, the elitist slant of the Protestant mission history. . . . Catholic missions did not fit tidily into the box marked Christianity and Progress. (Linden 1974:ix)

Linden's own story was one of Catholic priests, mostly themselves from European peasant families, bringing to rural Malawians "a Christianity filtered through centuries of European peasant culture." The result was an intensely *local* Christianity: "The focus of this book is the micro-events around Catholic mission stations, the interactions of European Catholic and African peasant conservatism" (Linden 1974:x).

More recently, in 1982, a history of the Dutch Reformed Church (DRC) in Zambia and Malawi was published, which also focused on microevents around rural mission stations. Its author noted

> the strong tendency in DRC mission policy to preserve the traditional structures of a people. The African should have access to the Bible in his own language. But he should not be lifted out of his traditional village life, or become a semi-European by following other white ways. . . . The DRC policy was turned to the needs of village life. Its deepest aim was the raising of a "Bible-loving, industrious and prosperous peasantry." . . . This policy did not stimulate and only reluctantly allowed these peasants to participate in a wider world. (Gilhuis 1982:108)

In such a context the African religious movements that swept through the DRC zone, along with all other mission zones in Zambia, seem to represent a macrocosmic invasion of a set of Christian microcosms!

It may be objected that Malawi has been a special case—"the most rural part of Central Africa." Alternatively it may be objected that I have been seizing upon a minority reactionary tendency within the overall progressive and expansive European missionary movement. Yet attitudes such as I have been citing were held not only by French peasant Catholics and Afrikaner ruralists and German cultural nationalists (Wright 1971). They were also held, for example, by university-trained Anglicans. My own recent work on the eastern districts of Southern Rhodesia, where there were certainly much more industrialization and urbanization than in Chanock's Malawi, has revealed how strongly focused on the village and on a self-supporting peasant church Anglican missionaries were. Canon Edgar Lloyd, for decades the leader of Anglican popular Christianity in Makoni district, spelled it out:

> The village work is extremely important . . . because it has to be done by themselves. . . . [The village out-station] is really a Christian community centre. It is wonderful to see in heathen Africa the religious devotion of so many villagers and the real influence the Christian religion has on

> their lives. . . . The particular work undertaken by this Mission is that of preaching Christ in the villages and in the country schools of the villages. Africa is a country of villages: of cultivated patches, often hand-tilled, of herds of small cattle, of wood-fires in huts and long nights of discussion. . . . To hold the villages for Christ is to hold Africa that now is. (Lloyd 1929).

In a series of recent articles I have described the local, rural, popular Anglicanism that emerged in Makoni district, with its network of small-peasant Anglican villages linked together and focused on a new symbolic center. But that center is nothing more macrocosmic than the district mission church and farm at Saint Faith's, to which regular pilgrimages were made (Ranger 1987a, 1987b).

In the preceding paragraphs I have concentrated on missionary perceptions. Such rural, microcosmic Christianities were the construct also, however, of African converts. As in the case of Yombe Protestantism, many of the converts to Makoni Anglicanism were returned migrant laborers concerned to find religious legitimacy for leadership roles in rural society. Others were the organic intellectuals who used mission literacy and the newly created written vernacular to elaborate myths of local ethnic identity. Much of the imagination that went into colonial immobilized societies came from them. But I am not, of course, saying that Catholic or Dutch Reformed Church or Anglican popular Christianity managed (or desired) to *preserve* small-scale rural society. They did something more and something less than that. They introduced their own changes—of ideas and practice and personnel—some of which articulated the notion of membership in a "universal" church. But they also participated crucially in that *narrowing* of scale that accompanied the colonial invention of "traditional" localism.

Village Christian societies were penetrated in many ways by colonial capitalism, but they were also in many ways *more* microcosmic than precolonial rural societies. When disillusionment set in with mission Christianity in Makoni district during the depression years of the 1930s, it was challenged by African-led churches that were much *less* local, whether these were prophetic Apostolic churches, which sprang out of migrant-labor experiences and which have become international in scope (Dillon-Malone 1978), or witchcraft eradication movements, like Mchape, which reached Makoni only after it had spread through Malawi, Zambia, Tanzania, and Mozambique (Ranger 1981).

CONCLUSION

My advocate's statement is, of course, partial and one-sided. Nevertheless, I hope it is enough in itself to challenge some of the established propositions about the essential contrasts between Christianity and African religion. Contrasts there certainly were, but these were not so much that the former was macrocosmic in its focus and the latter microcosmic. The contrast rather lay in how each operated *both* microcosmically and macrocosmically.

Jean Comaroff made a brilliant statement of this proposition in an oral presentation to the Boston conference. The volumes which she and her husband have produced on the interactions of Protestant missions with Tswana society concentrate upon unequivocally modernizing missionaries (see Comaroff and Comaroff 1991). Much of the Comaroffs' analysis shows how these men sought to introduce new concepts of time and space in order to integrate their converts into the wide world of industrial capitalism. Yet on *both* sides of this encounter—the Protestant and the "traditional"—the local and the global were in dialectic tension. The Tswana states had "an uneasy relationship of encompassment" with domestic and local religion; there were secessions and breakaways, as much religious as political; the states had to come to terms with incoming diviners and ritual specialists. "The whole question of politico-religious centralization was already on the Tswana agenda"; the nineteenth-century Tswana states were themselves recent constructs with as yet uncertain ideological legitimacy. For their part the Protestant missionaries were "marginal men," who came from societies in tension. Most aimed to create local-level communities of African yeomen.

Both for Tswana and for missionaries, argued Comaroff, the global and local dimensions were inseparable. Both had ideal notions of "global communities" but also a realization that no one actually lived in them. Real, everyday life took place locally, so that the overall Christian map of Botswana, or of southern Africa, was built up linking local Christian villages and mission stations into a network—rather as a territorial cult could put together a mosaic of local congregations.

Comaroff insisted, and rightly so, that there were real and important contrasts between the ways in which Protestantism and African religion conceived localism and globalism. "Some religions can do what others cannot." What she called "global monetarization" and "global literacy," at this period a mission monopoly, gave mission globalism a new potential. She concluded that "deconstruction can go too far."

No doubt in this chapter deconstruction *has* gone too far. So I should redeem my argumentative excesses by concluding that, restated in Jean Comaroff's terms, the tension between the local, the national, and the universal remains an important topic in African religious history. Perhaps I can make the point (and show that I do not owe it entirely to Jean Comaroff's gentle critique) by quoting from my 1987 article on Zimbabwean religious history. This deals with the ways in which Canon

Lloyd and his African converts took symbolic hold of the land, creating their own holy places amongst the sacred hills and caves of African religious imagination and generating their own pilgrimages. In this way, I argued, they legitimated an intensely local popular Anglicanism. But I go on to show how energetic Anglican bishops disliked the Saint Faith's brand of local Christianity and sought to undercut it, among other ways by establishing national pilgrimage centers. I concluded the piece by generalizing this tension between the local and the central: "There has been a constant oscillation in the [religious] history of Zimbabwe between the local and the central, the popular and the institutional. The holy place and the pilgrimage have sometimes served to validate the one and sometimes to validate the other. At times one has seemed to triumph and the other to collapse, but both have survived in continuous and creative tension with the other."

I go on to describe the challenge to local mission Christianity in the 1930s with the rise of African independent churches and the spread of African religious movements. It seemed then as if local Anglicanism and Catholicism had been swept away. Yet through movements of Christian Revivalism popular microcosmic Christianity was rescued and preserved. On the other hand:

> In the 1970s, when guerrilla war spread through Makoni, only local holy places and holy men seemed any longer relevant. The central, urban structures of Anglicanism and Catholicism were discredited and impotent and many commentators announced that legitimacy and authority had moved to the suffering rural and local churches. Indeed, there was an intense local interaction between the guerrillas, those men of the bush, and local holy places and their guardians. Guerrillas gained legitimate access to the caves and mountains by working with the representative figures of local religion—the spirit mediums guarding the burial hill of the Makoni chiefs, the Irish priests in charge at Triashill and St. Barbara's. . . . Yet since the end of the war in 1980 central church institutions have turned out still to have a great deal of life in them, and not only the vitality of material resources, placed at the service of the new government's educational and health policies. The symbolic resources of the ecclesiastical centre are not yet exhausted. (Ranger 1987b)

I might also have said, though I did not, that the resources of macrocosmic African religion were also not exhausted. Witchcraft eradication and witch-cleansing movements swept through Makoni and neighboring districts in the 1980s, providing opportunities for confession and absolution after the suspicions and tensions of the war. I *did* end that study of Makoni district by saying, as I shall end this chapter now by saying, that much of the continuing history of religion in southern Africa, whether of

Christianity or of African religion, lies in the working out of "this dialectic between the local and the central."

REFERENCES

Binsbergen, W. M. J. van. 1976. *The Dynamics of Religious Change in Western Zambia.* Ufahamu: University Press.

———. 1981. *Religious Change in Zambia: Exploratory Studies.* London: Kegan Paul.

Bond, George. 1978. "Religious Coexistence in Northern Zambia: Intellectualism and Materialism in Yombe Belief." *Annals of the New York Academy of Sciences* 318:23–26.

———. 1987. "Ancestors and Protestants: Religious Coexistence in the Social Field of a Zambian Community." *American Ethnologist* 14:55–72.

Brain, James. 1964. "More Modern Witch-Finding." *Tanzania Notes and Records* 62:44–48.

Chanock, Martin. 1972. "Development and Change in the History of Malawi." In B. Pachai, ed., *The Early History of Malawi*, pp. 429–46. London: Longman.

Comaroff, Jean, and John Comaroff. 1991. *From Revelation to Revolution: Christianity, Colonialism, and Consciousness in Southern Africa.* Volume One. Chicago: University of Chicago Press.

Crehan, Kate. 1978. "Khoi, Boer, and Missionary: An Anthropological Study of the Role of the Missionaries on the Cape Frontier, 1799–1850." Master's thesis, University of Manchester.

Cross, Sholto. 1972. "The Watch-Tower, Witch-Cleansing, and Secret Societies in Central Africa." Manuscript. Conference on the Religious History of Central Africa, Lusaka.

De Craemer, W., R. Fox, and Jan Vansina. 1976. "Religious Movements in Central Africa: A Theoretical Study." *Comparative Studies in Society and History* 18, 4:458–75.

Dillon-Malone, Clive. 1978. *The Korsten Basket-Makers: A Study of the Masowe Apostles.* Manchester: University of Manchester Press.

———. 1983. "The Mutumwa Churches of Zambia." *Journal of Religion in Africa* 14, 3:204–22.

———. 1985. "The Mutumwa Church of Peter Mulenga." *Journal of Religion in Africa* 15, 2:123–41.

Douglas, Mary. 1963. *The Lele of Kasai.* Oxford: Oxford University Press.

Fields, Karen. 1982. "Political Contingencies of Witchcraft in Colonial Central Africa." *Canadian Journal of African Studies* 16, 3:567–93.

———. 1985. *Revival and Rebellion in Colonial Central Africa.* Princeton: Princeton University Press.

Gelfand, Michael. 1959. *Shona Ritual with Special Reference to the Chaminuka Cult.* Cape Town: Juta Press.

Gilhuis, G. V. 1982. *From Dutch Mission Church to Reformed Church in Zambia.* Franeker: T. Wever Press.

Hilton, Anne. 1985. *The Kingdom of Kongo.* Oxford: Oxford University Press.

Ikenga-Metuh, E. 1987. "The Shattered Microcosm: A Critical Survey of Explanations of Conversion in Africa." In K. Holst Petersen, ed., *Religion, Development, and African Identity*, pp. 11–27. Uppsala: Scandinavian Institute of African Studies.

Iliffe, John. 1979. *A Modern History of Tanganyika*. Cambridge: Cambridge University Press.

Janzen, John. 1977. "The Tradition of Renewal in Kongo Religion." In N. S. Booth, Jr., ed., *African Religions: A Symposium*, pp. 38–62. New York: Nok Publishers.

———. 1979. "Ideologies and Institutions in the Precolonial History of Equatorial Therapeutic Systems." *Social Science and Medicine* 13B, 4:317–26.

———. 1982. *Lemba, 1650–1930: A Drum of Affliction in Africa and the New World*. New York: Garland Press.

———. 1985. "The Consequences of Literacy in African Religion: The Kongo Case." In Wim van Binsbergen and M. Schoffeleers, ed., *Theoretical Explorations in African Religion*, pp. 225–52. London: KPI.

———. Forthcoming. *Ngoma: Affliction and Ritual Therapy in Central and Southern Africa*.

Kopytoff, Igor. 1987. *The African Frontier: The Reproduction of Traditional African Societies*. Bloomington: Indiana University Press.

Lan, David. 1985. *Guns and Rain*. London: James Currey Press.

Last, Murray, and Gordon Chavunduka. 1986. *The Professionalization of African Medicine*. Manchester: University of Manchester Press.

Linden, Ian. 1974. *Catholics, Peasants, and Chewa Resistance in Nyasaland, 1889–1939*. London: Heinemann Educational.

Lelyveld, Joseph. 1985. *Move Your Shadow*. London: Michael Joseph.

Lloyd, Edgar. 1929. "Annual Report, St. Faith's." SPG Reports, SPG Archives, Rhodes House, Oxford.

———. 1935. St. Faith's Pastor Teacher Handbook. File ANG 16/1/10. National Archives, Zimbabwe.

McCracken, John. 1977. *Politics and Christianity in Malawi, 1875–1940*. Cambridge: Cambridge University Press.

MacGaffey, Wyatt. 1977. "Cultural Roots of Kongo Prophetism." *History of Religions* 17, 2:177–93.

———. 1986a. *Religion and Society in Central Africa: The Bakongo of Lower Zaire*. Chicago: University of Chicago Press.

———. 1986b. "Ethnography and the Closing of the Frontier in Lower Congo." *Africa* 56, 3:263–79.

Mackenzie, John. 1988. *The Empire of Nature: Hunting, Conservation, and British Imperialism*. Manchester: University of Manchester Press.

Madziyere, S. 1975. "Heathen Practices in the Urban and Rural Parts of Marendellas Area and Their Effects upon Christianity." In Terence Ranger and John Weller, eds., *Themes in the Christian History of Central Africa*, pp. 76–82. London: Heinemann Educational.

Mashingaidze, Elleck. 1976. *Christianity and the Mhondoro Cult: A Study of African*

Religious Initiative and Resilience in the Mazoe Valley Area of Mashonaland. In *Mohlomi: Journal of Southern African Historical Studies* 1:1:71–87.

Maxwell, Kevin. 1983. *Bemba Myth and Ritual: The Impact of Literacy on an Oral Culture.* New York: Peter Lang.

Mbiti, John. 1969. *African Religions and Philosophy.* London: Heinemann Educational.

Neckebrouck, V. 1984. "Inculturation et Identité." *Cultures et Développement* 14, 2:250–75.

Ranger, Terence. 1972a. "Missionary Adaptation of African Religious Institutions: The Masasi Case." In Ranger and Kimambo, eds., *The Historical Study of African Religion*, pp. 221–51. London: Heinemann Educational.

———. 1972b. "Mchape and the Study of Witchcraft Eradication." Manuscript. Conference on the History of Central African Religious Systems, Lusaka.

———. 1979. "European Attitudes and African Realities: The Rise and Fall of the Matola Chiefs of South-East Tanzania." *Journal of African History* 20, 1:63–82.

———. 1981. "Poverty and Prophetism: Religious Movements in Makoni District, 1929–1940." Manuscript. School of Oriental and African Studies, London.

———. 1982. "The Death of Chaminuka: Spirit Mediums, Nationalism, and the Guerrilla War in Zimbabwe." *African Affairs* 81:324, 349–69.

———. 1983. "Tradition and Travesty: Chiefs and the Administration in Makoni District, Zimbabwe, 1960–1980." In John Peel and Terence Ranger, eds., *Past and Present in Zimbabwe*, pp. 20–41. Manchester: University of Manchester Press.

———. 1985a. *Peasant Consciousness and Guerrilla War in Zimbabwe.* London: James Currey.

———. 1985b. "Religious Studies and Political Economy: The Mwari Cult and The Peasant Experience in Southern Rhodesia." In van Binsbergen and Schoffeleers, eds., *Theoretical Explorations in African Religion*, pp. 287–321. London: KPI.

———. 1986. "Religious Movements and Politics in Sub-Saharan Africa." *African Studies Review* 29, 2:1–69.

———. 1987a. "Religion, Development, and African Christian Identity." In K. Holst Petersen, ed., *Religion, Development, and African Identity*, pp. 29–57. Uppsala: Scandinavian Institute of African Studies.

———. 1987b. "Taking Hold of the Land: Holy Places and Pilgrimages in Twentieth-Century Zimbabwe." *Past and Present* 117:158–94.

———. 1989a. "The Politics of Prophecy in Matabeleland, 1953 to 1988." Manuscript. Conference on African Religion, Sattherwaite.

———. 1989b. "Religion and Witchcraft in Everyday Life in Contemporary Zimbabwe." In P. Kaarsholm, ed., *Culture and Society in Zimbabwe*, pp. 105–13. Copenhagen: Den NY Verden.

Ranger, Terence, and Isaria Kimambo, eds. 1972. *The Historical Study of African Religion.* London: Heinemann Educational.

Rennie, John Keith. 1973. "Christianity, Colonialism, and the Origins of Nationalism among the Noau of Southern Rhodesia, 1890–1935." Ph.D. diss., Department of History, Northwestern University.

Roberts, A. F. 1989. "History, Ethnicity, and Change in the 'Christian Kingdom' of Southeastern Zaire." In L. Vail, ed., *The Creation of Tribalism in Southern Africa*, pp. 193–214. London: James Currey.

Ross, Andrew. 1986. *John Philip, 1775–1850: Mission, Race, and Politics in South Africa.* Aberdeen: Aberdeen University Press.

Schoffeleers, Matthew. 1972. "The History and Political Role of the Mbona Cult among the Manganja." In Ranger and Kimambo, eds., *The Historical Study of African Religion*, pp. 73–94. London: Heinemann Educational.

———. 1974. "Crisis, Criticism, and Critique: An Interpretive Model of Territorial Mediumship among the Chewa." *Journal of Social Science* 3:17–34.

———. 1978a. "A Martyr Cult as a Reflection on Changes in Production." *African Perspectives* 2:19–34.

———. 1978b. *Guardians of the Land.* Gwelo: Mambo.

———. 1985. *Pentecostalism and Neo-traditionalism.* Amsterdam: Free University Press.

Vail, Leroy. 1989. *The Creation of Tribalism in Southern Africa.* London: James Currey.

Vansina, Jan. 1971. "Les Mouvements Religieux Kuba." *Etudes d'Histoire Africaine* 2:157–89.

———. 1973. "Lukoshi/Lupambula: Histoire d'un Culte Religieux." *Etudes d'Histoire Africaine* 5:51–97.

———. 1978. *The Children of Woot: A History of the Kuba Peoples.* Madison: University of Wisconsin Press.

Werbner, Richard. 1977. "Continuity and Policy in Southern Africa's High God Cult." In R. Werbner, ed., *Regional Cults*, pp. 34–56. London: Academic Press.

———. 1989. "Regional Cult of God Above: Alchemy and Defending Ifu Macrocosm." In R. Werbner, ed., *Ritual Passage, Sacred Journey*, pp. 18–36. Manchester: Manchester University Press.

Westerlund, David. 1980. *Ujamaa Na Dini: A Study of Some Aspects of Society and Religion in Tanzania, 1961–1977.* Stockholm: Almquist and Wiksell.

Wright, Marcia. 1971. *German Missions in Tanganyika, 1891–1941.* Oxford: Oxford University Press.

———. 1984. *Women in Peril.* Lusaka: Neczam Press.

Wrigley, Christopher. 1988. "The River-God and the Historians: Myth in the Shjire Valley and Elsewhere." *Journal of African History* 29, 3:367–83.

CHAPTER FOUR

Of Faith and Commitment: Christian Conversion in Muslim Java

Robert W. Hefner

Politics has always deeply affected Christian proselytization in Muslim Java. During the first two centuries of its rule (which began with a foothold in western Java in 1619), the Dutch government prohibited mission work outright for fear of antagonizing the island's Muslims and thereby jeopardizing colonial economic schemes. Founded in 1797 with the express purpose of working in the Dutch Indies, the Netherlands Missionary Society (Nederlandsch Zendeling Genootschap) was for several decades barred from working among the Javanese. Authorities confiscated the first Javanese translation of the New Testament, printed in India in 1831, on its arrival in the port city of Semarang. Eventually it rotted in a warehouse, because "the Bible was considered dangerous for the peace of the population" (van Akkeren 1969:55).

With its Muslim appeals for unity against the European infidel (Carey 1980), the Diponegoro rebellion (1825–1830) only served to impress more deeply on colonial bureaucrats the dangers of exciting Muslim passions. The colonial government thus continued to eschew any program of Christian proselytization, devoting its political resources to economic programs, especially the recently inaugurated "Cultivation System" (*cultuurstelsel*; see Geertz 1963; Hefner 1990). A key feature of Spanish and Portuguese initiatives in island Southeast Asia, the task of winning souls for Christendom was of decidedly less interest to the Calvinist Netherlanders.

Missionizing by European Christians in Java was finally tolerated only after the middle of the nineteenth century and even then only under watchful administrative eyes. Two developments facilitated the more liberal policy. First, European power was now firmly established in the countryside, and the likelihood of Christian missionization inciting serious Muslim resistance had diminished. In addition, and perhaps more important, several native Christian communities had sprung up at this time independently of European initiative, primarily as a result of the pastoral efforts of mestizo Euro-Javanese (van Akkeren 1969:55–91). Though suspicious that many natives converted because of a mistaken belief that they could escape compulsory labor, from which Europeans were spared, government officials were obliged after mid-century to tolerate a mission presence. After two centuries of exclusion, then, Christian missionaries were finally allowed to work among this overwhelmingly Muslim people.

The missionaries soon realized that Java's eastern territories offered some of the most promising areas for evangelization. They focused especially on the recently opened frontier of the southern and eastern reaches of the Brantas River basin, just to the east of Central Java's cultural heartland (see map 4.1). In this still sparsely populated countryside a Christian Javanese community—today estimated at about 4 percent of the seventy million ethnic Javanese—eventually took shape. Though in Central Java the church attracted some aristocratic supporters (Guillot 1979; Willis 1977:157), the East Javanese congregation was from its beginning rooted in the peasantry. Conversion among urban East Javanese began only after World War I and even then was unsuccessful, with the exception of a few Chinese converts, until Indonesian independence in 1949 (van Akkeren 1969:116).

In what follows I examine in greater detail this history of East Javanese conversion, striving to determine why people converted in some areas but not in others. My purpose is not to provide a general history of Javanese Protestantism, for which we already have several excellent, if mission-based, accounts (van Akkeren 1969; Willis 1977). Instead, I hope to analyze more closely the forces promoting this unusual Christian advance, accurately acclaimed by mission scholars as "the largest group of people [in modern times] ever to become Christians of a Moslem background" (Willis 1977:4). In doing so, I also hope to raise several questions for the analysis of religious conversion in general.

The social forces influencing East Javanese conversion have changed over the past 150 years. My discussion focuses on three moments in that history: first, the initial establishment of Christian communities in the East Javanese countryside in the 1830s; second, the abortive expansion of Christianity in the face of Islamic resurgence in the early twentieth century; and, third, the more recent mass conversions in the aftermath of the anticommunist massacres of 1965–1966. Although drawing on pan-Javanese data, my discussion of the last two periods centers on

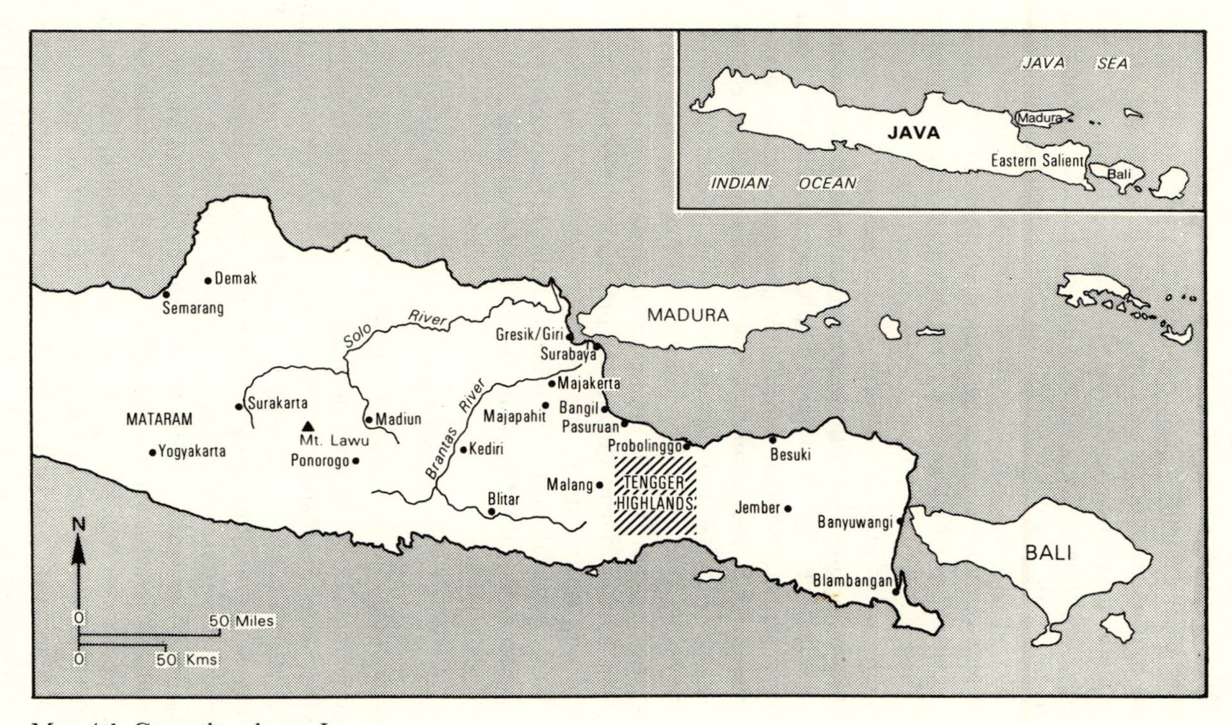

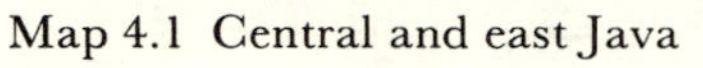

Map 4.1 Central and east Java

conversion in one particular region, a mountain district in the regency of Pasuruan in the province of East Java, where I conducted field research from 1978 to 1980 and again during eight months of 1985.

By linking social-historical influences to converts' life histories, I also hope to build on and qualify what are known as "intellectualist" accounts of religious conversion (Horton 1971; Skorupski 1976:183–204). Intellectualism explains conversion as a change in religious belief, where beliefs are viewed as instruments of explanation and control of actual time-space events. In line with this view individuals are assumed to change their beliefs as a result of social developments that promote comparison of the relative coherence of one set of beliefs with that of another: "rival sets of belief are in effect compared, and one is preferred, on grounds of explanatory force" (Skorupski 1977:205).

The intellectualist account correctly encourages us to think of individuals as active agents who at times are capable of critically evaluating their cultural heritage. But the model's emphasis on intellectual explanation and control neglects religion's vital role in conceiving and sustaining social community. It thus reinforces a widespread bias in conversion studies toward interiorist accounts of conversion, to the neglect of religion's importance in community, politics, and morality (see the introduction to this volume). Yet, as the Javanese example illustrates, social, political, and moral influences often take precedence over intellectualist explanation and control in the process of conversion. This simple insight has larger implications for our understanding of individual commitment to Christianity and the general reality of religious faith.

THE NINETEENTH CENTURY CRISIS OF TRADITION

From the beginning the spread of Christianity in eastern Java was a frontier phenomenon. It originated on the margins of mainstream society at a time of great social dislocation and in rural settings as yet undominated by the social and religious hierarchies of the Javanese heartland. The earliest expansion of Christian settlement into eastern Java illustrates this diffusionary pattern. The first village was founded in 1830 in the lower Brantas River basin, around the present-day city of Mojokerto. It was a fortuitous year for such a beginning. In nearby Central Java the five-year Diponegoro rebellion against Dutch colonialism had just come to a close. "The last stand of the Javanese aristocratic elite" against European colonialism (Ricklefs 1981:113), the war reduced Java's remaining principalities to the status of puppets of the colonial regime (Carey 1980:76). The conflict also consumed some two hundred thousand Javanese lives and drove tens of thousands of immigrants into the still sparsely populated territories of eastern Java (Palte 1984:19). Finally, among the Javanese themselves the turmoil set the stage for a crisis of cultural identity that has continued to the present day.

Located just to the east of nineteenth-century Java's most important population centers, the lower Brantas basin was well suited for both rice farming and river trade; at the beginning of the nineteenth century it was also sparsely populated. A thriving center of commerce and culture two centuries earlier, the territory had been depopulated as a result of warfare between Central and East Javanese kingdoms in the seventeenth and eighteenth centuries. The colonially imposed Pax Neerlandica eventually created the conditions for the reestablishment of population in this region, much of it consisting of migrants from the more densely populated territories to the west.

At first the communities founded in this eastern region were all Islamic. As in Central Java, however, they displayed wide variation in their commitment to religious orthodoxy. Popular Javanese traditions accord village founders (*cikal bakal*) great authority in determining the religious orientation of a community (see Jay 1963:33; Hefner 1985). Village founders might choose to erect a mosque and identify their village as devoutly Muslim (*santri*). Alternatively, they might devote their resources to the construction of a spirit shrine (*dhanyang*) and identify their community as "Javanist" (*kejawen*, *cara Jawa*). Most Javanists are Muslim but committed to distinctly Javanese ritual styles and only a perfunctory observance of the pillars of Islam (Geertz 1960:121–30; Jay 1963).

In keeping with this tradition of first-founder religious authority, a handful of Javanese and Euro-Javanese established Christian villages in the newly reopened Brantas River basin during the middle decades of the nineteenth century. The history of the first of these villages illustrates the tensions between European and Javanese identities that plagued the Christian congregation during its first years. The community's founder, C. L. Coolen, was the Javanized son of a Russian immigrant and a Javanese woman of minor aristocratic standing. Taking advantage of leasehold rights available only to Europeans (including their mixed-blood children), in 1830 Coolen acquired rights to 142 hectares of jungle land in the lower Brantas basin. Having established his own farm, he then leased the remaining territory to land-hungry immigrants (van Akkeren 1969:56).

Unlike some later Christian communities, Coolen did not bar Muslims from his settlement. All residents were obliged to conform to certain minimal Christian strictures, however, such as observing the sabbath and refraining from gambling and opium smoking. Renowned for his wealth and patriarchal leadership, Coolen also worked to adapt Christian practices to Javanese sensibilities. He peppered his sermons with Javanese mystical terms, incorporated references to Dewi Sri (the popular Javanist rice goddess) into his prayers, employed Sufi-style *dzikir* chanting for the Christian confession of faith, and sponsored such esteemed Javanese arts as gamelan music and *wayang* shadow theater, usually just after the sabbath worship. Later missionaries opposed Javanese aesthetic forms, viewing them as sensuous and sinful (van Akkeren 1969:62–92). Coolen also vigorously opposed policies later promoted by European missionaries, such as the requirement that converts adopt European dress, cut their hair, and take Christian names. Through his curious mixture of economic patronage, patriarchy, and cultural sensitivity, Coolen won hundreds of peasants to Christianity and established a thriving community in which his authority was, at first, unchallenged.

During the first twelve years of Coolen's settlement, European pastors in nearby Surabaya knew nothing of it. Shortly after its discovery by Europeans in 1842, however, the village was thrown into crisis. Torn between two worlds, Coolen cast his lot with his Javanese compatriots and tried to use his privileges as a Euro-Javanese in their favor. In the late 1840s he antagonized European administrators by attempting to circumvent the requirement that all natives, including his resident Christians, perform forced labor for the government's Cultivation System. Coolen's insolence eventually prompted the government to withdraw his lease and deed his lands to his tenants. These measures effectively stripped Coolen of his standing in the community.

Coolen's defiance of European authority also antagonized Dutch missionaries. He opposed baptism, claiming it was a European rather than a Christian custom. He expelled from his community all Javanese who, as European missionaries required, cut their hair, changed their dress, and took Christian names (van Akkeren 1969:73). In Coolen's eyes these were European customs that had nothing to do with Christianity and impeded the advance of the faith. Stripped of his land and despised by the missionaries, Coolen was gradually marginalized in the fledgling church.

Eventually, then, Coolen's community fell into disarray. The entire incident had provided European missionaries with important lessons on the dangers of allowing native Christians too much independence. In the years following the Coolen affair all Javanese congregations were made subject to the direct authority of the Dutch Reformed mission (van Akkeren 1969:108). Harsh measures prohibiting native dress, names, language, and arts were reimposed with full force. The consequences for the mission were immediate and far-reaching. Its advance stalled and in some areas even lost ground as converted Javanese came to be derisively identified as "Dutch Christians." Fruit of the missionary effort, this identification of Christianity with European culture impeded conversion efforts for decades to come.

Despite these setbacks several new Christian communities were established over the next few years. Almost all began in a manner similar to that of Coolen's experiment, combining "mission, migration, and clearance of jungle" (van Akkeren 1969:99; cf. Lombard 1990, I:84). The majority of the Christian settlements were new villages on frontier lands, not long-established communities, and their expansion eastward followed the steady advance of Central Javanese migrants. Having begun under Coolen in the lower Brantas plain, in a second phase (roughly 1860–85) Christian communities expanded further up the central Brantas valley toward Kediri. Shortly thereafter they continued their movement east and southeast along the curving course of the upper Brantas basin. Their final expansion was eastward into the last of Java's territories to be opened (or reopened) in modern times, the south coastal plains of Lumajang, Jember, and Banyuwangi (van Akkeren 1969:114).

This Christian expansion represented only a tiny portion of the total population movement from Central Java to the east. The great majority of the immigrants were Muslim Javanese, though they held to their faith with varying degrees of orthodoxy. Although European administrators provided some protection for Christians, and missionaries tried at times to organize estates to attract land-hungry peasants among whom they could proselytize, Javanese Christians, not their European superiors, provided most of the momentum for the establishment of Christian communities. By the beginning of the twentieth century a small network of Christian communities extended in a crescent from the lower Brantas basin through Kediri onward along the southern coast. This "Brantas crescent" remained the core territory of the East Javanese Christian Church (Gereja Kristen Jawi Wetan) well into the twentieth century. Conversion elsewhere in the province met with notably less success.

RESISTANCE TO CHRISTIANITY

Central Javanese were not the only immigrants to Java's eastern territories. Along the north coast around Surabaya, Pasuruan, Probolinggo, and Besuki, Madurese also arrived in large numbers. From the impoverished island of Madura just off the north coast of eastern Java, the Madurese eventually became the dominant ethnic group along eastern Java's north coast, where, centuries earlier, Javanese had predominated

(Elson 1978:32; Hefner 1990). The movement of Madurese had as distinctive a religious influence in this area as the immigration of Central Javanese did in the Brantas crescent.

Unlike Central Javanese immigrants Madurese entered modern East Java as a disesteemed ethnic minority. Javanese tended to regard these immigrants as coarse and ill-mannered (*kasar*). The dislocation involved in migration to a society where they were viewed as social inferiors was cushioned, however, by two distinctive features of Madurese social organization. First, their households were often built around extended families, a custom rare among ethnic Javanese. This domestic arrangement allowed for the pooling of resources and a more flexible adaptation to the rigors of Java's eastern frontier (De Vries 1931:31; Hefner 1990: 165). Second, Madurese organized their frontier communities around ties to Muslim religious teachers (*kyai*), with whom the migrants had first made contact back on the island of Madura. Families from different villages in Madura settled in areas of the East Javanese countryside previously opened by followers of their religious patron.

This latter aspect of Madurese social organization is important for understanding what many Javanese regard as the religious fanaticism of Madurese. As De Vries (1931:32) has noted, the immigrant Madurese established dispersed settlements, rather than the nucleated compounds preferred by Javanese. In general, in fact, Madurese displayed a weaker identification than Javanese with their villages of residence, committing their allegiances to their networks of kin on the one hand and of religious followers on the other. Kinship and religion thus provided the framework for the new lives immigrants established in an inhospitable environment. Those institutions also served to make Madurese more pious in their commitment to scriptural Islam than were many of their Javanese counterparts. This difference in religious commitment was not lost on Madurese, who responded to Javanese insults by accusing Javanese of being bad Muslims. In this fashion Islam became a boundary marker in Madurese interactions with a significant portion of the Javanese community.

These features of Madurese social organization also help to explain why Christianity made so little headway in the core regions of Madurese settlement along the northern coast of eastern Java. Like the Brantas crescent this coastal territory was a frontier area in the nineteenth century, having been depopulated in the seventeenth and early eighteenth century and resettled with Dutch support shortly thereafter (Alexander and Alexander 1979; Kumar 1979; Hefner 1990). But the north-coast Madurese resolved the moral and material dilemmas of migratory displacement by clinging all the more firmly to Muslim institutions, identifying Madurese ethnicity with the ideas and practices of scriptural Islam. To convert to Christianity was tantamount to repudiation of one's ethnicity, and a guarantee of social pariahdom.

Among the immigrant Central Javanese, by contrast, there was much less agreement on this equation of Islam and ethnic identity. A portion of the Javanese community was as orthodox as most Madurese. But others, probably the majority in the nineteenth century, were only nominally attentive to orthodox strictures, though they still identified themselves as Muslim. A few, however, were even explicitly anti-Islamic. In the course of the nineteenth century this emerging religious schism worsened.

This tension in the Javanese community was related to Java's earlier cultural history. Central Java had long had two related but in some ways competitive cultural traditions. In the inland areas of south-central Java official Islam had been tightly controlled by an aristocracy jealous of rival claimants to prestige or power. In this area of what is today regarded (a bit simplistically) as classical Javanese culture, Islam tended to take a more muted, Javanized form, emphasizing ritual and aesthetic forms not directly sanctioned by normative Islam. Some of these mystically oriented ritual forms are derived from South Asian variants of Sufi Islam (Woodward 1989). But others clearly owe their precedent to the Hindu traditions that predominated in Java until the sixteenth century (Geertz 1960; Hefner 1985; Ricklefs 1979).

The northern coast of Central and East Java, by contrast, had stronger ties to the insular Malay world, with its stricter and more vigorous commitment to scriptural Islam (Lombard 1990, I:77–208). In the sixteenth and seventeenth centuries, when the island was in transition to Islam, this coastal area produced Java's most influential Muslim leaders. Though from the seventeenth to the nineteenth century the inland courts brutally suppressed this region's political and economic autonomy, the coastal area remained Java's most important center of Islamic culture (Pigeaud 1967, I:6).

This regional difference in religious culture was reproduced in the course of the great eastward migrations of the eighteenth and nineteenth centuries. Javanist migrants established communities centered on shrines to guardian spirits (*dhanyang*) and graves of first-founding ancestors (*punden*) (Geertz 1960:26; Jay 1963:33; Hefner 1985:108). In these villages the most important annual rituals focused on food offerings to first-founding ancestors, guardian spirits, and deities of the earth, sky, and water (Hefner 1987b). Though usually acknowledged in prayer, Allah was conceived as a distant and relatively unapproachable divinity. Orthodox (*santri*) migrants, by contrast, downplayed, though by no means entirely, such Javanist customs. As in Madurese communities, in *santri* communities the Muslim boarding school (*pesantren*) was central to the socialization of children. Ritual activity was centered on the mosque rather than on a local spirit shrine. The focus of this ritual worship was Allah—immanent and transcendent—as well as his saintly intermediaries on earth. In the course of the nineteenth century the pesantren and mosque became increasingly influential in the diffusion of this more scripturally based, Islamic culture from Java's north coast into its hinterlands (Dhofier 1982; Geertz 1965; Hefner 1990).

Christianity established a toehold, then, only among Central Javanese immigrants to eastern Java, and even then primarily among Javanists. Virtually no north-coast Madurese became Christians. The appeal of Christianity among Javanists was related to a general crisis of authority and identity shaking Javanese society in the nineteenth century. In an earlier era, when the Dutch had not yet emasculated the courts, much of the Javanist population had looked to aristocrats (*priyayi*) for models of cultural excellence and moral anchors for their identity (Woodward 1989). In the early nineteenth century, however, the Dutch incorporated this aristocracy into the machinery of colonial exploitation, stripping them of many of their privileges and cutting them off from the rest of the population (Carey 1980:84). Not coincidentally, shortly after this time popular uprisings began to combine "violent hatred of foreigners" with an equally ferocious disdain for a Javanese aristocracy now regarded as mere lackeys of the Europeans (Kartodirdjo 1972:99).

Not surprisingly, in this context of social and cultural dislocation, even some Javanist peasants came to "rally . . . behind the kyai [Muslim religious teachers] against foreign rulers and against priyayi officials, who were alleged to have dishonored their religion by cooperating with the infidel" (Kartodirdjo 1972:100). In the late nineteenth and early twentieth centuries, then, a more pious form of Islam spread to segments of the previously Javanist population. This was the beginning of a deepening Islamization that has continued unabated into the twentieth century (see Benda 1983:32–60; Hefner 1987a; Nakamura 1983).

Not all Javanese rallied behind Islam. Indeed, in some respects the emergence of a resurgent Islam worsened ties between the orthodox and Javanist communities. As in other parts of the Muslim world the growing strength of nineteenth-century Islam brought demands for purification of the faith and the abolition of syncretic rites and traditions.

Among the Javanese, however, these Muslim initiatives provoked a strong countermovement. Up to that time most Javanists had thought of themselves as good Muslims; now the challenge of reform Islam prompted some to question their commitment to the faith. As Drewes has noted, several Javanese literary works of the late nineteenth century hint at a "rejection of Islam as being a religion foreign to Java and the Javanese" (Drewes 1966:310). Anderson (1990) and Ricklefs (1979:117; 1981:122) have demonstrated that among Javanese intellectuals in general there was growing resentment of Muslim puritanism; ethnohistorical studies of the peasantry find evidence of similar unease among segments of the rural populace (Onghokham 1975:32; Jay 1963:14–21; Hefner 1985:126–41). Though tensions between scriptural and Javanist Muslims had existed since the rise of Javanese Islam in the sixteenth century (De Graaf and Pigeaud 1974; Pigeaud 1967, I:78), evidence suggests that the Muslim resurgence of the nineteenth century strained ties even further.

Battered by European power and a revitalizing Islam, some in the Javanist community began to express interest in Christianity. In the years just after the Java War (1825–1830) the great court poet Raden Ngabehi Ranggawarsita, for example, composed a mythicohistorical chronicle in which the Javanese culture hero, Ajisaka—regarded in Javanese mythology as the carrier of civilization to Java (Poerwadhie-Atmohihardjo 1957; Hefner 1985)—is identified as having once converted to Christianity. Even though the tale reports he eventually leaves Christianity to study with the Prophet Muhammad, Aji displays no hostility toward Christianity, and Christ is sympathetically portrayed (van Akkeren 1969:46–48). In a similar vein one of the first native apostles of Christianity in Central Java was said to enjoy the quiet support of minor aristocrats at the Yogyakarta court (Guillot 1979:124). Like the earlier Coolen, this man failed to achieve his goal of establishing a Javanese church independent of European tutelage. Nonetheless, he is said to have had a generally sympathetic regard for the Dutch, whom he credited with having brought Christianity to Java.

Perhaps it is not surprising that Christianity attracted some attention among an aristocracy stripped of any real power and declining severely in status. In East Java, however, the church was rooted in the rural peasantry. Nonetheless, here, too, the growth of the church was related to this pan-Javanese crisis of identity and culture. As Ricklefs (1979:117) has noted, the rise of an exclusivist Islam produced a "growing awareness that there was, in some people's opinions, more to being a Muslim than merely saying that one was. . . . And a few learned that they were 'bad Muslims' and decided that, if this was so, they would rather not be Muslims at all."

What was at issue in all these conflicts was the nature of Javanese identity after the collapse of once-dominant traditions. Christianity was but one, and a minor one at that, of several religious movements seeking to fill this moral vacuum. Two counterinfluences, however, severely restricted the Christian appeal: first, the continuing identification of Christianity with the Dutch, a linkage reinforced by the austere strictures of European missionaries; and, second, the general paucity of Christian institutions in the countryside.

Both weaknesses underscore the important fact that mass conversion is rarely the outcome of intellectual appeal alone. Here, as in all cultures, a larger "political economy of meaning" (Eickelman 1979) determines which items of a cultural inventory are easily available and at what social cost. In the nineteenth century the cost of Christianity for most Javanese was still too high and its cultural utility too little. Events during the next period of Christian expansion, the early twentieth century, were to reveal this institutional limitation all the more clearly.

JESUS AND JAVANISM IN THE TENGGER HIGHLANDS

By the late nineteenth century the colonial government had dropped its blanket prohibition against missionary work in Java. It sought nonetheless to channel mission activity away from centers of Muslim orthodoxy and into Javanist territories, where Muslims would be less likely to object to the Christian presence. From this perspective there was no more appropriate locale for Christian proselytism than East Java's Tengger highlands. In the highest reaches of this rugged massif lived several thousand people who called themselves Hindu or Buddhist and refused Islam outright (Jasper 1926; Hefner 1985). In the middle altitudes of these same mountains most people called themselves Muslim. In fact, however, they were Javanist Muslims who rejected Islamic orthodoxy, borrowing freely from the traditions of their Hindu neighbors. Indeed, in the entire highlands there was not a single mosque and only a few prayer houses (*langgar, musholla*).

For European pastors, then, the Tengger highlands appeared to offer tantalizing opportunities.[1] Mission work began in the area in the 1880s. At first missionaries predicted quick and easy success, owing to what they called the "simple and unprejudiced" (Kreemer 1885:340) manner of the non- or nominally Islamic highlanders. A few years later, however, the missionaries had still won few souls to Christianity. Apparently, relations between orthodox Muslims and Javanists were still relatively pacific, and Javanists and Hindus alike felt little need to look to Christianity for protection from reformist Islam.

By the 1920s, however, all this had changed. Road construction at the end of the nineteenth century had brought an influx of Muslim traders and farmers from the lowlands (von Freijburg 1901:332). A booming demand for upland wood and cash crops created a lively trade network dominated by *santri* (orthodox) Muslims. In lower-lying mountain villages these Muslim immigrants eventually succeeded in shifting the balance of power in their communities of residence. Whenever they won control of village government, orthodox leaders forcibly abolished Javanist ritual and aesthetic traditions. In a region where Javanists, Hindus, and Muslims had long spoken of the need to respect each others' traditions (Hefner 1985:126–41), such bold moves provoked grave fears and deep resentment. These circumstances, then, prompted some in the upland Javanist community to contemplate converting to Christianity.

The dynamics of this crisis are nicely illustrated by events in the village of Wonorejo (a pseudonym), a community on the northwestern slopes of the Tengger highlands where I worked in 1979 and 1985. Wonorejo had long been a prominent center of Javanist religious activity. Its spirit shrine (*dhanyang*) was said to be home to an especially powerful guardian deity and attracted pilgrims from throughout the regency. Though Muslim by birth, the shrine's caretaker (*dhukun*) was militantly anti-Islamic. He met regularly with the Hindu priests who lived higher up the mountainside and proudly rejected orthodox Islam for what he called "true Javanese religion" (*agama Jawa asli*).

Around 1925 Wonorejo's shrine caretaker was challenged by a small group of wealthy Muslim merchants who had moved into the mountain region during commercial expansion at the beginning of the century. Criticizing his role as un-Muslim, these affluent immigrants demanded that the caretaker purge his rites of Hindu influences and publicly declare his loyalty to Islam. The caretaker refused, citing the long-established village belief that Javanism and Islam should live as one.

A strong follower of the local guardian-spirit cult, the village chief at first came to the defense of the shrine caretaker. Catching wind of new ways, however, he eventually acceded to the demands of the wealthy Muslim villagers and quietly counseled the caretaker to publicly identify himself as Muslim rather than as Hindu or Javanist. The caretaker retired rather than abide by this request. As village custom prescribed, the caretaker's son then inherited the ritual role. With great reluctance the new caretaker agreed to follow the chief's counsel. He swore allegiance to Islam, purged his prayers of Hindu referents, and even agreed to take part in Islamic religious classes organized by the Muslim merchants at a neighborhood prayer center (*langgar*) they had recently had built.

Secretly, however, the new caretaker was troubled by the Islamic advance. Unbeknownst to others in the community the caretaker had recently contacted a small circle of Javanese Christians in a community about twenty kilometers away. He had learned of the Christians after encountering a Javanese pastor who regularly visited the highlands, focusing his ministry on Javanist communities challenged by growing Muslim orthodoxy. This Javanese pastor had managed to establish a shadowy community of prospective converts in a dozen mountain villages. All his followers were exploring the Christian option secretly, however; none was yet willing to risk infuriating neighbors by openly breaking with Islam.

Eventually, however, Wonorejo's caretaker publicly declared his intention to convert to Christianity and sought to win the whole village to his new-found faith. He announced that Islam was contrary to the tradition of Wonorejo's ancestors and, he added, contrary to the ways of all Javanese. Christianity, he argued, *was* consonant with Javanese custom; in fact, he claimed its arrival on the island had been foretold by Javanese mystics centuries ago. Moreover, he added, Christianity has scripture and a prophet just as Islam does and is older than the religion of Muhammad. Finally, he said, conversion to Christianity was the only way to protect the village from the growing threat of *santri* Muslims.

For several days Wonorejo was thrown into turmoil. Respect for the shrine caretaker and antagonism toward the village's orthodox Muslims were sufficiently strong that the idea of Christian conversion was not dismissed outright. Despite their long-standing opposition to orthodox Islam, however, the village elders ultimately ruled against the new caretaker and demanded that he and his supporters leave the village.

The elders justified their decision by referring to issues of authority and identity, not fine points of theological doctrine. Did not our ancestors speak of the importance of respecting Muhammad, they said, even as they urged us to defend Javanese ways? Is it not also true, they said, that all of us are Javanese and, whatever their differences, Javanese are Muslims? Finally, the elders said, citing reports of Christian services in nearby towns, is it not true that Europeans forbid Javanese from worshiping alongside them in their churches? With these harsh words the elders stripped the caretaker of his role and expelled his family from the community.

Although dramatic, the caretaker's conversion and subsequent expulsion were not unique in this mountain region. As if by design a similar struggle for control of tradition unfolded in several nearby communities. Everywhere, it seems, there were a few Javanist families promoting Christianity as an alternative to an advancing Islam. In every case, however, the bittersweet fruit of their struggle was the same. The majority of villagers balked at the idea of openly breaking with Islam. The Christian sympathizers then had either to reject Christianity or, if they continued with their plans to convert, leave the village. Everywhere the argument against the would-be Christians was the same: Whatever their differences in matters of doctrine, Javanese are Muslims; Christians by contrast are European. In the end not a single mountain village converted to Christianity, and the movement for upland conversion disappeared without a trace.

BLOODSHED AND FAITH

The issue of Christian conversion was to arise again in this mountain region in the 1960s. This time the conversion controversy occurred not in the midslope Javanist region I have just discussed, which was now more or less securely Islamic, but higher up the mountain slope, in proto-Hindu communities that had been spared the Muslim influx at the turn of the century (Hefner 1985).

For these uplanders the 1950s had brought a heightened awareness of the perils facing non-Muslims in independent Indonesia. The Indonesian government now required all its citizens to profess one of five recognized religions: Islam, Catholicism, Protestantism, Buddhism, or, after 1962, Hinduism (Boland 1982:148). The tribal faiths of eastern Indonesia and syncretic or localized traditions like the proto-Hinduism of the Tengger highlands were not regarded as legitimate options. Technically, therefore, their adherents were obliged to convert to a new, officially recognized religion.

As a result of these pressures several Hindu communities converted to Islam in the early independence period (Hefner 1985, 1987b). In most villages, however, local leaders succeeded at forging an alliance with Balinese Hindus, who had managed to secure recognition of their religion as legitimate in 1962. The Tengger Hindus then adopted reforms intended to guarantee recognition of their religion as a legitimate branch of the national Hindu community (Hefner 1985:239–65). Though it had begun in 1962–1963, this reform movement in the Tengger highlands really gained strength only after the tumultuous events of 1965–1966.

On the night of September 30, 1965, left-wing officers staged an unsuccessful coup in the capital city of Jakarta. The Indonesian Communist Party (PKI) was quickly blamed for the coup attempt, and the military responded by joining forces with Muslim organizations to eliminate their powerful rival. Eventually, the PKI was outlawed, and hundreds of thousands of its followers were rounded up and killed in a massive bloodbath. Muslim youth groups worked in conjunction with representatives of the military to carry out the bloodletting, going from village to village arresting and executing suspected communists (Boland 1982:146; Willis 1977:92; Hefner 1990:202–21).

In this terrorized atmosphere it was extremely dangerous not to be able to claim affiliation with a recognized religion lest one be accused of atheism and, by implication, communism. Not surprisingly, then, the years following the coup saw a spectacular increase in conversions to Christianity and Hinduism. The vast majority of the converts were Javanists seeking protection from Muslim charges that they lacked religion (Lyon 1980; Boland 1982:231; Ricklefs 1979:124).

These, then, were the circumstances under which a Hindu reform movement spread throughout non-Islamic portions of the Tengger highlands in the 1970s (Hefner 1985). Evangelical Christianity also began to make headway at this time, however, though among a much smaller proportion of the upland population. The story of this Christian advance again illustrates the complex play of moral and political forces at work in conversion.

The Christian movement began in an upper-slope community that, for purposes of anonymity, I shall refer to as Sanggar. Later it spread to a neighboring village I shall call Petra. Sanggar and Petra were the only communities in this region where the Communist party had made significant inroads in the pre-1965 period (Hefner 1990). As in many other parts of Java the central issues that galvanized support for the communists had been political corruption and land reform (Mortimer 1974: 276–328). It is important to emphasize that the local communist leadership was *not* drawn from the ranks of the land poor. It consisted instead of a number of nouveau riche families, most of whom had earned their wealth working as traders in this region's lucrative vegetable trade. In the 1960s these "merchant communists" (as they were known) had challenged the monopoly hold of the traditional elite on village government.

In other parts of Java, of course, this upwardly mobile opposition might have joined a Muslim party to signal their dissatisfaction with the nationalist village establishment. But in a region with a long history of antipathy toward Islam, affiliation with Islamic parties was neither an attractive nor a realistic avenue for this aspiring counterelite. Like disaffected youth in many Javanist areas of the island (Feith 1957:32), they turned instead to the Communist Party. Their politics, one should note, were not at all radical. The highlands saw none of the physical confrontations or violence associated with communist mobilization efforts in other parts of East Java (Walkin 1969; Mortimer 1974:317).

Nonetheless, in the course of the bloodbath that swept Java in late 1965 the communist leaders in these upland communities were arrested and executed by Muslim youth groups who came from the lowlands to carry out the purge. Other communists were spared, but they were still subject to acts of severe public humiliation. All, for example, were confined to the village, had their heads shaved, forfeited their wealth, and were required to make public confessions of their putative treachery. In short, what had begun several years earlier as a relatively moderate effort to challenge an entrenched village elite ended with the death or disgrace of otherwise well-regarded families. Most of the village leaders who had been the focus of communist criticism, by contrast, remained in power after 1965. Indeed, their ranks supplied the leaders of the new movement for Hindu reform.

Shortly after these tragic events an Indonesian evangelical missionary, whom I will call Paulus, arrived in Sanggar. After a year of preaching, dispensing medicines, and traveling around the Hindu region, Paulus was greatly disheartened. Like non-Javanese missionaries before him, he had failed to win even a single convert to Christianity. In 1968, however, Paulus won approval from regency government to open a Christian junior high school in Sanggar. Because this was the only junior high in the region, it was the one option available for those who wanted to pursue higher education but could not afford boarding school in the lowlands.

Despite parental fears that they might be seduced by Paulus's Christian message, youths from the most prominent families in the mountain region quickly enrolled in the new junior high. Half went on to graduate. A large number were also eventually baptized as Christians. By 1977 (when I first met him), Paulus had 62 converts; by 1985, 130. Equally important, a small cadre of fifteen local youths had begun ministering on their own in villages around the highlands. Paulus had thus achieved a goal that had eluded all prior missionaries to this region: the routinization of congregational activities. An indigenous church was finally taking hold.

CONVERSION MEANINGS

As I interviewed Christian converts in 1980 and 1985, I was at first perplexed by their social profiles. As I had expected, a few were social outcasts, who seemed to have replicated their social marginality by adopting a fringe faith. I was surprised to learn, however, that the most active youths in the new church turned out to be not socially marginal but among the best-educated and most cosmopolitan villagers in the whole of the highlands. Most had lived at some time outside the village, and three had attended college—the first youths from the highlands to do so. Having spent eight years studying the Hindu reform movement and having developed a deep sympathy for its efforts, I found the high social standing and eager intelligence of these youths disturbing. It seemed to augur poorly for the future of the Javanese Hindu tradition that I so admired. Why were these bright youths deserting the venerable ways of their ancestors?

A simple answer soon presented itself. When I checked their backgrounds, I discovered that about three-fourths of the Christian converts were children or close relatives of communists who had been killed or disgraced in the events of 1965–1966. No convert had mentioned this fact in my interviews. But in conversation I *had* noticed that many of the young Christians displayed open hostility toward village leaders. These were the same village leaders who had taken the lead in promoting Hindu reform. Not surprisingly, the youths' resentment of the elite extended to the Hindu organizations with which the leaders were now associated. And so the puzzle of conversion seemed resolved. With Christianity these youths declared their independence from a village social order that, in their eyes, had brought their families pain and humiliation.

Was this Christian conversion, then, merely another expression of intravillage politics? At one level it was, in that it was strongly influenced by conflicts that had occurred a quarter century earlier. But at another level more was at issue here, I slowly realized, than a simple replaying of political factionalism.

One of the most consistent and, for these highlanders, unusual aspects of Paulus's evangelism was his emphasis on individual experience of the person of Christ. Though converts met regularly in small groups, Paulus stressed that the most important thing for all Christians was to pray and study the Bible every day. The quest for faith, Paulus explained, must be a deeply personal one. He emphasized that when first praying or reading scripture individuals might not find what they were seeking. God's word could be slow in coming. But it would come, he insisted, and when it did it would speak directly and with an intimate force like nothing ever before experienced.

Such ritually unmediated, individualized religiosity had no precedent in traditional village religion, which was communally based and ritualistic, organized around the hierarchical authority of the village chief and the Hindu Priest (Hefner 1985). In a powerful and only partially conscious fashion, then, Paulus coached the converts to do something they could not do in their traditional Hindu faith: create conversion narratives fitted to the peculiarities of their own life experiences. It was good, they were told, to seek personal meaning in scripture; when it was finally heard, Jesus' word would be profoundly personal. With this and other injunctions converts were encouraged to relate prayer and scripture to personal experience. Not surprisingly, when these youths turned to reflect on problems in their own lives, what they often focused on was the painful memory of their families' traumas.

Slowly, then, this evangelical socialization provided these youths with a religious language with which to declare their independence from village leaders, priests, and the social order of which they were part. To borrow terms from David Martin's (1990) brilliant study of evangelical conversion in Latin America, evangelicalism created a "free space" in which converts joined to declare their autonomy from the local social order without presenting it with an openly political challenge. The free space was more egalitarian than village society and provided new positions of initiative and authority for individuals who, by virtue of their family history, were barred from positions of prominence in the ordinary village.

The emotional trauma of breaking with one's neighbors and publicly professing a new faith, moreover, forced the youths to take their own actions seriously. Before going public with the news of their conversion, most reflected long and hard on the purpose and likely consequences of their commitment. This confessional gesture, again, had no real counterpart in traditional religion. Pressed by friends and officials to justify their radical act, the converts did indeed rethink their ideas on religion, most of them deeply. The social demand for public accountability, a moral and political demand, led to a very real rationalization of belief. What had begun as an act of political rebellion, then, eventually took on a deeper meaning. Whatever their initial motives, conversion had introduced these youths to a moral mission more impassioned than village factionalism.

Another, more painful, paradox accompanied the converts' experience. Early on in their conversion the Christians continued to identify strongly with their mountain heritage, even while rejecting the authority of the village officials responsible for its stewardship. Like East Javanese converts to Christianity a century earlier many believed that Christianity could be effective in defending local spiritual traditions from the predations of would-be reformists, in this instance both Hindu and Muslim.

Ironically, in fact, several Christian converts commented to me early in my research that they feared that recently introduced Hindu reforms were polluting indigenous customs with foreign (Balinese) ways. Like other nonpriestly villagers in this region, the Christians were largely ignorant of the liturgies preserved and performed by Tengger-Javanese priests. A detailed examination of their contents reveals that the old prayers are actually of Hindu-Javanese origin, with direct parallels to those used in modern Bali (Hefner 1985; Smith-Hefner 1990). This fact had been hidden from ordinary villagers by native priests' insistence on secrecy in the transmission of the liturgies (Hefner 1983) and by villagers' unfamiliarity with Balinese Hinduism. As contacts between Balinese and these Javanese Hindus increased in the 1970s, many uplanders were delighted to realize that Tengger and Balinese religions have much in common.

For Christian converts, however, this same recognition forced a tragic realization. It meant that, contrary to their original hopes, they could not follow both Christian and indigenous faiths at the same time. Conversion required repudiation of anything and everything Hindu. Having gone through the long and painful process of conversion, however, most could not entertain the idea of backsliding on their new faith. "I'm proud of our indigenous tradition," the leader of the Petra Christians and a close friend of mine told me, speaking with an underlying tone of sadness. Years earlier, before discovering Christianity, he had been active in an organization designed to preserve Tengger tradition. Now, however, his attitude had changed. "I must first and foremost place myself at God's command," he explained, "and those things that are not in accord with God's will I must leave behind. This is the meaning of being 'born again' (*melahirkan kembali*)."

As his statement indicates, conversion had reshaped this man's social commitments and sense of cultural priorities. There was no going back now. The social and moral consequences of his publically proclaimed conversion were far greater than those of intellectualist introspection alone. Sadly but with firm conviction, this man was resigned to living with doctrinal commitments contrary to what he had originally hoped for but which he accepted as essential to Christianity's truth.

CONCLUSION: CONVERSION IN CULTURAL CONTEXT

This Javanese example provides several general lessons for our understanding of conversion and the powerful appeal of confessional religions. First, and perhaps most important, the process of conversion evident in these three moments of Javanese history is the opposite of what one might expect in intellectualist or other primarily interiorist models of conversion. Widely influential in religious studies and, to a lesser degree, anthropology, intellectualism describes conversion as first and foremost a change in religious belief provoked by the need to develop more effective vehicles of explanation and control. To cite Robin Horton's (1971) intellectualist model, conversion occurs when an individual moves outside a restricted terrain into an expanded social world. Old ideas well suited to inward-looking villages cannot resolve the intellectual challenges of this bigger world. Individuals compare old beliefs with the new and then convert to world religions because they provide ready-made answers to the intellectual challenge of the macrocosm.

The intellectualist model is to be applauded for emphasizing the active, reflexive character of human beings. The model suggests that individuals do not simply passively internalize symbols and meanings but actively evaluate and adjust their understanding as demands and circumstances change (see Introduction). This emphasis on actors' reflexivity is a central theme in contemporary social theory's effort to understand the creative agency of social life (Giddens 1984:xvi; Hefner 1990). The intellectualist model of agency is flawed, however, by its narrow conception of just how and why individuals evaluate rival sets of cultural ideas. The assumption seems to be that individuals stand back from their social commitments and evaluate ideas as abstract or theoretical tools. There are two problems with this view. First, it simplifies the range of criteria referred to by actors in assessing beliefs, focusing on, as James Fernandez (1978:223) has put it, considerations of a largely technical, "natural science" sort. Second, in assuming that individuals evaluate beliefs in such a rarefied fashion, the intellectualist account gives a curiously solipsistic bias to the conversion process, as if religious choices are without moral and political consequences. In fact, conversion may deeply affect a person's identity and thus his or her ties to other people. Political and moral considerations influence conversion not simply as extrinsic constraints, therefore, but as intrinsic aspects of the conversion experience. This is no doubt what I. M. Lewis (1980:vii) had in mind when he observed that intellectualist characterizations overlook the role of religion in sustaining different kinds of social community.

These last issues, and the political mechanisms for their social management, need to be integrated into a larger theory of conversion even as we remain sensitive to its social psychology. Issues of community and identity were glaringly apparent in the three moments of Javanese conversion discussed here. In the nineteenth century, Christian conversion advanced but then stalled because of its identification with European colonialism. In the 1920s, Javanists in the Tengger highlands balked at converting to Christianity because it was still too closely linked to European life-worlds. By the 1970s that linkage had weakened, and the mountain Javanese described here, like Javanists in many other parts of Java, could more comfortably contemplate the possibility of converting to the Christian faith.

Converts in the Tengger highlands were drawn to the faith not so much by its explanations of space-time events in the world, as an intellectualist model would assume, as by its answers to problems of self-identification in a shattered social world. Christian answers to these questions became socially available only to the extent that individuals or groups were able to establish a free space in which conversion would not immediately result in severe social stigmatization. For most nineteenth-century Madurese no such social possibility ever existed; for most East Javanese of the same era conversion became a viable option only in frontier communities free from traditional social hierarchies. Then, as today, the Christian option required a loosening of the bond between religious commitment and received social community (cf. Martin 1990).

The example should not be taken to imply that the intellectual content of Christianity had no role in conversion. It did. But the precise role of Christian meanings was more complex, and sociological, than the technical evaluation of contrasting analytic grids suggested in the intellectualist model. The basic socioreligious institutions of society, and the sense of social identity they inspired, had to be placed in question before a significant number of Javanese could even begin to contemplate the Christian option. The events that brought about this loosening of tradition were quite varied, but their impact on individual evaluation was everywhere the same. People began to doubt the certainty of received ways, creating the disposition to look for new standards of self-identification.

Even among those who had converted, the intellectualist evaluation of doctrines was never free from the politics and morality of self-identification. After publicly committing themselves to Christianity most of the post-1965 converts still had an only elementary understanding of their new religion. Having put their conversion on public record, however, they had taken it from the realm of abstract reflection and made it a social fact, with far-reaching consequences for their social relationships. Even when converts discovered that Christianity had entailments other than those they had expected, they could not revert from their faith. Public profession of the faith had inspired an interior rationalization quite unlike anything that would have occurred on a purely individual basis. The faith of these young men and women had been made practically compelling by their public declarations and the intense self-legitimation those declarations inspired.

The converts had stumbled onto an essential feature of conversion to confessional faiths, one neglected in intellectualist and other largely interiorist accounts of conversion. The cultural knowledge embodied in a complex religion is always larger than any individual's understanding. So too are the institutions for its dissemination and defense. Over the long run, then, conversion (or, similarly, a child's learning of the faith) may have conceptual implications of which the individual is at first unaware. In other words, the allegiance professed early in conversion may be preliminary to a more radical and unanticipated resocialization. Inspired by the faith, converts may only later discover that their religion has moral and intellectual entailments greater than they had realized. Faith and the allegiance to cultural authority it implies always create a hierarchy of commitments. At some point these may require repudiation of ideals or desires once regarded as consistent with religion's truth.

There is a simple but important theoretical lesson here. An actor's identification with a particular religion implies an act of faith, which is to say the acceptance of a cultural authority whose full conceptual and sociological entailments may never be entirely clear. This acceptance can have the curious effect of hamstringing critical reflection, putting religion's doctrines beyond intellectualist scrutiny. Membership in a church or, for that matter, any social grouping can thus create moral and political pressures that preclude clearheaded evaluation of its ideas. This simple social fact refutes intellectualist accounts of religion and ideology. It suggests that, in our efforts to understand conversion, we have to pay as much attention to the moral and political consequences of membership in a community as we do to its intellectualist doctrines. This truth has been recognized by Christian theologians for centuries. As they stress so clearly, faith must be greater than reason.

This observation raises a second point. Scholars in the Weberian tradition often characterize traditional religions as more piecemeal in their approach to the problems of meaning. The world religions, by contrast, are seen as more rational and universalized (Bellah 1964:364). To quote Clifford Geertz, the world religions are "more abstract, more logically coherent, and more generally phrased. The problems of meaning, which in traditional systems are expressed only implicitly and fragmentarily, here get inclusive formulations and evoke comprehensive attitudes" (Geertz 1973:171). The study of conversion suggests that we should be careful about equating the more universalized doctrines of the world religions with superior rationality. Weber (1956:70) was right to insist that world religions codify their doctrines more abstractly and systematically. But to identify this quality of doctrinal formalization with a superior ability to address problems of meaning is to conflate the public codification of knowledge with its practical and psychological rationality. The two may be quite different. As Maurice Bloch (1989) has argued in another context, the formalization of religious or cultural media by no means guarantees that people will understand them; it may, in fact, lift doctrines beyond the reach of rational scrutiny (see introduction).

The example of these Christian Javanese converts, subscribing to the faith before having understood its entailments, indicates that not all believers need have thought through the conceptual implications of doctrines or beliefs they endorse as their own. This point—vital for any effort to understand the relationship between culture and experience—was raised years ago by Jean Piaget (1970:117) in a critique of the French anthropologist Claude Lévi-Strauss. One can assume, of course, that religious ideas or other cultural ideologies at some point originate in the mental processes of real people. But, to quote Paul Harris and Paul Heelas (1979:223), "they [the cultural ideas] need not reflect the thought processes of individuals currently utilizing the beliefs under consideration."

Thus, an individual can be committed to a particular belief system without fully understanding its conceptual truth or social entailments. One consequence of this fact is that when as social scientists we hear believers referring to certain doctrines as their "beliefs" we cannot automatically assume that they understand the intellectual content of those beliefs. If, in good Weberian fashion, we are interested in assessing the rationality of belief, we have to look more closely at how people actually engage the cultural truths to which they say they subscribe. Ultimately, this inquiry must take us beyond formal doctrine to an investigation of the practice and social psychology of religion.

This Javanese example reminds us, then, that the more doctrinaire, systematized canons of world religion are not mechanisms simply for the rational resolution of problems of meaning. Whatever their origins they are also social mechanisms for the authoritative control of identity, community, and knowledge across time and space. It is this simple fact, after all, onto which my mountain Javanese friends stumbled as they discovered that their local traditions are incompatible with their new Christian faith. There are limits to the flexible adaptation of the faith, it seems. To believe otherwise, church guardians would insist, is to backslide and risk the dissolution of absolute truth into relativism.

This is everywhere the claim of confessional world religions and one key to their revolutionary challenge to local cultures. It is a claim to universal truth and transcendental community. The claim has been given authority not through the compelling force of rationality alone but through the evolution of political and moral mechanisms for defending the Word against the babble of disparate truths. Civilization bears witness to the remarkable diffusion of these regimens, designed to sustain communities of faith and prohibit tampering with a truth deemed transcendent.

NOTES

1. Not all Europeans, however, supported the mission effort. In an unusual exchange of letters on the pages of a leading Indies journal, one writer protested that the government should protect the highlands' non-Islamic tradition as a

counterinfluence to the growing strength of Islam in East Java's lowlands (La Chappelle 1899:36). He also accused government officials of tolerating Muslim advances into the territory. In a blistering response the two Dutch *contrôleurs* for the upland district denied that there was any such policy or that it was even possible. Islam would continue to advance "slowly but surely," they said, because the mountain people are "dirty and undeveloped, and their religion is clearly beneath that of Muslim learning" (Bodemeijer 1901:327). One officer added, however, that Islam is a better "means of transition" to Christianity than the highlanders' traditional religion (von Freijburg 1901:334).

REFERENCES

Alexander, Jennifer, and Paul Alexander. 1979. "Labour Demands and the 'Involution' of Javanese Agriculture." *Social Analysis* 3:22–44.

Anderson, Benedict. 1990. "Professional Dreams: Reflections on Two Javanese Classics." In Anderson, *Language and Power: Exploring Political Cultures in Indonesia*, pp. 271–98. Ithaca: Cornell University Press.

Bellah, Robert N. 1964. "Religious Evolution." *American Sociological Review* 29, 3:358–74.

Benda, Harry J. 1983. *The Crescent and the Rising Sun: Indonesian Islam under the Japanese Occupation, 1942–1945.* Dordrecht: Foris Publications.

Bloch, Maurice. 1989. "From Cognition to Ideology." In M. Bloch, *Ritual, History, and Power: Selected Papers in Anthropology*, pp. 106–36. London: Athlone Press.

Bodemeijer, C. E. 1901. "Rapport naar aanleiding van de Nota betreffende het Tenggergebied van den heer H. M. La Chapelle." *Tijdschrift voor Indische Taal-, Land-, en Volkenkunde* 43:311–30.

Boland, B. J. 1982. *The Struggle of Islam in Modern Indonesia.* The Hague: Martinus Nijhoff.

Carey, P. B. R. 1980. "Aspects of Javanese History in the Nineteenth Century." In Harry Aveling, ed., *The Development of Indonesian Society*, pp. 45–105. Queensland, Australia: University Press.

De Graaf, H. J., and Th. G. Th. Pigeaud. 1974. *De Eeerste Moslimse Vorstendommen op Java.* The Hague: Martinus Nijhoff.

De Vries, Egbert. 1931. *Landbouw en Welvaart in het Regentschap Pasoeroean: Bijdrage tot de Kennis van de Sociale Economie van Java.* Wageningen: Veenman & Zonen.

Dhofier, Zamakhsyari. 1982. *Tradisi Pesantren: Studi Tentang Pandangan Hidup Kyai.* Jakarta: LP3ES.

Drewes, G. W. J. 1966. "The Struggle between Javanism and Islam as Illustrated by the Serat Dermagandul." *Biidragen tot de Taal-, Land-, en Volkenkunde van de Koninklijke Instituut* 122, 3:309–65.

Eickelman, Dale F. 1979. "The Political Economy of Meaning." *American Ethnologist* 6:386–93.

Elson, R. E. 1978. *The Cultivation System and "Agricultural Involution."* Department of History Research Paper No. 14. Clayton, Australia: Monash University.

Feith, Herbert. 1957. *The Indonesian Elections of 1955.* Interim Report Series, Modern Indonesia Project, Southeast Asia Program. Ithaca: Cornell University.

Fernandez, James W. 1978. "African Religious Movements." *Annual Review of Anthropology* 7:195–234.

Geertz, Clifford. 1960. *The Religion of Java.* New York: Free Press.

———. 1963. *Agricultural Involution: The Process of Ecological Change in Indonesia.* Berkeley: University of California Press.

———. 1965. "Modernization in a Muslim Society: The Indonesian Case." In Robert N. Bellah, ed., *Religion and Progress in Modern Asia*, pp. 93–108. New York: Free Press.

———. 1973. "'Internal Conversion' in Contemporary Bali." In Geertz, *The Interpretation of Cultures*, pp. 170–89. New York: Basic Books.

Giddens, Anthony. 1984. *The Constitution of Society: Outline of the Theory of Structuration.* Berkeley: University of California Press.

Goody, Jack. 1986. *The Logic of Writing and the Organization of Society.* Cambridge: Cambridge University Press.

Guillot, Claude. 1979. "Karangjoso revisité: Aux origines du christianisme à Java Central." *Archipel* 17:115–34.

Harris, Paul, and Paul Heelas. 1979. "Cognitive Processes and Collective Representations." *European Journal of Sociology* 20, 2:211–41.

Hefner, Robert W. 1983. "Ritual and Cultural Reproduction in Non-Islamic Java." *American Ethnologist* 10, 4:665–83.

———. 1985. *Hindu Javanese: Tengger Tradition and Islam.* Princeton: Princeton University Press.

———. 1987a. "The Political Economy of Islamic Conversion in Modern East Java." In William R. Roff, ed., *Islam and the Political Economy of Meaning: Comparative Studies of Muslim Discourse*, pp. 53–78. London: Croom Helm.

———. 1987b. "Islamizing Java? Religion and Politics in Rural East Java." *Journal of Asian Studies* 46, 3:533–54.

———. 1990. *The Political Economy of Mountain Java: An Interpretive History.* Berkeley and Los Angeles: University of California Press.

Horton, R. 1971. "African Conversion." *Africa* 61, 2:91–112.

Jasper, J. E. 1926. *Tengger en de Tenggereezen.* Batavia: Druk van G. Kolff.

Jay, Robert T. 1963. *Religion and Politics in Rural Central Java.* Cultural Report Series No. 12, Program in Southeast Asian Studies. New Haven: Yale University.

Kartodirdjo, Sartono. 1972. "Agrarian Radicalism in Java: Its Setting and Development." In Claire Holte, ed., *Culture and Politics in Indonesia*, pp. 70–125. Ithaca: Cornell University Press.

Kreemer, J. 1885. "Veertien Dagen in Pasoeroeansch Tengger." *Mededelingen vanwege het Nederlansch Zendelinggenootschap; tijdschrift voor zendingswetenschap* 19:337–84.

Kumar, Ann. 1979. "Javanese Historiography in and of the 'Colonial Period': A

Case Study." In A. Reid and D. Marr, eds., *Perceptions of the Past in Southeast Asia*, pp. 187–206. Singapore: Heinemann.

La Chapelle, H. M. 1899. "Nota Betreffende Het Tengger-Gebied." *Tijdschrift voor Indische Taal-, Land-, en Volkenkunde* 41:32–54.

Lewis. I. M. 1980. "Introduction." In I. M. Lewis, ed., *Islam in Tropical Africa*, pp. 1–98. Bloomington: Indiana University Press.

Lombard, Denys. 1990. *Le carrefour javanais: Essai d'histoire globale*. 3 vols. Paris: EHESS.

Lyon, M. L. 1980. "The Hindu Revival in Java: Politics and Religious Identity." In James J. Fox, ed., *Indonesia: The Making of a Culture*, pp. 205–20. Canberra: Research School of Pacific Studies.

Martin, David. 1990. *Tongues of Fire: The Explosion of Protestantism in Latin America*. Oxford: Basil Blackwell.

Mortimer, Rex. 1974. *Indonesian Communism under Sukarno*. Ithaca: Cornell University Press.

Nakamura, Mitsuo. 1983. *The Crescent Arises over the Banyan Tree: A Study of the Muhammadiyah Movement in a Central Javanese Town*. Yogyakarta: Gadjah Mada University Press.

Onghokham. 1975. *The Residency of Madiun: Priyayi and Peasant in the Nineteenth Century*. Ph.D. thesis, Department of History, Yale University.

Palte, Jan G. L. 1984. *The Development of Java's Rural Uplands in Response to Population Growth*. Yogyakarta: Gadjah Mada University, Faculty of Geography.

Piaget, Jean. 1970. *Structuralism*. New York: Harper and Row.

Pigeaud, Th. G. Th. 1967. *Literature of Java*. 3 vols. The Hague: Martinus Nijhoff.

Poerwadhie-Atmohihardjo. 1957. "Adjisaka Sanes Babad Utawi Sedjarah." *Djaja Baja* 11, 20:13–20.

Ricklefs, M. C. 1979. "Six Centuries of Islamization in Java." In N. Levtzion, ed., *Conversion to Islam*, pp. 100–128. New York: Holmes and Meier.

———. 1981. *A History of Modern Indonesia*. Bloomington: Indiana University Press.

Skorupski, John. 1976. *Symbol and Theory: A Philosophical Study of Theories of Religion in Social Anthropology*. Cambridge: Cambridge University Press.

Smith-Hefner, Nancy J. 1990. "The Litany of 'The World's Beginning': A Hindu-Javanese Purification Text." *Journal of Southeast Asian Studies* 21, 2:287–328.

van Akkeren, Philip. 1969. *Sri and Christ: A Study of the Indigenous Church in East Java*. London: Lutterworth Press.

von Freijburg, G. G. L. 1901. "Rapport." *Tijdschrift voor Indische Taal-, Land-, en Volkenkunde* 43:331–48.

Walkin, Jacob. 1969. "The Moslem-Communist Confrontation in East Java, 1964–1965." *Orbis* 13, 3:822–47.

Weber, Max. 1956. *The Sociology of Religion*. Boston: Beacon Press.

Willis, Avery T. 1977. *Indonesian Revival: Why Two Million Came to Christ*. Pasadena: William Carey Library.

Woodward, Mark R. 1989. *Islam in Java: Normative Piety and Mysticism in the Sultanate of Yogyakarta*. Tucson: University of Arizona Press.

PART THREE

The Political Economy of Religious Identity

CHAPTER FIVE

Conversion and Colonialism in Northern Mexico: The Tarahumara Response to the Jesuit Mission Program, 1601–1767

William L. Merrill

The escape of human history from human intentions, and the return of the consequences of that escape as causal influences on human action, is a chronic feature of social life.

ANTHONY GIDDENS, *Central Problems in Social Theory*

The conversion of colonial subjects to one version of Christianity or another has been central to most European colonial endeavors, but nowhere has it figured more prominently than in the Spanish conquest of the New World. Inspired by the Christian reconquest of Iberia, completed in 1492, Spain's monarchs made the conversion of New World peoples to Catholicism a principal goal of the conquest (Lockhart and Schwartz 1983:9–10). The responsibility for evangelizing the native inhabitants of the Spanish New World fell primarily to priests of four religious orders—Franciscans, Dominicans, Augustinians, and Jesuits (Ricard 1966:2–3). The Spanish Crown provided these missionaries with an annual subsidy and exempted the mission populations from taxation until their conversion was complete. In return the priests were expected not only to convert the native peoples to Christianity but also to organize them into a labor force for Spanish economic enterprises and to establish their mission communities as economically viable units that could then become taxpaying parishes (Radding de Murrieta 1977:155; Polzer 1976:53–54). In the naïveté of the early years of the conquest this transformation was envisioned to require only a decade or so, but in many areas it remained incomplete long past the collapse of the Spanish empire in the nineteenth century (Farriss 1984:90–96; Polzer 1976:54; Ricard 1966; Spicer 1962).

The complexities of religious conversion in Spanish colonial history are well illustrated by the Catholic mission to the Tarahumara (or Rarámuri) Indians of Chihuahua, Mexico, one of the oldest Christian missions in the New World.[1] Jesuit missionaries first contacted the Tarahumaras around 1601 and proselytized among them until 1767, when

Charles III of Spain expelled the Jesuits from his New World holdings (González Rodríguez 1984:14–15, 147; Dunne 1948). The responsibility for administering the Jesuits' missions was then divided between Franciscan missionaries and secular (i.e., nonmonastic) priests under the bishop of Durango until 1859, when all the missions were turned over to the secular clergy. Four decades later the Jesuits returned to Tarahumara country, where they have continued their missionary efforts until the present (Merrill 1988:30–43; Ocampo 1966; Spicer 1962:25–45).

The duration of the Catholic mission program among the Tarahumaras testifies not only to the missionaries' dedication to their calling but also to their inability to transform the Tarahumaras as a whole into orthodox Catholics able and willing to support parish priests. Today the vast majority of the approximately seventy thousand people who identify themselves as Tarahumaras call themselves "baptized ones" (*pagótame* or *pagótuame*) (Secretaría de Programación y Presupuesto 1982–1984).[2] These "baptized" Tarahumaras attend Mass, celebrate the major holy days of the Catholic ritual calendar, and accord special spiritual status and ritual functions to representatives of the Catholic church, but they have incorporated only a few Catholic beliefs and have radically transformed Catholic ritual (Bennett and Zingg 1935; Velasco Rivero 1983; Merrill 1988).[3] The remaining Tarahumaras, estimated at 3 percent of the population, reject any affiliation with the Catholic church. They refer to themselves and are referred to by the baptized Tarahumaras and non-Indians in the area as *gentiles* (heathens) and *cimarrones* (fugitives or wild people) (Kennedy 1970:37–40; Kennedy 1978).

To these two groups of Tarahumaras can be added a third, composed of the descendants of the thousands of Tarahumaras who over the centuries have lost their separate Indian identity. For the most part these people deny or are unaware of their Tarahumara ancestry, identifying themselves as mestizos or whites (*blancos*). They practice a way of life that they consider to be non-Indian, and, with the exception of a few who have converted in the twentieth century to one of several Protestant sects, they regard themselves as Catholics (Champion 1955, 1962; Velasco Rivero 1983).

This tripartite division of Tarahumara identity is among the most significant (albeit unintended) consequences of Catholic missionary efforts to convert the Tarahumaras to Christianity. These internal divisions emerged during the colonial Jesuit mission period as different Tarahumaras responded in distinct ways to the Jesuits' mission program and to the larger colonial endeavor of which it was a part. Here I address the issue of the Tarahumaras' conversion to Christianity by attempting to determine why these diverse responses took place and by evaluating the role of the Jesuit missionaries in creating and perpetuating these divisions. I also consider why, at the time of the Jesuits' expulsion in 1767, only a small minority of Tarahumaras appear to have been well instructed in the basic tenets of the Catholic faith. I suggest that conflicts and contradictions both within the mission program itself and between it and the encompassing colonial system undermined the missionaries' ability to achieve their intended goals and that these and other factors enabled the Tarahumaras to control to a considerable extent the conversion process. To conclude I examine some of the limitations of the view that conversion entails a radical shift in the religious beliefs of individuals and then briefly outline a more relativistic concept of conversion that I feel is better suited to understanding religious conversion, especially in transcultural, colonial settings.

THE TARAHUMARA MISSION SYSTEM AND THE SPANISH FRONTIER

In the half century following the Spanish conquest of the Aztec capital of Tenochtitlan in 1521, a series of mining strikes, mostly of silver, propelled Spanish settlement a thousand kilometers northward from central Mexico to the edge of Tarahumara country, where the Mexican states of Chihuahua, Durango, and Sinaloa are found today (see map 5.1). This vast expanse of mountains, plains, deserts, and tropical lowlands was organized in 1562 into a single political unit called Nueva Vizcaya, with its capital at Guadiana (today Durango) (Gerhard 1982:10; Porras Muñoz 1980a:10–17; Porras Muñoz 1980b; Cramaussel 1990). Nueva Vizcaya's first missionaries were Franciscans, joined in the 1590s by Jesuits, who soon established several missions north of Guadiana and also to the west across the Sierra Madre mountain chain in Sinaloa (Dunne 1944). These missions became the staging points for the first missionary expeditions to the Tarahumaras.

In 1601 the Jesuit Pedro Mendes left the Sinaloa missions to enter what is now the westernmost section of Chihuahua. There he contacted Indians closely related to the Tarahumaras known as the Chínipas (González Rodríguez 1984:31–41; Tardá and Guadalaxara 1676:389; Pennington 1963:10). Local Indian resistance, probably stimulated by hostile encounters with Spanish miners, delayed the founding of the Chínipas missions until the 1620s. A decade later neighboring Guazapar and Guarijío Indians killed the two priests there and destroyed the missions, which the Jesuits did not reestablish until 1676 (Almada 1937; Decorme 1941:II, 123–46; González Rodríguez 1984:42–61).

On the eastern side of the Sierra Madre the Jesuit Juan Font first

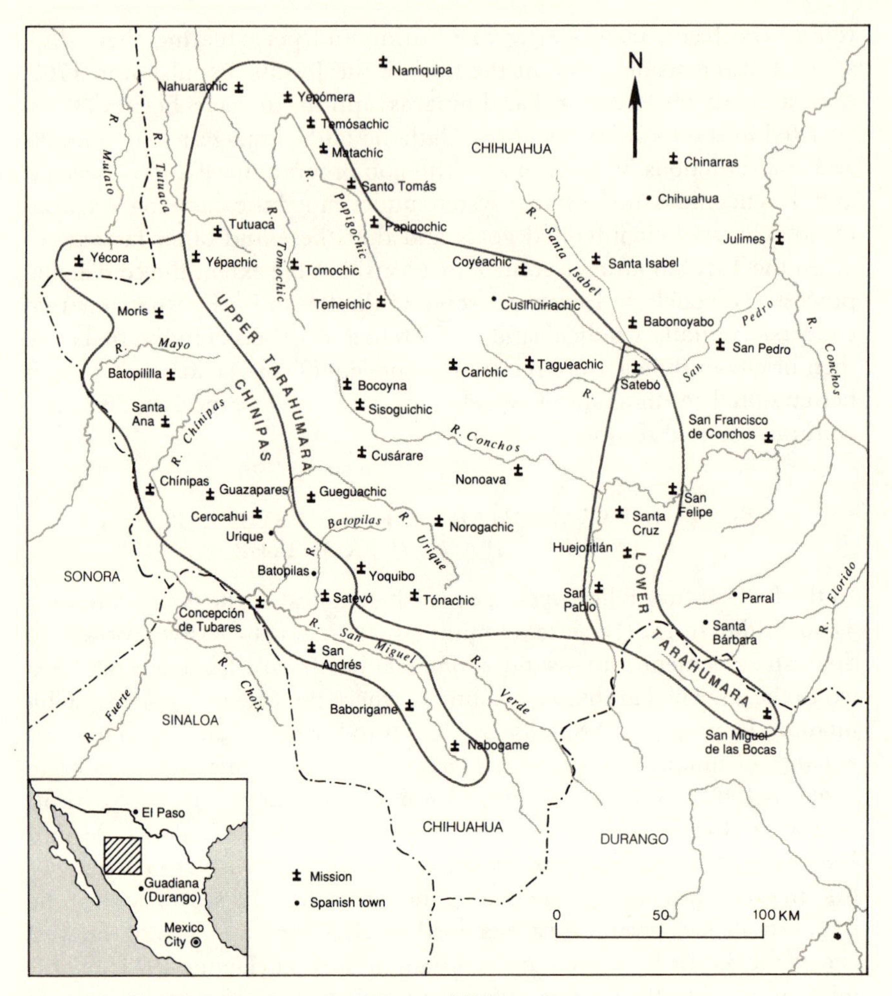

Map 5.1 The Tarahumara missions, ca. 1767

contacted the Tarahumaras around 1604, soon convincing a number of them to join Tepehuanes in missions he had created in the San Pablo Valley, near the border between the two groups (Contreras 1638; González Rodríguez 1984:145–95; Dunne 1948:18–22). Rebellions in 1616–1618, 1648–1652, and 1690–1700 disrupted mission expansion, but by the time of their expulsion in 1767 the Jesuits had established a network of missions that stretched across much of Tarahumara country (Alegre 1956–1960; Bancroft 1886; Dunne 1948; Spicer 1962; Zepeda, in González Rodríguez 1984:241–47; Neumann 1969; Pascual 1651; Pascual, in Sheridan and Naylor 1979:17–31; Naylor and Polzer 1986; Lizassoain

1763; Tamarón y Romeral 1937; Roca 1979). These missions were organized into three divisions. The first was the Misión de la Natividad, or Tarahumara Baja (Lower Tarahumara), which included missions founded for the most part before 1648. By the early 1700s these missions had been merged with the Tepehuan missions to the south to form a single province, and then in 1753 and 1754 they were transferred to secular clergy under the bishop of Durango (Medrano Ybarra 1691; Guendulain 1725; Burrus 1963; Deeds 1981). The second division was the Misión de San Joaquin y Santa Ana, or Tarahumara Alta (Upper Tarahumara), composed of missions founded in 1673 or later. The third were missions to the west of the Upper Tarahumara area, which the Jesuits organized into the Chínipas mission province in 1734 (Decorme 1941:II, 230, n. 16). These Chínipas missions included Tarahumaras as well as Guarijío and Guazapar Indians, both closely related linguistically to the Tarahumaras, and the more distantly related Pima Bajos, Tubares, and Tepehuanes (Guadalaxara 1683; Pennington 1963:1–11; Miller 1983).

Tarahumaras also lived in and around several Franciscan missions, most located in the far northeastern section of the Tarahumaras' aboriginal territory, along their border with Conchos Indians (Bravo de la Serna 1640; Tardá 1677; Arlegui 1851; Griffen 1979; Dunne 1948:124–27). In fact, in the 1670s a Franciscan missionary in one of these missions challenged the Jesuits' right to establish a mission in a nearby Tarahumara community. The confrontation, which paralleled similar conflicts between Jesuits and Franciscans in other areas of New Spain, was resolved in Mexico City in the Jesuits' favor, but the Franciscans continued to proselytize among the Tarahumaras and took over many of the Jesuits' Tarahumara missions following the Jesuits' expulsion in 1767 (Dunne 1948:124–27; Alegre 1956–1960:IV, 237, 322–23; Arlegui 1851; Alcocer 1958:147–63).

During the century and a half of the colonial Jesuit mission period, around three hundred Jesuits served as missionaries among the Tarahumaras (González Rodríguez 1969:xlvii; González Rodríguez 1989: personal communication). At the time of their expulsion thirty-one Jesuits administered over twenty thousand adult Indians in the Upper Tarahumara and Chínipas missions, which covered an area exceeding thirty-five thousand square kilometers (Lizassoain 1763; [Aguirre] 1765; Zelis 1871). Not all Tarahumaras, however, had been incorporated into the mission system. Small pockets of "gentiles" were scattered among several of the missions, and an estimated five hundred "gentile" and "apostate" families lived along the rugged canyons of the Urique and Batopilas rivers between the Upper Tarahumara and Chínipas missions (Miqueo 1745; Escalona 1744; Tamarón y Romeral 1937:133). Other refuge areas were located in the rough terrain to the north and west of the Upper Tarahumara and Chínipas missions, where rebels from the seventeenth-century revolts had fled (Cubedu, in González Rodríguez 1984:337; Fernández de Abee, in Sheridan and Naylor 1979:82–83; Fernández de Abee 1744). The Jesuits had not established missions in the southernmost section of Tarahumara country along the Río Verde and between this river and the Lower Tarahumara missions to the east.

In 1767 the Jesuit mission system extended far beyond the main areas of Spanish settlement. The largest concentration of non-Indian settlers was found in the Lower Tarahumara area where, in 1765, almost 40 percent of the people living in the immediate vicinity of the former mission pueblos were non-Indians. When the residents of the major Spanish economic centers located nearby are taken into consideration, Indians constituted only about 20 percent of the population in this area (Tamarón y Romeral 1937; Deeds 1981). These non-Indians included Spaniards, small numbers of other Europeans, individuals of European descent born in the New World, black slaves, and mestizos, mulattoes, and other people of mixed descent who tended to be free laborers. In addition, substantial numbers of Indians from central Mexico and Sinaloa had settled in the area, typically to work as skilled laborers in the mines (West 1949).

In the Upper Tarahumara, silver strikes in the late seventeenth and early eighteenth centuries near the northeastern borders of Tarahumara country drew large numbers of miners to the area and stimulated the expansion of Spanish farming and stockraising down the well-watered Río Papigochic valley (West 1949; Gerhard 1982; Neumann 1969:56, n. 2). In 1765 non-Indian settlers lived in the vicinity of all the Tarahumara mission *partidos* (districts) in the Papigochic valley, making up about 16 percent of the local population (Tamarón y Romeral 1937). The most extensive mining activity in the eighteenth century, however, took place to the west, in the Chínipas region. Between 1690 and 1750, mines were opened along the borders of the entire Chínipas province, but they often were short-lived and appear not to have produced an influx of non-Indian farmers and ranchers into the mission partidos (Gerhard 1982). In 1765 the largest Spanish settlement in the Chínipas region was the mining town of Batopilas, where a mixed population of 227 Indians and non-Indians lived; a second mining camp, San Juan Nepomuceno, included fifty-five Indians and thirty-six non-Indians (Tamarón y Romeral 1937:169–70).

Outside these mining centers and agricultural zones the non-Indian presence in the Upper Tarahumara and Chínipas regions was negligible. In 1765 no non-Indians were reported from the remainder of the Upper

Tarahumara mission area, and only fifty-three were noted near the Chínipas missions, dispersed among four separate partidos. These same missions included more than twenty thousand Indians (Tamarón y Romeral 1937). Although the Indians in these Upper Tarahumara and Chínipas missions came in contact with non-Indians who traded in the area and also were drafted for labor in Spanish economic enterprises, their everyday interaction with non-Indians was restricted for the most part to their missionaries and the few non-Indian servants and ranch hands who worked for some of the priests.

THE JESUIT MISSION STRATEGY

To convert the Tarahumaras to Christianity and transform them into loyal and productive Spanish subjects, the Jesuits attempted to apply a comprehensive program of directed social and cultural change.[4] This program involved radical changes in aboriginal settlement patterns; in social, political, and economic relations; and in the scheduling of daily life. The missionaries also tried to eradicate indigenous practices, such as polygamy and drunkenness, that were contrary to Christian teachings or European mores. They did not, however, aim toward a complete replacement of the indigenous way of life (cf. Farriss 1984:91). They were committed, at least in principle, to learning the languages of their converts, and they adjusted their behavior to conform to the dictates of local etiquette. They also recognized the value of indigenous medical remedies and agricultural techniques; they consumed, if they did not always relish, the Indians' foods; and they even encouraged the performance of native rituals that they felt complemented or reinforced Catholic practices.

In creating new missions the missionaries placed equal emphasis on establishing the missions' economies, developing an infrastructure to organize mission life, and instructing their neophytes in religious matters. Upon arriving at a new mission the missionary first designated sites where mission pueblos were to be established, selecting one of these pueblos as his principal residence. This site served as the head mission, or *cabecera*; the other pueblos, typically numbering from two to four, were mission stations, or *visitas*, which the missionary was supposed to visit regularly. Together the cabecera and visitas formed a unit known as the *partido*. The Indians who lived near each of these places were expected to build a church and a house for the priest as well as houses for themselves. The priests often adopted as the model for the spatial organization of their mission pueblos a grid pattern derived from town plans that the Romans had developed centuries before for their colonies in Spain (Spicer 1962:283; Tardá and Guadalaxara 1676).

The annual subsidy that the royal treasury provided the missionaries was intended to cover basic needs, not all the missions' operating expenses. Each mission pueblo or partido was expected to become self-sufficient and if possible to produce a surplus to support further mission expansion. To achieve this goal, the missionary in residence attempted to enhance local agricultural productivity by introducing Old World livestock, domesticated plants, and European agricultural technology, like plows and irrigation. He also organized the mission populace into a labor force to care for the mission's herds, cultivate its fields, and perform household chores for him. If the mission did not have its own separate fields, the Indians were supposed to provide a portion of their own crops to support the missionary.

A hierarchically organized group of political officials administered the civil affairs of the mission pueblos. Considered representatives of the Spanish Crown, the Indian men who held these offices usually were appointed by the missionaries and were expected to follow their orders. The missionaries also selected other local people to serve as religious officials to care for the church, to assist in organizing and performing Catholic rituals, and to teach prayers, the catechism, and other elements of church doctrine to the remaining members of their communities.

In the realm of religious conversion the missionaries concentrated first on baptizing as many people in their new missions as possible, both to ensure their salvation in the afterlife and to mark their incorporation into the Christian community. Before administering the sacrament of baptism, the priests were required to teach their new converts elementary church doctrine; the Catholic church allowed only small children and seriously ill adults to be baptized without such instruction (Polzer 1976:42, 47). Following baptism the priests attempted to involve their new converts in a program of regular religious instruction that would enable them to participate in the general confessions usually held once or twice a year and eventually to partake in the sacrament of Holy Eucharist. Although the missionaries accepted minimal familiarity with Christian precepts as sufficient for baptism and confession, they were expected to restrict communion to those people who could demonstrate a more extensive understanding of church doctrine, including especially the concept of Christ embodied in the communion host (Polzer 1976:62–63, 71–73, 108).

The Jesuits considered the rite of baptism a transformation of a person from the status of heathen or *gentile* to that of convert or neophyte, and they often used the term *conversiones* to label their mission pueblos during the initial period of missionization. Nonetheless, they envisioned conversion as a gradual process that commenced rather than concluded with baptism. They believed that more thorough conversion could be accomplished through both doctrinal instruction and participation in the sacraments and other rituals of the church, which would engender a spiritual transformation in their neophytes. As evidence of such internal change the missionaries looked for displays of religious fervor during rituals, demonstrations of devotion and obedience to the priests, behavior that conformed to the standards of Christian morality, and indications that the Indians' understandings of the Catholic faith surpassed mere rote memorization of doctrine.

THE TARAHUMARA RESPONSE TO THE JESUIT MISSION PROGRAM

The Tarahumaras did not respond uniformly to the colonial Jesuit mission program but were varied in their responses at different times and places and also with respect to different components of the program. To evaluate these responses, it is useful to divide the Jesuit mission program into three basic components: (1) mission creation, (2) social, political, and technological innovations, and (3) religious life.

Mission Creation

As a basic principle of their mission policy the Jesuits assigned missionaries to unmissionized areas only when at least some of the Indians living there requested them. The Spanish apparently never resorted to military force to compel the Tarahumaras to allow missionaries into their communities or to accept baptism. After missions were established, Spanish soldiers sometimes tried to force Indians to live in them or to return to the missions they had abandoned, and in the seventeenth century they moved rebel Tarahumaras into mission communities that had remained loyal to the Spanish (Pennington 1963:5–17). But the Tarahumaras who participated in the initial stage of mission formation seem to have done so voluntarily.

The factors that motivated the Tarahumaras' initial requests for missionaries remained relatively constant over the Jesuit period even though their responses to the mission program as a whole varied considerably during this same period. These factors did not include the perception that Catholic doctrine and a life structured by European Christian values were superior to indigenous beliefs, values, and practices. Although Tarahumaras outside the missions apparently were impressed by the colorful Catholic ceremonies and other aspects of mission life, they were largely unaware of the specifically religious teachings of the mission program until after they were incorporated into it.

The Tarahumaras appear to have been initially attracted to the Jesuit mission program for three reasons. The first was to gain access to the priests' supernatural power, especially for curing the Old World diseases that periodically devastated the Tarahumara population throughout the colonial period (Castillo, in González Rodríguez 1984:256–57; Font, in González Rodríguez 1984:190; Tardá and Guadalaxara 1676:106; Reff 1987). The second was to seek the protection that a series of laws and royal decrees afforded Christian Indians and their communities against military conquest, enslavement, and encroachment by non-Indian settlers (Spicer 1962; Sheridan and Naylor 1979:88–101; Velasco Rivero 1983:229). The third was to acquire European goods, either directly from the missionaries or indirectly through trading with or working for the non-Indian settlers, to whom the missions offered them greater access (Ratkay 1683:26–27).

The members of the Lower Tarahumara communities contacted by the Jesuits in the initial decade of the seventeenth century seem to have responded in a uniformly positive fashion to the missionaries (Font, in González Rodríguez 1984:178–95). Very soon, however, an alternative perspective on the missions emerged to counter the pro-mission view promulgated by the missionaries and their Indian supporters. This counterideology, in addition to detailing the abuses of the missionaries and settlers, proposed that the missionaries were interested in establishing missions only to collect the royal subsidies and to take the Indians' land from them. It portrayed the priests as the sorcerers of the Spanish and warned that conversion would render the land sterile. It also claimed that baptism caused illness and death and that the church bells that regulated mission life attracted the diseases from which so many Tarahumaras had died (Tardá and Guadalaxara 1676; González Rodríguez 1969:lv).

Developed primarily by Indians who had entered the missions, this counterideology diffused widely among Tarahumaras outside the mission system. Many of these Tarahumaras already recognized that the mission program was inseparable from the less desirable aspects of the larger Spanish colonial endeavor. As the two Jesuits who led the conversion of the Upper Tarahumara reported in 1676,

> When they go out among the Spaniards or see them in their lands they see so much work in the mines, the haciendas, the houses, and irrigation works. . . . They also see that it is the Indians who do the heaviest work and for this reason, seeing these things and knowing of others, they are afraid to become Christians, thinking, these ignorant people, that all this work is God's law and necessary to go to heaven. Some whom we have asked if they want to be Christians have responded that they are now old and have no strength, implying that they cannot be Christians because

> they cannot work. Others clearly say that they do not want to be Christians because they do not want to work, that the Christians work very much and, although the truths of our holy faith are presented to them, they believe that they are being tricked and afterward they will be made to work, which is what they refuse. (Tardá and Guadalaxara 1676:364v)

Despite the missionaries' disclaimers, the Indians' fears that conversion would lead inevitably to the exploitation of their labor proved fully justified (Estrada, in Sheridan and Naylor 1979:74; Andonaegui 1744; Deeds 1989).

Missionary visits to the unmissionized areas of Tarahumara country typically produced intense and often acrimonious debates between community members who favored accepting the missionaries and those who were ambivalent or opposed to them. The advocates of missionization often included Christian Indians from the missions who had married into the *gentile* communities and local Indians who had ventured into the mission pueblos and were impressed by what they had seen. The most vehement opponents of missionization tended to be indigenous ritual specialists joined by rebels and apostates who had settled in these communities. These people sometimes threatened to murder those who accepted baptism or warned that spirits or sorcerers would kill them. The missionaries, often informed by the Christian Indians of the arguments being made against them, attempted to challenge these arguments in their sermons and discussions and to undermine the influence of their principal adversaries by characterizing them as sorcerers (*hechiceros*) whose supposed evil inclinations endangered the lives and well-being of their fellows (Tardá and Guadalaxara 1676).

In the mid-seventeenth century and again between 1690 and 1700, Tarahumara opposition to the expansion of the Jesuit mission system and the Spanish frontier exploded in a series of organized revolts. In these revolts the rebel Indians attacked a number of Spanish settlements, directing their animosity particularly toward the poorly defended mission pueblos (Dunne 1948; Neumann 1969; Pascual 1651; Deeds 1989:439; González Rodríguez n.d.). In the revolts of the 1690s, for example, they killed two missionaries and burned more than twenty missions in Sonora and the Upper Tarahumara along with a few Franciscan missions on the Tarahumara-Concho border (Neumann 1969; González Rodríguez n.d.). The rebels' intent apparently was to eradicate all traces of the missionary presence, as vividly indicated in one missionary's account of the attack on the Upper Tarahumara mission of Echoguita:

> With impious hands they first pulled down a lofty cross which had been erected in the cemetery and burned it. They then surrounded the group of

> buildings, battered open the doors of the church, and with wild and furious yells rushed in. They climbed upon the altars, tore from their places the images of the Mother of God and of the Saints, rent them asunder, and cast the pieces into the river which flowed close by. They smashed the altars and the baptismal font of carved stone, pillaged the sacristy, tore to ribbons six chasubles and all the other vestments, and scattered the fragments. They beat the chalice against a rock and broke it into three pieces and laid sacrilegious hands upon everything else, destroying and ruining all. . . . Finally, they kindled fires around the dwelling house and the church and burned them to the ground. As the flames mounted, they cried: "Here is a pleasant sight to see! This is more interesting than hearing Mass, being baptized, and listening to the fathers while they say strange things." For they looked upon the missionaries as the magicians, or sorcerers, of the Spaniards, and hoped soon to be free of them. (Neumann, in Sheridan and Naylor 1979:54–55)

The revolts of the 1690s differed in several respects from the Tarahumara revolts of the mid-seventeenth century. Although the violence in both periods centered on the Upper Tarahumara area from the Río Papigochic valley west, the Tarahumara rebels in the later revolts were for the most part baptized Indians living within the mission system rather than *gentiles* from outside the missions as had been the case in the mid-century revolts. In the earlier rebellions the rebels were almost exclusively Tarahumaras, whereas in the later revolts a number of different Indian groups were allied in opposition to the northward expansion of the Spanish frontier. The division of the Tarahumaras into pro- and anti-Spanish factions also was more clearly drawn in the later revolts, with fewer than half of the Tarahumara missions supporting the rebels (Neumann 1969:126–27 n. 169). Perhaps most significantly, the 1690–1700 revolts did not succeed as the earlier revolts had in expelling the Spanish from the Upper Tarahumara region. Although Indian resistance in a few Upper Tarahumara missions prevented their reestablishment until the eighteenth century, the Jesuits were able to return immediately to their other Upper Tarahumara missions and to resume their program of mission expansion (Neumann 1969:127).

The formation of the Jesuit mission system among the Tarahumaras in the seventeenth century thus was characterized not by slow, continual growth but by cycles of rapid mission expansion soon challenged by violent native resistance that was followed by consolidation of the mission frontier and then renewed efforts at expansion. The Tarahumaras tended to respond most positively to mission formation and baptism during times of crises, when the advantages of the mission program appeared to outweigh the disavantages. Epidemics in the early 1600s and 1670s, for example, apparently motivated some Indians in the Lower and Upper Tarahumara areas, respectively, to request missionaries in the belief that the priests could cure the diseases plaguing them (Tardá and Guadalaxara 1676; Reff 1987; cf. Font, in González Rodríguez 1984:190). Similarly, encroaching Spanish settlement in the Lower Tarahumara region in the 1640s and fear of the Spanish military in the Upper Tarahumara after the revolts of the 1690s seem to have encouraged Indians in these areas to seek the protection that the mission system offered (Neumann 1969). In the absence of such adverse conditions the Indians were more reluctant to enter the mission system.

After 1700 the Tarahumaras did not organize any large-scale revolts against the Spanish and their missionaries. Nonetheless, in the eighteenth century the Jesuits failed to extend the mission network much beyond its limits prior to the revolts of the 1690s (Ortiz Zapata 1678). Their efforts were hampered by the consolidation of opposition to the mission program among the Indians in many of the areas remaining to be missionized as well as the ruggedness of the places in which these Indians lived. The mission program also suffered from a shortage of competent missionaries. The Spanish Crown was reluctant to provide additional missionary subsidies for the north, and few priests were eager to serve in these difficult and often dangerous missions (Dunne 1948:101–3; Decorme 1941). By the mid-eighteenth century, however, an influx of new and better-qualified priests resulted in renewed efforts to expand the mission network into the most remote reaches of Tarahumara country (Decorme 1941:II, 245). These efforts came to an abrupt halt in 1767 when the Bourbon King Charles III of Spain ordered the expulsion of the Jesuits from his New World holdings and the expropriation of their properties (Dunne 1937, 1948; Benedict 1972).

Social, Political, and Technological Innovations

The Tarahumaras who accepted baptism and affiliation with the Jesuit mission system responded positively to several other components of the mission program. Like the Tarahumaras who remained outside the mission system, they eagerly adopted elements of European technology, like axes, hoes, and plows, and Old World livestock and plants, all of which enhanced their own agricultural productivity. They embraced the pueblo form of community organization with its hierarchically organized set of native political officials. They also accepted the religious officials appointed by the priests and began using the mission pueblos and churches as centers for community ceremonial and political activities.

Yet, although the Jesuits succeeded in introducing many aspects of the pueblo organization, they failed almost entirely to congregate the Tarahumaras into compact mission villages.

The reasons for the failure of the congregation program differed somewhat between the Lower Tarahumara missions on the one hand and the Upper Tarahumara and Chínipas missions on the other. In the Lower Tarahumara area, demand for the Indians' labor in the region's agricultural and mining enterprises proved to be the most significant factor affecting the presence of the Indians in the mission pueblos. Less than ten years after these missions were founded, the majority of Indians were absent from the mission pueblos, either because they had been drafted for work by Spanish settlers or had deserted the missions to avoid labor drafts (Zepeda, in González Rodríguez 1984:211–12). During the eighteenth century, demands for Indian labor and abuses of Indian workers increased to the point where government officials attempted to intervene, but their efforts apparently had little effect (Deeds 1981).

These labor demands undermined the missionaries' ability to produce enough food locally to support substantial numbers of Indian converts in the mission pueblos. Although some of the Lower Tarahumara missions apparently produced surpluses that were sold to non-Indian settlers, they seem to have been unable to develop their economies to the point where they could support more than a small resident population (West 1949: 68–69; Polzer 1976:55). Of course, droughts, floods, and the occasional raids of nomadic Indians also disrupted the missions' economies, but the labor drafts were especially detrimental because they pulled Indians out of the missions at critical points in the growing cycle of maize, the mainstay of the local diet (Governor of Chihuahua, in Sheridan and Naylor 1979:96).

The availability of labor to grow maize appears to have been the principal factor limiting the size of the populations in the Lower Tarahumara mission pueblos, since most of these missions had access to adequate land and water and were well supplied with livestock, especially cattle. With maize in relatively short supply in the missions, the Indians were forced either to continue working in the mines and haciendas or to abandon the area to search for food in the interior (Zepeda, in González Rodríguez 1984:211–12).

In the more rugged areas of the Upper Tarahumara and Chínipas missions permanent congregation of large numbers of people in mission pueblos was impractical because arable plots were small and scattered (González Rodríguez 1969:liv; Sheridan and Naylor 1979:3). By living adjacent to their fields, the Tarahumaras were better able to protect their crops against pests and invading livestock. They also minimized the time and effort they would have expended traveling to their fields and transporting their harvests had they moved into the mission pueblos. Nonetheless, they could have lived at their farms during the growing season and then assembled at the mission pueblos for the remainder of the year, using horses to move their harvests from farm to pueblo (Pennington 1963:141–42). The Indians in some of the Upper Tarahumara missions possibly did adopt this modification of the congregation program, at least for a few years (Andonaegui 1744; Osorio 1744). In most areas, however, including those where arable land was more abundant, the people continued the indigenous pattern of year-round dispersed settlement.

Because of perennial labor shortages on the northern frontier, Indians in several of these missions were subjected to work levies, especially in the eighteenth century (Andonaegui 1744; [Glandorff] 1744; Miqueo 1745; Lizassoain 1763). Their resistance to congregation was motivated in part by their desire to avoid forced labor and pressures from the missionaries and non-Indian settlers to modify their indigenous way of life. By the early eighteenth century some Tarahumaras also had concluded that settling in the mission pueblos increased the likelihood of dying in the periodic epidemics of Old World diseases. Others were reluctant to move closer to the churches for fear that they would lose their lands to Spanish settlers, who would claim that they had abandoned them (Miqueo 1745: 22v). In addition, as in the Lower Tarahumara area, non-Indian settlers sometimes encouraged the Indians to remain outside the missions, presumably to maintain access to their labor (Estrada 1730; Fernández de Abee, in Sheridan and Naylor 1979:80–81; Lizassoain 1763:23).

The Jesuits had little alternative but to accept, albeit begrudgingly, the Indians' rejection of congregation, for the priests lacked the means to force the Indians to live in the mission pueblos. The Spanish military presence on the northern frontier was quite small during most of the Jesuit period, and the soldiers usually were occupied fighting nomadic Indians outside the Tarahumara area; a permanent military garrison was never established in Tarahumara country. In addition, Spanish officials often refused to order Indians to return to their missions, in some cases heeding the Indians' complaints that the priests treated them harshly (Fernández de Abee, in Sheridan and Naylor 1979:80–81). As with the Spanish settlers these officials frequently regarded the missionaries as impediments to the development of the local economy and as threats to their own political power and control over the Indians' labor.

Religious Life

The Tarahumaras in most of the Jesuits' missions appear to have participated enthusiastically in the elaborate religious ceremonies introduced by the missionaries to celebrate the principal holy days of the Catholic ritual calendar, to the point, in some areas at least, of adopting the colonial Catholic practice of ritual flagellation (Tardá and Guadalaxara 1676; Velasco Rivero 1983). This enthusiasm was not restricted to Tarahumaras who lived within the mission system. In the mid-eighteenth century, missionaries in the Upper Tarahumara complained that Indians who had abandoned the missions said Mass, performed baptisms, and heard confessions on their own in the unmissionized areas to which they had fled (Escalona 1744). In at least one instance these "apostates" created the ritual utensils required for Holy Eucharist, using a clay cup for the chalice, the top of a round box (*una rueda de cajeta*) for the paten, and a small metal mortar with a stone suspended inside for the bell. Even the *gentile* Indians, who reportedly argued that "neither priest nor sacraments were required for salvation," created their own sacraments, which they considered to have the same effect as those used by the Christians (Miqueo 1745:19).

The Tarahumaras' favorable response to the Catholic rituals and other components of the Jesuits' mission program apparently did not extend to instruction in formal Catholic doctrine. The progress of formal religious instruction in the Tarahumara missions is difficult to determine because the missionaries seldom provided detailed evaluations of the extent to which they had indoctrinated their converts, and reports that the Indians participated in Catholic religious ceremonies. Their participation in the sacraments of baptism, marriage, and confession cannot be taken as evidence that they were well instructed, because such participation required little or no understanding of church doctrine. In contrast, the colonial Catholic church discouraged priests from administering communion to anyone who failed to demonstrate a solid grounding in church doctrine. The receipt of communion, though by no means indicating a replacement of indigenous religious belief and practice by Catholicism, does at least suggest substantive progress in religious instruction and in the process of conversion as the Jesuits themselves envisioned it (Polzer 1989, personal communication; Polzer 1976; cf. Ricard 1966:122–26).

The Jesuits apparently achieved some success in indoctrinating their converts in the Lower Tarahumara missions during the early years of the mission period. In 1662 priests at the mixed Tarahumara-Tepehuan missions of San Miguel de las Bocas and San Pablo reported that many of the Indians in the missions took communion (Castillo, in González Rodríguez 1984:252, 260; Figueroa 1857:219). Rodrigo del Castillo, the Jesuit at San Miguel de las Bocas, enthusiastically wrote:

> They are well informed in the matters of the faith because since the founding of this mission [thirty-two years before] the missionary fathers in charge have attended to them with untiring work and fervent zeal. Every day the young people come to them to be taught the doctrine; . . . they usually repeat the doctrine in unison and then when they are finished the teacher questions each of them individually so that if they are ignorant of something it is repeated so they will learn. As a result, no girls or boys reach the state of matrimony who do not know the catechism well. (Castillo, in González Rodríguez 1984:251)

Thirty years later, however, a rough census of the fifteen Lower Tarahumara missions indicated that only around 10 percent of the residents took communion, and the number of Tarahumaras participating in the sacrament apparently did not increase in the eighteenth century. By the 1740s few Indians in the Lower Tarahumara missions partook of communion, and their missionaries, unversed in the Tarahumara language, could not provide them effective religious instruction (Deeds 1981:156–61). In 1747, only six years before the Lower Tarahumara missions were secularized, the Jesuit José María Miqueo (1745:22–23v) lamented that the Indians there were as "impolitic and crude" as they had been at the founding of these missions a century before and that the majority of their priests refused to administer communion to any of them, even when they were dying. The Indians' limited command of Catholic doctrine at this time is indicated by Miqueo's inquiry of his superior why it should not be possible to offer communion at least to the dying if they could demonstrate "a rough understanding of the sanctity of the sacrament and the existence of the Lord in it" (Miqueo 1745:23v).

The Jesuits who worked in the Upper Tarahumara and Chínipas missions apparently made even less progress in instructing their converts. In 1683 the missionary at the recently established Upper Tarahumara mission of Carichíc reported that his new converts participated enthusiastically in the Easter and Christmas ceremonies staged at the church but that "all the Indians are utterly incapable of receiving the blessed Eucharist, for the reason that they do not sufficiently grasp the idea of God, concealed in the Host. The sacrament of the Eucharist is not administered in any of these Tarahumara missions—not even to the dying" (Ratkay 1683:36). By 1699 everyone at this mission confessed at least once a year during Lent, they continued to perform these and other Catholic ceremonies, and they also played various musical instruments during the observance of religious holidays, but forty-five years later they were still unable to recite the catechism (Neumann 1969:133–35; Fernández de Abee, in Sheridan and Naylor 1979:80).

The reports of two Jesuit Visitors, Ignacio Lizassoain (1763) and Manuel de Aguirre (1765), offer a unique opportunity to evaluate the extent of Catholic doctrinal instruction in the Tarahumara missions at the end of the Jesuit period (Merrill 1991). Unlike previous Visitors, Lizassoain and Aguirre provided counts of the people who were taking communion in the Upper Tarahumara and Chínipas missions; they did not visit the Lower Tarahumara pueblos, which had been secularized in the 1750s.[5] According to their reports, the twenty-five partidos of the Upper Tarahumara and Chínipas mission divisions included 20,266 adults, of whom only 3,394 (16.7 percent) participated in communion. There was, however, considerable variation among the different partidos. Proportionally, more than twice as many adults took communion in the ten Chínipas missions than in the fifteen Upper Tarahumara missions (28.6 percent versus 13.8 percent). Moreover, in two Chínipas partidos (Yécora and Moris) and in three partidos (Santo Tomás, Tomochic, and Tutuaca) and one cabecera (Temeichic) of the Upper Tarahumara, three-quarters or more of the adults partook of communion.

I have discovered no feature or constellation of features shared by these missions that would distinguish them from the other Upper Tarahumara and Chínipas missions, where the percentage of adults who received communion was much lower. The Indians in these six missions apparently did not congregate in pueblos to any greater degree than the Indians in other pueblos, nor did they hold a more positive attitude toward the mission program. To the contrary, the Indians in five of the six missions fought against the Spanish in the revolts of the 1690s, and continuing discontent disrupted the mission program there throughout much of the eighteenth century (Andonaegui 1744; Estrada, in Sheridan and Naylor 1979:73; [Glandorff] 1744; Guendulain 1725; Lizassoain 1763:23; Neumann 1969:127). In addition, although they were more or less contiguous, these missions varied in their physiographic setting, the ethnic composition of their populations, and their proximity to non-Indian settlers. Finally, there is no evidence that the missionaries assigned to these six missions were more dedicated or competent than those found in the other Upper Tarahumara and Chínipas missions (Dunne 1948:206–13; Gera, in González Rodríguez 1984:338–39; Fernández de Abee 1744; González Rodríguez 1969:xliv). In fact, the missionary assigned from 1751 to 1761 to the Pima mission of Yépachic (a visita of Tutuaca in 1765) was described as incompetent and ill-tempered; at the end of his tenure the spiritual and temporal affairs of the mission were in disarray and many of the Indians had left (Braun 1765). Yet in the 1760s a higher percentage (90.1 percent) of adults reportedly took communion there than in any other Upper Tarahumara or Chínipas mission.

There is no reason to doubt that the majority of Indians in these six missions were taking communion in the 1760s; that the counts provided by the two Jesuit Visitors are close but not identical suggests that they compiled their information independently. The factors responsible for the high level of participation in communion may have been too localized or subtle to be readily identified in the existing historical record. An alternative possibility is that the Indians in these missions were not markedly better instructed in Catholic doctrine than those in other missions but their missionaries placed less stringent requirements on whom they admitted to the sacrament. Other religious orders operating among Indian groups in other parts of colonial Mexico varied in the application of the rules regulating access to communion (Ricard 1966:122–27). If such variation existed within the Jesuit order as well, it might also account for the slightly higher percentage of adults taking communion in the Chínipas missions as a whole compared to the Upper Tarahumara missions, because the Indians' attitudes toward the mission program and the general conditions within which they lived appear to have been much the same in the two areas.

Thus, by the conclusion of the Jesuit mission period in 1767 the priests' early successes in indoctrinating the Indians in the Lower Tarahumara missions appear to have disappeared, and except for six missions, instruction in formal Catholic doctrine in the Upper Tarahumara and Chínipas areas seems to have progressed little beyond the minimal knowledge required for baptism. The progress of religious instruction in the Tarahumara missions under Franciscan control is poorly known. Griffen (1979:55–56; cf. Polzer 1976:54–57) suggests, however, that the Franciscans experienced even greater difficulties than the Jesuits in indoctrinating the Indians in their missions.

The inability of the missionaries to indoctrinate the majority of Indians in the Upper Tarahumara and Chínipas missions is directly linked to the failure of the congregation program there. Because the Indians were so dispersed, opportunities for teaching them doctrine were limited to the occasions when the Indians themselves chose to assemble at the mission churches, and the number of missionaries required to minister to them directly always far exceeded the number available. As a result, native catechists, many of whom were only minimally trained in church doctrine, were given the responsibility of instructing the other Tarahumaras, especially those who lived at or near the mission stations that the priests visited irregularly.[6]

In addition, by living apart from their missionaries and remaining marginal to the Spanish colonial economy and society, the Tarahumaras preserved more or less intact many facets of their indigenous way of life.

Among other things, they maintained the integrity of their local societies as moral communities and continued to practice their native religion as they wished. The persistence of their traditional culture probably was responsible in part for the lack of interest in church doctrine that apparently characterized the majority of Tarahumaras in these missions (e.g., Ratkay 1683:35–36; Fernández de Abee 1744).

In the Upper Tarahumara and Chínipas missions the missionaries were unable to indoctrinate most of their converts primarily because they could not disrupt the production and reproduction of the native religious beliefs and the social and cultural practices that sustained them. They were confronted by a continuingly vital native ideology in terms of which Catholic doctrine was largely irrelevant and often meaningless. The Indians in the Lower Tarahumara missions, in contrast, were experiencing extensive disruptions in their lives as a consequence of their participation in the Spanish colonial economy and society. Their identity as Tarahumaras, along with their religion and most other dimensions of their lives, was undergoing significant changes. In transforming their society and culture to meet the demands of their changing world, these Indians presumably drew upon many foreign practices and ideas from the multiethnic and multicultural milieu in which they found themselves (Ortiz Zapata 1678; Castillo, in González Rodríguez 1984:250–51). Despite being part of this milieu, however, Catholic doctrine appears not to have replaced an undoubtedly seriously challenged and changing system of native religious belief.

In 1743, a decade before the Lower Tarahumara missions were turned over to secular priests, none of the missionaries in the four principal Tarahumara missions could preach in the native language, and the temporal and spiritual affairs of the missions were in disarray (Deeds 1981:156–61). The missionaries' efforts to indoctrinate the Indians also were complicated by the considerable turnover in the mission populations throughout the mission period, as Indians who died in epidemics or abandoned the missions were replaced by Indians from outside the missions for whom the process of religious education had to be repeated. Yet formal religious instruction in the Lower Tarahumara was unsuccessful primarily because the Indians who were affiliated with the missions frequently were absent from the missions, working in Spanish economic centers.

Although *gentiles* sometimes were baptized while on work levies, the Indians apparently received little or no religious instruction while outside the missions. In fact, the Spanish settlers tolerated and frequently promoted native practices, like drinking and switching marriage partners, that the priests were attempting to eradicate. Many Indians also assimilated the antimissionary attitudes of the non-Indian settlers with whom they came in contact, an animosity that derived primarily from the settlers' competition with the priests for land and the Indians' labor (Fernández de Abee, in Sheridan and Naylor 1979:82; Deeds 1981, 1989). Contrary to the initial assumptions of both the priests and many Spanish officials, the integration of these Indians into the colonial system did not depend upon their conversion to the Catholic religion but instead tended to preclude their incorporation into the Catholic church.

THE FORMATION OF TARAHUMARA COLONIAL IDENTITIES

Stern (1983) has argued that the emergence of internal divisions within New World Indian communities is a crucial dimension of Spanish colonial history, but one often obscured by the tendency of scholars to concentrate on the external relations of these communities and their evolution into closed corporate societies. He emphasizes in particular the development of social and economic distinctions within these Indian communities that often mirrored the hierarchical relations of Spanish colonial society. Although I have found little evidence for the emergence of such stratification within colonial Tarahumara communities, the members of many of these communities were divided in their attitudes and responses to Spanish colonialism. As is often found in colonial contexts, these attitudes and responses ranged from enthusiastic acceptance through accommodation to near total rejection (Dozier 1962).

Over the course of the colonial period these differences became increasingly associated with groups of communities located in different regions of Tarahumara country rather than being replicated within each Tarahumara community. By the conclusion of the colonial Jesuit period in 1767 the Tarahumaras who rejected most aspects of the Spanish colonial system lived in the remoter reaches of western and southern Tarahumara country. These Indians maintained a radical anticolonial consciousness based on the experiences and attitudes of rebels and apostate Indians who had fled from the missions and Spanish economic centers. They rarely participated in the colonial economy, and because of their isolation from Spanish colonial society they experienced little economic disruption from it. They apparently did not reject Catholic religion entirely but rather the institutional structures of the mission program and its articulation with the encompassing colonial system. Although they undoubtedly were aware of the priests' mistreatment of Indians in the missions, their reluctance to enter the mission system appears to have been motivated primarily by their desire to avoid the abuses that the

Indians suffered while living and working in the colonial society outside the mission pueblos.

At the opposite extreme were the Indians who lived in and around the Lower Tarahumara missions and the Spanish economic centers of east-central Chihuahua and northern Durango. Less than forty years after the founding of the Tarahumara mission system, the missionaries were characterizing many of them as "acculturated Indians" (*ladinos*). The Tarahumaras who lived between these two groups, in the Upper Tarahumara and Chínipas missions, maintained an intermediate stance toward the Spanish colonial system. They retained much of their indigenous way of life as well as their identity as Indians, although they apparently modified this identity to reflect their affiliation with the Jesuit mission system.

At the end of the colonial Jesuit period the regionalization of Tarahumara identity was neither complete nor without exceptions. The boundaries between the different areas were often blurred, reflecting gradations in the proximity of Indian communities to Spanish economic centers and the fact that Indians moved from one area to another. Tarahumara identity was not, however, an unbroken continuum but three fairly distinct divisions, which represented complex responses to the Spanish colonial program in general and especially to the colonial economy. These internal divisions emerged primarily because of differences in the circumstances within which the Tarahumaras operated while living outside the missions, beyond the direct control of their missionaries.

In the Lower Tarahumara area the transformations in indigenous society and culture occurred primarily because of the Indians' extensive participation in the regional colonial economy. Despite their commitment to acculturating the Tarahumaras, the Jesuit missionaries opposed this process because they were disturbed by the direction the acculturation was taking and the detrimental impact it was having on the Indians' religious instruction. The missionaries attempted to reassert control over the process of assimilation and to isolate the Indians from the less desirable elements of frontier society, but their efforts proved ineffective against the enormous local demands for Indian labor.

The Indians in the Upper Tarahumara and Chínipas areas were more reluctant than those in the Lower Tarahumara missions to enter the colonial economy, having developed a negative or ambivalent attitude toward the colonial system before missions were established among them. They also were more buffered from labor drafts and the loss of their lands to non-Indians because they lived farther from major Spanish settlements and economic centers.[7] Given the relative isolation of these missions, the priests potentially had the opportunity to assimilate the local Indians along the lines they originally envisioned in their mission program, but they were unable to do so largely because the Indians refused to congregate in concentrated settlements.

The missionaries' role in creating the internal divisions among the Tarahumaras thus was clearly secondary, but it was not entirely negligible. In the case of the *gentile* Tarahumaras, of course, the priests did little more than provide a label for the group and serve as a focus of their opposition to Spanish colonialism as a whole. In the Lower Tarahumara, in contrast, the Jesuits set the stage for the Indians' incorporation into Spanish colonial society. They convinced the Indians to move into the mission partidos, thereby making them more accessible to labor drafts and disrupting aboriginal patterns of land tenure and social relations. They also exposed the Indians to many aspects of European culture and taught them skills necessary for the operation of the missions that prepared them for work in the Spanish mines and haciendas.

The Indians in the Upper Tarahumara and Chínipas missions, although they rejected the Jesuits' congregation program, did adopt some of the principal institutions and idioms of the mission program as the basis for defending their political and cultural autonomy within the colonial system and for creating a new identity distinct from both non-Christian Indians and non-Indian Christians. The Indians who served as pueblo political officials, for example, became the principal mediators between the mission Indian communities and the external colonial society. As a group these officials provided a higher level of community integration and coordination than had existed aboriginally, often enabling the members of their communities to resist incorporation into the colonial system more effectively. Similarly, the elaborate Catholic ceremonies that the Indians staged at the mission churches substantiated their status as Christians in the eyes of the missionaries and Spanish colonial officials and thus afforded them and their lands some protection against exploitation and expropriation. These ceremonies also symbolized to the Indians themselves the existence of a new kind of community in which they were now members.

The interaction of a number of factors undermined the Jesuits' ability to implement their mission program fully among the Tarahumaras as a whole. From the outset the environmental, demographic, and social conditions in the Tarahumara region—the vast and often rugged terrain, the at times unpredictable climate, the dispersed and relatively small Indian populations and their diffuse political organization—presented major obstacles that the missionaries never entirely overcame. During the colonial period these conditions brought out contradictions within the Spanish colonial program that also subverted the priests' efforts. The colonial system was rife with competing interests and unresolved conflicts: within and between the religious orders, between the regular and secular clergy, between the Catholic church and the royal government, between creoles and European-born subjects, and, perhaps most significantly, between the missionaries and the non-Indian settlers. These adverse conditions and contradictions frequently rendered the consequences of the missionaries' actions considerably different from and sometimes diametrically opposed to their original intentions.

The weaknesses in the mission and colonial programs ultimately prevented the Jesuits from establishing the level of direct control over the Tarahumaras that they believed, with justification, was necessary to convert them to orthodox Catholicism. The Indians did not enjoy untrammeled freedom, of course, for they were subjected to the rules and demands of the missionaries, settlers, and royal officials while living in the missions and Spanish settlements. They also could not always avoid forced labor, which sometimes amounted to slavery. Nonetheless, they often could play the conflicting segments of the colonial society against one another to their advantage and could also retreat to the many areas both within and beyond the mission system where Spanish dominion was minimal or absent. As a consequence the Indians were able to control their integration into Spanish colonial society and the extent to which they incorporated Catholic beliefs and practices into their lives.

CONVERSION AND THE TARAHUMARAS

The history of the colonial Jesuit mission program among the Tarahumaras closely resembles the histories of Catholic missionary efforts among Indian societies across colonial Latin America.[8] The variations through space and time in the Indians' responses to the mission and colonial programs; the modifications in indigenous society, culture, and identity; and the transformations of both native and Catholic religions are widespread and familiar processes.[9] The complexity of these processes tends to obscure the fact that they all were linked ultimately to the pursuit of a single goal: the conversion of the New World's inhabitants to Christianity. While the religious dimension of the colonial encounter cannot be reduced to matters of religious conversion alone, it is nonetheless appropriate to ask whether or in what sense the Indians of Spain's New World colonies converted to Catholicism. Directing this question to the case at hand, we can ask: Did the Tarahumaras convert to Christianity by the end of the colonial Jesuit period?

The answer obviously depends upon how religious conversion is defined. In an overview of sociological studies of conversion Snow and Machalek (1984) argue that conversion entails changes in the values, beliefs, identities, and most significantly, the universes of discourse of individuals, the latter evidenced by changes in their speech and reasoning styles. They argue, however, that public displays of conversion unaccompanied by private acceptance should not be taken as examples of conversion, nor should cases in which people participate in a new religion and its rituals but do not change their preexisting views of the world. Their position on this issue is similar to that of Horton (1975:394), who considers the application of the term "conversion" inappropriate unless a radical change in personal cosmology takes place.

Snow and Machalek's perspective shares with most notions of religious conversion an emphasis on internal changes in individual converts, especially in their beliefs. Although perhaps useful to a point in the investigation of conversion in contemporary Western societies, this perspective immediately encounters both methodological and theoretical problems when applied to the historical study of conversion in transcultural contexts.

The methodological problems derive from the type of information about conversion that is available in the historical record. The principal sources of information in these contexts are written documents typically produced by missionaries rather than the converts themselves. Native voices are notoriously absent from most of these documents. Even when colonial missionaries provide examples of what appears to have been radical individual religious change, their accounts inevitably are structured by their own universes of discourse and bear an unknown relationship to the actual experiences of the converts.

Apart from these practical problems this internalist view of religious conversion tends to elevate the activities and experiences of discrete individuals above social and political processes. In culture contact situations the establishment of political and cultural domination, the resistance to such domination, and other aspects of the power relations between the engaged societies all influence the process of religious conversion. Similarly, the diffusion and ultimate institutionalization of religious innovations within a society are significantly affected by the power relations among the members of the society (Weber 1963). These internal power relations are also important in determining the rhythm of the conversion process. The members of hierarchically organized societies, for example, might embrace a new religion rapidly following the conversion of a political elite; in more politically diffuse societies like the Tarahumaras', such acceptance might take place quite gradually on an individual-by-individual or family-by-family basis (Sahlins 1983:519).

This view of conversion also obscures the fact that belief and practice are inextricably linked and that practices may be of greater significance than beliefs at different points in the conversion process. Participation in religious rituals, though not necessarily an indicator of profound internal change, can contribute to the internalization of the religious ideas portrayed or embedded in the rituals. Such participation also can promote a sense of identity with the new religion, which in turn provides the basis upon which changes in beliefs proceed (Rappaport 1979).

The primacy assigned to belief in such conceptions of religious conversion reflects an intellectualist bias of some European scholarly and Christian traditions that is not necessarily shared by the adherents of all religions. Geertz (1973:177) argues, for example, that the Balinese are more concerned with performing rituals correctly than with establishing conformity in religious doctrine or ritual exegesis, stressing "orthopraxy, not orthodoxy." The Tarahumaras of today maintain a similar attitude, in part because they consider their ritual actions to be complete unto themselves and to some degree intrinsically efficacious, and also because the intellectual foundations of their religious rituals are to a large extent embedded in their commonsense understandings of the world, which are usually implicit and seldom questioned (Hefner 1987).

Where such perspectives prevail, both the converts and missionaries can agree, on the basis of religious practices alone, that conversion has taken place even though a major transformation in belief has not occurred. Moreover, the connections between beliefs and ritual practices are never so determined that a specific set of beliefs automatically produces a single ritual expression or that only one interpretation is possible for a particular ritual (Merrill 1988:145–50). In other words, the possibility always exists that orthodoxy can accompany heteropraxy and orthopraxy can accompany heterodoxy. Depending upon the religion in question, either state of affairs—or for that matter, one in which heterodoxy accompanies heteropraxy—can be regarded as qualifying as conversion.

These considerations lead directly to the conclusion that no single, universally applicable definition of conversion is possible or even desirable. Instead, conversion is better conceived more relativistically. A relativistic notion of conversion acknowledges that different religions define and evaluate conversion differently. It also recognizes at least two perspectives in any conversion situation—that of the existing adherents of the new religion and that of the supposed converts—and that these perspectives can differ. By allowing for multiple perspectives this view accommodates the complexities and political dimensions of conversion. It recognizes, for example, that the status of "convert" can be withheld, refused, or contested as well as bestowed and accepted and that people can appropriate the beliefs and practices of a religion at the same time that they reject formal affiliation with it.

This view of conversion is particularly appropriate when addressing the question of whether the Tarahumaras converted to Catholicism during the colonial Jesuit period. The perspectives of both the missionaries and the Indians presumably coincided with regard to the Tarahumaras who remained unbaptized and entirely outside the mission system (the *gentiles*) and also with respect to those Tarahumaras who enthusiastically embraced Jesuit mission life and Catholic beliefs and practices (the "good Christians"). Between these two extremes, however, the categories are more ambiguous, the perspectives more at odds.

The missionaries seem to have divided the Tarahumaras whom they considered to be converts into at least three categories in addition to that of "good Christians." The first were the "bad Christians," typically Indians in the older missions who were familiar with basic Catholic beliefs and rituals but who shared the anticlerical attitudes and "vices" of many non-Indian settlers. The second were what might be called "unformed Christians," typically Indians in the newer missions who, from the missionaries' perspective, required only religious instruction and protection from the Devil and other evil influences to become good Christians. The third category of Tarahumaras were the people whom the missionaries labeled "apostates," that is, people who had been baptized but subsequently rejected the mission program.

The historical record reveals little information on how these Indians viewed themselves in relation to these missionary categories. In 1662 a priest at one of the older Tarahumara missions reported that the baptized Tarahumaras referred to unbaptized Indians as "Jews"; in the local terminology of the day "Jews" and "gentiles" were both used to label Indians who remained outside the Catholic church. In contrast, how these baptized Indians labeled themselves in the process of defining their new identity as mission Indians is not recorded (Castillo, in González Rodríguez 1984:250). Today the terms "baptized" (*pagótame* or *pagótuame*) and *gentile* (or *cimarron*) are used by both groups of Tarahumaras to label themselves. Even though phrased in a religious idiom, however, these labels are best understood as metaphors for the essentially political stances that the different Indian communities assumed toward the Spanish colonial system as a whole, not as simple characterizations of their relationships to the Catholic religion.

Although there are undoubtedly significant variations in different areas of Tarahumara country, the contemporary "baptized" Tarahumaras for the most part do not view themselves or their ancestors as converts to Catholicism, nor do they identify themselves as "Catholics" (*católicos*), "Christians" (*cristianos*), or otherwise as the members of a "universal" church. Instead, they regard themselves as *Rarámuri pagótame* (baptized Tarahumaras) whose religious beliefs and rituals, including the sacrament of baptism, were given to them by their deities at the beginning of the world. Yet an explicit affiliation with local institutions of the Catholic church is a central component of their distinctive identity. This affiliation is publicly expressed through the orthodox baptism of each new generation of Tarahumaras by the official representatives of the church. The symbolic significance of baptism as both the principal rite of incorporation into the baptized Tarahumara community and the preeminent marker of their link to the local Catholic church presumably explains why they have not modified this sacrament as they have other Catholic rituals and why they continue to rely on Catholic priests to perform it for them (cf. Velasco Rivero 1983:77).

When the Jesuits resumed their missionary activities among the Tarahumaras in 1900, they considered the Tarahumaras' religion to be a mix of pagan ritual, superstition, and distorted Catholicism. They attempted for several decades to introduce orthodox Catholicism but were largely unsuccessful (Ocampo 1966). The religion that the baptized Tarahumaras had created in the colonial period by reworking Catholic beliefs and practices within an evolving indigenous framework had become a key element in the formation of their colonial and postcolonial identity and their resistance against political and cultural domination (Velasco Rivero 1983). By the 1960s, inspired by the liberation theology associated with the Second Vatican Council, many Jesuits working in the Tarahumara missions began to integrate elements of Tarahumara religion into their own religious practices and to argue that contemporary Tarahumara religion should be regarded as a legitimate form of Catholicism (Velasco Rivero 1983; Robles O. 1987). This shift in perspective, which entails a radical change in the criteria for defining and evaluating conversion, has affected Catholic mission policy and practice in other parts of the world (e.g., Shapiro 1987). The ideology of at least some segments of the Catholic church has now been so transformed that the missionaries themselves can contemplate the possibility of converting to the native religion.

NOTES

Acknowledgments. I am grateful to the Smithsonian Institution for grants from the Scholarly Studies Program and Research Opportunities Fund, which allowed me to complete the research upon which this essay is based. I also thank Susan

Deeds, Luis González Rodríguez, Martha Graham, Robert Hefner, Robert Jackson, Charles Polzer, Cynthia Radding, Cecilia Troop, Richard Werbner, and Peter Wood, whose insightful commentaries proved invaluable in making final revisions.

1. Today the people known in Spanish as the Tarahumaras refer to themselves as Rarámuri. The term *Rarámuri* does not appear in the literature until the nineteenth century (Deimel 1980:12; Tellechea 1826:95, 116, 120); *Tarahumara* was used throughout the Spanish colonial period. I follow the colonial usage here.

2. Basic ethnographic information on the Tarahumaras can be found in monographs by Lumholtz (1902), Bennett and Zingg (1935), Plancarte (1954), Pennington (1963), Kennedy (1970, 1978), González Rodríguez (1982), and Merrill (1988). Brief ethnographic overviews include Fried (1969), Pennington (1983), and Merrill (1983).

3. The religious beliefs and practices of the contemporary Tarahumaras have been investigated in only a few communities. The available evidence suggests considerable regional variation, including a closer approximation to orthodox Catholicism in those communities more heavily influenced by Jesuit missionaries (González Rodríguez 1985:40–70; Kennedy and López 1981; Velasco Rivero 1983).

4. This overview of the Jesuit approach to missionization is based on a number of colonial Jesuit documents, but especially Tardá and Guadalaxara (1676) and Ratkay (1683), as well as the excellent analyses provided by Spicer (1962: 288–98) and Polzer (1976).

5. I have assumed that the unsigned 1765 report was prepared by Aguirre, who served as the Jesuit Visitor in that year. In analyzing the reports of these Visitors, I have interpreted Aguirre's category *individuos por todo* (total individuals) to include adults only. I also have followed Aguirre's organization of the partidos, excluding the partidos of Baborigame and Nabogame for lack of data and the mission of Chinarras, which was located outside the Upper Tarahumara–Chínipas area. When the figures provided by the two Visitors differed, I use the larger except in the case of Matachic, where Lizassoain's count for people confessing exceeds Aguirre's figure for "total individuals." When they reported only that few people (*pocos*) in a mission took communion, I used an estimate of 5 percent of the total adult population to arrive at a figure, except for three visitas of the mission of Sisoguichic. For them, I used 0.75 percent, the percentage of adults taking communion in the head mission of Sisoguichic and one visita (Bocoyna), for which Aguirre provided figures. For a more detailed evaluation and analysis of these Visitors' reports, see Merrill (1991).

6. An analysis of the data provided by Lizassoain and Aguirre reveals that, except in the partido of Temeichic, the percentage of adults taking communion did not vary significantly between the head missions, where priests resided, and their visitas. Also, the variations in the percentage of adults taking communion among these different partidos does not correlate with differences in the number of years a missionary had resided in them. This suggests that direct contact with

a missionary was not the most important factor affecting the progress of religious instruction (Merrill 1991).

7. In the eighteenth century some of the priests in the Upper Tarahumara missions were themselves a threat to the Indians' livelihood, taking over Indian lands for their personal use (Dunne 1948:212–13).

8. The Christian evangelization of Indians in colonial Mexico has been the subject of a number of recent studies. The majority of these studies concentrate on the complex societies of central and southern Mexico (e.g., Burkhart 1989; Clendinnen 1987; Farriss 1984; Jones 1989; and Klor de Alva 1982). Spicer's (1980) monumental study of Yaqui cultural history combined with Hu-DeHart's (1981) more focused work provide detailed material on the colonial religious history of some of the Tarahumaras' closest neighbors.

9. Although the Tarahumaras clearly transformed their indigenous religion and the Catholicism to which they were exposed during the Spanish colonial period, no study of this process and its variations in different areas of Tarahumara country has been completed for this period. Moreover, the development of Tarahumara religion during the period following the expulsion of the Jesuits in 1767 and their return in 1900 remains to be investigated. The only systematic accounts of Tarahumara religion and its relationship to Catholicism come from the twentieth century (e.g., Bennett and Zingg 1935; Kennedy 1978; González Rodríguez 1982; Velasco Rivero 1983 and 1990; and Merrill 1983, 1988, and n.d.).

REFERENCES

[Aguirre, Manuel de.] 1765. *Noticia de las Misiones q.e administran los P.P. de la Comp.a de Jesús en esta Nueva España, año de 1765.* W. B. Stevens Collection, University of Texas, Austin.

Alcocer, José Antonio. 1958. *Bosquejo de la historia del Colegio de Nuestra Señora de Guadalupe y sus misiones, año de 1788.* Rafael Cervantes, ed. Mexico City: Editorial Porrúa.

Alegre, Francisco Javier. 1956–1960. *Historia de la provincia de la Compañía de Jesús de Nueva España.* Ernest J. Burrus and Felix Zubillaga, eds. 4 vols. Rome: Institutum Historicum S. J.

Almada, Francisco R. 1937. *Apuntes históricos de la región de Chínipas.* Chihuahua: Talleres Linotipográficos del Estado de Chihuahua.

Andonaegui, Roque de. 1744. Letter to Lorenzo Gera, 5 December 1744, Themeychic. Bolton Papers, Bancroft Library, University of California, Berkeley.

Arlegui, José. 1851. *Crónica de la provincia de N.S.P.S. Francisco de Zacatecas.* 2d ed. Mexico City: Cumplido.

Bancroft, Hubert H. 1886. *History of the North Mexican States and Texas.* Vol. 1, *1531–1800.* San Francisco: History Company.

Benedict, H. Bradley. 1972. "El saqueo de las misiones de Chihuahua, 1767–1777." *Historia Mexicana* 22:24–33.

Bennett, Wendell C., and Robert M. Zingg. 1935. *The Tarahumara: An Indian Tribe of Northern Mexico*. Chicago: University of Chicago Press.

Braun, Bartholomé. 1765. Letter to Francisco Zevallos, 17 June 1765, Yoquibo. Archivo Histórico de Hacienda, leg. 17, exp. 57. Mexico City.

Bravo de la Serna, Francisco. 1640. *Petición*, 4 January 1640, Parral. Archivo General de la Nación, Jesuitas I–16. Mexico City.

Burkhart, Louise M. 1989. *The Slippery Earth: Nahua-Christian Moral Dialogue in Sixteenth-Century Mexico*. Tucson: University of Arizona Press.

Burrus, Ernest J. 1963. *Misiones norteñas Mexicanas de la Compañía de Jesús, 1751–1757*. Mexico City: Antigua Librería Robredo de José Porrúa e Hijos.

Champion, Jean R. 1955. "Acculturation among the Tarahumara of Northwest Mexico since 1890." *Transactions of the New York Academy of Sciences* 17:560–66.

———. 1962. "A Study in Culture Persistence: The Tarahumaras of Northwestern Mexico." Ph.D. diss., Columbia University.

Clendinnen, Inga. 1987. *Ambivalent Conquests: Maya and Spaniard in Yucatan, 1517–1570*. Cambridge: Cambridge University Press.

Contreras, Gaspar de. 1638. Letter to Andrés Pérez, 5 August 1638, Santiago Papasquiaro. Archivo General de la Nación, Misiones 25, 284–87v. Mexico City. [English translation in Sheridan and Naylor 1979:11–13.]

Cramaussel, Chantal. 1990. *Primera página de historia colonial Chihuahuense: La provincia de Santa Bárbara en Nueva Vizcaya, 1563–1631*. Chihuahua: Universidad Autónoma de Ciudad Juárez.

Decorme, Gerard. 1941. *La obra de los Jesuitas Mexicanos durante la epoca colonial, 1572–1767 (Compendio Histórico)*. 2 vols. Mexico City: Antigua Librería Robredo de José Porrúa e Hijos.

Deeds, Susan M. 1981. "Rendering unto Caesar: The Secularization of Jesuit Missions in Mid-Eighteenth Century Durango." Ph.D. diss., University of Arizona.

———. 1989. "Rural Work in Nueva Vizcaya: Forms of Labor Coercion on the Periphery." *Hispanic American Historical Review* 69:425–49.

Deimel, Claus. 1980. *Tarahumara: Indianer im Norden Mexikos*. Frankfurt, West Germany: Syndikat.

Dozier, Edward P. 1962. *Differing Reactions to Religious Contacts among North American Indian Societies*. Akten des 34, pp. 161–71. Internationalen Amerikanistenkongresses, Vienna, 18–25 July 1960. Vienna: Verlag Ferdinand Berger, Horn.

Dunne, Peter M. 1937. "The Expulsion of the Jesuits from New Spain, 1767." *Mid-America* 19:3–30.

———. 1944. *Pioneer Jesuits in Northern Mexico*. Berkeley: University of California Press.

———. 1948. *Early Jesuit Missions in Tarahumara*. Berkeley: University of California Press.

Escalona, Joseph de. 1744. *Carta annua*, 7 June 1744, El Santissimo Nombre de María [Sisoguichic]. Bolton Papers, Bancroft Library, University of California, Berkeley.

Estrada, Ignacio Xavier de. 1730. Letter to Juan Antonio de Oviedo, 23 November 1730, Themeichic. Archivo Histórico de Hacienda 278, exp. 7. Mexico City. [English translation in Sheridan and Naylor 1979:73–78.]

Farriss, Nancy M. 1984. *Maya Society under Colonial Rule: The Collective Enterprise of Survival.* Princeton: Princeton University Press.

Fernández de Abee, Juan Isidro. 1744. *Razón de la fundación y progressos que ha tenido esta Misión de Jesús Carichíc desde el día 8 de noviembre del año de 1675.* 8 July 1722, Jesús Carichíc. Bolton Papers, Bancroft Library, University of California, Berkeley. [English translation of excerpts in Sheridan and Naylor 1979:78–86.]

Figueroa, Gerónimo de. 1857. "Puntos de Anua de estos diez años que he asistido en este partido de San Pablo . . . desde el año de 1652 hasta este de 1662." In *Documentos para la Historia de México*, 4th ser., vol. 3, pp. 217–22. Mexico City: Imprenta de Vicente García Torres.

Fried, Jacob. 1969. "The Tarahumara." In *Ethnology*, pt. 2, Evon Z. Vogt, ed., pp. 846–70. *Handbook of Middle American Indians*, vol. 8, Robert Wauchope, gen. ed. Austin: University of Texas Press.

Geertz, Clifford. 1973. "'Internal Conversion' in Contemporary Bali." In C. Geertz, *The Interpretation of Cultures*, pp. 170–89. New York: Basic Books.

Gerhard, Peter. 1982. *The North Frontier of New Spain.* Princeton: Princeton University Press.

Giddens, Anthony. 1979. *Central Problems in Social Theory: Action, Structure, and Contradiction in Social Analysis.* Berkeley: University of California Press.

[Glandorff, Franz Hermann.] 1744. *Carta annua*, n.d., Tomochic. Bolton Papers, Bancroft Library, University of California, Berkeley.

González Rodríguez, Luis. 1969. "Introduction." In *Révoltes des Indiens Tarahumars (1626–1724)*, Luis González R., ed. and trans., pp. xxxv–lxiii. Paris: Institut des Hautes Etudes de l'Amérique Latine de l'Université de Paris.

———. 1982. *Tarahumara: La sierra y el hombre.* Mexico City: Fondo de Cultura Económica.

———. 1984. *Crónicas de la sierra Tarahumara.* Mexico City: Secretaría de Educación Pública.

———. 1985. "Los Tarahumares" (The Tarahumares). In *Tarahumara*, photographs by Bob Schalkwijk, texts by Luis González Rodríguez and Don Burgess, pp. 13–70. Mexico City: Chrysler de México.

———. n.d. "Las Guerrillas de Resistencia Etnica en el Noroeste (1690): Un Análisis de la Documentación Oficial." Unpublished manuscript.

Griffen, William B. 1979. *Indian Assimilation in the Franciscan Area of Nueva Vizcaya.* Anthropological Papers of the University of Arizona, no. 33.

Guadalaxara, Tomás de. 1683. *Compendio del arte de la lengua de los Tarahumares, y Guazapares.* Puebla: Diego Fernández de León.

Guendulain, Juan de. 1725. Letter to Gaspar Roder[o], 22 December 1725, Cocorim. Archivo General de la Nación, Jesuitas 2–4, exp. 32. Mexico City.

Hefner, Robert W. 1987. "The Political Economy of Islamic Conversion in Modern East Java." In *Islam and the Political Economy of Meaning: Comparative Studies of Muslim Discourse*, William R. Roff, ed., pp. 53–78. London: Croom Helm.

Horton, Robin. 1975. "On the Rationality of Conversion." *Africa* 45:219–35, 373–99.

Hu-DeHart, Evelyn. 1981. *Missionaries, Miners, and Indians: Spanish Contact with the Yaqui Nation of Northwestern New Spain, 1533–1820.* Tucson: University of Arizona Press.

Jones, Grant D. 1989. *Maya Resistance to Spanish Rule: Time and History on a Colonial Frontier.* Albuquerque: University of New Mexico Press.

Kennedy, John G. 1970. *Inápuchi: Una comunidad Tarahumara gentil.* Mexico City: Instituto Indigenista Interamericano.

———. 1978. *Tarahumara of the Sierra Madre: Beer, Ecology, and Social Organization.* Arlington Heights, Ill.: AHM Publishing.

Kennedy, John G., and Raúl A. López. 1981. *Semana Santa in the Sierra Tarahumara: A Comparative Study in Three Communities.* Occasional Papers of the Museum of Cultural History, University of California, Los Angeles, no. 4.

Klor de Alva, J. Jorge. 1982. "Spiritual Conflict and Accommodation in New Spain: Toward a Typology of Aztec Responses to Christianity." In *The Inca and Aztec States, 1400–1800: Anthropology and History,* George A. Collier, Renato I. Rosaldo, and John D. Wirth, eds., pp. 345–66. New York: Academic Press.

Lizassoain, Ignacio. 1763. *Noticia de la visita general de P. Ignacio Lizasoain . . . Visitador General de las Missiones de esta Prov.a de Nueva España.* W. B. Stevens Collection, University of Texas, Austin.

Lockhart, James, and Stuart B. Schwartz. 1983. *Early Latin America: A History of Colonial Spanish America and Brazil.* Cambridge: Cambridge University Press.

Lumholtz, Carl. 1902. *Unknown Mexico.* 2 vols. New York: Charles Scribner's Sons.

Medrano Ybarra, Francisco de. 1691. Letter to Ambrosio Oddon, 2 March 1691, Santiago [Papasquiaro]. Archivo Histórico de Hacienda 279, exp. 116. Mexico City.

Merrill, William L. 1983. "Tarahumara Social Organization, Political Organization, and Religion." In *Southwest,* Alfonso Ortiz, ed., pp. 290–305. *Handbook of North American Indians,* vol. 10, William C. Sturtevant, gen. ed. Washington, D.C.: Smithsonian Institution.

———. 1988. *Rarámuri Souls: Knowledge and Social Process in Northern Mexico.* Washington, D.C.: Smithsonian Institution Press.

———. 1991. "La Doctrinación Religiosa en la Tarahumara Colonial: Los Informes de los Visitadores Lizasoain y Aguirre al Final de la Epoca Jesuita." In *Actas del Segundo Congreso de Historia Regional Comparada 1990.* Ciudad Juárez: Universidad Autónoma de Ciudad Juárez.

———. n.d. "Rarámuri Easter." In *Lent and Holy Week in Northwest Mexico and Southwest United States,* N. Ross Crumrine and Rosamond B. Spicer, eds. Lanham, Md.: University Press of America. In press.

Miller, Wick. 1983. "Uto-Aztecan Languages." In *Southwest,* Alfonso Ortiz, ed., pp. 113–24. *Handbook of North American Indians,* vol. 10, William C. Sturtevant, gen. ed. Washington, D.C.: Smithsonian Institution.

Miqueo, José María. 1745. Letter to Christóbal de Escobar, 7 March 1745,

Yoquibo. Archivo General de la Nación, Jesuitas I–16, 19–24v. Mexico City.
Naylor, Thomas H., and Charles W. Polzer, comps. and eds. 1986. *The Presidio and Militia on the Northern Frontier of New Spain: A Documentary History.* Vol. 1: *1570–1700.* Tucson: University of Arizona Press.
Neumann, Joseph. 1969. *Révoltes des Indiens Tarahumars (1626–1724).* Luis González Rodríguez, ed. and trans. Paris: Institut des Hautes Etudes de l'Amérique Latine de l'Université de Paris.
Ocampo, Manuel. 1966. *Historia de la Misión Tarahumara (1900–1965).* 2d ed. Mexico City: Editorial Jus.
Ortiz Zapata, Juan. 1678. *Relación de las misiones . . . 1678.* Archivo General de la Nación, Misiones 26, 251–69v. Mexico City.
Osorio, Francisco. 1744. *Carta annua,* 1744, Papigochic. Bolton Papers, Bancroft Library, University of California, Berkeley.
Pascual, José. 1651. Letter to Jesuit Provincial, 23 June 1651, San Felipe. Archivo General de la Nación, Templos y Conventos 153, exp. 45, 385–86v. Mexico City.
Pennington, Campbell W. 1963. *The Tarahumar of Mexico: Their Environment and Material Culture.* Salt Lake City: University of Utah Press.
———. 1983. "Tarahumara." In *Southwest,* Alfonso Ortiz, ed., pp. 276–89. *Handbook of North American Indians,* vol. 10, William C. Sturtevant, gen. ed. Washington, D.C.: Smithsonian Institution.
Plancarte, Francisco. 1954. *El problema indígena Tarahumara.* Memorias del Instituto Nacional Indigenista, vol. 5. Mexico City.
Polzer, Charles W. 1976. *Rules and Precepts of the Jesuit Missions of Northwestern New Spain.* Tucson: University of Arizona Press.
Porras Muñoz, Guillermo. 1980a. *Iglesia y estado en Nueva Vizcaya (1562–1821).* Mexico City: Universidad Nacional Autónoma de México.
———. 1980b. *La Frontera con los Indios de Nueva Vizcaya en el siglo XVII.* Mexico City: Fomento Cultural Banamex.
Radding de Murrieta, Cynthia. 1977. "The Function of the Market in Changing Economic Structures in the Mission Communities of Pimería Alta, 1768–1821." *The Americas* 34:155–69.
Rappaport, Roy A. 1979. *Ecology, Meaning, and Religion.* Richmond, Calif.: North Atlantic Books.
Ratkay, Juan María. 1683. *An Account of the Tarahumara Missions,* 20 March 1683, Carichic. Marion L. Reynolds, trans. Bolton Papers, Bancroft Library, University of California, Berkeley.
Reff, Daniel T. 1987. "Old World Diseases and the Dynamics of Indian and Jesuit Relations in Northwestern New Spain, 1520–1660." In *Ejidos and Regions of Refuge in Northwestern Mexico,* N. Ross Crumrine and Phil C. Weigand, eds., pp. 85–94. Anthropological Papers of the University of Arizona, no. 46.
Ricard, Robert. 1966. *The Spiritual Conquest of Mexico: An Essay on the Apostolate and the Evangelizing Methods of the Mendicant Orders in New Spain: 1523–1572.* Lesley B. Simpson, trans. Berkeley: University of California Press.

Robles O., J. Ricardo. 1987. "Los Rarámuri-Pagótuame." Unpublished manuscript.

Roca, Paul M. 1979. *Spanish Jesuit Churches in Mexico's Tarahumara*. Tucson: University of Arizona Press.

Sahlins, Marshall. 1983. "Other Times, Other Customs: The Anthropology of History." *American Anthropologist* 85:517–44.

Secretaría de Programación y Presupuesto. 1982–1984. *X Censo general de población y vivenda, 1980*. Mexico City: Secretaría de Programación y Presupuesto.

Shapiro, Judith. 1987. "From Tupã to the Land without Evil: The Christianization of Tupi-Guarani Cosmology." *American Ethnologist* 14:126–39.

Sheridan, Thomas E., and Thomas H. Naylor, eds. 1979. *Rarámuri: A Tarahumara Colonial Chronicle, 1607–1791*. Flagstaff: Northland Press.

Snow, David A., and Richard Machalek. 1984. "The Sociology of Conversion." *Annual Review of Sociology* 10:167–90.

Spicer, Edward H. 1962. *Cycles of Conquest: The Impact of Spain, Mexico, and the United States on the Indians of the Southwest, 1533–1960*. Tucson: University of Arizona Press.

———. 1980. *The Yaquis: A Cultural History*. Tucson: University of Arizona Press.

Stern, Steve J. 1983. "The Struggle for Solidarity: Class, Culture, and Community in Highland Indian America." *Radical History Review* 27:21–45.

Tamarón y Romeral, Pedro. 1937. *Demonstración del vastísimo obispado de la Nueva Vizcaya, 1765: Durango, Sinaloa, Sonora, Arizona, Nuevo México, Chihuahua, y Porciones de Texas, Coahuila y Zacatecas*. Vito Alessio Robles, ed. Mexico City: Porrúa.

Tardá, Joseph. 1677. Letter to Thomas de Altamirano, 22 July 1677, San Bernabé. Archivo General de la Nación, Jesuitas I–16. Mexico City.

Tardá, Joseph, and Tomás de Guadalaxara. 1676. Letter to Francisco Ximénez, 15 August 1676. Archivum Romanum Societatis Iesu, Mexicana 17, 355–92v. Rome.

Tellechea, Miguel. 1826. *Compendio gramatical para la inteligencia del idioma Tarahumar*. Mexico City: Imprenta de la Federación en Palacio.

Velasco Rivero, Pedro de. 1983. *Danzar o morir: Religión y resistencia a la dominación en la cultura Tarahumar*. Mexico City: Centro de Reflexión Teológica.

———. 1990. "Sincretismo o reformulación y apropriación de propuestas religiosas: Reflexión a partir del cristianismo tarahumar." In *Los Rarámuri Hoy (Mesa-Debate)*, Françoise Brouzés Pelissier, ed. Chihuahua: Dirección General de Culturas Populares.

Weber, Max. 1963. *The Sociology of Religion*. Ephraim Fischoff, trans. Boston: Beacon Press.

West, Robert C. 1949. "The Mining Community in Northern New Spain: The Parral Mining District." *Ibero-Americana* 30. Berkeley: University of California Press.

Zelis, Rafael de. 1871. *Catálogo de los sugetos de la Compañía de Jesús que formaban la provincia de México el día del arresto, 25 de Junio de 1767*. Mexico City: I. Escalante.

CHAPTER SIX

Conversion and "Community" in Amazonia

Donald K. Pollock

Portuguese sailors first sighted the mainland of Brazil on April 22, 1500. During the nine days of this initial European visit, local indigenous peoples—the Tupi groups that had recently occupied the coast (Hemming 1978:28–31; Balée 1984)—had their first exposure to Christian ritual, a Catholic mass performed on the beach. In his description of this event Pero Alvares Cabral remarked on how easily the Portuguese sailors convinced their Indian hosts to participate. He wrote in a letter to King Manoel I that "at the elevation of the Host, when we knelt, they placed themselves as we were with hands uplifted, and so quietly that I assure Your Highness that they gave us much edification." The apparent innocence of these Indians convinced Cabral that "if we could understand their speech and they ours, they would immediately become Christians" (quoted in Hemming 1978:2–3).[1]

Cabral's optimism now seems innocent; nearly five hundred years later the conversions he anticipated have not taken place. Although many indigenous societies in Central America and along the Andean highlands succumbed to Spanish conquest, and thus to new economic, political, and religious forms (Duviols 1977), the indigenous cultures of Amazonia, the lowland region drained by the Amazon River, to a remarkable extent resisted conversion to Christianity. In this essay I explore some aspects of this resistance, to consider whether an understanding of this failure to convert can shed light on the nature of conversion as a general phenomenon.[2]

The debate surrounding conversion to "world" religions concedes that the phenomenon is a particular kind of response to social and cultural change. The key issues are the kind of response conversion represents and the relationship between social organization and religious belief. In proposing that the example of indigenous Amazonian groups represents a large-scale failure of *religious* conversion, I do not want to suggest that no change of any kind has taken place. Instead I suggest that the intercultural contact and social change that provide the hypothesized context for conversion to world religions present not religious or cosmological crises so much as moral dilemmas and challenges to culturally informed notions of person and identity. Within a context of change new foundations of morality and person *may* be provided by the frameworks of world religions—in Amazonia, by various forms of Christianity—but such frameworks are not adopted where social formations do not support the benefits of conversion. In Amazonia, Christianity has not offered such formations and has often instead been identified by indigenous groups as a primary source of the social dislocation provoking cultural change (cf. Muratorio 1984). In effect, Christianity is the problem, not the solution. In the 1980s missionaries have tried to lay a secular foundation for the consciousness of a wider social universe in pan-Indian movements that provide ideologies for understanding political and economic change as well as new conceptions of morality and person that must accompany such change. I suggest that in Amazonia the new cosmology of *comunidade*, or "community," represents this foundation.

My strategy here is to explore some of these issues in the context of one particular ethnographic case, specifically that of the Culina Indians. The Culina have been subject to the pressures of intercultural contact for a relatively short time, perhaps less than one hundred years, and to varying degrees within that period. Moreover, the Culina have been exposed to several varieties of missionary contact, and their reaction to each has been illuminatingly different. Here I consider how the Culina have responded to two different forms of missionization, one Catholic, the other Protestant. In view of the largely unsuccessful efforts of Catholic missionizing over nearly five hundred years, it may be useful to consider also the new forms of missionizing that are taking place. I must note, however, that the Culina had, at the time of my research, resisted conversion not only to Christianity but also to the ideology of *comunidade* that has become the focus of contemporary Catholic missionizing in Brazil. My consideration of failed conversion considers both the religious and the secular forms, which I believe the Culina understand to be fundamentally similar.

The failure to convert can be understood only in the context of the missionizing and evangelism that have confronted Amazonian Indians and in the social context of the conversion experience. Surely Robin Horton is correct when he notes that conversion is as much a response to expanded cultural and social interaction as it is to the efforts of missionaries; Islam or Christianity serves primarily as a "catalyst," giving a particular content to an otherwise independent process (Horton 1971:103–4). In Amazonia the missionary has often provided the most intensive intercultural contact and the new cosmology to bridge that interaction.

MISSIONIZING AMAZONIA

The history of missionary activity in Amazonia is too long and complex to detail adequately here, but I want to give some indication of the scope of proselytizing, if only to underscore its ineffectiveness. I have noted that the first Portuguese sailors to arrive in Brazil thought immediately of converting the Indians they met. Visitors, explorers, merchants, and soldiers for the next thirty years marveled at the Indians' apparent lack of knowledge of religion and law: "[they are] nothing more than brute beasts who are led by their sentiments alone" (Hemming 1978:14).[3] As the Portuguese and Spanish began to exploit the riches of the new continent, the "brute" Indians became first their partners in barter and exchange and soon thereafter their virtual slaves.

The arrival of the Jesuits in 1549 in Brazil—the first foreign country in which the newly formed society set up missions—threatened to halt the enslavement of Indians. The Jesuits were welcomed by the coastal Tupi-Guaraní groups, who sought refuge from brutal Portuguese and Spanish soldiers and merchants. The Jesuits created large mission settlements called *aldeias* ("villages"; *reducciones* in Spanish) in which thousands of Indians were brought to live and work under the rigorous and ascetic Jesuit rule. In the early years of the aldeias the Jesuits performed mass baptisms and wrote ecstatically of mass conversions of Indians to Christianity. The Jesuits soon discovered, however, that the conversions were superficial at best. Indians were happy to perform meaningless rituals in return for protection from the colonists, gifts from the missionaries, and the supernatural benefits of the powerful European shamans. As early as 1551 the Jesuits suspected that their successes were only apparent and sought new methods for conversion. They went so far as to send Indian boys to Portugal for intensive training; they were then dismayed when these boys quickly reverted to traditional tribal life after their return to Brazil. The Jesuits' response was a more concerted suppression of Indian culture; monogamy, the use of clothes, rejection of shamanism, and sedentariness represented at least an implicit understanding of the relationship between way of life and the discipline of religious belief.

The Jesuits' system of permanent aldeias, and their obsession with maintaining a high count of souls saved, ultimately proved fatal to the

Indians. In 1565 smallpox appeared in two aldeias. Of 60,000 Indians who had been baptized near Bahia between 1559 and 1583, only 300 remained by 1590, and the loss of lives in other areas was nearly as great. The Jesuits responded by restocking the aldeias, to maintain the conversion rate that justified their presence in the New World, which only continued to fuel epidemics and the starvation that followed. By the beginning of the seventeenth century and the end of the first waves of epidemics, the Jesuits faced attacks from colonists seeking Indian slaves. The Jesuit Antonio Ruíz de Montoya reported that in 1630 slave hunters from São Paulo began attacking the missions in the Guairá area of Paraguay, and within a few years they had killed or captured some 300,000 Guaraní; another 8,000 Guaraní died during the evacuation of eleven reducciones, as Montoya tried to lead the remaining population to safety (Métraux 1945:78; cf. Caraman 1974:57–68). By the time the Jesuits were expelled in 1767 they had inadvertently contributed to the complete destruction of the coastal Tupi peoples and had driven other Tupi-Guaraní peoples into the interior. They had converted virtually none of these Indians (see Marzal 1981, Kiemen 1954; Mörner 1965).

The Jesuit missions represent one of the most extensive efforts to convert indigenous peoples, and their impact on Amazonian Indians cannot be underestimated; even the contemporary distribution of groups throughout the Amazon Basin can be attributed, in part, to the activities of the Jesuits on the coast in the seventeenth century. Even the most sympathetic observers concede, however, that the Jesuits' impact on Tupi and Guaraní religion was short-lived. The most that apologists such as Rippy and Nelson (1936:356) can claim is that "if the padres succeeded in winning one generation of Indians from savage practices to a degree of civilization, they were a success for that generation." Nonetheless, as Schaden (1982:2) put it: "Above all, the fundamental character of [Guaraní] religion demonstrates particular resistance to contact with representatives of the Christian world."

During the hundred years following the expulsion of the Jesuits, no large-scale missionizing occurred in Amazonia, and the activities of rural priests in baptizing and "converting" local Indians failed to yield any more genuine conversions. Indeed, Hemming notes that in 1846 only two missionaries lived in the Brazilian province of Pará, which at that time included the whole of the Brazilian Amazon. The Italian Capuchins arrived among the Kraho Indians in central Brazil that year, to assist them in impeding the expansion of cattle ranching. By 1850 the Kraho had been decimated by disease, and when their priest, Friar Raphael, died in 1875, no mission priest was available to replace him. Missionizing among the Kraho had produced no converts; the provincial president commented of Friar Raphael that "making the Indians Christians seems to him a task beyond his capacity" (quoted in Hemming 1987:388).

A new wave of missionary activity began in 1870, when another group of Italian Capuchins arrived in the rubber territories where Indians were once again being enslaved by or forced to work for Peruvian, Bolivian, and Brazilian rubber tappers. Failing to establish missions in the Purus-Juruá area of what is now the Brazilian state of Acre, the Capuchins moved to the Uaupes and Rio Negro region northwest of the Amazon in 1880, where they also found the enslavement and exploitation of Indians. The Capuchins' efforts to suppress numerous aspects of traditional religious life among the Tukuna, Tariana, and Kobewa led to their expulsion by the Indians in 1884. The Capuchins were invited to the Putumayo region in northern Peru in 1893, an area made infamous twenty years later in Roger Casement's account of the brutal system of debt-peonage. Taussig (1987:313–14) quotes from a 1906 broadside from the region, in which the head of the mission laments the outcome of the Capuchins' efforts: "But when the most delightful hopes shone forth from the highest minister presaging that the light of the Evangelist was going to be diffused rapidly into these dens of savagery, unexpected events, civil wars, or political changes obliged the missionaries to leave, destroying in a few days the work of many years, leaving those wretches yet again enveloped in the darkness of infidelity. . . . Poor Indians, eternally savages."

A four-hundred-year-old pattern emerges from this summary account of attempts to convert Amazonian Indians. Catholic missionaries tended to move into areas in which Indians were already disputing with whites over land or were being enslaved for their labor. Even though the missions protected the Indians against the settlers, they contributed to the rapid spread of diseases against which the Indians had little immunity. Moreover, the disciplinary zealotry of missionaries led them to suppress traditional practices, particularly, shamanism and religious rituals. It is no surprise that many Indians equated baptism with death; if disease did not follow, cultural death would. Throughout this period, missionaries were welcomed by indigenous groups precisely to the extent that they did not proselytize. Pro-Indian groups in Brazil today actively promote this particular interpretation of colonial events. For example, a recent history of indigenous peoples, written ostensibly by Indians themselves and published by the Brazilian Conselho Indigenista Missionário, describes early missionaries as agents of "white" modes of life who brought measles, chicken pox, colds, and tuberculosis (CIMI 1986:124–27).[4]

In 1910 the Brazilian Indian Protection Service was created, and

Indians were no longer forced to accept Christianity or Brazilian culture. Since then, ironically, Protestant proselytizing has been more successful than four hundred years of Catholic efforts. The most extensive missionizing has been mounted by the Summer Institute of Linguistics (Hvalkof and Aaby 1981) and its institutional alter ego, the Wycliffe Bible Translators (Stoll 1982); other large Protestant groups in South America include the New Tribes Mission, the World Radio Missionary Fellowship, and the Gospel Missionary Union. Robinson (1981:43) identifies some thirty Protestant missionary groups in Ecuador alone. I should note that indigenous populations are not the only targets of Protestant proselytizing; Protestantism has gained converts among the traditionally Catholic "white" populations of Brazil and other Latin American countries, and in recent years the rate of conversion has accelerated. Willems (1967:249) describes the basis of Protestant conversion in Brazil and Chile in terms that would be agreeable to Horton: "The Catholic pantheon is predominantly local; the cult of saintly helpers is centered around local shrines and concerned with rural problems. Migration to cities and rural frontiers tends to alienate people from their local pantheons and the problems they have to face in their new environment call for different solutions." Ironically, efforts to protect Indian rights, and traditional Indian cultures, may have facilitated Protestant missionizing, because missionaries can proselytize among groups that are not, at the moment, struggling for their sheer existence. I consider the work of two of the principal missionary groups, the American Protestant Summer Institute of Linguistics and the Brazilian Catholic Conselho Indigenista Missionário, in my discussion of the Culina.[5]

CONVERSION, AVERSION, AND DIVERSION IN AMAZONIA

The Tupi and Guaraní Indian cases raise questions about the concept of conversion and point not only to historical changes in the concept but also to differences in how various world religions conceive of conversion. "Conversion" in its most usual sense seems to presume that religious beliefs and practices form an internally coherent and comprehensive whole that is appropriately acquired (if not always acquired) en bloc by converts. Moreover, religions, in this view, are preferentially exclusive; a person is Catholic or Muslim or Protestant but not some hybrid combination; "syncretic" religions are interesting precisely because they seem to violate these basic assumptions. Conversion in Nock's (1933) sense, as a subjective or phenomenological experience, appears to be a more recent notion, though it perhaps has always characterized the Protestant vision of conversion and has been adopted only to a lesser degree by Catholicism. Heirich's (1977) notion of conversion as a change in one's "sense of ultimate grounding" that goes beyond a simple change in beliefs is a logical extension of this essentially Protestant view.

Contemporary social science approaches to conversion consider at least two conceptually different kinds of religious change. Sociologists have, in recent years, turned to the study of individuals who convert to unorthodox, "new" religious movements (Snow and Machalek 1983; 1984). Within this paradigm conversion is an expression of individual deviance, and the cognitive dimensions of religious experience are embraced to the exclusion of the social and cultural contexts in which religious change takes place. This approach also makes an implicit assumption of relative social stability, within which religious conversion, particularly to heterodox beliefs or fringe religious groups, becomes deviant. The explanation of conversion is consequently not to be found in the social system that supports orthodox religious beliefs and groups but in the psychological makeup of the individuals who divert from orthodoxy (cf. Staples and Mauss 1987; Bankston, Forsyth, and Floyd, 1981).[6]

Anthropologists and historians, in contrast, have been interested in religious change as a dimension of broader social change, particularly as traditional, small-scale societies encounter and subsequently enter the contemporary spheres of global politics and economics. Anthropologists are heir to the sociology of religious change outlined by Weber and have proposed several neo-Weberian accounts of religious conversion among social groups. Geertz, for example, has adapted the Weberian notion that world religions provide a more "rationalized" framework for understanding the changes that accompany the entry of traditional societies into the broader world (Geertz 1973b). Horton's influential reworking of the Weberian view challenges the notion that world religions are inherently more rational than local, traditional religions and suggests instead that what we might think of as the cosmological geography of traditional religions is ultimately too limited: "The essence of the pre-modern situation is that most events affecting the life of the individual occur within the microcosm of the local community, and that this microcosm is to a considerable extent insulated from the macrocosm of the wider world" (Horton 1971:101). In Horton's view religious change—in particular, conversion to world religions—is less the direct result of missionizing than of social and political changes that demand an expanded cosmology and a revised morality. World religions are often available to meet this need and, indeed, are so termed not because they have adherents worldwide but because their cosmological geography encompasses heterogeneity on a global scale. If Horton's framework appears excessively "intellectualist," it has the virtue of locating these hypothetical cognitive dilemmas within contexts of social change. The possibility that his framework is inadequate is suggested, however, by its limited ethnographic scope; part of my argument here is that Horton's conditions for religious conversion have existed for centuries in lowland South America but substantial conversion has not taken place.

The ambiguities in the notion of conversion make it difficult to assess the claims of Europeans that they converted indigenous peoples in South America, and it is impossible to judge what indigenous peoples may have believed about their "conversion" in the first few centuries of European colonization. Todorov (1984) has noted that Columbus considered conversion to consist minimally or essentially of the performance of acts such as baptism or making the sign of the cross, that is, the performance of acts whose effectiveness is independent of the belief, will, or intention of the actor. Catholicism of the late fifteenth century offered a conceptual space for such rituals, one that could be filled by indigenous practices to produce syncretic forms and which presumably resonated with indigenous modes of knowledge and power. Columbus's belief that he converted Indians by teaching them to kneel during prayer was not naive in the context of his contemporary Catholicism. Indeed, accounts of Jesuit missions in southern Brazil and Paraguay until the expulsion of the Jesuits from South America—accounts detailing the conversion of thousands of Indians—must be evaluated in this light. Caraman (1974:24), for example, mentions the Guaraní family, who believed themselves to have been converted to Christianity when, as they entered a church, water fell from a rafter onto their heads in a charade of baptism.

The absence of detailed accounts of indigenous views of conversion among the Tupi and Guaraní further cautions against the application of Christian, and in particular Protestant, conceptions of conversion. There is little evidence to suggest that indigenous peoples shared missionary views of the exclusivity of religious affiliation (or, indeed, of the very notion of religious affiliation itself) or identity, except perhaps as a form of identity in a political-economic context. Jesuit accounts are replete, however, with evidence that Christian ritual forms were easily adopted and elements of Christian mythology were readily incorporated into the framework of traditional indigenous beliefs.[7] In the end it is difficult to judge what may have constituted Christianization apart from compliance with the rules of mission life, such as monogamy and the avoidance of fermented beverages, and submission to the authority of the mission.

In Amazonia, conversion to Christianity appears to have taken place primarily among individuals within small groups, not throughout whole villages or cultures. The Siriono, however, offer an interesting case of a group that conceives of itself as having converted to Protestantism on a larger scale. Stearman (1987) notes that the last remaining village of this Bolivian group, now totaling fewer than three hundred people, has been missionized by Protestant groups more or less continuously since the 1930s (cf. Holmberg 1950). Within the past thirty years missionaries of the Summer Institute of Linguistics (SIL) have pursued their characteristic strategy among the Siriono of translating the Bible through the assistance of young men who are removed from the village to assist in linguistic work. During their time away these men are also trained as teachers, and those who convert in this process are assigned to positions in the village school. Ultimately, such a strategy places SIL converts in positions of political and economic leadership in which they control access to medical care and education and serve as role models and "culture brokers" for other village members. SIL has had considerable success among the Siriono; the village considers itself *creyentes*, Protestant true believers surrounded by ignorant Catholic Bolivians.

As in most extended interethnic contacts in Amazonia, Siriono conceptions of self and morality were fundamentally shaken by intensive interaction with Bolivians. Here I cannot review the extensive social changes experienced by the Siriono in the twentieth century, but these include periods of endemic starvation brought about by marginalization along unproductive frontiers, a more recent shift from nomadism to settled horticulture in a region populated largely by Bolivians, and a dramatic loss of population, from an estimated three thousand in the mid-1940s to fewer than three hundred today. A profound demoralization of Siriono was reported by Holmberg in his 1950 monograph: the Siriono had all but given up hope of surviving as a culture.

Significantly, Protestantism, a high-status religion associated with the technological riches of North American missionaries, may be the source of a new and enhanced sense of self that, far from integrating the Siriono into a broader social system, actually strengthens the social and conceptual boundaries between them and local Bolivians (Stearman 1987:148). Their conversion is far from complete, however. Stearman (1987:118–19) notes that "Christianity seems to have layered over, rather than replaced" traditional religious beliefs, that Protestantism appears primarily in church on Sundays, and that Siriono do not question whether their two sets of religious belief might conflict. Siriono conversion, then, while providing a new sense of identity for an indigenous society threatened and enclaved by an encroaching Bolivian world, does not overtly contradict or replace traditional religious belief.

The Siriono are unusual but not unique in adopting Protestant identity as a means of strengthening social and cultural boundaries between themselves and non-Indians; Colson (1971) suggests that the same process is taking place among the Patamona Indians of the Guiana Highlands. An interesting and perhaps more common variation on this theme is illustrated by the Palikúr (Arnaud 1980). The single Brazilian village of Palikúr, with a population of about five hundred, converted almost en masse to Protestant Christianity beginning in 1967. The principal social change that seems to have accompanied this conversion was an increased level of work performed by members of the community. By 1978, however, only twenty members of the village retained their *crente* identity; it appears that Christianity simply failed to resonate effectively with the largely traditional forms of life retained in the village. In particular, there seems to have been no obvious benefit inherent in one of the major features of Protestant Christianity: its rather extreme control of forms of "body practice," including sexuality, consumption of tobacco and alcohol, and dress.

By contrast, the Central Brazilian Kraho have strongly rejected conversion, and their encounters with Protestant missionaries and local Catholic Brazilians have only revitalized a distinctly Kraho identity. Their contemporary aversion to Christianity contrasts with an earlier messianic, millenarian phase focused on an anticipation of spontaneous conversion to Christianity (discussed below). I noted that nineteenth-century Capuchin friars failed to produce conversions; Melatti (1967: 46–48) notes that Baptist missionaries now working among the Kraho have also failed to convert a single individual. Indeed, Kraho consider the adoption of Protestantism to require that they abandon valued aspects of their traditional life, among which they mention mythology, rituals, extramarital sexual liaisons, cattle stealing, nudity, log races, and alcohol and tobacco (Mellati 1967:129).

The Kraho recognize the difference between two varieties of *cristaos*: categorical non-Kraho who are *crentes* (Protestants) and *catolicos*. The latter are known to smoke, drink, carry guns, use obscene language, and engage in sexual infidelity. Sharing, at least in practice, aspects of a moral universe with these catolicos, Kraho now welcome Catholic baptism, not as a sign of conversion but as a means of creating ritual sponsors (i.e., godparents) among the Brazilians with whom they trade or for whom they work (Melatti 1967:130–31). Indeed, Melatti mentions cases in which wages paid by a ritual coparent have been doubled following the baptism of a child. It should be noted that this custom represents no radical shift in traditional Kraho social life: every individual is expected to have one or more ritual sponsors from whom one receives one's "social identity," which includes a category of names and ritual roles, as opposed to the "physical identity" deriving from one's parents (Melatti 1976).

The Kraho messianic movement coalesced for a period of about two months, probably in October and November 1951, in one particular village. A Kraho man, about thirty years old, began to hear voices and have visions and believed himself in contact with Tati, the Kraho spirit of rain and thunder. He took the name Jose Nogueira and described Tati as a "new man" with black hair, a large beard, and a rifle in his hand. Nogueira reported that Tati had come to punish Christians and to transform the Kraho into *civilizados*. Nogueira's brief movement had most of the features of the well-known Melanesian cargo cults: he ordered the construction of a large house to hold the goods he predicted were going to arrive, and a large corral was built to pen the cattle that were miraculously to appear.[8] Nogueira prohibited the eating of meat on one day of the week, in imitation of Catholic practice; forbade body painting; and traditional Kraho baskets were thrown out and replaced by Brazilian-style baskets. He promised that, on a night to be revealed to him by Tati, a large boat would arrive, loaded with manufactured goods. It appears that most of the younger members of his village, in addition to the mature men, participated in the messianic movement, accepting the idea of transformation into civilizados and the destruction of the "Christians."

Inevitably, the predicted miracles failed to occur, and the boats laden with manufactured goods never arrived. Nogueira blamed several successive failures on witchcraft by his enemies, but eventually his followers lost faith in his message and he was abandoned. Melatti found him in 1962 to be "suicidal"; by 1966 he had left the village. Nogueira was not the only sign of a propensity for messianism among the Kraho, however. After Nogueira's failure his wife's brother experienced similar visions and also urged the construction of a corral to hold cattle that would appear. His village members responded that if he could produce a single cow they would follow his every order. This attempt to revive Nogueira's movement was unsuccessful. Melatti notes that as late as March 1967 a shaman named Patrício Chiquinho revealed that he had received from God the power to kill Brazilians with rain, and he announced that an inundation would occur in February 1968, killing all the local Brazilians as well as those in Brasília and Rio de Janeiro.

The cases of the Siriono and the Kraho, despite their apparent differences, offer a similar insight. Both groups appear to have self-consciously engaged Christianity either as a source of cultural and social identity or as the identity of the "other" against which they identify themselves. Neither group has embraced Christianity as a means of resolving whatever hypothetical cosmological dilemmas may accompany intensive contact with the macrocosm of Christian—or at least Protestant—society.

Rather, and perhaps paradoxically, a world religion has been embraced as a means of preserving local, traditional identity and microcosmic social integrity in the midst of encroaching national societies.

Amazonian examples of explicit conversion and aversion to Christianity are relatively rare; it appears that indigenous groups, subjected first to Catholic and then more recently to Protestant missionaries, move between superficial acceptance of ritual forms, such as baptism and music, and sometimes violent rejection of efforts to suppress their traditional modes of life. The relationship between Indians and missionaries has had a kind of approach-avoidance quality, in which the benefits offered by missionaries are offset by their identification with the social forces that destroy indigenous life. Missionaries in Amazonia have commented on this frustration for centuries; the Christian message they teach is contradicted by the Brazilians with whom Indians interact and who are often explicitly identified as *crentes*, *católicos*, or *cristaos*. As I noted earlier, for many indigenous groups Christianity has long been regarded as the source of the problem, not as the solution.

Though Indians in Amazonia have not converted to Christianity on any appreciable scale, many Brazilians living in Amazonia have to an extent "diverted" to indigenous beliefs. The propensity of the Brazilian backwoodsmen called *caboclos* to adopt indigenous modes of life is not particularly remarkable; what is striking, however, is the rise of religious beliefs among these settlers that parallel the "low cosmology" forms of religion found among Indians. These include beliefs in local forest and river spirits and the frequent use of local Indian shamans for curing illness (cf. Moran 1974; Parker 1985). As Taussig (1987:386) commented, referring to the "apostolic excursion" of the Capuchin priest Father Gaspar de Pinell in 1926: "Poor old Gaspar! Could he have envisioned that now, many decades later, it would be the white colonists . . . who would be inculcating into their traditions what they held to be Indian magic and religion?" One might also mention the recent urban Brazilian trend of adopting various forms of Afro-Indian belief, including macumba and candomblé, the worship of deities and spirit powers derived from West African religions (e.g., Bastide 1960; Pollak-Eltz 1972; Brown 1986).

Shapiro (1987) comments on another form of religious diversion among Brazilians: the incorporation of Tupi cosmology into Catholic theology, or "the missionary as convert." As she notes, this identification with indigenous cosmology is not a strategy to gain the trust of Indians but constitutes a self-directed discourse (Shapiro 1987:136). I consider this phenomenon in my discussion of contemporary Catholic missionaries among the Culina.

THE CULINA

The Culina are an Arawak-speaking group, numbering between twenty-five hundred and three thousand individuals, who live in western Brazil and Peru. They are one of several Arawakan groups in this general region, having been pushed into the area, according to one account, by Tupi-Guaraní groups moving up the Amazon. Europeans knew of the Culina by rumor in the mid-nineteenth century; Chandless, who ascended the Juruá River in 1867, reported that other local Indians kept to one side of the river to avoid the dangerous Culina on the other. European contact with the Culina was not reported until about 1911, when Constant Tastevin, a Catholic missionary priest, collected a Culina word list during his extensive travels through the region (Rivet and Tastevin 1921:462–63). Tastevin noted, however, that the Culina had had contact with Brazilian rubber tappers at least as early as 1890, when the groups living near the Eru River fled to the south, to the Envira and Purus rivers; he mentioned the *aba madiha* (fish people) on the Purus in a paper published in 1938 (Rivet and Tastevin 1938:74).

By the time of Tastevin's travels some Culina were working for rubber tappers rather than fleeing from them. Braulino de Carvalho (1931:245) mentions Culina along the Gregório River, with a large group at the rubber camp (*seringal*) called Ituxi at the mouth of the river, where they maintained gardens for the camp and worked extracting latex from rubber trees. According to their own accounts, the Culina, particularly those groups living among the Juruá, have worked off and on for rubber tappers since that time. Indeed, in 1950 Schultz and Chiara (1955) found a group of Culina on the Purus who had been working for local rubber tappers long enough that they were reported to speak fairly good Portuguese.

The recent history of the Culina is linked closely to the rubber tappers. The Culina were originally deep forest dwellers; after initially fleeing from Brazilians, they were finally attracted to the riverbanks by the availability of metal tools, pots and pans, guns, and other manufactured products: formerly luxuries, ultimately necessities. The exchange of their labor for manufactured items created an economic dependence on rubber tappers that was threatened by the collapse of the Brazilian rubber industry when cheaper South Asian rubber became available on world markets. Since the 1920s the Culina on the Purus have been itinerants, moving from seringal to seringal and performing menial labor.

Although the Culina and other groups in the region do not appear to have been enslaved by nineteenth-century rubber tappers (cf. Taussig

1987), the desire for Western goods, and the intimate contact with Brazilians it required, proved fatal to many of them. In particular, introduced diseases decimated local populations; several groups have become extinct since the turn of the century. The Culina probably experienced a major measles epidemic as early as 1877, and as late as 1950 a similar epidemic on the Purus killed half of the Culina living in the village of Cupichaua, at the site of the current Cashinaua village called Fronteira (Schultz and Chiara 1955:183). Though the Culina have been spared the worst of violent attacks by Brazilians, the density of Brazilian and indigenous communities on the Juruá and Envira rivers has exhausted the game in the surrounding forests, and Indian villages have difficulty finding sufficient protein resources to support large populations.

Maronaua, the village in which I did research, sits on a bank of the upper Purus River near the Peruvian frontier and represents the southwestern-most expansion of Culina who fled from the exploitative rubber tappers of the late nineteenth century. The members of this village call themselves the *kurubu madiha* (the "kurubu" fish people); they are probably the descendants of the "fish people" mentioned by Tastevin on the Purus in the first decades of this century. They are certainly the remnants of the group encountered by Schultz and Chiara; the effect of the reported measles epidemic in 1950 is evident in a gap in the village population of anyone who would have been an infant at that time.

The older members of this group remember childhoods spent in forest villages, before contact with Brazilians, where they lived "without clothes or metal pots." Groups of families seeking work at the seringals moved to the rivers and established small villages near the rubber camps. These small groups moved up and down the local rivers for about thirty years, following the rubber camps that were disappearing as Brazilian rubber became less profitable. Maronaua has been their home only since the 1960s, when a Culina man named Codo and his family moved to the site. The current population coalesced in the early 1970s, when the Paulist priest from the town of Sena Madureira constructed a school house in the village.

The opportunity for education, and work at the nearby Seringal Sobral, attracted a number of families, particularly several of Codo's siblings and their families, who had not settled in any more or less permanent area since the 1950 epidemic, which they understood to be the result of powerful withchcraft. The promise of education was especially attractive to these Culina, who believed that education would enhance their ability to deal with Brazilians in the region. They were also familiar with the experience of Culina in the Peruvian village of San Bernardo, which had been essentially created by missionaries of the Summer Institute of Linguistics in the late 1940s. The San Bernardo SIL missionaries have had some success at teaching Spanish to Culina children and promoting literacy, and the Culina at Maronaua hoped for similar benefits. Moreover, the owner of the Seringal Sobral was considered a good "patron," who even used his plane to fly sick individuals to the state capital at Rio Branco for medical care. The Culina were working at Sobral as late as 1978; it was abandoned soon after (see Viveiros de Castro 1978:1–3).

At the time of my research in 1981–1982 the Culina at Maronaua numbered about 160, 30 of whom lived a short way downriver from the main village at the site of the abandoned Seringal Sobral. The village enjoyed a stable subsistence economy based on the familiar Amazonian pattern of slash-and-burn horticulture combined with hunting, fishing, and gathering. The forest surrounding Maronaua was relatively rich in game, and ample horticultural land ensured a varied and adequate diet. Members of the village had access to a small range of manufactured goods from itinerant Brazilian traders who plied the Purus River, supplying the small settlements of rubber tappers along the river. These traders usually stopped at Maronaua for meat or produce, though occasionally an individual Culina man might have a small ball of rubber to exchange as well. Traders charged very high prices for their wares, and Culina acquired manufactured goods only sporadically. Their close acquaintance with a variety of attractive but largely unattainable goods left Culina in something of a state of frustrated ambitions, a condition that both the National Indian Foundation (FUNAI) and the local Catholic mission (CIMI) were anxious to exploit in gaining the allegiance of the village.

The Culina at Maronaua are more isolated from non-Indians than their cousins some five days downriver at the village known as Santo Amaro, half a mile from a large, permanent Brazilian farm. Certainly they are more isolated than the Culina along the Juruá River to the north, where the Culina work for local Brazilian farmers, ranchers, and rubber tappers. Nonetheless, the Maronaua Culina have had nearly one hundred years of contact with non-Indians in which to broaden their cosmological horizons.

MISSIONARY ACTIVITY AMONG THE CULINA

During most of their residence at Maronaua, the Culina have been served by Catholic missionaries of the Brazilian Conselho Missionário Indigenista (CIMI). A succession of CIMI missionaries has staffed the school, conducting classes in reading and writing, providing medical care, and promoting *conscientização*, the "consciousness raising" designed to create a sense of pan-Indian history and identity (cf. Shapiro 1981:144; 1982:16). CIMI pursues no overtly evangelical goals among the Culina; it expresses an interest only in ensuring and defending the legitimate rights of indigenous groups to land, self-determination, and cultural integrity.

Although CIMI missionaries do not overtly proselytize, CIMI is nonetheless interested in the conversion of Indians (Altmann 1990). As Shapiro (1981:142) has noted, CIMI distinguishes between faith and religion; "faith" is a universal experience that can be channeled through various forms of "religion" as an institutional complex. The destruction of traditional culture is also the destruction of those institutional frameworks best suited to the experience of "faith" for any group. Consequently, CIMI missionaries have adopted the model of Christ's "hidden years" in Nazareth and expect to devote their own thirty years to *encarnação*, the "incarnation" of Indian culture, to experience it personally, as Indians do, so that the message they ultimately offer addresses the concerns of Indians and not those of the missionaries.

This version of a theology of liberation is not easily implemented. Among the Culina, CIMI has worked to achieve economic and political stability within villages, to insure that Culina are free to live in their traditional manner. Conversion is encouraged, not to a new religious cosmology, however, but to an elevated consciousness of the broader social forces that threaten Culina and Indians in general. I call this "conversion" in the sense that it demands that Indians adopt a new perspective on the social universe of which they are a part. They are encouraged to believe that they are a part of a wider social universe, a moral system they share with others and in which they can meaningfully participate. CIMI has tried to foster this perspective through the promotion of a pan-Indian identity summarized by the concept of *comunidade*, or "community."

The CIMI missionaries who work in this region (and among other indigenous groups, including the Cashinawa and Campa) have been singularly unsuccessful in rallying Culina behind either local economic projects or the pan-Indian movements promoted by CIMI at a national level. This failure parallels the historic failures of conversion, and to the extent that we can understand the Culina reluctance to convert to comunidade we might also understand the more general failure of religious conversion. In particular, I want to explore the suggestion that these Brazilian missionaries have attributed to Culina a notion of personhood "embedded" in comunidade, a conception that rests on a Western articulation of such critical dimensions of person and identity as individualism versus communalism and cooperation versus conflict. Indeed, these Brazilian missionaries are struggling with challenges to their own ideology of personhood, one reflecting the essential tension between individualism and collectivism and another their awareness of their own "embeddedness" in a repressive social order. This ideology is carried over into their work with the Culina, but within the promotion of a benign, utopian communalism. The sense of *person* that emerges from and is implicit within the activities of the missionaries fails to resonate with the Culina, leading to the ultimate failure (or irrelevance) of projects whose goals the Culina nonetheless value and embrace. It is also worth noting, if only parenthetically, that CIMI missionaries appealed to various anthropological writings to legitimate their beliefs about indigenous life; these works reinforce missionary fantasies about indigenous life because they too diminish the social salience of individuals.

I noted earlier that one aspect of the debate over conversion is the nature of the relationship between social life and religious cosmology. I assume here that social practices and cultural meanings are dialectically interconnected and that notions of person and identity emerge from and in turn inform practice. (This interdependence of social formations, practice, and personhood is nicely illustrated by, for example, Foucault's (1977) demonstration of the reciprocity between the historical emergence of individualism and the growth of prisons.) Any adequate account of personhood and identity must therefore be attentive to the dialectic of structure and process at times of social and cultural transformation and of the articulation of social and individual levels of agency. To this end I consider the ways in which Culina persons emerge in processes of "signifying practice" (Comaroff 1985:6).

As I mentioned above, CIMI missionaries have initiated several projects among the Culina, all of which have so far failed to stimulate interest or villagewide support. These have included economic schemes such as a rubber-tapping cooperative and the introduction of a cow and a bull into the village. They have also tried to create a wider sense of "Indian" identity by engaging Culina in indigenous movements on a larger, national scale. I consider two of the projects here: the rubber-tapping cooperative and the promotion of literacy.

The rubber-tapping cooperative is instructive of an unsuccessful economic project. Rubber collected by villagers was to be first aggregated and then sold in a single sale in the town of Sena Madureira, where the best local price for rubber could be obtained. For the only sale that the cooperative made, village members gathered about two hundred kilos of rubber. The CIMI missionary couple resident in the village managed the process: they purchased goods with the income from the rubber and maintained the account books in which each man's contribution was noted. The villagers collectively decided what to have the missionaries purchase with the income from the rubber. In Sena the missionaries purchased a large quantity of goods, including such valued items as ammunition, cloth, kerosene, salt, and sugar, and back in Maronaua they distributed these goods to the village men in proportion to the amount of rubber each man had contributed.

The rubber cooperative was driven primarily by the missionaries' own zeal. They harangued the village almost daily about the benefits of cooperating within a "community," in particular of providing for the collective welfare through productive labor. The missionaries reported to me a familiar set of beliefs about and stereotypes of indigenous people: selflessly communal, practicing the virtues of egalitarian pragmatism; and harmonious and gentle, a view disturbingly reminiscent of Cabral's first impressions ("good and of pure simplicity") in 1500 and common in much of the nineteenth-century literature produced by critics of the brutal system of debt-peonage under which Indians worked in the rubber boom (Taussig 1987). The missionaries felt that the rubber collective simply operationalized this "naturally" Culina ethos.

After the first sale, however, the Culina resisted any further participation in the collective and complained about the distribution of the goods that were purchased. The principal headman of the village, in particular, felt that missionary control of distribution undercut his traditional role as guarantor of village welfare. Moreover, one young man had refused to participate from the outset. Because he was extraordinarily productive in rubber tapping, he earned a personal fortune by local standards. He also retained control over the disposition of his earnings, thereby eliciting bitter resentment from other village residents. His example encouraged every other man in the village to quit the collective.

Several points emerge from this example. First, although the rubber collective and other economic projects may have failed in part because they did not reproduce local economic structures, they also failed because they were ultimately insensitive to the Culina notions of agency, responsibility, and morality that constitute their view of persons and are implicit in traditional economic practices, but which conflicted with the new forms of economic practice. Initially, however, Culina had agreed to the rubber collective because it appeared to conform generally to their own economic practices and certainly promised outcomes of value to village members.

Ultimately, however, CIMI's approach to the rubber collective violated Culina views of sociability. Despite the apparent radicalism of CIMI, these Brazilian missionaries were caught within an ideology of social relations mediated by commodities and of individualism emerging from types of economic production shaped also by a pervasive bureaucratic rationality. This ideology was expressed implicitly in the allocation of goods according to the contribution of each participant and in the distribution of goods only to participants who needed them. The power to draw from the store of goods was related to individual productivity, reflecting a structure of individuation that acquires moral dimensions in a surplus economy. The Culina, by contrast, were more likely to imbue the goods with social affect, to consider the entire store of goods a powerful symbol of village sociality to which all village members should equally have access and which distinguished their village from others; "individuals" did not emerge from their traditional social structure. It was not especially important that everyone had contributed, or how much they had contributed, but rather that everyone should benefit.

By contrast, the set of missionary practices implied that the production of commodities was the principal measure of a form of sociability toward a community, which an individual, understood in the Brazilian-Western sense, enters into as an act of moral judgment. The error was perhaps less in the organization of economic activities according to the wrong set of rules than in the initial, hidden assumption that economic productivity is the primary practical arena of agency, responsibility, and morality in which persons and identity are constituted, an assumption that accords with most Western cultures but is, as yet, an uncomfortable if not foreign one to the Culina.

The example of the young man who refused to cooperate in the rubber-tapping collective adds an additional dimension to Culina notions of person and property. (His refusal to participate also underscores the fact that the collective lacked the kind of "corporate" structure that could enforce its own rules. In this respect only the collective replicated the normal structure of Culina political life, in which participation in group activities is encouraged rather than coerced and in which headmen lead through personal power and charisma rather than through bureaucratically supported authority.) This young man, whom I will call Akwo, had also essentially violated the same norms of production and consumption that the missionaries' rubber collective had violated. Unlike the missionaries, however, Akwo did so in a way that was consistent with the basic terms of the system. He was already something of a renegade in the traditional moral economy of Culina life. In brief, Akwo and his wife lived with his father, contravening the Culina custom of uxorilocal postmarital residence that gives a wife's parents access to the economic productivity of the husband. The Culina expect that the head of a household will control the use and distribution of the economic products of the household's members. This expectation parallels the assumption that, at the broadest social level, the village headman is the "owner" of the economic product of the village as a whole, a privilege that also carries the burden of providing if necessary for the economic welfare of all village members. Akwo's father did not end up the principal beneficiary of Akwo's economic productivity, however; in practice the conflicting expectations pitting the rights of a household head against those of a father-in-law left Akwo free to enjoy his economic output himself. For the Culina the social and moral principle at issue was that Akwo's father-in-law was denied the right to control the products of Akwo's work.

In the missionary-run rubber collective the Culina were expected to turn over control of the allocation and distribution of economic goods to the missionaries. The missionaries believed themselves to be simply managers of a system that conformed to traditional Culina economic practice, but the Culina understood the missionaries to be usurping the role legitimately belonging to the village headman. Akwo's refusal to participate in the collective was an open rejection of the missionaries' implicit and unintended claim to this role, but this time his rebellion was legitimate, and other men followed suit.

The closest Culina analogue to the missionary rubber cooperative might be the collective hunting that takes place almost every day during the rainy season (Rüf 1972). Ideally every man in the village participates in the hunt, and even if men become separated during the day they return to the village as a single group. There they deposit their game in a single pile in front of their assembled wives, who distribute the meat among the various households. Moreover, before arriving in the village, the men also divide the meat among themselves so that every man can make a contribution to the whole.

In such a system the output of labor is not in the form of commodities, "productivity" is not a critical aspect of moral discourse, and relations of production and consumption are not individualizing in our Western sense. Rather, proper personhood entails, for example, the provision of appropriate substances within a system of production and consumption ordered by the symbolic properties of such paradigmatic sets as meat and vegetables, male and female, and wild and sociable (Pollock 1985). Where the Culina are concerned with the symbolic qualities of consumables, the CIMI missionaries are concerned with the practical quantity of producibles. (Culina have adopted the Portuguese term *trabalho* for "work," the normal productive activity of men and women not being "work" in any traditional sense.)

CIMI's efforts to ensure the economic viability of the village are complemented by an education program, especially to encourage literacy.

Literacy, it is proposed, would serve comunidade by linking dispersed Culina villages; CIMI imagined a network of correspondence, newsletters, and even newspapers in the Culina language that would forge a sense of collective participation and pan-Culina identity.[9] The husband of the missionary couple taught reading and writing to the village men, after which his wife gave classes to the village women. The missionaries held classes more or less every day during the dry season, at those times when they both were in the village. At the Culina request only adults participated in the classes.

The potential success of the literacy program was compromised by several factors. First, classes were held irregularly, and lessons could not be reinforced continuously by daily practice. Second (and here I do not speak with any educational authority), it appeared that adults did not learn as rapidly as children might, a judgment that I base in part on the relative success of the literacy program managed by the Summer Institute of Linguistics in the Peruvian Culina village of San Bernardo.[10] Third, the essential functions of literacy were unclear to the Culina. Intervillage communication through written letters was a novelty, but its value was reduced by the political tensions that normally characterize intervillage relations. In one memorable instance the only genuinely literate adult man (who had been taught by SIL missionaries in Peru as a child) destroyed a letter en route to another village rather than bear the politically inflammatory news it contained. By the time of my departure none of the adult villagers had acquired more than a rudimentary sense of the concept of reading and writing; instead they found it easier by far to memorize lessons that could be recited.

The struggle to teach Culina to read and write may have been all the harder for acquiescing to the Culina's own views of how they should learn. Unlike the rubber cooperative and other economic projects, which tended to fail because they did not conform to traditional Culina practices, the education program seemed destined to fail precisely because it *did* conform to those practices. This should not be surprising; reading and writing are not easy concepts for a preliterate community and even "ethnoeducational" practice is not likely to be effective in accomplishing a radically new task.

Perhaps more fundamentally, however, written communication is unable to convey the richer meanings available in oral communication, especially in oratorical forms of speech. For the Culina, verbal performance is a principal dimension of the expression of identity. The acquisition of personhood by infants is gauged by their increasing comprehension of language and by their ability to produce proper speech. Like many other indigenous societies in South America, the Culina distinguish among verbal styles, and the ability to produce them constitutes a measure of one's agency; for example, the great degree of social power attributed to headmen derives precisely from their compelling forms of speech, which other village members "hear and obey." At the extreme, the special songs of shamans, inducing spirits to cure illness, are maximally directive verbal displays.

The dramatic, even theatrical verbal performance of a headman or prominent adult male, the songs of shamans, and the shy, hesitant, stumbling speeches of young men making their first public addresses do not translate well into written form. The few letters that did arrive from other villages had an anemic quality and often contained simple recitations of a village census or the game shot on a hunt, as though their authors realized that this impoverished method of communication was appropriate only for lists. Although the headman of my own village asked me to transcribe a number of letters for him, he vastly preferred to send (and receive) audio tapes that could more accurately capture the subtleties of speech.

Culina villages are distinguished by dialect variations, as are their members as kinds of persons, and language is said to be the focal difference between Culina and other indigenous groups. Culina thus become distinctly uncomfortable in multiethnic or pan-Indian contexts, in which they have a sharp sense of their own isolation from levels of meaning being shared by others. For CIMI the Culina presence in national pan-Indian settings is a form of symbolic power, but for the Culina in these settings an inability to speak and understand either Portuguese or other indigenous languages is a form of impotence, a kind of infantilization that strips them, in their own terms, of personhood. The broader community in which CIMI has tried to enroll Culina is one in which they lack precisely the dimension of agency that would qualify them to engage that community as persons.

Verbal facility is a primary means of individuation among Culina. Each member of the village has attributed to him or her the basic performative competence appropriate to age, gender, and marital status, but beyond this, individuals are known to be more or less adept at more sophisticated speech styles as well. Indeed, it might be said that economic or productive activities tend to be collectivizing, but verbal performances tend to be individualizing. This is almost completely the inverse of the meanings inherent in these practices for the Brazilian missionaries; for them, literacy as a basic skill is shared in more or less equal degree by all literate people, but economic productivity individuates members of social groups. The program of literacy education was, consequently, intended to promote the communalism of comunidade, in which a "people" (*um povo*) would have their collective identity reified and expressed in various written forms: newsletters, contracts, government documents. As a set of discursive practices these written forms submerged the individuating potential that was highly valued by Culina in their own speech practices.

Missionary fantasies of a primitive communal utopia are already familiar to us through the writings of the earliest Europeans to reach the coast of Brazil. It is significant that these sixteenth- and seventeenth-century images of South American Indians were, at that time, a powerful counterpoint to and critique of the implanted political-economic orders, some of which would soon collapse under popular revolutions. CIMI's images of indigenous life, likewise, are responding to an implicit appreciation of a paradox inherent in their beliefs about their own, and hierarchical, social system, in which individual action is enjoined to continually reproduce a repressive social order that individuals are nonetheless powerless to transform.

I referred to this conception as one of "embeddedness," referring to an individual in the familiar Western sense, but one whose capacity for agency is constrained by membership in a social group. Inevitably, CIMI impressed this conception of embedded identity onto indigenous societies, explicitly through a fantasy of selfless communalism that could be harnessed to the goals of comunidade, implicitly through the signifying practices of economic and educational projects.

CIMI regularly appealed to anthropological writings to legitimate its conception of indigenous society, to imbue it with a supposed objectivity. Undoubtedly the most commonly cited work is Betty Meggers's *Amazonia* (1971). This study combines several assumptions, both explicit and implicit, that reinforced fundamental missionary views. For example, Meggers's paradigm is that of evolutionary biology, and her principal theme is adaptation to ecological constraints. Missionaries perceived this theme in the moral discourse of indigenous life shaped by a balanced, harmonious relationship to the environment, a reflection of the innate and marvelous wisdom possessed by Indians in their "natural" habitat. The subtitle of the Brazilian version of the book (Meggers 1977) seems to certify the CIMI interpretation: *Um Paraiso Perdido*, a "lost paradise," lost through the destructive force of Brazilian expansion and the technological order of civilized life. (Meggers was not so certain in her original subtitle, "Man and Culture in a *Counterfeit* Paradise" [my emphasis].) Moreover, Meggers stresses the theme of cooperative utilization of resources by indigenous peoples, a theme that resonates with missionary exaggerations of communalism and with misplaced Western notions of rationality. Among the other works regularly cited by CIMI for their scientific authority are those minor classics of Amazonian cultural ecology that attribute food taboos or hunting-gathering patterns to the (unconscious?) calculation of protein resource availability and environmental carrying capacity (e.g., Gross 1975; Ross 1978). Such conceptions deny indigenous peoples various forms of agency and leave them responding instead to the essentially instinctive behavioral imperatives of animals.

Although the Culina have passively resisted CIMI efforts to instill a pan-Indian consciousness, to develop in them a sense of identity as "Indians" in opposition to non-Indian Brazilians, they have, ironically, already accommodated themselves in one sense to the structure of local Brazilian society. For the Culina are quite convinced that Brazilians are persons—though the reverse is not always true—and thus feel compelled to locate themselves somehow within the broader social universe represented by their relations with local Brazilians. In this context Culina refer to themselves as *caboclos*, or "backwoodsmen," a telling, if technically inaccurate, use of the term that expresses their relative lack of agency within this wider context. If CIMI has failed to convert Culina to the ideology of comunidade, it may also be because Culina have already begun to identify with this broader and more heterogeneous social universe, one in which they already interact as relatively powerless agents.

The Protestant Summer Institute of Linguistics has been the most active missionary group among the Culina, having established the village called San Bernardo on the Purus River in Peru during the late 1940s.[11] Early on SIL created a school at San Bernardo in which Culina children have been taught to read and write (at times under contract from the Peruvian government) and in which they received the basic teachings of fundamentalist Protestantism. The promise of education was a powerful attraction for the Culina in Peru, and the village is now a large one of some three hundred people. Because SIL has brought together Culina from a number of subgroups, the village has little of the cohesion found in smaller, socially more homogeneous villages, which has to some extent helped the missionaries to create new forms of social solidarity.

The SIL strategy at San Bernardo appears similar to that pursued in other areas of Amazonia. As with the Siriono, this strategy consists of removing literate young men to SIL headquarters at Yarinacocha, Peru, where they receive training as bilingual teachers and are encouraged to convert to Christianity. They return to San Bernardo to form classes and to turn classes into congregations (cf. Stoll 1982:99–100). SIL normally hopes that such young men will ultimately become village leaders and thereby even more powerful agents of religious conversion. Bilingual

Culina are also taken to Yarinacocha to assist in translating the Bible; at the time of my research several books of the Bible had been published in the Culina language.

Not surprisingly, the SIL system profoundly changes Culina life. The primary organizing structure of SIL village activity is shaped by its ideology of Western market capitalism and the emergence of individual identity through economic production. CIMI missionaries were unsuccessful in enrolling Culina in economic cooperatives that were based on implicit individualizing practices and succumbed to Culina refusal to participate in such schemes. SIL has been more successful in imposing a market economy on the Culina at San Bernardo by introducing trade goods at reduced prices. The Culina there came to rely on these goods, and SIL quickly won them over by creating opportunities for cash labor and for the sale of produce. The system appears to have succeeded in part because of the economic infrastructure maintained by the missionaries, but also because it has been flexible enough to allow for the kind of communal sharing of resources and income that characterizes normal Culina life. For example, by serving essentially as merchants whose manufactured products are available for sale to village members, SIL missionaries have not usurped the roles of village leaders, who remain free to organize the distribution of goods purchased from the missionaries. The hallmark of the CIMI rubber-tapping collective was an accounting system that contradicted traditional Culina assumptions about the moral implications of distribution; the concerns of the SIL system are, first, to create opportunities for the accumulation of surplus wealth and, second, to provide access to a market in which this surplus can be exchanged for manufactured goods.

The system has not been a complete success, however. First, SIL established a dispensary for medications and trained a nurse to provide basic medical care, which must be purchased like any other commodity. The problems presented by the sale and purchase of medical care are not unrelated to SIL suppression of traditional Culina religious activities. At the least the missionaries have interpreted Culina cosmology in a Christian idiom: for example, the Culina spirit Kira, traditionally believed to be a "culture hero" from the mythological past who long ago retired to his village in the sky, has been identified with the Christian God, but the *tokorime* spirits with whom shamans interact have been identified with Satan. The latter identification has posed a serious problem for village members. Traditionally, all adult Culina men were shamans, and they had important roles in protecting the village from witchcraft and in curing the illness that results from witchcraft. Because so many illnesses are considered to be caused by witchcraft, the suppression of public shamanistic activity has forced these Culina to perform curing rituals at night, deep in the jungle, or on the river far from the main village. More seriously, the SIL insistence that medical care be bought and sold contravenes a fundamental principle of sociability that defines the curing of illness as a particularly valued expression of kinship obligations. Indeed, a number of individuals who believed themselves to be the victims of witchcraft came from San Bernardo to Maronaua, calling upon extensive kin ties to obtain treatment by traditional shamans.

Conversion of the San Bernardo Culina to Christianity has been slow; several individuals identified themselves to me as creyentes, but they complained that almost none of their village members shared this faith. My impression is that they are less converted, so to speak, than the Sirionо; many do not even maintain the pretense of participating in Christian rituals. The unconverted Culina from the village expressed the greatest ambivalence about their ability to maintain the obligations of "siblingship" in the face of their expanding market economy and the suppression of their traditional religious beliefs. Participation in the market economy ultimately means entering the local social system as peasants. These Culina recognized that embedded within this new economic system were new moral imperatives that they could not adopt without threatening their traditional identities. Christianity offered a powerful and compelling source of legitimation of the new conceptions of identity that were emerging in a wider context, but the promise of conversion was entry into the lowest levels of the local social system, not unlike the Culina at Maronaua, who unwittingly used the ironic term "caboclo" as a synonym for Indian.

SIL left Peru during my research, and many of the effects of the social changes SIL missionaries produced did not persist after their departure. It appears fairly certain that there were insufficient converts within the village to maintain any continued, indigenous efforts to proselytize. Indeed, one of the village's most prominent converts, a literate man who worked as the nurse, acquired a second wife, scandalizing even the polygamous Culina by marrying his first wife's mother.

CONVERSION AND COMUNIDADE

Coversion to Christianity has no doubt taken place among the Amazonian Indians, but there is not enough information about the cases in which it may have occurred to adequately understand how it has taken place. On the contrary, while missionaries have probably exaggerated their success in converting, anthropologists studying indigenous groups have usually ignored the signs of conversion that would challenge or compromise the exotic images that finally appear in our accounts.

Nonetheless, conversion has been rare enough in Amazonia that its general absence deserves comment. I have suggested that, if new forms of intercultural contact provide the context for conversion, one factor historically inhibiting this option was precisely the nature of Indian contacts with Western peoples. Specifically, when it was identified with death from epidemics, with enslavement and forced labor, and with the suppression of traditional ways of life, Christianity did not present itself as an attractive source of new identity. In this regard we may note the frequency with which Indians identify Brazilians or Bolivians as cristaos, creyentes, or catolicos, recognizing, at least implicitly, that religious ideologies do constitute the frameworks of identity. Messianic movements express the ambivalence toward Christianity, in promising to destroy Christians at the same time that they create Christians of Indians.

The more recent efforts of Brazilian Catholic missionaries explicitly recognize this ambivalence in Christianity and substitute the concept of "community." The notion of comunidade is the structural equivalent of "macrocosm," the expanded social universe that world religions order for the converted. It is in this sense that I have suggested that CIMI has promoted conversion to comunidade, because comunidade incorporates new conceptions of self and identity and new moral imperatives among Indians.

The experience of the Culina with CIMI's comunidade should not be generalized to other indigenous groups. As with any other notion of conversion, various groups have embraced the concept in varying degrees; Mario Juruna, for example, a Kayapo Indian headman, has even represented Brazilian Indians at the Bertrand Russell War Crimes Tribunal in Stockholm. Rather, the experience of the Culina underscores Hefner's comment on world religions that "they cannot assume the same depth of shared experience reflexively verified in the day-to-day interactions of a small scale society" (1987:75). Comunidade is an abstraction that transcends the particular circumstances of local groups. Remaining relatively isolated, the Culina at Maronaua find the abstract quality of comunidade largely irrelevant to the conduct of their lives, and missionary efforts to enroll Culina in various economic and educational activities have failed to anchor those activities in the concrete modes of signifying practice that resonate with a meaningful discourse on identity and morality.

The Protestant SIL strategy has been different and in a sense has attempted to duplicate the history of European Protestantism on a smaller scale, to provoke the kind of social change for which Protestant Christianity provides the rationalizing ideology. This strategy is almost the complete inverse of that of CIMI. While CIMI promoted what it believed to be forms of economic communalism, SIL promoted individual participation in a surplus, market economy. Where CIMI saw literacy as a means of linking dispersed Culina groups in a grand network that forged a sense of being *madiha* ("Culina," rather than distinct kinds of persons in distinct villages), SIL saw literacy as a means to deliver the Word of God to individuals, in effect to extinguish their Indian identity. By initiating intentional social change, SIL missionaries may have been better social engineers. Certainly by the time of their expulsion from Peru in the early 1980s they had succeeded in converting more Culina at San Bernardo to Christianity than CIMI had converted Culina at Maronaua to comunidade.

Ultimately, both Culina villages will be enrolled in the wider social universe of encroaching Brazilian and Peruvian societies. Although CIMI has attempted to forestall this integration by promoting the isolation of the Culina in a demarcated territory, I do not believe that the Culina will give up Brazilian manufactured goods, and their isolation from other groups may lead them to participate more deeply in the national society before they will be able to assess the benefits of the comunidade movement. And although SIL has promoted just that kind of participation in the national society, the Culina at San Bernardo may not be integrated deeply enough in the wider social system to maintain their interaction without SIL assistance. Christianity might provide the ideological foundation for such participation, but with the Culinas' option of retreating into relative isolation widespread conversion is unlikely to take place.

NOTES

1. Cabral's letter, and Columbus's experiences earlier, raises the point that what constitutes "conversion" may depend upon contemporary understandings of the nature of religion. Todorov (1984) comments on the fifteenth-century assumption that merely performing the rituals of Catholicism, such as uttering prayers and crossing oneself, constituted conversion, and identifies Cortés as the first European in the New World to consider "belief" an element of religious adherence.

2. Limitation of the scope of this essay to Amazonia is not entirely arbitrary. At the time of the conquest the indigenous societies of the South American highlands and Andes, and areas of Mexico and Central America, tended to be seden-

tary, and were subject to the political and economic control of powerful centralized states, such as the Maya, Aztec, and Inca. Religious conversion among these groups, and the well-known forms of "syncretic" Catholicism it has produced, was part of a broader process of subjugation beyond the scope of this essay. It should be noted, however, that various Central American groups, small-scale shifting horticulturalists, were not "conquered" and remain for the most part unconverted to Christianity. At the same time, I do not wish to exaggerate the "aversion" of Amazonian Indians to various forms of Christianity. At least one group, the Terena, appears to have converted to Catholicism, retaining few, if any, traditional features of religious life; indeed, Terena have been among the most modernized of Amazonian Indians, even participating in regional and national political systems since at least 1846. Cardoso de Oliveira (1976) addresses the interesting problem of how a group maintains a distinctive sense of identity with such intensive integration into national society, but his discussion of Terena religion—Catholic or otherwise—is too brief to be used as a detailed example.

3. I draw upon Hemming's (1978; 1987) two extremely detailed accounts of the history of Brazilian Indians.

4. This history indicts the motives of most Europeans in the New World but, perhaps not surprisingly, exempts early missionaries from the strongest condemnation. Those missionaries are presented as well meaning, though misguided.

5. Wallis (1960) provides a representative account of the work in Ecuador by missionaries from the Summer Institute of Linguistics. She identifies the Indian in her account as "Aucas," however, apparently without realizing that this is a derogatory Quichua term for "non-Quichua" (see Taussig 1987:97ff.). Lewis (1988) presents a popular, critical account of American Protestant missionaries in South America.

6. A more radical critique of this literature might note that most religious beliefs and groups support the status quo. By considering individual forms of conversion to be "deviance," this literature also implicitly supports that status quo.

7. Sullivan (1988:19) approvingly cites Figueiredo's extreme view that indigenous, European, and African cultural elements have blended seamlessly into a single religion (Figueiredo 1975:183). Although the claim may be true only of a few particular indigenous cultures, it is probably also true that numerous Amazonian Indians have adopted—and later shed—Christian religious notions.

8. Information on the Kraho messianic movement is drawn from Melatti (1972). He states that such "cargo cults" have appeared in only two groups in Amazonia, the Kraho and the Tukuna of the Northwest Amazon region (Melatti 1972:80), though messianic movements are more common (cf. Clastres 1975; Métraux 1967:12–41; Regan 1988).

9. CIMI actually employs the Culina autodenomination *madiha*, which can be glossed at various levels of contrast as "person" (versus nonpersons), "Culina" (versus other Indians), or "human" (versus nonhumans).

10. SIL missionaries have produced a number of publications to assist in literacy training and have translated several books of the Bible into the Culina language. At the time of my research CIMI was compiling its own pamphlet for literacy training, which incorporated strong political messages promoting Culina land rights.

11. Although I have not visited San Bernardo, I have interviewed numerous members of the village. The reports of the Culina from the village are consistent with accounts of SIL work in other areas (Stoll 1982; Hvalkof and Aaby 1981). I should note also that the American-based New Tribes Mission, a Protestant group, has been working with the Culina in the village of Piau on the Juruá River since 1969; however, I have no reliable information on their work.

REFERENCES

Altmann, Lori. 1990. *Convivência e solidaridade: Uma experiência pastoral entre os Kulina (Madija)*. Cuiaba: Grupo de Trabalho Missionário Evangélico.

Arnaud, E. 1980. "O Protestantismo entre os Indios Palikúr do Rio Urucauá (Oiapoque, Brasil)." *Revista de antropologia* 23:99–102.

Balée, William. 1984. "The Ecology of Ancient Tupi Warfare." In Brian Ferguson, ed., *Warfare, Culture, and Environment*, pp. 241–65. New York: Academic Press.

Bankston, W. B., C. J. Forsyth, and H. H. Floyd. 1981. "Toward a General Model of Radical Conversion: An Interactionist Perspective on the Transformation of Self-Identity." *Qualitative Sociology* 4:279–97.

Bastide, Roger. 1960. *Les religions afro-brésiliennes*. Paris: Presses Universitaires de France.

Bonilla, V. D. 1972. *Servants of God or Masters of Men?* New York: Penguin Books.

Braulino de Carvalho, J. 1931. "Breve Notícia sobre os Indígenas que Habitam a Fronteira do Brasil com Peru." *Boletim do Museu Nacional* 7:225–56.

Brown, D. G. 1986. *Umbanda Religion and Politics in Urban Brazil*. Ann Arbor: UMI Research Press.

Caraman, Philip. 1974. *The Lost Paradise: The Jesuit Republic in South America*. New York: Seabury Press.

Cardoso de Oliveira, R. 1976. *Do Indio ao bugre: O processo de assimilação dos Terêna*. Rio de Janeiro: Francisco Alves.

Centro Ecumênico de Documentação e Informações (CEDI). 1981 *Povos indígenas no Brasil 5: Javari*. São Paulo: CEDI.

Chandless, William. 1869. "Notes on a Journey up the River Juruá." *Journal of the Royal Geographical Society* 36:86–118.

CIMI (Conselho Indigenista Missionário). 1986. *História dos povos indígenas: 500 anos de luta no Brasil*. Petrópolis: Editora Vozes.

Clastres, H. 1975. *La terre sans mal: Le prophétisme tupi-guarani*. Paris: Editions du Seuil.

Colson, A. B. 1971. "Hallelujah among the Patamona Indians." *Antropologica* 28:25–58.

Comaroff, Jean. 1985. *Body of Power, Spirit of Resistance: The Culture and History of a South African People*. Chicago: University of Chicago Press.

Duviols, Pierre. 1977. *La destruccion de las religiones andianas*. Mexico City: Universidad Nacional Autonoma de Mexico.

Figueiredo, Napoleão. 1975. "Religiões mediúnicas na Amazônia: O batuque." *Journal of Latin American Lore* 1:173–84.

Foucault, Michel. 1977. *Discipline and Punish: The Birth of the Prison*. New York: Pantheon.

Galvão, E. 1979. *Encontro de sociedades*. Rio de Janeiro: Editora Paz e Terra.

Geertz, Clifford. 1973a. "Person, Time, and Conduct in Bali." In C. Geertz, *The Interpretation of Cultures*, pp. 360–411. New York: Basic Books.

———. 1973b. "'Internal Conversion' in Contemporary Bali." In C. Geertz, *The Interpretation of Cultures*, pp. 170–89. New York: Basic Books.

Gross, Daniel. 1975. "Protein Capture and Cultural Development in the Amazon Basin." *American Anthropologist* 77:526–49.

Hefner, Robert. 1987. "The Political Economy of Islamic Conversion in Modern East Java." In W. R Roff, ed., *Islam and the Political Economy of Meaning*, pp. 53–78. London: Croom Helm.

Heirich, M. 1977. "Change of Heart: A Test of Some Widely Held Theories about Religious Conversion." *American Journal of Sociology* 83:653–80.

Hemming, John. 1978. *Red Gold: The Conquest of the Brazilian Indians, 1500–1760*. Cambridge: Harvard University Press.

———. 1987. *Amazon Frontier: The Defeat of the Brazilian Indians*. London: Macmillan.

Holmberg, A. 1950. *Nomads of the Long Bow: The Sirlono of Eastern Bolivia*. Institute of Social Anthropology Monograph, no. 10. Washington, D.C.: Smithsonian Institution.

Horton, R 1971. "African Conversion." *Africa* 41:87–108.

Hvalkof, S., and P. Aaby. 1981. *Is God an American?* Copenhagen: International Work Group for Indigenous Affairs.

Kiemen, M. C. 1954. *The Indian Policy of Portugal in the Amazon Region, 1614–1693*. Washington, D.C.: Catholic University Press.

Lewis, Norman. 1988. *The Missionaries: God against the Indians*. New York: McGraw-Hill.

Marzal, M. M. 1981. "Las reducciones indígenas en la Amazonia del virreinato peruano." *Amazonia peruana* 5:7–45.

Meggers, Betty. 1971. *Amazonia: Man and Culture in a Counterfeit Paradise*. Chicago: Aldine.

———. 1977. *Amazonia: Um paraiso perdido*. Rio de Janeiro: Editora Vozes.

Melatti, J. C. 1967. *Indios e criadores: A situação dos Kraho na area pastoril do Tocantins*. Rio de Janeiro: Instituto de Ciências Sociais da UFRJ.

———. 1972. *O messianismo Kraho*. Rio de Janeiro: Editora Herder.

———. 1976. "Nominadores e genitores: Um aspecto do dualismo Kraho." In E. Schaden, ed., *Leituras de etnologia brasileira*, pp. 139–48. São Paulo: Companhia Editora Nacional.

Métraux, A. 1945. "The Guarani." In J. Steward, ed., *The Handbook of South*

American Indians, vol. 3, pp. 69–94. Washington, D.C.: Bureau of American Ethnology.

———. 1967. *Religions et magies indiennes*. Paris: Editions Gallimard.

Moran, Emilio. 1974. "The Adaptive System of the Amazonian Caboclo." In C. Wagley, ed., *Man in the Amazon*, pp. 136–59. Gainesville: University Press of Florida.

Mörner, Magnus, ed. 1965. *The Expulsion of the Jesuits from Latin America*. New York: Alfred Knopf.

Muratorio, Blanca. 1984. "Evangelisation, Protest, and Ethnic Identity: Sixteenth-Century Missionaries and Indians in Northern Amazonian Ecuador." In J. Bak and G. Benecke, eds., *Religion and Rural Revolt*, pp. 414–23. Manchester: Manchester University Press.

Nock, A. D. 1933. *Conversion: The Old and the New in Religion from Alexander the Great to Augustine of Hippo*. New York: Oxford University Press.

Parker, Eugene P., ed. 1985. *The Amazon Caboclo: Historical and Contemporary Perspectives*. Williamsburg: College of William and Mary.

Pollak-Eltz, A. 1972. *Cultos afroamericanos*. Caracas: Universidade Catolica Abdres Bello.

Pollock, Donald. 1985. "Food and Sexual Identity among the Culina." *Food and Foodways* 1:25–42.

Ranger, T. 1978. "The Churches, the Nationalist State, and African Religion." In E. Fashole-Luke, R. Gray, A. Hastings, and G. Tasie, eds., *Christianity in Independent Africa*, pp. 479–502. London: Rex Collins.

Regan, J. 1988. "Mesianismo Cocama: Un Movimiento de Resistencia en la Amazonia Peruana." *América Indígena* 48:127–37.

Rippy, J. F., and J. T. Nelson. 1936. *Crusaders of the Jungles*. Chapel Hill: University of North Carolina Press.

Rivet, P., and C. Tastevin. 1921. "Les tribus indiennes des bassins du Purus et des régions limitrophes." *La Geographie* 35:449–82.

———. 1938. "Les langues Arawak du Purus et du Jurua." *Journal de la société des americanistes de Paris* 30:71–114, 235–88; 31:223–48; 32:1–55.

Robinson, S. 1981. "Fulfilling the Mission: North American Evangelism in Ecuador." In S. Hvalkof and P. Aaby, eds., *Is God an American?* pp. 41–50. Copenhagen: International Work Group for Indigenous Affairs.

Roe, Peter G. 1982. *The Cosmic Zygote*. New Brunswick: Rutgers University Press.

Ross, Eric. 1978. "Food Taboos, Diet, and Hunting Strategy: The Adaptation to Animals in Amazon Cultural Ecology." *Current Anthropology* 19:1–36.

Rüf, Isabelle. 1972. "Le 'dutsee tui' chez les Indiens Culina du Perou." *Bulletin de la société suisse des americanistes* 36:73–80.

Schaden, Egon. 1982. "A religião guaraní e o cristianismo." *Revista de antropologia* 25:1–24.

Schultz, H., and V. Chiara. 1955. "Informações sobre os Indios do Alto Rio Purus." *Revista do Museu Paulista* n.s. 9:181–200.

Shapiro, Judith. 1981. "Ideologies of Catholic Missionary Practice in a Postcolonial Era." *Comparative Studies in Society and History* 23:130–49.

———. 1982. "Missionary Radicalism on the Brazilian Frontier." Paper presented at conference, "Religion and Power," Providence, Rhode Island.

———. 1987. "From Tupã to the Land without Evil: The Christianization of Tupi-Guaraní Cosmology." *American Ethnologist* 14:126–39.

Snow, D. A., and R. Machalek. 1983. "The Convert as a Social Type." In R. Collins, ed., *Sociological Theory, 1983*, pp. 259–89. New York: Jossey-Bass.

———. 1984. "The Sociology of Conversion." *Annual Review of Sociology, 1984* 10:167–90.

Staples, C. L., and A. L. Mauss. 1987. "Conversion or Commitment? A Reassessment of the Snow and Machalek Approach to the Study of Conversion." *Journal for the Scientific Study of Religion* 26:133–47.

Stearman, A. M. 1987. *No Longer Nomads: The Siriono Revisited.* Lanham, Md.: Hamilton Press.

Stoll, David. 1982. *Fishers of Men or Founders of Empire?* London: Zed Press.

Sullivan, Lawrence. 1988. *Icanchu's Drum: An Orientation to Meaning in South American Religions.* New York: Macmillan.

Taussig, Michael. 1987. *Shamanism, Colonialism, and the Wild Man: A Study in Terror and Healing.* Chicago: University of Chicago Press.

Todorov, T. 1984. *The Conquest of America.* New York: Harper and Row.

Viveiros de Castro, Eduardo. 1978. "Os Kulina do alto purus-acre: Relatório de viagem realizada em janeiro-fevereiro de 1978." Brasília: Fundação Nacional do Indio.

Wallis, E. E. 1960. *The Dayuma Story: Life under Auca Spears.* New York: Harper.

Willems, E. 1967. *Followers of the New Faith: Culture Change and the Rise of Protestantism in Brazil and Chile.* Nashville: Vanderbilt University Press.

CHAPTER SEVEN

"We Are *Ekelesia*": Conversion in Uiaku, Papua New Guinea

John Barker

The Maisin people of Uiaku village, in Papua New Guinea's Oro Province, have been Christians since the early 1900s. The New Guinea mission of the Australian Anglican church settled New Hebridean and Solomon Islander teachers in the village in 1901, and after 1911 large numbers of the villagers began to accept baptism. A Papuan priest has performed services in the church since 1962 on the site of the first mission station. All but a handful of villagers have been baptized and received a Christian name, attended school and worshiped in the church, and contributed labor and money to the upkeep of the priest.[1] Six Uiaku men have entered the priesthood, and many more villagers have worked for the church elsewhere in Papua New Guinea as nurses, medical orderlies, and teachers.

If conversion is understood simply as a change in religious affiliation, the Maisins' conversion lies far in the past. The church has long been an important and accepted part of their lives. But if conversion is understood in a broader sense, as a transformation of a people's cosmological and moral assumptions as they move from a localized "traditional" religion to a universal "world" religion, then one must say that the process is still continuing. Scholars approach conversion in this broader sense from different points of view. Some begin with missionary activities and would agree with Beckett (1978:209) that "Christianity in the South Seas must, in the final analysis, be understood in terms of colonization" (cf. Beidelman 1982). Others start with the modalities of conversion itself: the dialectic or dialogue in a converted community between introduced and received ideas and values (e.g., Kaplan 1990, Macintyre 1990). A third possibility is to start with the perspectives of converts on their own conversion (e.g., Thune 1981, Young 1977).[2]

These three perspectives are not mutually exclusive. In this essay I draw on each for insights into the significance of Maisin Christianity and the conversion process. As an agency of change the Anglican church in Uiaku has furthered colonial and postcolonial incorporation by equipping the Maisin for work in governmental and church bureaucracies and by introducing key Western values and forms into the heart of the community. As we shall see, the long-term engagement of the clergy with the Maisin has produced an anomalous result that neither party could have anticipated: the continuing coexistence of two social environments, the mission station and the village. The mission station *looks* like an imposed Western institution run by foreigners, while the village looks like a pristine, traditional society. In reality they are separate domains or subsystems of one society. All Maisin participate in both domains. I examine these domains in the first part of this essay.

The two social environments yield two variations on the conversion process, which I examine in the second part of the essay. The station, intimately associated with the outside economic and political culture of Papua New Guinea, generates a modality of "external conversion" that at time seems like straightforward acculturation. The village, rooted in exchange and subsistence activities, generates a modality of "internal conversion" in which people adjust preexisting moral assumptions and cultural elements to new situations and challenges. The wider historical process of Maisin conversion, then, has developed two dimensions by virtue of the practical routines and dualism of the colonial situation. Although all Maisin participate in the two modalities, they rarely perceive any contradiction between them because the social environments in which the modalities are embedded usually address distinct concerns and form autonomous aspects of local existence.

It is important in these preliminary remarks to clear up a possible misunderstanding. Although the station and the village would seem to oppose the requirements of a "world" religion against those of a "traditional" religion, Maisin do not and cannot convert from one to the other because they are involved in both environments. In addition, Christian elements are important in both domains and in both modalities of conversion. Indeed, they form flexible tools used by Maisin to deal with their rapidly changing world.

The indigenous perspective that I consider in the last part of this essay is the most concrete and in many ways the most interesting. It is expressed in a public commentary made by a Maisin leader that links the formation of a village cooperative society in the 1950s with the people's acceptance of Christianity. The rhetoric of conversion, of which this commentary is an example, reconciles external and internal conversion, producing a powerful statement of the moral significance many Maisin find in the church. But, given the inherent incompatibilities of the station and the village, and of external and internal conversion, reconciliation cannot actually occur but can only be acknowledged rhetorically. Although the rhetoric presents a positive image of past conversion, its message to present-day Maisin is one of tragic failure.

My analysis, then, is of Maisin conversion from three related points of view; I gradually narrow the analytic focus, discussing first the mission agency, then local experiences of transformation, and finally the rhetoric of conversion. Along the way I discuss several theoretical approaches that influence my approach. In the conclusion I offer some general comments on the political aspects of the Maisins' conversion and on the relationship between hegemonic structures reflected in the station and in external conversion and consciousness.

THE DEVELOPMENT OF THE MISSION STATION AND VILLAGE DOMAINS IN UIAKU

Uiaku consists of two beach villages, separated by a broad shallow river, on the southwest shores of Collingwood Bay in Oro Province in northeastern Papua New Guinea. In 1981–1983 there were about 500 Maisin in Uiaku and between 250 and 300 more who had migrated to work elsewhere in the country. The local economy depends on the subsistence activities of gardening, gathering, fishing, and hunting, and people make extensive use of local trees and plants in their material culture. Far from markets and roads, the Maisin have had little success in producing cash crops. They have developed a small market in distant urban centers for their beautifully designed tapa (bark) cloth. They receive most of their cash and commodities, however, as remittances and gifts from employed migrants.

Uiaku is divided into eighteen contiguous hamlets, each occupied by one or two named patriclans and patrilineages called *iyon* ("divisions"). The Maisin distinguish several levels of iyon on the basis of shared putative patrilineal descent, origin and migration stories, village lands, and various emblems (*kawo*), which may include tapa cloth designs, songs, names, ritual prerogatives, and respected birds and plants. Some Maisin claim that the iyon also own garden lands; but in practice minimal lineages control and pass on land.

Because of extensive outmigration, Uiaku's population has been shrinking, but it remains one of the largest communities on the northeast coast. Its size and its accessibility made it an early target of missionary efforts. In the early 1970s the national government assumed control of education and the teachers' salaries. Villagers bear almost all other expenses and requirements of the local church and school. The station and the hamlets continued to coexist in the 1980s as two distinct social systems rooted in different histories and economic systems.

The Anglican Mission and Colonial Incorporation

I begin this analysis by exploring the contribution of the Anglican mission to the Maisins' incorporation into the wider politico-economic structures of the colonial order. Similarly, Jean and John Comaroff (1986) in a masterful essay have explored missionary activities among the Tshidi people in southern Africa. They argue that the missionary enterprise needs to be studied on two levels. At the level of manifest events and actions the motivations and the consequences of Methodist missionary initiatives, and of Tshidi responses, were variable and indeterminate: "the missionary project was everywhere made particular by variations in the structure of local communities, in the social and theological background of the evangelists, and in the wider politico-economic context and precise circumstances within which the encounter took place." At another level, however, the missionaries were able "to exert power over the common-sense meanings and routine activities diffused in the everyday world." By participating in the mission routines, the Tshidi gradually internalized "a set of values, an ineffable manner of seeing and being" that laid a conceptual basis for their "incorporation into the industrial capitalist world" (Comaroff and Comaroff 1986:1–2). At the level of practice, then, the missionary enterprise induces a generic, cultural patterning.

The Anglican mission in Papua never attained the proportions of Methodist organization in southern Africa, but the Comaroffs' insights are still applicable. The Anglicans began work on the northeast coast of Papua in 1891, a few years after the annexation of the territory by Britain. Shortages of cash and staff retarded the mission's expansion and left the missionaries dependent upon local villagers for much of their support (Wetherell 1977). In addition, the Anglican leaders were hampered by ambivalence about their work. They expressed admiration for village life and showed a marked reluctance to interfere directly with native customs. The Reverend Henry Newton, for instance, wrote in 1914 that the church "is not to be a body distinct from the native life, but rather one that permeates the whole by its influence. . . . The Mission has not come . . . to change native life into a parody of European or Australian civilization" (Newton 1914:251).

Yet this sentiment was not accompanied by systematic study of village societies or by more than a piecemeal development of mission policies on culture. Local missionaries might share the views of their leaders, but they had to work out their own approaches to the customs they found in the districts. The poverty and vague policies of the mission in combination with staff turnover, differences in personal approaches, and the varying responses of local peoples made for a high degree of flux in the early years of the Uiaku mission. (For a detailed study see Barker [1987].)

The Anglicans did make an impact on local societies through their routine work. Most of their efforts were geared to reproducing in Papua the liturgy, institutional structure, religious programs, educational system, and discipline of the home church. Maintaining the infrastructure to support this work occupied the rest of the missionaries' and teachers' time. The mission followed a common pattern of expansion (see Heise 1967). The Anglicans gradually built a network of district stations, headed by white priests, and substations (village schools and churches), run by non-European teachers. Although they were small affairs constructed from bush materials with the aid of villagers, the substations were still discrete "model communities" that reproduced and exaggerated the routines and values of the home churches (cf. Guenther 1977: 457). Creating a separate environment within village societies seemed the best way to impart to villagers, particularly the young in schools, what one missionary called "a christian habit of life" (Gill 1929).

Although the missionaries sometimes clashed with villagers and government agents, forming one point of what Burridge (1960) calls the colonial "triangle," they facilitated the incorporation of villagers into the colonial system in three main ways. First, the presence of missionaries and teachers in the coastal villages undermined resistance to the colonial administration. Second, the local school and church provided villagers with some preparation and a resource for employment in the territory. Finally, the mission stations introduced elements of the colonial hegemonic order into the village itself.

Many Maisins were willing, and often eager, to participate in the developing colonial system. From the start of the Uiaku mission, teachers reported consistently strong attendance at the church and school (Barker 1985a:100). By 1920 young unmarried men routinely left the village after finishing school to work for one or more eighteen-month stints as plantation hands and mining laborers. Others left for even longer periods, joining the government police force or the mission as teachers. In 1942 the administration conscripted all able-bodied men for the brutal Kokoda campaign against invading Japanese forces. When the war ended, the administration and mission rapidly expanded educational facilities and occupations for native peoples in the territory in preparation for eventual independence. The Maisin were well positioned to take advantage of the situation. Many of the postwar generation went to high school and then landed permanent, well-paying jobs as teachers, civil servants, businesspeople, doctors, nurses, dentists, and priests. By the time of independence in 1975 the export of elite and expert labor had become a bulwark of the local economy (cf. Carrier 1981).

The mission station was also a conduit for certain Western institutions and practices. As was the case with many multinucleated coastal societies, Uiaku at the time of European contact was not a single polity but was made up of shifting alliances formed around various rising and falling big men and war leaders. The mission provided the basis for a sense of wider community unity. The church and school served the entire community regardless of loyalties and divisions. The first church council, set up around 1918, was composed of representatives from each hamlet. Following the Second World War the Maisin began experimenting with cooperative societies and cash cropping, inspired by a mission-sponsored cooperative elsewhere on the coast. By 1982, Uiaku boasted nine organizations serving a variety of needs including maintaining the church and school, running a community store, and organizing youth sports (see Barker 1986).

The Village and the Station

Drawing on Bourdieu's (1977) idea of *habitus*, the Comaroffs imply that by regularly participating in mission routines converts internalize the commonsense culture of its Western inventors. In Uiaku, however, the mission's social system has not replaced or absorbed the indigenous social system (cf. Bond 1987, MacGaffey 1986). In the early 1980s in Uiaku, two social systems coexisted, with incongruous practical environments, which the Maisin distinguished as the "village" and the "mission station." The Maisin have for some time participated in both practico-moral environments and internalized their variant values.[3]

The village is home to "tradition." Each hamlet is made up of two or more uneven lines of houses facing a bare earth plaza. Men build their houses near their birthplaces. The spatial divisions in the villages thus mark genealogical connections and distinctions that Maisins believe date from the original emergence of the people from the earth. Historical memory is evoked by emblems, place names in the bush, and migration stories and genealogies, all owned and defended by the patriclans and lineages. The elders, particularly those belonging to the upper-ranking kawo clans, possess the greatest knowledge of the traditions and so receive the greatest respect from the villagers. They speak first on formal occasions, resolve or mediate disputes, and possess the knowledge in some cases to strike others through sorcery. The rhythms of village life are equally localized. Time in the villages flows according to the rhythms of subsistence gardening and frequent exchanges of food and valuables to mark births, marriages, and deaths. Although the village has undergone many changes, it continues to embody the values and practices of the pre-European past.

Villagers continue to call the central block of land originally purchased by the mission the "mission station" and to refer to the indigenous clergy and the government-employed teachers as "missionaries." This is not as archaic as it might seem, for the station continues to reflect the orientations of its founders. The station buildings are organized into a large rectangle around a grassy playing field. Wide, straight avenues, bordered by croton hedges (maintained by school children), connect the buildings. Temporal regularity parallels the spatial organization. A bell beside the church divides each day into periods. It rings to mark school hours; to signal the Angelus every noon; and to call the people to matins, evensong, and Sunday services. One normally enters the station to engage in a specific activity (religious instruction, choir practice, school, organized sports, and so on) for a specific amount of time under the direction of a specialist. The language of the station is English (in 1982 neither the priest nor two out of the three teachers could speak Maisin).[4] In the church and classroom the clergy and teachers are figures of authority who announce and enforce nationally mandated rules and regulations. They are also professionals: the teachers receive a wage from the government, and the clergy are supported by the villagers. Although their spouses make gardens in land donated by villagers, the "missionaries" depend heavily upon purchased commodities for survival. In several respects, then, the station reflects its historical roots and reproduces key practices and orientations of present-day urban society in Papua New Guinea.[5]

Villagers often speak of the station and village as two distinct societies inhabited, respectively, by foreign "missionaries" and "villagers." One friend advised me to take pity on the poor "missionaries":

> They are station people. They follow the time and they do their things at time. As a village man I eat breakfast when I want. Or I make my garden or go fishing. It is not like . . . mission staff. They cannot just run off. That is the greatest difference. If the station people use their money unwisely they have to pray that people will help them. We in the village just need to look for food and anything we can collect will do. For the mission staff, it can be hopeless.

This perspective celebrates the power of the villagers over the station staff, but it is misleading in two respects. First, it ignores the fact that the village has become increasingly oriented toward a cash economy in recent decades and depends on the station for entry into the national education system and thus for jobs. Second, it ignores the fact that villagers spend a considerable amount of their lives engaged in station activities. My friend, for example, attended the village school, went to high school and the church teachers' college, and then became a teacher before returning to care for his ailing father. Besides participating in village activities he spent some time each month collecting stewardship funds in the village to support church work. And he occasionally gave the Sunday sermon. Like other leaders of village organizations he periodically acted as a "missionary" himself.

PATTERNS OF CONVERSION

Although the establishment of the mission station in Uiaku followed typical church practice, the continued coexistence of station and village subsystems in Maisin society well after the end of the missionary period is an anomaly, unintended by the missionaries and the Maisin. The dual environment of Maisin life gives rise to distinct patterns of transformation. Anthropological approaches to conversion elsewhere are useful for analyzing Maisin transformation but need to be adapted to the special circumstances of the Uiaku case.

Humphrey J. Fisher (1973, 1985) and Robin Horton (1971, 1975) have exchanged views in the journal *Africa* on two theories of conversion to world religions, characterized by Fisher as the "Juggernaut" of Islam and Christianity and the "Phoenix" of resurgent indigenous religions. I refer to them as "external" and "internal" conversion, respectively.

Fisher argues that the broader worldview of an incoming world religion gives religious conversion an unstoppable momentum. He defines three stages: quarantine, mixing, and reform. During the quarantine stage the missionaries of the new religion attract only those people already estranged from their community. At first this small group maintains the imported religion in a pristine form, unaffected by the influences of the surrounding community. Gradually, however, more local people seek membership in the new religion, often attracted less by its precepts than by its association with outside sources of wealth and power. At this "mixing" stage the new converts do not renounce their former ideas and ways of life but hold them to be broadly compatible with the introduced religion. Over time the doctrines and orientations of the world religion increasingly make themselves felt as people become more familiar with them and aware of possible contradictions with their present life. A period of conscious reform may then fellow. Fisher acknowledges that Islam and Christianity in Africa have been reshaped by local cultural, economic, and political conditions; but he also insists that the ways of life of African converts have been reshaped by the key doctrines, dynamics, and practices of the world religions themselves. Viewed from the position of the African convert, this is a theory of external conversion (Fisher 1973:31; cf. Berkhofer 1965; Burridge 1978; Laitin 1986:23–38; Nock 1933).

Horton, in contrast, develops a theory of internal conversion: "the crucial variables [in conversion] are not the external influences (Islam, Christianity), but the pre-existing thought-patterns and values, and the pre-existing socio-economic matrix" (Horton 1975:221).[6] He bases his approach on two assumptions,

> first, that where people confront new and puzzling situations, they tend to adapt to them as far as possible in terms of their existing ideas and attitudes, even though they may have to stretch and develop them considerably in the process. Second, that where people assimilate new ideas, they do so because these ideas make sense to them in terms of the notions they already hold. (Horton and Peel 1976:482)

Horton suggests that traditional African worldviews are "two-tiered," with local spirits underpinning the microcosm of the subsistence community and a distant supreme being underpinning the encompassing "macrocosm." The relative development of the microcosm or the macrocosm depends on whether people are more involved in local community or cross-community relations (as in long-distance trading). Colonization drew rural Africans into the affairs of a larger society in which the familiar, local spirits no longer seemed credible, and they began to develop the preexisting concept of a supreme being. In his provocative "thought experiment" Horton (1971) says that this basic transformation in African cosmology "might well have occurred in some recognizable form even in the absence of [the] world faiths" (Horton and Peel 1976:482). The Africans were highly selective, taking from Islam and Christianity only those ideas that fit in their preexisting cosmology. The world religions are "catalysts," stimulating and accelerating changes that are "in the air" and triggering reactions in which "they do not always appear among the end-products" (Horton 1971:104). Although I know of few anthropologists who have directly adopted Horton's ideas, many would be sympathetic to his stress on indigenous cultural structures in conversion (e.g., Hefner 1987, Hughes 1984, Kahn 1983, Morrison 1981, Schwimmer 1973, Schieffelin 1981).[7]

Horton (1975) insists the two theories are incompatible, but they share a number of striking features: notably the Weberian emphasis on the transformation of converts' worldviews from localized and largely tacit cosmologies to more universal, coherent, and consciously ordered conceptions of the divine. Moreover, both approaches view conversion as a unitary process. The difference between them would seem to be one of emphasis, as indeed Fisher (1985) suggests. More recently, also drawing upon Weber, Laitin (1986:24–29) has developed a model that simultaneously considers theological orientations, the practical organization of the religion, and the cultural and social conditions of the converts' lives.

Another possibility, however, is that internal conversion and external conversion are determined in large part by the practico-moral environments in which conversion takes place. Indeed, I shall argue that both types of "conversion" occur in Maisin society as variations within the larger historic conversion process outlined in the first part of the paper. In the station domain, conversion has a strong "external" character, to the point that the Maisin in this context appear to be acculturating. In the village domain, conversion has an "internal" quality, drawing upon received notions. The Maisin as a whole experience both types of transformation; but, limited to the distinct orientations and issues of the different domains, the processes rarely come into conflict.

External Orientations in the Station Domain

From the mission station, Uiaku appears a Christian community. The church is its largest building and the site of its largest celebrations. Villagers devote a considerable amount of time, labor, and money to the upkeep of the station and its staff. People grouse about this or that group of villagers not meeting their share, but nobody questions the obligation of Christians to support the church. The church is the outward face of Uiaku. Important visitors, such as bishops and politicians, stay on the mission station. The most spectacular feasts and traditional dances take place on the station on the saint's day and Easter; in addition, regional sports meets are held there, and women's church groups from regional villages gather at the station for meetings.

The village organizations provide the most interesting evidence of external conversion. Historically rooted in and borrowing from the authority of the church, their stated aims have a reformist bent: to encourage church attendance, to comfort the sick with prayers, to develop cash crops, to involve young people in community projects, and so forth. As customary occasions for political maneuvering—bride-price negotiations, puberty ceremonies, death rites—have declined with outmigration and increasing involvement in the cash economy, the organizations have become the major locus of village politics. All of the leading men and many women have served as committee members and as leaders in the organizations (see Barker 1985a: Ch. 5).

When a man becomes a church councillor or a woman the head of the Mothers Union, they do not forget the values they learned growing up in the village. But they also grew up attending school and church and model their roles (if not always their moral attitudes) on the teachers and on their ideas of Europeans. Like the "missionaries," the committee leaders assume a singular authority to judge what is best for other villagers and to order certain work done. One man, for example, described the church council in this way: "The councillors do the same work as the government, except they work on the mission side, telling the people what work needs to be done." Other informants added little: "They tell the people to work when anything is needed in the church." As better-educated migrants return to the village, after several years of employment, they gravitate to—and are pushed toward—leadership positions in village corporations, where they can, in a popular phrase, "help the villagers." Some leaders build and take advantage of networks with regional and national organizations in which they find people of similar education and experience. During October and November 1986, for example, a delegation of the Mothers Union flew to Popondetta, the provincial capital, for an annual conference; the youth club hosted visitors to discuss future regional games; a village councillor lobbied the provincial government to invite a timber firm into the Collingwood Bay area; and a retired dentist organized a welcome for a visiting World Health Organization team operating a project on the station.

But this picture of rampant Westernization is misleading when applied to Uiaku as a whole. Indeed, from a number of standpoints the eighty-year attempt to plant Christianity has been an abysmal failure. Only a small minority of Maisins—mostly women and children—regularly attend church services; few individuals have more than the vaguest notion of church doctrine; most villagers are firmly convinced of the reality of local bush spirits and sorcerers; and individuals frequently disregard church strictures on marriage and divorce. The village organizations, too, although run by villagers, tend to be ineffectual when they turn their attention to the village; instead they concentrate on the school, the church, and other public institutions.

Perhaps the Maisin are at the "quarantined" or "mixed" stage of conversion in Fisher's model, rather than the "reform." But these terms also are unsatisfactory. The Maisin are very much involved in the station. They want their children to attend school and to find good jobs, they desire a suitably impressive church and other public institutions, and they hope that participation in village organizations will attract government and business money to the region. The station reflects the desires and energies of villagers as much as it does the structures of the outside world. For their collective advancement in the outside politico-economic system, the Maisin are quite willing to reform, to obey the authoritative voice of the priest or teacher, and to adopt new bureaucracies. But the concerns of the station domain have little direct relevance to the subsistence cycle, the experience of sickness, or the attack of a ghost. The ideas and routines of the station domain seldom mix in with those of the village because there is no need for them to do so.

Internal Orientations in the Village Domain

The most consequential restructurings of cosmology and morality since the Anglicans set up their base in Uiaku have taken form in the village domain. But these changes are hard to detect not only because reliable historical sources are rare but also because the ideas and structures in question continue to look "indigenous"; one must have a considerable familiarity with the culture before internal modifications are recognizable.[8] The Maisin case poses an additional problem: villagers talk about their customs in ways that mask the nature of change. The nature of this masking, however, is revealing. On the one hand, Maisins often insist that their customs are unchanged from the time of creation. On the other, they credit missionaries with making fundamental changes in the very bases of the community. These apparently contradictory statements are complementary aspects of a single ideology that legitimates change within ostensibly unchanging moral truths. The ideology is a product of the internal modality of conversion in Uiaku. It is generated from the two related tendencies discussed by Horton: the tendency of people to try to comprehend new things in terms of what they already know; and the tendency of people to assimilate new ideas into preexisting frameworks.

The first tendency is apparent in Maisin notions of cosmology. The Maisin assume that Christian figures exist in the same cosmos as the more familiar entities of the microcosm. One informant told me: "Before the time of the missionaries the people did not know of God. But God was in the place. There was no word for Him." Others told me that the ancestors were *toton*, "ignorant," until the missionaries came to tell them about the people and truths in the Bible. Like many other Melanesian Christians most Maisins accept literally the events and persons they hear of in the church (Ryan 1969). And, as Horton's theory suggests, they understand Christian cosmological notions in terms of what they already know of the invisible world. A few people told me of their encounters with Jesus, the Virgin Mary, and Jacob's ladder in dreams when they were ill and how these experiences led to their recovery (much as a father or mother appearing in a dream may signal a return to health). Other informants speculated that God may be responsible for major natural disasters, such as typhoons and the disastrous 1951 eruption of Mount Lamington (cf. Schwimmer 1969), which (much like a sorcerer) He administers as punishments on local peoples.

Horton's theory also suggests that the emphases within a cosmology shift as the social contexts of peoples' lives widen. Here, too, the Maisin evidence is supportive. Oral testimonies show a clear decline in villagers' interactions with local spirits over the past eighty years. For example, people no longer make sacrifices to ancestral spirits before beginning a garden or engaging in a communal hunt. Villagers also say that sorcery is not the problem it was even a decade ago. I never heard a Maisin dispute the reality of the spiritual forces of the microcosm. But people do say that the power of God is greater, and if one has faith one need not fear the wrath of ghosts or sorcerers (cf. Tonkinson 1981:260). Several people also suggested that the recent dead, all Christians, now obediently follow the priest's suggestions at their funerals and go to heaven without pestering their remaining relatives (cf. MacGaffey 1986:170). Over the years, then, experience with the spiritual forces of the microcosm has diminished, but this trend has not led to the rejection of the received cosmology (for more detailed studies see Barker [1983, 1990a]; cf. MacGaffey 1986). In thinking about spiritual powers in the Christian macrocosm, the Maisin have had to stretch their received assumptions about them. This adjustment has not been minor, but at the same time it has affirmed the truth about the essentials.

Maisins say, however, that manifestations of God are rare compared with those of local spirits, ghosts, and sorcerers. Unlike the microcosm, where personal experience is an important source of knowledge, the macrocosm is revealed primarily through church teaching and the *giu* (authoritative advice based on sacred knowledge). The giu is the basis of the authority of the "missionaries" (the clergy and the teachers on the station) and, by extension, those villagers who serve on community organizations. It is their knowledge of greater things, acquired primarily through the ability to read and to write, that gives them authority to speak of wider "truths."

Although the knowledge of God and the Bible might be beyond the ken of most villagers, the role of the missionary is accessible. Villagers assimilate the missionary's function within their received notions of morality. They often speak of the relation between the missionaries and themselves as an exchange: the "missionaries" give church services, perform baptisms and marriages, pronounce the giu, and educate the children in return for attendance, labor, food, and wages. This mind-set becomes apparent when one side or the other feels that obligations are not being met. For example, after a period of sparsely attended services, one church councillor made the following speech, identifying attendance as a kind of prestation:

> If nobody goes to church the priest wastes his time. So you must think that when the priest starts to work in the church to go and attend church first and then come back to do your own work. When the attendance is down it shows that we hate the priest and the deacon. If we want them to stay we must show the sign by attending.

The "exchange" ideology reinforces the differences and complementarity of the two sides. Each brings distinct things to the exchange. And, as is often the case where exchange items are not identical, there is a strong element of asymmetry and hierarchy.

Maisins often say of the missionaries: "They take care of the people." They say the same of the relationship of parents to children, older to younger siblings, and senior to junior lineages. The key prototype for the missionary-villager relationship, however, is the symbolic opposition between the two types of patriclans, *kawo* and *sabu*. Kawo are higher-ranking clans that possess a number of ritual prerogatives, including the right to speak first at gatherings and to hold feasts and dances in their hamlets. Associated with several kawo clans are a number of lower-ranking sabu groups. The sabu have fewer ritual prerogatives than the kawo—for example, they cannot beat drums or hold feasts in their hamlets—but they do have one definitive right: to begin fights with enemies. Kawo and sabu are in a permanent asymmetrical alliance. Maisins say that the kawo "look after" their sabu. They temper the warrior group by forging alliances between groups through feasting and exchanging. The sabu reciprocate by providing their kawo "older brothers" with food and labor at feasts. The sabu must show "respect" for their kawo. If they do not, the kawo will be unable to establish and maintain conditions of peace and amity in the village and beyond, for they will be unable to sponsor feasts. The state of "amity," *marawa-wawe*, is clearly the ideal. Because tribal warfare lies so far in the past, we cannot take the above description as evidence of the way precontact Maisin society really was. But these historic memories survive today and form a kind of "social science" that Maisins use to make sense out of the dynamics between "villagers" and "missionaries" (cf. MacGaffey 1986).

As it is with parents and children, and kawo and sabu, so it is with missionaries and villagers. Here is a typical description of the duties of the clergy: "They bring the Bible and give good giu [here meaning religious instruction or advice] to the people, pray for the sick, and tell the people not to do bad things." Many villagers credit the priest for stopping fights in the village.[9] The Maisin sometimes make the same contrast between the Christian people of the present and the "heathen" people (*eteni*) of the past. "The heathen village is different," one man explained, "because they have no giu [i.e., Christian knowledge]. If they want to do anything they can. They will not respect you. They will put you in a bad place and kill you. Christians welcome you, put you up, and give you food." Like the young child, or the angry sabu, the heathen have little moral conscience; they act without constraint. To employ a Freudian idiom, the Maisin treat the kawo, elders, parents, missionaries, committee leaders, and Christians as instances of the controlling superego; sabu, junior siblings, children, villagers, and pagans constitute the untempered forces of the id. The "ego" oscillates between these extremes, but ideally it is in a position of social amity, suspended between the social good and personal interests.

Villagers often credit or blame the missionaries for ending particular customs (for example, betrothals and selfmutilation in mortuary ceremonies). Yet there are problems with taking such statements at face value. Not only is there little evidence of missionary opposition to all but a handful of practices, but few villagers agree or even seem interested in the list of customs the mission may have opposed. The Maisins' conception of change is better understood within the moral framework I have been outlining, as a tempering of the energies of an inferior by a moral superior. One informant described conversion in this way: "When the first [missionaries] came, they wanted the people to stop all the customs that they had brought to the place and to join the mission in 'amity.' The people were really ignorant so they kept on. Now they know and have left those bad things. . . . If the thing is good, the people will carry on doing it. If it is bad, the missionaries keep on talking and the people give up these things." The description is one of pruning away the bad to leave only the good. There is change, but there is also a deeper, enduring truth, the "good" that people continue.

Rather than adopt the framework of mission Christianity, then, the Maisin conceptualize church teachings on cosmology and the moral order in terms of received ideas. In so doing the Maisin must stretch their understandings of familiar concepts. *Marawa-wawe* ("amity"), for instance, probably once meant no more than a temporary condition of balanced exchange between groups. But today Maisins often use it as an equivalent to the Christian notion of universal brotherhood under

God. Similarly, sorcery has not disappeared from the community, but the Maisin speak of it as a form of personal sin (*rature*, or "telling lies") that inevitably rebounds on the sorcerer (Barker 1983).

These conceptions of "missionaries" and "villagers" form an ideology that partly masks and distorts actual change in several ways. First, the ideology greatly exaggerates the impact of missionaries on Maisin society. To hear villagers talk about how missionaries stopped particular customs and prevented fights, one would never realize that European missionaries actually spent little time in Uiaku in the past (and that they are long gone), or that the teachers and present-day station staff participate minimally in village life. As I have tried to indicate here, "missionary" denotes a more general category of moral relation; a "missionary" represents the voice of conscience. Second, the ideology masks various economic and political conditions that impinge on and force adjustments in village life. It perceives such forces and their effects in ways that confirm itself and gives the impression that the cosmology and moral order are continuing even as their manifest symbols and practices are dramatically modified.

Once I became aware of this "change in continuity," I began to find it everywhere: in notions of sickness and sorcery, marriage practices, and women's facial tattooing (Barker 1983, 1985a, 1989; Barker and Tietjen 1990). Mortuary exchanges especially are a prominent instance of the accommodation of the ideology to change.[10]

Mortuary rituals were easily the most elaborate religious activities of the contact culture. Missionaries wrote about their violent aspects, about weeping women gashing their foreheads and breasts with sharp rocks. The Maisin credit missionary opposition for the ending of these and many other practices. In fact the opposition was sporadic at best, and most of the offending practices continued well after the population had converted. To the extent that we can reconstruct the colonial history of the rites, their modification has been haphazard, with villagers leaving out at different times a certain exchange, type of apparel, or ritual act (most of which were never opposed by the mission). By the early 1980s the sequence of the death rites bore a family resemblance to the one described by missionaries in 1904, but it was much simplified and incorporated an unadorned Christian burial rite at its center.

As in other kin-based societies, a death in Uiaku incurs long-term exchanges and obligations. The most important are between the deceased's kin and affines. In the early 1980s mortuary exchanges still absorbed substantial time, labor, and goods. When a married adult died, the surviving spouse left her or his house to stay with an affine. The kin of the deceased destroyed the couple's house and gardens and distributed the property and food among themselves. The widow or widower was at first immobile, kept hidden behind a sheet of tapa in the relatives' house. Gradually, the affines reintroduced her or him to normal routines: the bereaved was fed various foods, taken to the bush to relieve her- or himself, given a garden knife, taken to church, and so on. This stage was followed by a period of light mourning, lasting weeks to several years, in which the mourner allowed her or his hair to grow unkept and uncut, grew a beard (if a man), wore dark clothing, and avoided public gatherings. Other villagers might join in if they felt close to the deceased. Eventually, the kin and affines of the mourners set a time for a *roi babasi*, or a "face cleaning" ceremony. The affines cut the mourner's hair, decorated him or her in new tapa and ornaments, and presented gifts of tapa cloth, pots, mats, and food. Ideally, these gifts balanced the things taken at the time of death. The final ceremony strongly resembled traditional puberty rites. Now the widow or widower could remarry.

Such was the situation in 1981–1982. But many people were expressing unhappiness with the rites. They complained that because the roi babasi was not prepared quickly enough, people remained in mourning too long. Villagers also complained that affines rarely gave as much to surviving spouses as they took at the time of death. These grievances had clear economic roots. First, mourning obligations had become a public nuisance. An untimely death can knock out a long-planned church festival, sports meet, or development project. Those involved in the death must donate labor and food to the mortuary exchanges. Others are afraid to participate in the festival (and certainly to dance) for fear of offending mourners. When two people died just before the bishop and a regional member of parliament were to arrive for a festival in Uiaku in December 1981, the organizers were nearly driven to distraction negotiating for the mourners to be "cleaned up" so that the people could dance. Second, the Maisins' uneven incorporation into the cash economy had made it difficult to balance the exchanges. People who have worked or who have relatives in towns have more money and more possessions. When a relatively well-off person dispenses property at a death or as the organizer of a roi babasi, the other side often cannot balance the exchange.

These may have been the underlying causes of the Maisins' complaints, but the villagers did not refer to them in explaining their problems. Instead, they held that the mortuary exchanges posed a moral issue. The lack of balance indicated that people were being "greedy" and were not in "amity." Even though the forms were being observed, people sensed that custom itself was being violated.

Their objections began to increase in 1980 after a young boy died. His family had recently returned to Uiaku after his father resigned from a management position on an oil palm project. The grieving parents surrendered most of their goods to the wife's people and went into mourning for almost two years. Several enraged kinsmen claimed that the wife's people had become too greedy for the property of these people and too lazy to help end their mourning, and so the bereaved stayed too long in their unhappy condition. The church deacon, who was a Maisin man related to the mourning parents, and several other villagers took these arguments further. They argued that amity between villagers should be a feature of the death rites from the start rather than a final goal. The critics took the opportunity of a funeral for another youngster in September 1982 to point out that *marawa-wawe* (amity) not only was the customary goal of the rites but was also in accordance with the church teaching that people should love and support their brothers and sisters. Most of the people at the funeral agreed and left the bereaved household in possession of its property and gardens. In addition, three days after the death the respective affines took the husband and wife out of mourning with small ceremonies, thus drastically curtailing the mourning period. Most of the funerals I witnessed later, in 1983 and 1986, followed the abbreviated pattern.

Two related points are significant in this example. First, Christian ideas were important in making these modifications possible. But, as Horton might argue, people were able to accept the Christian teaching on universal love because they had assimilated it into a received notion of social amity based upon an ideal of balanced reciprocity. The related point is that this transformation in the death rites, important as it was, did not involve the adoption of Western-style funeral rites. People operated within what they already knew, especially their collective memory of "tradition." I strongly suspect that an anthropologist working in Uiaku ten years from now will be told, as I was in the early 1980s, that the death rites she or he observes "come from the ancestors." And, of course, in a sense they do.

The external and internal orientations examined here are best understood as aspects of a larger conversion process emerging from the historical particularities of the Maisins' colonial situation. On the one hand, Maisins are involved in regional and global ideologies and politico-economic systems through the church and the school, and the village committees modeled after them. On the other hand, Maisins continue to look to received identities and traditions in their local world to find an authoritive basis for governing community life. Thus all Maisins participate in the macrocosm and the microcosm, and all engage in station and village activities and ideas that together influence the overall direction of conversion. Understood in this way, Maisin conversion cannot be adequately understood in unilinear terms as either capitulation or resistance. Instead, we must view the Maisin as active participants in a much more complicated and ambiguous conversion process, participants who draw upon a variety of old and introduced tools to refashion themselves in a more complex world.

THE RHETORIC OF CONVERSION

So far I have considered conversion as an aspect of colonial incorporation and as a process of social and ideological transformation. In this section I turn to the ways in which converts themselves talk about conversion, how they construct rhetorics of transformation within more diffuse religious discourses. Robert Hefner's study of the Islamization of Besuki in eastern Java is helpful. He notes that "in all religious and ideological discourse there is a dual economy of knowledge, in which explicit doctrinal knowledge is informed by and mutually informs a less discursive, tacit knowledge constructed in a wider social experience" (Hefner 1987: 55). The key difference between traditional and world religions is not rationality per se, as a strict Weberian might have it, but the characteristic social organization in which each develops a distinctive voice. Embedded in small-scale communities, in which spiritual knowledge is woven into the fabric of everyday life, traditional religions are relatively silent, supported by tacit moral and cosmological assumptions. In contrast, "world" religions are more explicit and ordered; they "provide the discourse for the elaboration of a secondary moral and ideological identity beyond that given in the immediacy of local groupings." World religions may form "a kind of secondary community built above and between those given by local social circumstances" (Hefner 1987:74–75).

Hefner's two-tiered model of religious discourse fits the case of Uiaku. Although the station and the village are not discrete religious orders, they do represent different levels of social organization. External conversion addresses the "secondary community" that links Uiaku with other people in Papua New Guinea; internal conversion draws on the "local social circumstances" of received culture. As Hefner's study shows, the two tiers may coexist for long periods in a community. Both can flexibly be drawn upon to make sense of increasingly complex social experiences. But as people are drawn into the larger culture of the surrounding society and struggle with difficult questions of self-definition and cultural legitimation, the contradictions between the two levels of community come to the fore. This experience of the secondary community challenges tacit assumptions about morality and cosmology—"shakes the foundations"—and so brings these assumptions into conscious discussion.

The representation of conversion I examine here is an example of such a reconsideration of moral assumptions and identity emerging from a sense of moral crisis. In June 1983 a meeting was held in Uiaku to discuss the latest closing of the cooperative trade store. Several men alluded to the origins of the society that had run the cooperative. Among those who spoke was a man whose father had opened the first village trade store in 1946. He began:

> When people got married and grew up, they did what their fathers taught them. They had their own kawo. When they built the church, they all put their kawo into the church for God. No one held theirs back. No clan got it back. When I was a small boy, I saw them break the spear and club and end fighting [between the clans]. They did this because the missionaries came and wanted peace. It was the sign. They told us to live in amity. . . . You must all know this and not be confused. We must follow the right way. We are *ekelesia* [Christians]. We are leaders. We are government. We look after our own place. We do all of the work.

He ended by quietly reading out a list of the first shareholders of the cooperative society, most of them now dead.

This commentary was unique, but it drew on events and themes familiar to the audience. It is best understood as "transitory ingenuity" (MacGaffey 1986:62): an attempt to find meaning in a difficult situation by improvising a plausible rhetorical structure. In the following analysis, I want to show that this sort of rhetoric is unrealistic and problematic for the Maisin. To do this, I first need to put the commentary in context by examining the historical background of the cooperative society, its association with the church, and its utility to Maisins as a symbol of conversion.

Inspired by the Christian Socialist movement in Australia, the Reverends James Benson and A. Clint set up an experimental cooperative at nearby Gona village in 1946, the first in Oro Province (Dakeyne 1966). The missionaries hoped cooperatives would simultaneously improve the material conditions of villagers and deepen their understanding of Christian teachings through the discipline of daily prayer and regular work. In 1948 a Maisin returned from the Gona cooperative bearing seed rice and new ideas. He called a meeting of clan allies, who had traditionally formed rival factions in Uiaku. Together they proclaimed a new era of peace and prosperity at the meeting, ritually breaking a spear and club. Members of the Uiaku-Ganjiga Christian Co-operative Society then planted the rice and other cash crops, selling the first harvest to the missionaries at Wanigela.

The mission soon abandoned its Gona experiment and interest in village cooperatives, but the Maisin continued their cooperative activities with what several observers felt was religious fervor. "All the peoples of Collingwood Bay," wrote a worried Patrol Officer Bell,

> are very co-operatively minded and have been ever since the war. The failures they have had in the last few years have in no way deterred them. They have seized upon co-operation as a means towards an end, a complete new order, by which they will advance both economically and socially. Any attempt to talk them out of this immediately breeds suspicion in their minds and they imagine they are being robbed of their chance of advancement. (Patrol Reports 1955)

What particularly concerned Bell and his brother officers was the "communalism" of the cooperatives: the idea that "all participants were supposed to work at the same time and to undertake whatever work was allotted to them by the group leaders, and benefits derived were to have been shared equally" (Crocombe 1964:29). But not all men gave as much time to the plantations. And what was to be done about those who donated land? The Maisins temporarily overcame those obstructions when they organized a cooperative to build an iron-roofed church, the first in the district. After the missionary in Wanigela agreed to take care of the books, the villagers raised funds through selling copra and then purchased sheet iron and church fixtures from centers up the coast. The venture was successful. Bishop George Ambo, the first Papuan bishop, inaugurated Saint Thomas Church in 1962 and installed the Reverend George Nixon Simbiri as Uiaku's first priest.

At other times, however, society leaders kept cooperative monies in jars hidden away in their houses. As officer Bell observed, the native-run cooperatives discouraged individual entrepreneurship. And theft by the leaders was a real possibility. In 1952 and again in 1962 government agents disbanded unofficial societies and distributed the hoarded funds. In 1962–1964, the government sponsored its own cooperative society in Uiaku, providing training and occasional supervision for the participants. Around the same time, Uiaku began to suffer from extensive outmigration and a steep decline in coastal shipping, which together put an end to cash cropping. The society store has survived, but its survival is very shaky. It now depends entirely on monies sent to the village by migrants and on the occasional government grant. As incoming funds ebb and flow, so do the fortunes of the store. It was closed through most of 1982–1983.

The cooperative society seems an unlikely candidate for an image of conversion given its repeated failures and its relative lack of importance in the local economy. The Maisin do not need the society store; they can and often do buy goods much more cheaply at stores near the regional airstrip in Wanigela. Yet most meetings I attended in Uiaku dealt in one way or another with the problems of the store. It soon became clear that the villagers treated the society less as an economic problem than as a moral issue. Talk about the store ran in predictable channels. Some people looked for scapegoats: they called the educated younger men running the store "big heads," too lazy to take care of the books and responsible for siphoning off the store's funds; they accused the storekeepers of secretly extending credit and giving goods to their kinsfolk; and they warned young women not to tempt the storekeepers into sexual encounters and thereby weaken them. The society leaders in turn admonished villagers to avoid rumor mongering, because such gossip drove good storekeepers from their jobs. The store acted as a magnet for many of the tensions, suspicions, and open conflicts in the community.

I suggest that the cooperative society carries such moral weight precisely because for the Maisin it is a powerful symbol of conversion, of movement toward a "new order." Part of the society's symbolic strength comes from its close association with the key symbols of hegemonic power: business and money. Throughout Papua New Guinea, rural peoples see the development of locally controlled businesses as the road to economic salvation, a view that politicians enthusiastically reinforce. As studies of the so-called cargo cults show, "bisnis" has a strong ideological message for many Melanesians; it carries a notion of moral equivalence with Europeans and the ability to exercise power over their own lives (Burridge 1960). The commentary we are examining develops these notions of external conversion in such phrases as "We are leaders. We are government. . . . We do all of the work." The speaker claims autonomy for the Maisin, perhaps defiantly, but in terms that accept the external hegemonic culture of state authority, governmental bureaucracy, organized labor, and, by implication, money.

The society also gathers symbolic strength from its association with the village church. In the commentary the church does not participate in external conversion, linking the Maisin with the outside system, but instead is assimilated to received moral values within a process of internal conversion. The commentary refers to an actual event at the consecration of Saint Thomas church in 1962. As the bishop's party approached the church, they found it surrounded on three sides by a low fence of crisscrossed sticks. The different trees making up the fence were kawo, emblems of the clans, linked together in a sign of unity. In building this fence, Maisins had symbolically transformed the mission station from a foreign social order to a village center; these kinds of emblems had hitherto been set up only on feast days in the central plazas of the higher-ranking clans. In effect, the Maisin converted the mission station into the village and thus encompassed external conversion within the idiom of internal conversion.

This event forms the rhetorical core of the commentary. The Maisin had accepted baptism and the presence of the mission, of course, decades before the cooperatives and the new church. Older Maisins are aware of this, but the postwar events strike many of them as marking much more of a transformation, a movement toward a new order. The commentary begins with the asymmetrical reciprocity between missionary and convert that makes peace possible. By insisting that all of the clans gave their emblems to the church and that none took them back, the speaker suggests that the clans sacrificed their different identities for a higher unity, a more general state of "amity" that embraced the entire community. His reading of the names of the original shareholders suggests that the giving of shares to form the cooperative society was also a sacrifice for a higher unity. This unity, in turn, made the society prosperous and gave Maisins their church. The speech thus interweaves themes of internal conversion with those of external conversion: leadership (of committees), government, work. A condition of dependence and difference becomes one of empowerment where the opposition between missionary and villagers is obviated. Amity, equality, collective empowerment, and prosperity are all conjoined in a single powerful statement identifying the society and the church within conversion. This is the full meaning of "We are ekelesia" (ecclesia): we have become the church.

I suggested earlier that the commentary represented "transitory ingenuity" and that it was problematic. It is ingenious in the way it is fabricated from certain key events and symbols. For many Maisins the society is a mirror of their moral condition. Its failure reflects their own moral collapse. Speakers at meetings contrast and reinforce this negative image with a positive one of the society at the time of its founding. Such representations of conversion can take on the quality of charter myths. Especially interesting is that the Maisin leaders speak of the fortunes of the society with images of conversion drawn from both external and internal processes, suggesting that those were once (and can be again) reconciled.

The commentary is problematic in that it portrays the society's relations with the outside world as being governed by village morality. This is clearly mistaken. This image of conversion encourages the Maisin to think the failure of the society reflects their own moral failure. This is similar to the situation of the death rites described earlier. And, as in that case, leaders at the meetings admonish the people to be respectful of the leaders ("missionaries"), to stop rumor mongering, to live in amity, and so forth. The rub is that the moral order of the village has little relevance to the fortunes of the society and other business ventures. A variety of extrinsic economic forces conspire to undermine the society's success. The ingenious rhetoric of conversion considered here might make Maisins feel good about the "new men" of the 1950s but it makes them feel bad about themselves in the present.

CONCLUSIONS

I have presented Maisin conversion in this essay from three related points of view. First, I examined the contribution of mission Christianity to the people's long-term incorporation into the colonial and post-colonial system. As the Comaroffs (1986) suggest for the Tshidi, the most systematic and influential controls of the mission enterprise were the routines of teaching, preaching, and setting up a supporting infrastructure. The founders of the mission foresaw a village-based Christianity following the forms of the medieval church. This has indeed developed in Uiaku, although not quite in the way that the early church leaders imagined. Village society is still distinctly "Melanesian," rooted in subsistence production and kin-based exchange, and it has also remained distinct from the station establishment, which finds its roots in Western culture. To see the station as a foreign imposition, however, would grossly misrepresent the situation. A presence in Uiaku for more than eighty years, the station continues with the participation of Maisins in the church, in the school, in work committees, and in raising funds. It connects Uiaku into a larger network of education, jobs, government, and capitalism, and it brings these forces into the heart of local experience. The relation of village to station is the long-term product of interactions between Maisin and outside agents, one that could not fit the expectations of either. Uiaku society, I would suggest, has a dual culture that has to be understood in the context of a multicultural Papua New Guinea.

Conversion may also be understood as an ongoing process for the converts themselves. Examining the situation in the 1980s, I have suggested that the Maisin today experience two modalities of conversion corresponding to the two practical environments in which they conduct their lives. While engaged in the church, the school, or the village committees, they experience "external conversion," a process that reforms or remodels local ways according to imported values and orientations. External conversion draws from the hegemonic culture of the country (and its former colonial masters) and emphasizes bureaucratic rule, singular authority, and obedience. While engaged in subsistence activities, exchanges, or rituals, Maisins experience "internal conversion," an ongoing modification of preexisting traditional elements. Internal conversion is harder to detect because much of local cultural understanding is tacitly shared and because the Maisin explicitly credit missionaries and their successors with changing their society. As their mortuary exchanges show, however, the Maisin make sense of the action of these outsiders and manipulate elements of the received culture by projecting a strongly held moral ideology. This ideology sees "missionaries" as superior but reciprocal players interacting with villagers in a relationship that clarifies and enlarges the understanding of tradition. In the village domain, then, Maisins experience conversion as change within an enduring tradition. Both the external and internal modalities contribute to the overall historical process of conversion in which all Maisins are involved.

Finally, I examined the rhetoric of conversion as a discourse about the nature of community. Taking a cue from Hefner's (1987) study of the conversion of Javanese Hindus, I suggested that the external and internal dimensions of conversion relate to two different levels of social structure, which in turn correspond to the distinction between "world" and "traditional" religions. Through the process of external conversion, the Maisin identify with the common interests, forms, and political values of the larger community in Papua New Guinea. Through internal conversion, they attempt to harmonize the present conditions of their lives with their understanding of received morality. Much of the time they experience no conflict between these two perceptions of community. Indeed, they provide Maisins with flexible cultural tools for dealing with an increasingly complex world. But there are exceptions, triggered by difficult endeavors such as the cooperative society. On the one hand, the society is the epitome of engagement in the external cash economy and bureaucratic system. On the other hand, Maisins perceive the act of cooperation itself as part of inherited village morality. These two discourses inform each other in representations of the happy days of the 1950s, when, so it is said, success in one domain lent itself to success in the other: the people were united in "amity" and the society was a booming success.

Maisin commentaries on conversion present the church and the cooperative society together as the embodiment of that success, the mark of the "true" conversion of the people. But if this unity did come about it was temporary and fragile. Its representation in the present is mythic and perhaps overly wishful: for village morality has at best an indirect influence on the success or failure of business ventures. The main effect of such representations of conversion is to make villagers feel at once frustrated and guilty. The engagement in Christianity and commerce certainly at times "shakes the foundations" of the village moral order. But, for the moment, the Maisin are left with no clear alternatives to their dualistic environment.

Clearly the introduction of Christianity in Uiaku has been inseparable from incorporation into larger political and economic systems. The support of the station and the moral ideology linking villagers and missionaries indicate a general acceptance of the hegemonic system, even if the villagers do not entirely understand it. In Uiaku, unlike in southern Africa, where missionization was more thorough and oppression is institutionalized, discourses of protest and resistance have not taken discernible shape, either in organized Western forms or within seemingly apolitical symbolic forms (cf. Comaroff 1985). Rural Maisins often do express resentment about the lack of economic development and opportunities in their area. But they are as likely to blame themselves as to look to causes outside the community (cf. Smith 1984, 1990). In contrast, Anglican Christianity has been partly assimilated to village ways and may even give new life to old values. The situation resembles that described by Laitin in his model of hegemony and culture among the Yoruba. Laitin argues that in a multicultural society a cultural subsystem may become hegemonic, defining the commonsense symbols and issues of the larger political and economic order, the domain of political power. Other cultural subsystems "do not necessarily threaten the political order," although they may "hold within themselves the sources for counter-hegemony" (Laitin 1986:181, 182). This latter development, of course, depends on historical circumstances and the sense Maisins and other political actors make of them.

Conversion, then, often has the kind of dual economy observable in Uiaku, where people are able to cope simultaneously with two or more practico-moral orientations to the world. The overall direction of a people's conversion depends upon the precise mix of local and extra-local elements present, however, which in turn depends upon the contact situation and the authority of mission and colonial bodies. Among the Maisin, indigenous ideas and values may have maintained a greater social presence than in many other instances of missionization because of the relatively benign attitudes of the Anglicans, limited economic intrusion (no land alienation, for example), and the diffuse nature of the pre-contact religion. Such conditions do not hold everywhere and may even be rare. Converts in southern Africa, for example, were often required to live in mission-directed communities separate from their pagan kin; Native Americans for the most part lost their lands; and Polynesians found their overt politico-religious hierarchy a vulnerable target for external challenge. The peculiarities of the Maisin case, then, should not be overgeneralized. My theoretical point, however, is that conversion may have two faces: one turned inward, toward the microcosm of the local community, and one turned outward, toward a people's differential involvement in the macrocosm. This point, I think, can be explored elsewhere.

External and internal conversion differ not only in modalities but also in content. External conversion deals in bureaucracies, rules, and roles. Internal conversion is rooted less in activities than in consciousness of cosmological notions and moral orientations. This difference in content may help to explain how Maisins engage simultaneously in both types of conversion without experiencing sharp contradictions. One may *act* like a "missionary," for instance, but rationalize one's actions in terms of village morality. Anne Marie Tietjen's study of the moral reasoning of male leaders and nonleaders in Uiaku is revealing in this regard. Adapting psychologist Lawrence Kohlberg's model and test of moral reasoning to Maisin society, Tietjen found that all of her respondents placed a strong ideological emphasis on reciprocity and equivalence, regardless of differences in education and experience outside the village (Tietjen and Walker 1985). Village morality, then, along with basic cosmological notions, is highly flexible and adaptive. Maisins draw upon it to make sense of the mission station and outside world and to make them more or less tolerable. If the material conditions of Uiaku change drastically, as they no doubt will once a major forestry company begins operations in Collingwood Bay, support for the station will probably weaken as villagers put their energies into activities with higher apparent returns. But the people's characteristic moral and cosmological ideas will probably continue in new and developing forms. The situation is reminiscent of MacGaffey's comment on the duality of Kongo society: "whereas in political and economic reality the bureaucratic sector dominates the customary, in popular consciousness the indigenous cosmology retains its primacy because only in the customary sector are [the people] at home" (MacGaffey 1986:248).

NOTES

Acknowledgments. I wish to acknowledge the support of the Killam Foundation, the National Geographic Society, and the Social Sciences and Humanities Research Council of Canada for work in Uiaku in 1981–1983 and 1986. The staffs of the Anglican church, National Archives, and New Guinea Collection of the U.P.N.G. library in Papua New Guinea were extremely helpful and generous with their time. I thank them for permission to cite material appearing in this chapter. Anne Marie Tietjen, Miriam Kahn, William Merrill, and Robert Hefner provided helpful suggestions on earlier drafts. Finally, I wish to express my gratitude to the people of Uiaku and Ganjiga villages, especially to Father Wellington Aburin, Father Giles Ganasa, Deacon Russell Maikin, Macsherry Gegeyo, and Roland Wawe.

1. The exceptions in 1982 included one old woman who had never attended school and several young children in polygamous families. The Anglican church baptizes infants except in disapproved marriages. Older unbaptized children are usually baptized upon completing school.

2. By drawing on these three perspectives I do not mean to slight others. Some anthropologists have recommended approaching conversion in terms of the dialogue or encounter between missionaries and converts (Burridge 1978, Clifford 1980). Others have analyzed the differing conversion experiences of women and men or the young and old (Comaroff and Comaroff 1986, Jolly and Macintyre 1989). Psychologists, historians, sociologists, and theologians also have distinct approaches (see Rambo [1984] for a summary of the literature).

3. For a more detailed analysis of the village-station relationship in Maisin social practice and ideology, see Barker (1990b).

4. I was surprised to find in 1986 that the newly arrived Maisin priest continued to conduct services in English even though a Maisin translation existed. He did, however, deliver the sermon in the vernacular.

5. Many older Maisin also refer to urban centers as "stations."

6. Geertz (1973) originated the term "internal conversion" in his study of the "disenchantment" of modern Balinese religion. Although set in a Weberian framework, Geertz's general perspective is compatible with Horton's (cf. Hefner 1987, Laitin 1986).

7. Horton has provided the most theoretically explicit analysis of internal conversion, but he has intellectualist predecessors. In Melanesia the most influential has been Peter Lawrence. Lawrence (1964) understands so-called cargo cults, for example, as extensions of traditional magico-religious beliefs into new circumstances and has argued that Christianity and other Western influences have barely touched the deep-seated assumptions of indigenous worldviews. For a critique of Melanesianists' analyses of indigenous Christianity, see Barker (1992).

8. The Melanesian literature has tended to treat village societies as autonomous wholes unaffected by outside political and economic forces. Excellent critiques are presented by Carrier and Carrier (1987) and Howard (1983).

9. In the two years I have worked in Uiaku I have never seen a non-Maisin venture into the village to stop a fight. When I asked the village priest about this, he told me that the intrusion of a stranger into village affairs would be strongly resented. Maisin statements about modern "missionaries," as about past ones, should be considered ideological constructions that reveal more about Maisin notions of change than about actual behavior.

10. I have discussed changes in Maisin mortuary practices at greater length elsewhere (Barker 1985b).

REFERENCES

Barker, John. 1983. "Missionaries and Sorcerers: Changes in Sorcery Beliefs among the Maisin of Collingwood Bay, Oro Province." *Research in Melanesia* 7 (3/4):13–24.

———. 1985a. "Maisin Christianity: An Ethnography of the Contemporary Religion of a Seaboard Melanesian People." Ph.D. diss., University of British Columbia.

———. 1985b. "Missionaries and Mourning: Continuity and Change in the Death Ceremonies of a Melanesian People." In Darrell L. Whiteman, ed., *Anthropologists, Missionaries, and Cultural Change*, pp. 263–94. Studies in Third World Societies, No. 25. Williamsburg: College of William and Mary.

———. 1986. "From Boy's House to Young Club: A Case Study of the Youth Movement in Uiaku and Ganjiga Villages, Oro Province." In Maev O'Collins, ed., *Youth and Society: Perspectives from Papua New Guinea*, pp. 81–107. Political and Social Change Monograph, No. 5. Canberra: Department of Political and Social Change, Research School of Pacific Studies, Australian National University.

———. 1987. "Optimistic Pragmatists: Anglican Missionaries among the Maisin of Collingwood Bay, Northeastern Papua, 1898–1920." *Journal of Pacific History* 22 (2):66–81.

———. 1989. "Western Medicine and the Continuity of Belief: The Maisin of Collingwood Bay, Oro Province." In Stephen Frankel and Gilbert Lewis, eds., *A Continuing Trial of Treatment: Medical Pluralism in Papua New Guinea*, pp. 69–94. Dordrecht: Kluwer.

———. 1990a. "Encounters with Evil: Christianity and the Response to Sorcery among the Maisin of Papua New Guinea." *Oceania* 61:139–55.

———. 1990b. "Mission Station and Village: Cultural Practice and Representations in Maisin Society." In John Barker, ed., *Christianity in Oceania: Ethnographic Perspectives*, pp. 173–96. ASAO Monograph, No. 12. Lanham, Md.: University Press of America.

———. 1992. "Christianity in Western Melanesian Ethnography." In James Carrier, ed., *History and Tradition in Melanesian Anthropology*. Berkeley: University of California Press.

Barker, John, and Anne Marie Tietjen. 1990. "Female Facial Tattooing among the Maisin of Oro Province, Papua New Guinea: The Changing Significance of an Ancient Custom." *Oceania* 60:217–34.

Beckett, Jeremy. 1978. "Mission, Church, and Sect: Three Types of Religious Commitment in the Torres Straits." In James A. Boutilier, Daniel T. Hughes, and Sharon W. Tiffany, eds., *Mission, Church, and Sect in Oceania*, pp. 209–30. Ann Arbor: University of Michigan Press.

Beidelman, T. O. 1982. *Colonial Evangelism: A Socio-Historical Study of an East African Mission at the Grassroots*. Bloomington: Indiana University Press.

Berkhofer, Robert F., Jr. 1965. *Salvation and the Savage: An Analysis of Protestant Missions and American Indian Response, 1787–1862*. Lexington: University of Kentucky Press.

Bond, George C. 1987. "Ancestors and Protestants: Religious Coexistence in the Social Field of a Zambian Community." *American Ethnologist* 14:55–72.

Bourdieu, Pierre. 1977. *Outline of a Theory of Practice*. Cambridge: Cambridge University Press.

Burridge, K. O. L. 1960. *Mambu: A Study of Melanesian Cargo Movements and Their Social and Ideological Background*. New York and Evanston: Harper and Row.

———. 1978. "Missionary Occasions." In James A. Boutilier, Daniel T. Hughes, and Sharon W. Tiffany, eds., *Mission, Church, and Sect in Oceania*, pp. 1–30. Ann Arbor: University of Michigan Press.

Carrier, James G. 1981. "Labour Migration and Labour Export on Ponam Island." *Oceania* 51:237–55.

Carrier, James G., and Achsah H. Carrier. 1987. "Brigadoon: or, Musical Comedy and the Persistence of Tradition in Melanesian Ethnography." *Oceania* 57:271–93.

Clifford, James. 1980. "The Translation of Cultures: Maurice Leenhardt's Evangelism, New Caledonia, 1902–1926." *Journal of Pacific History* 15:2–20.

Comaroff, Jean. 1985. *Body of Power, Spirit of Resistance: The Culture and History of a South African People*. Chicago: University of Chicago Press.

Comaroff, Jean, and John Comaroff. 1986. "Christianity and Colonialism in South Africa." *American Ethnologist* 13:1–22.

Crocombe, R. G. 1964. *Commercial Cash Cropping among the Orokaiva*. New Guinea Research Bulletin, No. 4. Canberra and Port Moresby: New Guinea Research Unit.

Dakeyne, R. B. 1966. "Co-operatives at Yega." *Orokaiva Papers*. New Guinea Research Bulletin, no. 13, pp. 53–68. Port Moresby and Canberra: New Guinea Research Unit.

Fisher, Humphrey J. 1973. "Conversion Reconsidered: Some Historical Aspects of Religious Conversion in Black Africa." *Africa* 43:27–40.

———. 1985. "The Juggernaut's Apologia: Conversion to Islam in Black Africa." *Africa* 55:153–73.

Geertz, Clifford. 1973. "'Internal Conversion' in Contemporary Bali." In Geertz, *The Interpretation of Cultures: Selected Essays*, pp. 170–89. New York: Basic Books.

Gill, S. R. M. 1929. "Committee Appointed to Enquire into the Interrelationship between Native Ideas and Christianity." Anglican Archives, box 25, University of Papua New Guinea.

Guenther, Mathias George. 1977. "The Mission Station as 'Sample Community': A Contemporary Case from Botswana." *Missiology* 5:457–65.

Hefner, Robert W. 1987. "The Political Economy of Islamic Conversion in Modern East Java." In William R. Roff, ed., *Islam and the Political Economy of Meaning*, pp. 53–78. London: Croom Helm.

Heise, David R. 1967. "Prefactory Findings in the Sociology of Missions." *Journal for the Scientific Study of Religion* 6:39–58.

Horton, Robin. 1971. "African Conversion." *Africa* 41:85–108.

———. 1975. "On the Rationality of Conversion." *Africa* 41:85–108.

Horton, Robin, and J. D. Y. Peel. 1976. "Conversion and Confusion: A Rejoinder on Christianity in Eastern Nigeria." *Canadian Journal of African Studies* 10: 481–98.

Howard, Michael C. 1983. "Vanuatu: The Myth of Melanesian Socialism." *Labour, Capital, and Society* 16:176–203.

Hughes, Philip J. 1984. "The Assimilation of Christianity in the Thai Culture." *Religion* 14:313–36.

Jolly, Margaret, and Martha Macintyre, eds. 1989. *Family and Gender in the Pacific: Domestic Contradictions and the Colonial Impact*. Cambridge: Cambridge University Press.

Kahn, Miriam. 1983. "Sunday Christians, Monday Sorcerers: Selective Adaptation to Missionization in Wamira." *Journal of Pacific History* 18:96–112.

Kaplan, Martha. 1990. "Christianity, People of the Land, and Chiefs in Fiji." In John Barker, ed., *Christianity in Oceania: Ethnographic Perspectives*, pp. 127–48. ASAO Monograph, No. 12. Lanham, Md.: University Press of America.

Laitin, David D. 1986. *Hegemony and Culture: Politics and Religious Change among the Yoruba*. Chicago: University of Chicago Press.

Lawrence, Peter. 1964. *Road Belong Cargo: A Study of the Cargo Movement in the Southern Madang District*. Manchester: Manchester University Press.

MacGaffey, Wyatt. 1986. *Religion and Society in Central Africa: The BaKongo of Lower Zaire*. Chicago: University of Chicago Press.

Macintyre, Martha. 1990. "Christianity, Cargo Cultism, and the Concept of the Spirit in Misiman Cosmology." In John Barker, ed., *Christianity in Oceania: Ethnographic Perspectives*, pp. 81–100. ASAO Monograph, no. 12. Lanham, Md.: University Press of America.

Morrison, Kenneth M. 1981. "The Mythological Sources of Abenaki Catholicism: A Case Study of the Social History of Power." *Religion* 11:235–63.

Nock, A. D. 1933. *Conversion: The Old and New in Religion from Alexander the Great to Augustine of Hippo*. Oxford: Oxford University Press.

Patrol Reports. 10–15 March 1955. Assistant District Officer, Tufi Subdistrict. Port Moresby: National Archives of Papua New Guinea.

Rambo, Lewis R. 1982. "Current Research on Religious Conversion." *Religious Studies Review* 8:146–59.

Ranger, Terrence. 1978. "The Churches, the Nationalist State, and African Religion." In E. Fashole-Luke, R. Gray, A. Hastings, and G. Tasie, eds., *Christianity in Independent Africa*, pp. 479–502. Bloomington: Indiana University Press.

Ryan, D. 1969. "Christianity, Cargo Cults, and Politics among the Toaripi of Papua." *Oceania* 40:99–118.

Schieffelin, Edward L. 1981. "Evangelical Rhetoric and the Transformation of Traditional Culture in Papua New Guinea." *Comparative Studies in Society and History* 23:150–56.

Schwimmer, Erik G. 1969. *Cultural Consequences of a Volcanic Eruption Experienced by the Mount Lamington Orokaiva*. Eugene, Ore.: Department of Anthropology, University of Oregon.

———. 1973. *Exchange in the Social Structure of the Orokaiva: Traditional and Emergent Ideologies in the Northern District of Papua*. New York: St. Martin's Press.

Smith, Michael French. 1984. "'Wild' Villagers and Capitalist Virtues: Perceptions of Western Work Habits in a Preindustrial Community." *Anthropological Quarterly* 57 (4):125–39.

———. 1990. "Catholicism, Capitalist Incorporation, and Resistance in Kragur." In John Barker, ed., *Christianity in Oceania: Ethnographic Perspectives*, pp. 149–72. ASAO Monograph, no. 12. Lanham, Md.: University Press of America.

Thune, Carl. 1981. "Normanby Island Historiography." *Bikmaus* 2:3–9.

Tietjen, Anne Marie, and Lawrence J. Walker. 1985. "Moral Reasoning and Leadership among Men in a Papua New Guinea Society." *Developmental Psychology* 21:982–92.

Tonkinson, Robert. 1981. "Church and Kastom in Southeast Ambrym." In M. Allen, ed., *Vanuatu*, pp. 237–67. Sydney: Academic Press.

Wetherell, David. 1977. *Reluctant Mission: The Anglican Church in Papua New Guinea, 1891–1942*. St. Lucia: University of Queensland Press.

Young, Michael W. 1977. "Doctor Bromilow and the Bwaidoka Wars." *Journal of Pacific History* 12:130–53.

PART FOUR

Modalities of Religious Exchange

CHAPTER EIGHT

Religion, Morality, and Prophetic Traditions: Conversion among the Pitjantjatjara of Central Australia

Aram A. Yengoyan

Religious conversion to world religions has long been of historical interest to anthropology, comparative religion, and sociology, but most analysis has been devoted to understanding how and why world religions spread at the expense of traditional cultures and societies. Though the literature on Africa (as exemplified by the works of Horton 1971, 1975a, 1975b; Peel 1968; and Fisher 1985) might diverge in its analyses of the spread of Christianity and Islam throughout sub-Saharan Africa, one would have to admit that Islam's juggernaut, to paraphrase H. J. Fisher (1985), is more than simply an argument between Horton and Fisher. The logic and movement of forms of religious conversion exist apart from the theories of historians and anthropologists. In Southeast Asia, Hinduism of an early era spread at the expense of localized societies just as Christianity and Islam moved into the area before and after European contact in the sixteenth century. And throughout Melanesia and Polynesia the Christian missionary effort has left a marked imprint on local cultures, one which still haunts the development of contemporary cultural identity in most parts of Polynesia.

Although most areas of the ethnographic world have been affected differently, world religions have generally overwhelmed local cultures. Whether the theoretical models of this conversion process are expressed as the contrast between and shift from traditionalism to rationality (Weber 1956), or the differences in logic between traditional religions and world religions (Geertz 1973), or the move from microcosmic beliefs to macrocosmic thought as expressed by Horton (or the two-tier model of religious structuration), in case after case we are left with a range of conversion examples in which local cultures, small-scale societies, and even more complex groups are cast as passive agents in a long historial process.

Yet in a relatively few but critical cases, religious conversion did not take place, or, if it did, the resultant religious creations and changes have been unexpected either from the viewpoint of world religion or from the viewpoint of the local cultures. In this chapter I discuss some of the ethnographic and theoretical debates on why the Pitjantjatjara of the western desert of central Australia have not converted to Christianity. To understand the theoretical issues which this case might illuminate, I first discuss some of the more important features of Pitjantjatjara religion as they bear on the conversion process. I aim to demonstrate that certain facets of Pitjantjatjara religion and morality are not only essential ontological features of Pitjantjatjara religious thought and behavior but also constraints on the openness of Aboriginal religion. I then examine the political and economic manifestations of Pitjantjatjara religious thought through which the ontological framework of society is sustained.

We cannot say that the relationship between Christianity and Pitjantjatjara religion is one of a lack of convergence or one in which religious syncretism is absent or could not occur; rather, we must approach this case as one in which the religion of the economically and politically dispossessed society (the Pitjantjatjara) does not have a "prior text" that facilitates religious conversion—that is, one that relates to prior texts in Western thought which do embrace Christianity. It does, however, have a prior text constituted by combined moral and categorical assumptions that underlie Pitjantjatjara social and collective life and that explain the constraints to change. I analyze how this prior text works and how it differs from the essential tenets of Christian dogma to make the religious conversion of individuals or groups a virtual impossibility. It should be stressed, however, that to a certain extent the case of the Pitjantjatjara parallels that of other Aboriginal societies. Although religious conversion to Christianity has occurred in Aboriginal Australia, when we understand the socioeconomic context in which conversion has taken place we quickly realize that conversion is usually related to economic need or social deprivation or both. In such examples, the tribal ethic or structure has been destroyed with much of the Aboriginal population.

Because my analysis generally stresses the intellectualist aspect of why conversion did not occur among the Pitjantjatjara, the context in which intellectualistic explanations are set forth is important. Economic as well as sociopolitical attributes are essential for comprehending the extent to which "traditional" identities are sustained and fostered. The issues of cultural maintenance and reproduction, which are intellectualistic as well as sociopolitical, rest on one major philosophical component, namely, the role of person and the creation of the individual as they are sustained and expressed through Christian thought.

While Islam has been interpreted as an integration of belief, behavior, and social structure which, in theory, reworks social thought and action, Christianity is interpreted as a system of thought and action which affects the individual but does not render a particular social form. In Christianity, one finds that encountered social orders are negated through the identification of sources of indigenous "evil" or "falseness," which are gradually replaced by new sources of "goodness" and "truth." Although a new social order need not emerge—as Burridge (1978:19) notes, Christian communities are expressed in a wide range of types of social organization—another form of self must emerge within a dynamic Christian context. The individual becomes a distinct and responsible unit who has rights and bears responsibilities toward fellow humans as well as to an evolving social order.

The evolving social order may take different manifestations, however, and, again from our knowledge of different ethnographic cases in which Christianity has had an impact, it is apparent that Christianity embraces a wide variety of social forms. Some of these social forms are more compatible with Christianity, others less so; however, in each case individuality is the feature which is constant in each different social milieu. As Burridge (1978:15) concludes, the concept of individuality, a hallmark of Christianity, is generalized in some cases; this, in turn, may create new social forms in which the cultural logic is based on individualism; in theory these social structures are harmonious with the way in which individualism has reemerged. However, individualism can evolve in a variety of social forms or social milieus. In contemporary America, for example, society simply does not restrict or constrain the individual as a motivating agent to the same extent that Pitjantjatjara society does. At this end of the spectrum, one may find the individual as a self-reflexive and critical thinker who can step outside the social milieu, scrutinize its customs, and create (or at least envision) a new moral foundation for emerging social orders. New social orders and new moralities in turn create what Burridge (1978:15) terms the "new man," a conception of the individual closely linked to Christian visions as expressed through the resurrection.

All societies depend upon the activities of individual agents, who mediate social, structural, religious, and philosophical tenets in dealing with daily contingencies. And from this process emerge new cultural and moral imperatives. Cultures differ, however, in the extent of the constraints imposed on the individual. Such challenges are clearly exemplified by the Australian Aboriginal for whom an intricate and detailed set of structural constraints in the form of totemic affiliations, subsection systems, marriage arrangements, and kinship relations embed the individual in a complex mesh of groups and relationships.

In such a social context the dilemma for Christian conversion is not simply how to substitute one set of religious tenets for another but how to develop new forms of individuality from the complex matrix of Aboriginal social rules through which all individuals are intricately related. While Christianity posits a strong sense of the individual and the ability to move between group identity and individual identity, the social structures and relationships of Aboriginal Australia make problematic any such free-floating individuality, and thus the process of Christian conversion itself.

THE CONTEXT OF PITJANTJATJARA RELIGION

The Pitjantjatjara make up one of the largest language groups in the western desert, ranging from Warburton east to Ernabella, north to the western Macdonald Ranges, and south to Yalata and Ooldea. The population of Pitjantjatjara speakers in this vast area of several thousand miles is about one thousand individuals. Their geographic spread started in the 1920s and 1930s, during which Elkin and Tindale noted a population movement toward the east and southeast. Currently, most of the Pitjantjatjara live in small communities in western Australia in a chain of mountain ranges extending from the Musgraves on the east to the Petermanns and Tonkinsons on the west. Traditionally, they had a classic hunting and collecting economy, but over the last four decades they have shifted toward a mixed cash economy, mild to extreme dependence on social welfare funds, and occasional entrepreneurial activities fostered by government agencies.

In spite of these economic transformations and the demise of full-time hunting and collecting, the social and religious structures of the Pitjantjatjara have remained intact. Initiation rituals are precisely followed and emphatically supported both internally, for example, by the virtual prohibition of marriage for noninitiated males, and externally, through the Red Ochre ceremonies performed by individuals from different areas. The purpose of Red Ochre ceremonies is to enforce the full cycle of male initiation rites, which must be completed before a marriage is sanctioned.

In the Aboriginal worldview, ritual and religious totemism are still the essential ground of all human activity. In fact, rituals of different scales of intensity and scope are now conducted with much greater frequency and emphasis than in the past. During a period of sixteen months in 1966–1967, at least 150 to 200 ceremonial activities and initiation rites were performed at Amata (a Pitjantjatjara settlement in the Musgrave Ranges). The increasing sedentarization of the population, along with the recent increased mobility through the use of motor vehicles (which have replaced the camel), has resulted in more "leisure" time for ritual reproduction. Motor transportation also makes it possible to participate in rituals held farther away. Not only is the ritual life of the 1960s and 1970s probably as rich as that of the precontact past but the intensity and frequency of performances have also reached heights which the tribal elders could not have anticipated.

Missionary influence among the Pitjantjatjara started in the late 1930s with the establishment of a Presbyterian mission at Ernabella, located in the eastern section of the Musgrave Ranges. Besides its evangelical purposes, the original mission was charged in the late 1930s with buffering the Pitjantjatjara to the west from the gradual encroachment of European influences from the east and south. Since that time the mission has successfully cared for the people by providing employment, purchasing dingo scalps, supplying gasoline and mechanical assistance for vehicle repairs, offering medical aid, and selling commodities and provisions through the local store.

Local economic activities that were started by the Presbyterian mission have had a marked impact on the native population. Beginning in the 1940s, Pitjantjatjara were hired to work as shepherds throughout the eastern Musgrave Ranges. Sheep provided meat and the wool was spun to make small rugs, one of the major hallmarks of the work done by the Pitjantjatjara at Ernabella. These rugs were designed with Aboriginal motifs and symbols, and were sold to tourist shops in Alice Springs; many made their way to art galleries throughout Australia. Besides providing income for about a dozen Pitjantjatjara workers, the rugs established a sense of pride and identity with the people's cultural heritage.

But by the middle 1970s the sheep industry was phased out because of high costs. "Traditional" rug making gave way to the production of similar designs and motifs in batik on fabric which was imported and dyed for local use. By the late 1970s the mission was "secularized" and headed by government administrators. Since the early 1980s most of the local population has been employed through an assortment of different jobs. In general, both employment and employment opportunities have increased in recent years. At various times the Pitjantjatjara have moved temporarily to the west or to small outstations closer to ancestral lands, but because sustained employment exists and Ernabella is the traditional home for the majority of the population, most Pitjantjatjara have stayed in the community.

Even though the church built an economic infrastructure for the benefit of the Pitjantjatjara, native Aboriginals were not required to convert to Christianity to avail themselves of church resources. Although a good portion of the population attended church services and pageantry with some regularity, the majority of Pitjantjatjara were not actively committed to Christianity. They looked still to their own traditions for the basis for their identity and commitments.

GENERAL THEMES OF PITJANTJATJARA RELIGION

The most coherent themes which maintain the integrity of Pitjantjatjara society and culture combine religious dogma and faith, along with a keenness of pride. These themes set blacks apart from the dominant whites. In fact, the Pitjantjatjara use terms like "blackfella" and "whitefella" not only to establish and reassert the contrast between Aboriginal life and the white world but also to show that what defines Aboriginality is a set of cultural features which white Australians can never understand, let alone possess. One particular example of this ability to invoke cultural structures to maintain the difference between both societies comes to mind. Pitjantjatjara males would emphatically state, with much laughter, that Europeans are like dogs. Why? Because dogs and whites possess no marriage rules and indiscriminately mate with anyone of their own species. In contrast, Aboriginal marriages are exogamous, structured by prescriptive rules which dictate the category into which one will marry; the system of marriage is specifically coded to bring forth desired relationships based on marriage.

The Aboriginals' pride in their own tradition is not only astutely developed but is also intellectualized in part as a means of telling the "other" that they are the "other" and that certain basic cultural, religious, and philosophical boundaries cannot be crossed or even minimized. Pride, combined with an intellectual arrogance of how the "blackfella" life differs from that of all white Australians, is the very essence of cultural differentiation. It provides a foundation for the cultural reproduction of Aboriginality as a coherent set of abstractions whose integrity can be understood only by the Pitjantjatjara and, to a certain extent, other Aboriginal peoples.

As in the religion of neighboring Central Australian Aboriginals, Pitjantjatjara religion emphasizes a morality which puts great value on social collectivities and the incorporation of the individual within them. The dominance of the moral is expressed in the realm of myth, to such a degree that, in most perspectives, one could argue that all Pitjantjatjara religion is based on myth. I will attempt to expand on the general theme of mythic importance before relating it to the moral basis of ritual action and everyday reality.

Myth is the most pivotal link to the ancient past, as expressed in the Dreamtime, as well as to all accounts of cosmogony and cosmology.

Myths not only explain how the world came to be and how the Pitjantjatjara are part of a universal scheme but they also inform the activities of daily life. The classic division between sacred and secular (which has a critical impact on human activities among the Pitjantjatjara) is central to how myth underwrites the sacred side of this contrast. Virtually all sacred activities, implements, songs, and rituals are the ongoing expression of particular myths. Thus, seldom, if ever, does one find myths which are not relegated to the most ancient past. The taxonomic worlds of fauna, flora, marriage sections, and cosmology are all explained by particular myths which give intellectual and emotional sustenance to those categorizations.

How does myth project itself into the present and into the most distant future? The essence of Aboriginal religion as myth, and the reproduction of myth, which is basically the reproduction of religion, has two primary vehicles: physical markers and the structure of linguistic tenses. All myths, regardless of their intratribal, intertribal, or extratribal scope, have physical referents; these are vital to the myths' persistence. For all social and spiritual purposes the Dreaming unifies the social with the spiritual. Interestingly, dreaming "tracks" employ only land and physical features as icons; the sky is never used. Most of the environment is carved and demarcated with the tracks of mythic heroes and ancestral beings who move from locality to locality. Some of these tracks are on the earth's surface, but most are below the surface. In dramatizing myths, Pitjantjatjara males state what happened at a particular locality, where the events moved to, and all the intricacies of how each event relates to all other events; these "tracks" and movements code and maintain the myth. Each story also conveys a particular moral and shows how this moral is reflected in Pitjantjatjara existence. Each physical step or track signifies a story, myth, or legend, emblematically expressing what is happening in a highly overt and literal way. The symbolism is always there, and from it a number of accounts can be derived for each physical referent. But the symbolic constitution is only one aspect of expressive culture; the environment and what it means consequently trigger the kinds of rituals which must take place. Even more important, certain rituals are enacted only in the appropriate physical context. Since the meaning of a ritual or a larger ceremony has a physical referent, nearly all physical and environmental features also possess a spiritual counterpart.

Just as myth is visually present throughout the landscape as a set of markers on and below the ground, myth is also propelled from the most ancient past into the present through certain forms of tense and aspect in language structures. The past tense is used only for secular actions and events which have no sacred counterpart. More important, the use of the past tense implies that an action or event is concluded. For the Pitjantjatjara, sacred activities and sacred thoughts have no beginning or end. The major features of Pitjantjatjara humanity as expressed in myth are part of an almost unbroken existence from the ancient past as unfolded in the Dreaming.

In the recording of myths and sacred stories the "past" is completely absent. Most mythic and religious accounts are narrated in the imperfective and continuing imperfective, which stress the continuity of action. Thus, in versions of the eaglehawk myth, for example, one hears "eaglehawk was falling off the branch," not "eaglehawk fell off the branch." In the first version the imperfective is used as aspect and not as tense. Myths stress the continuity of the most distant past with the most recent past and the present. This form of narrative places the myths and other sacred stories in the present and propels them into the future.

Using the past tense for myths and sacred accounts would imply that the action has ended and will never recur, that once an event has transpired its impact on the present could be only marginal, and that over time it would have no impact on or meaning in spiritual thought and action. Not only is the past tense absent then in mythic narrative, but its use is not tolerated in the culture. The combination of the imperfective as aspect and the use of physical referents for all mythic accounts provides a collective means of maintaining religious value in the present, even though its source is in the most distant past. Thus the sacred is manifest in a particular linguistic structure, and this structure continuously maintains itself into the realm of the present.

The past tense is used for nearly all activities which might be labeled secular or profane. Thus eating, going on a trip, or seeing another person are conveyed in the past. "I saw him four days ago" represents a completed action and implies that the action will never recur. As recent history, secular actions are not subject to the structure of religion and myth. The past tense is often used for events which have occurred within living memory, and these events are commonly pegged to particular historical events. For one of my older informants, the events during and just after World War I established his sense of historical time. He placed other accounts in this context and discussed each account as something which had happened once.

Ideally all sacred events (myth and religion) are cast in the imperfective, and all secular events are expressed in the past. Certain other forms of narrative occasionally modify this pattern; however, in its contrast of structure and history, of the sacred and the secular, and of different perspectives of time, the use of the past as tense and the imperfective as aspect allows the Pitjantjatjara to maintain the sacredness of their existence.

One other factor is vital in understanding why myth is the critical feature in Pitjantjatjara religion. Throughout the social anthropological literature on religion, myth and ritual have almost always been coupled together. From Malinowski to Radcliffe-Brown and to contemporary writers, ritual is conceived as the enactment of myth, and myth is the charter or the justification of ritual and how it is performed. Within the Aboriginal context, and specifically for the Pitjantjatjara, I argue that most rites are mythless and most myths are riteless. This is not to say that rite and myth are not connected, for in many cases rituals are performed in terms of particular legends which serve as the moral justification of the ritual action. But in most cases ritual and myth have their own, differently structured, logic and properties. For the Pitjantjatjara, rituals are more a social than a mythic expression. Just as social groups adjust to everyday experiences, rituals also respond to life's contingencies, and thus they are caught up in the social milieu. Myths as stories with particular narrative devices not only stand apart from human intervention, however, but also exist as testimonials of the ancient past and the moral imperatives the past reveals in, and through, the narratives. Rituals can be reorganized or restructured to accommodate new social needs and conditions, either through internal change or external borrowing. Thus, one might question the assumption that all rituals are invariant, for they are the basis of social action which establishes how rituals are to be performed (for a more detailed discussion, see Yengoyan 1979, 1980, 1986, 1989, 1990). Residing in the unconscious, myth has a logic that in theory is immutable. The realm of myth, based on emblematic markers, its own form of narrative in language structure, and its semiseparation from ritual, not only constitutes all that is religious but also escapes accommodation to the social forces of everyday life.

Earlier, I had mentioned how the collective is stressed in religious thought and in all knowledge. Pitjantjatjara understand that knowledge and wisdom should coexist. Any individual who has been fully initiated should have equal access to spiritual and economic knowledge, which is understood as a given and is always group based. Thus, all individuals within their own groups have equal knowledge; and knowledge itself is only comprehended as something which individuals possess because they belong to particular groups. Knowledge is never a private matter, nor is it considered characteristic only of a particular individual. In fact, Pitjantjatjara have a marked fear of any form of personalized knowledge which does not have collective roots; socialization is linked to patterns of social interaction which strongly deny any attribution of special knowledge to any single individual.

One possible exception to this conception of knowledge is the existence of medicine men. The Pitjantjatjara would like to deny their existence, but they do exist, and they are feared. Seldom, if ever, would anyone talk to me about them. They fear not only what medicine men can do because of their putative powers but also the secret knowledge of the medicine men, knowledge that is highly individual, not collective, knowledge which others cannot understand.

All knowledge is not common knowledge, however. Social markers, such as age and gender, affect the imparting and content of knowledge. Knowledge denied at earlier ages will be made available at later periods in life. Spiritual knowledge and wisdom are never fully attained until an individual reaches a relatively old age.

Differences in knowledge along gender lines are the most striking. Both sexes identify a body of knowledge belonging to only their gender and of no interest to the other. For example, in attempting to understand how certain myths were linked with the constellations, I soon realized that almost all astronomical knowledge and all accounts of stars and planets are highly differentiated as either male or female. The Southern Cross and the Big Dipper belong to men, but Venus is only in the female canon. If males do possess knowledge of Venus, I could not obtain it from them. Pitjantjatjara males would relate only knowledge which they considered male knowledge, and they also made it very clear that they had no awareness of female knowledge and would make no attempt to understand it because female knowledge was inferior. Unfortunately, because of my limited contact with women, I cannot provide their knowledge of the galaxy or perspective on male knowledge. This division of knowledge by gender reflects the dualistic contrast and oppositions inherent in group knowledge, which is based on principles of inclusion and exclusion.

The moral foundations of social action are thought to be derived from the ancestral beings and events of the mythic past and present. Throughout Pitjantjatjara society one finds a close connection between what individuals do, how they argue and justify their actions, and what occurs in mythic stories and accounts. The realm of myth provides cultural truths in terms of action and how action is understood by individuals and groups. But the moral truths should not be associated with righteous behavior and are far from being considered as ideals. One example might suffice to express the range of behaviors which are established and justified in mythic life. Deception is one of the best examples of how moral truths, as expressed in myth, have a strong counterpart in social life. Many Pitjantjatjara myths have plots in which an individual, usually a fully initiated male, can control events and individuals by deceiving others. The deceived parties are usually young male novices or women, but at times they are other initiated males. In the myths the deceiver gets his way by threatening, injuring, or possibly killing his victims. The injured parties unite to correct the situation; but even though they have been wronged, no one can claim that the deceptive behavior was outside the law. Deception is part of a moral grounding of truths which one must learn to live with. In most myths, at the final stage of the story, the deceiver ends up as a hero; his actions, however repulsive, are still within acceptable limits. Thus, the deceiver is sometimes a physically injured hero, but a hero nonetheless.

In daily life deception may occur again between the same groups just as in the myths. One must be on guard, but one must also understand that a deception which has its basis in the moral givens of myth is tolerable and socially accepted. Deception beyond what myths and plot structures embrace is severely punished by the community. In this sense action is primarily moral action, and moral action expresses the cultural givens of the mythic past and present.

THE CONVERSION PROCESS: POLITICS AND CULTURAL IDENTITY

In attempting to understand Pitjantjatjara religious structures as collective, moral givens derived from mythic primacy, my concern is to analyze how these cultural givens establish a prior text which might allow us to explain and understand what kinds of religious change, through conversion, may or may not occur.[1] Christianity among the Pitjantjatjara was introduced by the Presbyterian church, which started a mission in the late 1930s at Ernabella. The mission was staffed by white Australians and by a minister who, until about 1982, was always a European. More recently, after the South Australian government replaced the Presbyterian church as the financial backer of the mission and in other outreach responsibilities, the church has attempted to turn over mission operations to Aboriginals.

By the middle 1980s, but even as far back as the middle 1960s, when I first worked in this area, the missionaries counted about eight or ten "true" converts, meaning individuals who had given their souls to the Christian church. From the perspective of the Pitjantjatjara, however, conversion was manifested by the rejection of initiation rites. Thus, a good proportion of the community came to Sunday services, but it was obvious that they were primarily interested in the music and choral singing and some of the ritual of the Presbyterian service. Conversion had little or no attraction, in part because of the enlightened policies of the church, which did not try to save souls just for the sake of doing so, but also because of the foreignness of the message of Christianity, which, apart from the ritual and singing, was in many ways incomprehensible to the Pitjantjatjara. Thus, after nearly fifty years of church and missionizing activities, conversions were so few as to be nearly inconsequential.

The same pattern of low conversion rates or even the absence of conversion occurs in other Aboriginal contexts throughout the interior. In 1970, I spent about a week in Yuendumu, which is the largest of the Walbiri communities. The Walbiri, who reside to the northwest of Alice Springs, are probably the largest Aboriginal "tribe" in central Australia. The local white Australian minister indicated that during twenty-one years among the Walbiri, he had had only one convert to Christianity.

In contrast to the Pitjantjatjara and Walbiri, the Aranda of the Alice Springs–Hermannsburg area converted to Christianity after nearly one hundred years of missionary activity. Yet Strehlow (1956, 1970), the leading Aranda ethnographer and the son of one of the first missionaries among the Aranda, notes that Christianity per se was never ideologically acceptable to the Aranda; rather, the important inducements to at least "hear out" Christianity were the economic consequences of conversion.

In western Australia, Tonkinson (1974) demonstrates how the Mandjildjara of Jigalong overcame the forces of Apostolic Christianity, not by accommodating Christian themes, but by maintaining their own religion, whose basic axioms are simply not represented in Christianity. Mandjildjara rates of religious conversion are comparable to those of the Pitjantjatjara and Walbiri. Tonkinson (1974:118) notes that Apostolic missionaries in Jigalong failed in the conversion process partly because of the nature of Mandjildjara religion, but also in part because of their values and attitudes toward the people. In twenty-four years they had only one committed convert.

From these cases it is apparent that the Pitjantjatjara and other desert-dwelling Aboriginal societies simply do not convert to Christianity—a fact that has been noted by anthropologists of differing theoretical persuasions. Explanations for the absence of conversion must be sought within the cultural foundations of society and within the social and political conditions that reproduce and defend popular commitment to cultural truths. Both Strehlow and Tonkinson note that the "basic axioms" of the spiritual and sacred life are such that Christian doctrine simply does not provide the intellectual or spiritual underpinnings which relate to Aboriginal life. Thus we need to understand the features of Christianity that render religious conversion a moot, if not impossible, task.

The Presbyterian mission at Ernabella was not, and is not, fundamentalist in its orientation to religious thought and the role of the Pitjantjatjara in it. Although the teachings of the Bible are critical, they are not taken literally, and the mission is not committed to the emergence of a "new man" among the Pitjantjatjara. Most of the mission employees had a good command of spoken Pitjantjatjara, services were given in the native language, and evil or false beliefs were not stressed; in general the excessive paternalism evident in Jigalong was simply absent. At the same time, many of the mission employees tried to learn about Pitjantjatjara life, and some have published accomplished works on their experiences as well as on their understanding of Pitjantjatjara culture.

Politically, the Pitjantjatjara realize that whites have resources and are able to "produce" things like roads, vehicles, ample food, cigarettes, and so forth. They also acknowledge, however, that mission folk were different from other whites, especially those who worked for government agencies or private companies. The mission folk lived frugally, and they did not smoke, drink, or swear. But above all, many stayed for a number of years; some mission staff stayed from fifteen to thirty years. The Aboriginals consider this exceptional behavior; nonmission whites usually smoke, they generally drink or are not averse to drinking, and they also do not stay long at the mission or the settlement. In fact, the major points of discussion include when "so-and-so" is leaving or that someone has made "big money" and now wants to move to Alice Springs for comfort. These differences between Christian and non-Christian whites have also generated a suspicion that there is a lot of government money for blackfellas but that none of it is in the people's hands. Thus, the Pitjantjatjara realize that the mission folk did not come for money, and they respect the long-term commitment made by the mission, even if that commitment was generated by beliefs marginal to the people.

Throughout the 1960s and into the late 1970s, when the Presbyterian church was phased out, the Pitjantjatjara, as a political entity, were brought into consultation with the mission staff on local matters of work and other community concerns. It was always assumed, however, that the mission would make the final decisions and that daily operations were under its control. Individual Pitjantjatjara might have balked at this political hierarchy, but overall, relatively few complained since the status quo did not tax people of their time in order to reach decisions. Thus Pitjantjatjara could leave the mission for various lengths of time and go to the bush or move west to ancestral lands.

By the early 1980s all of this changed. With the Pitjantjatjara Land Rights Act in 1981 and the departure of the white missionaries, who left the care of the church to a lay native minister, the political scene was radically altered. Because the Pitjantjatjara now had rights over what was the Northwest Reserve of the state of South Australia, they assumed a more dominant position relative to other aboriginal groups and were brought into the political process in conjunction with white government agencies and their local white representatives. This meant not only a proliferation of committees and the necessity to make decisions but also a great influx of money. By the middle 1980s, Ernabella had seventy to eighty whites in various capacities, ranging from school teachers to technicians, and had experienced an inmigration of urban and semiurban blacks from Adelaide and other South Australian communities. Jobs were available, goods flowed throughout the community, motor traffic rapidly increased (all heads of households desired a Toyota), and the bureaucracy became an infrastructure.

The effects of these changes have been drastic. Native Pitjantjatjara claim that Ernabella is no longer the same community. There are foreigners whom no one knows and other Aboriginal peoples who are black but speak no native language and who have taken jobs there (which in reality many Pitjantjatjara would not accept). In fact, the semihomogeneous community of the middle 1970s has taken on the appearance of a boom town. White administrators, who define their role as advisers and consultants, in theory are there to assist native peoples in their tasks. Aboriginal council leaders are caught up in meetings and committees which in many cases are not part of their lifestyle. The process of political socialization requiring decision making, responsibilities, and obligations, which in many cases rest with a number of individuals, is difficult to comprehend, let alone to accept. In short, although the Pitjantjatjara are the controllers, they are in turn controlled by a legal and political structure which is imposed from the outside, which does not reflect their culture, and which limits the freedom of movement they value so highly.

In retrospect, the influence of the Presbyterian mission and the process of Christianization had minimal impacts on the cultural and religious foundations of Pitjantjatjara society. The church provided a focus for gatherings and also maintained the collectivity of action, but it never became an integral part of Pitjantjatjara life. The Pitjantjatjara realized that the church came with the whites, and it helped articulate Aboriginal-White relations in a harmonious way. Politically, the local people were powerless, but one can also ask what resources were to be controlled and how. Indeed, that the mission staff lived a frugal life and, at the same time, did not interfere with Pitjantjatjara society might be why the Pitjantjatjara have remained a viable culture. To this day few individuals are bilingual, almost all males have been initiated in the customary way, and the destruction of Aboriginal society which occurred elsewhere did not take place. School children were never housed and monitored by mission staff, nor were they sent to church schools in urban areas for prolonged periods.

Burridge (1978) notes that once Christian conversion has created the individual and individuality is expressed through rights and duties this form of individuality can be sustained only through the emergence of money as the medium of exchange. As Simmel ([1907] 1978), followed by Burridge, stresses, money establishes markers between individuals as well as between groups, statuses, interest groups, and eventually classes. In some sense the individuality which is so vital and essential to Christianity is based on money because "Christianity was founded in a monied environment" (Burridge 1978:18). Money is the initial opening to the gradual evolving of new political relationships, for once individuals acknowledge the value of money, they acknowledge their participation in a foreign political economy.

The political economy of money and Christianity had not yet crystallized during the era of the Presbyterian mission in Ernabella. Money was present and wages were paid, but the small supplies of money and a limited cash economy meant that money per se did not alter Aboriginal social structure. Again, all of this has changed. In the 1980s, money has become one of the major barometers of change in individual and social cleavages, which are expressed in the consumer culture of vehicles and other goods. A social structure is evolving which emphasizes material wealth; consequently, the acquisitiveness of individuals has partly eroded the communal system of reciprocity and exchange that kept individuals embedded in a collective framework. Possessions now belong to the individual who purchases them, and many Aboriginals show a marked reluctance to share them with neighbors and kin.

On various occasions when Pitjantjatjara are asked by a European if they are Christian, many will respond in the affirmative, as an act of social accommodation which may or may not have a political or ideological basis. Furthermore, Pitjantjatjara never tell each other that they are Christians even if they have leanings in that direction. An avowal of one's Christianity might imply a negative attitude toward others in the community, and, at the same time, one might be excluded from community and ritual activities because of one's "alleged" Christian commitment.

If the social context of political economy was not conducive to Christian conversion at Ernabella, the disjunctions between Christianity and Pitjantjatjara religion are even greater, both in their philosophical tenets and in how each religion embodies the prophetic tradition in doctrine and practice.

All forms of Christianity have a futuristic orientation. The life hereafter is one of the central beliefs in Christianity. It is within one's power as an individual, either through faith, or reason, or good deeds, to achieve salvation in the form of paradise. The Catholic church stresses faith as the essential ingredient for salvation. Most Protestant churches temper faith with good deeds and hard work and thus emphasize that how well one does on this earth is an indicator of what might happen in the future, and that lack of faith, lack of good deeds, or a wasted life is the path to eternal damnation.

For the Pitjantjatjara, salvation, damnation, and the future of each person are non-issues. It is not the future which is important but the message of the ancient past that lives in the present to determine what will happen. In an unchanging life, an understanding of the past is the key to explaining what is happening and what will happen. In this sense, the eternal is always present. Pitjantjatjara, who possess the eternal through their totems, would take delight in refuting Tillich's statement that "there are no societies which possess the eternal." For Christians the act of prayer implies that life can be changed and improved: for Aboriginals, betterment is insured by adhering more firmly to the eternal laws and by minimizing group and individual violations of correct social conduct.

A second critical difference between Christianity and Pitjantjatjara religion is the way the sacred is conceptualized. God, the Holy Spirit, and the Trinity exist in Christianity as concepts which might or might not have a physical referent. For the Catholic, Jesus is God, but God's existence is also translated in other ways; God's powers, in one sense, are omnipresent as well as omnipotent.

In Pitjantjatjara religion there is no single omnipotent force. Although Maddock (1972) discusses the existence of transcendental powers, that is, those which surpass and override totemic powers, most Australian ethnographies come from either Arnhem Land or southeast Australia. The religions of most desert groups do not have beings with transcendental powers; that is, powers are not linked to any particular totemic center. Apart from this absence, however, ideas and concepts in Christian dogma are not acceptable primarily because they do not have a physical referent. If myths maintain their existence through emblematic signification and are thus visibly present to native believers, ideas such as the universal God preclude the Aboriginals' comprehension and the possibility of internalization. (In fact, given the firm conviction that the natural and supernatural express one another and that one cannot exist without the other, it would be interesting to examine how and why those religions we call "world" religions, which are proselytizing religions, were able to break from the limitations of local social contexts and local environments.) Thus, the Pitjantjatjara understanding of the continuity of myth as religious symbolism in and through physical referents virtually excludes the possibility of accepting, let alone converting to, a religious system heavily biased toward omnipresence.

The last factor, and probably the most important one, in limiting religious conversion is the role of the individual as expressed in prophetic traditions. As mentioned earlier, the stress on collective action and knowledge is not only diagnostic of social and cultural life but is also dramatically revealed in negative attitudes toward individual volition and the privatization of knowledge. Thus, the Pitjantjatjara are suspicious of individuals who either have left the local area for various purposes or are attempting to obtain a political base of power and influence through the manipulation of other people.

The emphatic cultural denial of the importance of the individual is critical in explaining why the Pitjantjatjara have almost no understanding of the prophetic tradition which is a vital component of early Christianity and even more so of the New Testament. Prophets, in early Christianity, delivered a message about future events; but this message was at times based on visions or miracles which were central to a religious plot or mode of operation. The vision combined with prophecy was extolled and eulogized by the prophet, thereby forming the issues which would draw followers and eventually converts to the prophet's mission. But in early Christianity the basis for these visions is personal; it is linked to the endeavors and tribulations of an individual who in turn spreads the word through other individuals as disciples.

When the Pitjantjatjara hear prophetic accounts from the Bible, and when they understand that they are the words of one individual, their first reactions are distrust and caution; eventually they express denial through lack of involvement. They cannot accept that this edifice of religiosity emerged and evolved from biblical characters like Moses, Abraham, Christ, and the disciples. These are acting individuals and not the creation of group action or collective knowledge. Even today, a new Christian movement may try to spread throughout the desert, but in each case the suspicion toward the individual as prophet is very strong. The Christian message is foreign because it is individualized, but the message is also nearly always based on what the future will reveal and what it will mean for the average person. Both revelations are cultural events which have no prior text in and no linkage to the Pitjantjatjara worldview; thus they stand outside the Pitjantjatjara creation of life.

CONCLUSION

The contrast between Christianity and Pitjantjatjara religion indicates the degree of religious conjunction and disjunction which exists and the extent to which these factors can explain the dynamics of religious conversion among the Pitjantjatjara. Using certain religious structures as the prior text(s) which establish the framework for conversion, my aim was to discuss the cultural conditions which limited conversion not only for the Pitjantjatjara but also to a certain extent for the Walbiri, who share a number of religious features with the Pitjantjatjara. What is ideal about this case is that the process is still continuing and is far from any resolution. If other desert groups are affected by economic deprivation or social dislocation as were groups historically along the coast and in areas just inland, conversion will no doubt occur—but again mainly from necessity. As long as the tribal and ritual integrity of these societies is maintained, conversion to Christianity in any of its differing versions will not occur or will be quite minimal. Although such conditions do have strong utilitarian overtones, the utility of conversion is not simply limited to biological and individual survival but is also in part a reconstruction of a sense of community and identity as it relates to Aboriginal existence in a multicultural world of ideas and things.

Critical to our understanding of the success or failure of conversion is a careful reading of the ethnographic foundations and the language that capture social and cultural life. The combination of language and certain cultural features as ontological axioms forms the prior text as the critical component in comprehending and, to a lesser degree, predicting what will happen and what will be the implications of events as they unfold (Yengoyan 1989, 1990).

Ernabella was a "total social institution" from its inception to the middle 1970s. In fact, the history of missions throughout Australia indicates that in more isolated contexts (such as Ernabella) total institutions embracing Aboriginal societies and Europeans were quite widespread, although they appeared at different times. Through federal and state governmental intervention, as well as Aboriginal self-determination, the missions have been phased out from the pivotal authority position in the total institution (Rose and Swain 1988:1–11). Within this background the diversity of Aboriginal-mission relationships is apparent not only for dealing with the impact or lack of impact of conversion but also in establishing the political and social contexts within which conversion and religious activity might have taken place. The Presbyterians, through their dedication to enlightened policies regarding the people and their cultural institutions, maintained a viable indigenous cultural system. They did not regard native culture as evil, nor did they regard the bearers of that culture to be children or products of the devil. Surely what is described by Tonkinson (1974, 1988) is almost the opposite of what transpired at Presbyterian Ernabella for a period of nearly forty years, but one can also conclude that the mission did seal the community from outside forces which it felt were "dangerous or harmful." This paternalism not only limited economic change but it also restricted the mobility or outmigration which might have taken place.

The arrival of external social institutions, including a new, secular political structure, the beginnings of a semiheterogeneous community, the extensions of Australian bureaucracy into the local level, the emergence of a Pitjantjatjara "elite" as heads of community and committees, a full money economy, the spread of consumerism and an exchange system based on commodities as opposed to labor, also brought a number of damaging social processes. In the 1980s petrol sniffing, alcoholism, and a gradual breakdown of parental control over children have taken place partly as a response to a changing authority structure in which the power of tribal elders has shifted into the hands of a new quasi-elite.

These problems have occurred, however, in many Aboriginal communities. They are not restricted to former missions, nor are they simply a response to creeping Europeanization. In fact, one of the major forces behind such conditions in many Aboriginal societies is the context of internal colonialism within a welfare state (see Beckett [1985] for a detailed account of these issues). The social services which are now in full blossom under the welfare state were all pioneered by the early missions, but in general their negative impacts have only emerged since the mid-1970s.

Religious movements in recent times which incorporate certain aspects of Christianity have been noted among the Pintubi and other neighboring groups in the Balgo area by Myers (1986) and further to the west by Kolig (1981, 1988). These cults use Christian narrative to bridge local differences as a means of identity formation. As a cult, Christianity does not convey a whole message nor does it embody a system of belief and action which in any way promotes the "new man." Ideally, these Christian narratives effectively promote a type of individuation which permits the emergence of a negotiated social framework which again brings forth the production of self. The focus on the individual and the production of self in terms of Christian ends does not imply, however, that the social structure of local Christianity is completely voluntaristic or loose.

In 1982 a number of these movements spread through the Balgo–Halls Creek area. But again, as cults, their existence depended on how Aboriginals as cultural or religious brokers were able to maintain their dominance over a small entourage. The cults were also open to religious opportunism by the Aboriginals who might use them to achieve certain ends or for an economic "payoff." Many cults will meet short-term needs, but few will translate themselves into long-term, enduring social movements. Of particular interest is the fact that cults do address the question of the emergence of the individual but only with the parallel emergence of a negotiated social organization.

The contrast between Aboriginal Australian cultures and Melanesian societies presents some interesting problems relating to how and why conversion occurs. The anthropological literature on New Guinea presents numerous cases in which conversion to Christianity is rapid and lasting. Schieffelin's (1981a, 1981b) accounts of the Kaluli and Onabasulu indicate an almost wholesale rejection of a cultural tradition that was unable to transform itself during the period of missionary contact. The evangelical intimidation by the indigenous missionaries provided the natives with no choice but to gradually reject traditional ceremonies and food exchange, a move that led to a decline in the local political authority structure. Of more importance is that futuristic events within the canon of traditional Kaluli belief were integrated into the Christian myth of the coming of Christ.

Among the Telefolmin of Melanesia the breakdown of the ceremonial system based on the *Yolam* (men's cult house) and a set of contrastive male-female domestic relations is even more dramatic. In a brilliant analysis Jorgenson (1981) notes how various Telefol communities became split between traditionalists and revivalists as a response not only to Christianity but also to the presence of copper-mining ventures. With the destruction of the *Yolam* in some communities, he found a rapid and irreversible change as missionaries moved throughout the area, working in part through women (who were not part of the traditional system) and in part through uninitiated young novices. Change was so drastic that Jorgenson, the ethnographer, was contacted in Canada in 1979 by the traditionalists and requested to return as soon as possible to record the traditional lore before it disappeared with the death of the older generation. In other cases, massive and quick conversion occurred when a generation of young men, in their desire to take control from elders, sided with a missionary and used Christianity both as a spiritual and political means to bring about a new social order.

Both cosmological and sociopolitical factors help explain conversion in the two societies. The achieving of individuality (which is difficult in Aboriginal societies because of the intricate system of relationships and structures in which the individual is embedded) is more evident in many Melanesian societies, where the dominant structural and organizational configuration is determined by brother-sister relations and affinal exchanges (Burridge 1978:17). Furthermore, the existence and meaning of tradition as a bonding of individuals in an existing framework is almost absent in some Melanesian societies. As Stephen (1979) stresses, an unchanging coherent tradition sanctified only by the distant past is always played off against daily contingencies. The discourse with the past does not have to do with what the past said through its ancestors but with what those ancestors are saying in the present. If older, static traditions no longer work under present circumstances, other answers must be sought. These pragmatic attitudes are interpreted through what individuals say and do, not through what the past unfolds as a static form of thought and action. In such cases, one would expect to find revelation as it emerges in and through the individual. Pragmatism as a cultural force is not only embedded in individual action but is also found in the continuous interpretation and evaluation of community. Gods need not be relegated to the past; Stephen (1979:15) correctly concludes that new gods and new deities might choose to live and exist in contemporary communities. The dominance of the present and the cultural commitment to pragmatism explain some of the conditions which promote and support the existence of sorcery even in heavily Christianized areas (Stephen 1987).

The contrast between Aboriginal Australia and Melanesia is expressed not only in the marked differences in religious conversion. The Melanesian ethnography yields numerous accounts of cargo cults and messianic movements, and again, these accounts indicate that the social polity of individuals and groups works toward influence, gain, and status. In the Aboriginal ethnography accounts of messianic movements and cargoes, even in their most rudimentary forms, simply do not exist (Burridge 1973, 1988). A close reading of the one reported case shows that the "mini-messianic movement" was directed against the ethnographer, though the ethnographer was not aware that he was the target.

How might we try to explain these differences? Here, I argue that the rapidity of change in Melanesia through conversion, cargo cults, and messianic movements might be explained in at least two ways. It is my impression that the prophetic tradition is widespread in many New Guinea religions and that it existed prior to contact. Where we find cultural pockets of "big men" (and now "great men"), we would expect a prophetic tradition; in many ways the big man complex is prophetic itself. If this is the case, I would predict that an indigenous system of prophets has a prior text which might allow us to explain the absence or presence of religious conversion in different sociocultural contexts.

Of further interest, and on problems which are more anthropological and linguistic, the prior text model should also include a framework of inquiry which attempts to identify how indigenous religious structures relate myth into the present through visual markers, language structures, or both. I do not expect to find parallels in the Melanesian case; in fact, ideally we would find linguistic structures of myth and the nature of myth as a transcendental power or localized phenomena which might be contrasted with the Pitjantjatjara case.

Epistemological and ontological differences are evident both in culture and in language when we try to find explanations (at least on the cultural level) of how and why conversion in many Melanesian societies differs from that of Aboriginal Australia. Yet the sociopolitical environment in which conversion is embedded is as important as "intellectualistic" or "psychological" forces. Native experience and identity structure among the Pitjantjatjara might have led them to reject Christianity as a religious force, but in most cases they did not reject the social organization of the missions. Again, the development of each mission is vital in assessing the contemporary impact of missions and Christianity on the Pitjantjatjara as well as other groups.

Missions had an impact on local cultures in part by extending a set of services and introducing socioeconomic relations which reorganized day-to-day Aboriginal life (Rose and Swain 1988). In turn, most missions and missionaries were the first advocates of Aboriginal causes, for better health, employment within the white Australian economy, and eventually self-determination. It is difficult to assess the degree to which missions and Christian conversion succeeded or failed; in fact, the question may not even be appropriate. Christianity might have failed, but the mission movement did have a lasting impact, one, however, that may not be generalizable. If Jigalong failed in all senses of the word, as Tonkinson (1974, 1988) notes, Ernabella lies at the other end of the spectrum. It did succeed most admirably in allowing the Pitjantjatjara sense of identity to flourish, although this may have been a consequence which the missionaries neither intended nor desired.

In either case, the mission structure was, and is, part of the internal colonization of Australian Aboriginals, and within this colonization the Euro-Australian majority held the missionary effort in low esteem. As Burridge (1988:28) emphatically concludes, white Australians not only disdained the mission, the missionary, and Christianity but also "in so many ways preferred that Aborigines *not* be Christians, *not* have a status equivalent to other Australians." In whatever context, mission or non-mission, or Christian or non-Christian, the dilemma is similar for both whites and blacks, namely, how is faith sustained in a world forged by secular materialism and based on increasing individuation? Christianity did not create a moral crisis among the Pitjantjatjara, although it did lessen the traditional bonds of their culture; however, the moral crisis might yet occur as a by-product of continuous colonialization based on state-operated capitalism.

As an epilogue to the issue of Christian conversion, we might ask whether and how Aboriginals converted Europeans. Religious conversion of whites to Pitjantjatjara religion has seldom, if ever, occurred. As Pitjantjatjara explained to me on a number of occasions, whites cannot experience a Dreaming. But conversion, at least among the Pitjantjatjara, has occurred in another form: the initiation of white males into adulthood through the practice of subincision. In 1982 I was told of at least eight cases in which Europeans had submitted to subincision, and I suspect that there were a few more cases not brought to my attention. Whatever the motives of those individual Europeans and the Pitjantjatjara practitioners, this practice did mark the re-creation of a whitefella as a blackfella. In some cases, conversion worked, that is, whites realized the social and moral implications of the initiation. In other cases, they did not. In all cases, however, the initiates adopted Aboriginal traditions to some degree. Just how different this is from the Pitjantjatjara understanding of Christianity and mission life is an unanswerable question, one which can only draw forth their speculations and our puzzlement on something which should remain moot.

NOTES

Acknowledgments. I wish to thank Robert Hefner for his clarification of a number of issues raised in this paper. Also special thanks are extended to Heinz Fenkl, Linda Callis-Buckley, and Laura Stork for their critical and creative reading of various drafts of this paper.

1. The coherence dimension of the prior text provides a mutual set of symbols and understandings which individuals use to make sense of societal events; texts bind individuals to individuals and groups to groups. But more important, "coherence" allows individuals to create new texts and interpret old texts for other members of society. Yet "new" texts can only be understood, created, and transmitted through the prior text of language structure and cultural meaning (for a more detailed statement on prior texts, see Becker 1979).

REFERENCES

Becker, A. L. 1979. "Text-Building, Epistemology, and Aesthetics in Javanese Shadow Theater." In *The Imagination of Reality: Essays in Southeast Asian Coherence Systems*, A. L. Becker and Aram A. Yengoyan, eds., pp. 211–43. Norwood, N.J.: Ablex.

Beckett, Jeremy. 1985. "Colonialism in a Welfare State: The Case of the Australian Aborigines." In *The Future of Former Foragers in Australia and Southern Africa*, Carmel Schrire and Robert Gordon, eds., pp. 7–24. Cambridge, Mass.: Cultural Survival.

Burridge, Kenelm O. L. 1973. *Encountering Aborigines: Anthropology and the Australian Aboriginal.* Elmsford, N.Y.: Pergamon Press.

———. 1978. "Introduction: Missionary Occasions." In *Mission, Church, and Sect in Oceania*, James A. Boutilier, Daniel T. Hughes, and Sharon W. Tiffany, eds. ASAO Monograph, no. 6, pp. 1–30. Lanham, Md.: University Press of America.

———. 1988. "Aborigines and Christianity: An Overview." In *Aboriginal Australians and Christian Missions*, Tony Swain and Deborah B. Rose, eds., pp. 18–29. Bedford Park, South Australia: Australian Association for the Study of Religions.

Fisher, Humphrey J. 1985. "The Juggernaut's Apologia: Conversion to Islam in Black Africa." *Africa* 55:153–73.

Geertz, Clifford. 1973. "'Internal Conversion' in Contemporary Bali." In Clifford Geertz, *The Interpretation of Cultures*, pp. 170–89. New York: Basic Books.

Horton, Robin. 1971. "African Conversion." *Africa* 41:85–108.

———. 1975a. "On the Rationality of Conversion: Part I." *Africa* 45:219–35.

———. 1975b. "On the Rationality of Conversion: Part II." *Africa* 45:373–99.

Jorgenson, Dan. 1981. "Life on the Fringe: History and Society in Telefolmin." In *The Plight of Peripheral People in Papua New Guinea*, vol. 1, *The Inland Situation*, Robert Gordon et al., eds., pp. 59–79. Cambridge, Mass.: Cultural Survival.

Kolig, Erich. 1981. *The Silent Revolution: The Effects of Modernization on Australian Aboriginal Religion.* Philadelphia: ISHI.

———. 1988. "Mission Not Accomplished: Christianity in the Kimberleys." In *Aboriginal Australians and Christian Missions*, Tony Swain and Deborah B. Rose, eds., pp. 376–90. Bedford Park, South Australia: Australian Association for the Study of Religions.

Maddock, K. 1972. *The Australian Aborigines: A Portrait of Their Society.* London: Penguin Press.

Myers, Fred R. 1986. *Pintupi Country, Pintupi Self: Sentiment, Place, and Politics among Western Desert Aborigines.* Washington, D.C.: Smithsonian Institution Press.

Peel, J. D. Y. 1968. *Aladura: A Religious Movement among the Yoruba.* London: Oxford University Press.

Rose, Deborah Bird, and Tony Swain. 1988. "Introduction." In *Aboriginal Australians and Christian Missions*, Tony Swain and Deborah B. Rose, eds., pp. 1–8. Bedford Park, South Australia: Australian Association for the Study of Religions.

Schieffelin, E. L. 1981a. "Evangelical Rhetoric and the Transformation of Traditional Culture in Papua New Guinea." *Comparative Studies in Society and History* 23:150–56.

———. 1981b. "The End of Traditional Music, Dance, and Body Decoration in

Bosavi, Papua New Guinea." In *The Plight of Peripheral People in Papua New Guinea*, vol. 1, *The Inland Situation*, Robert Gordon et al., eds., pp. 1–22. Cambridge, Mass.: Cultural Survival.

Simmel, Georg. [1907] 1978. *The Philosophy of Money*. London: Routledge and Kegan Paul.

Stephen, Michele. 1979. "Dreams of Change: The Innovative Role of Altered States of Consciousness in Traditional Melanesian Religion." *Oceania* 50:3–22.

———., ed. 1987. *Sorcerer and Witch in Melanesia*. New Brunswick: Rutgers University Press.

Strehlow, T. G. H. 1956. *The Sustaining Ideals of Australian Aboriginal Societies*. Adelaide: Aborigines Advancement League Inc. of South Australia.

———. 1970. "Geography and the Totemic Landscape in Central Australia: A Functional Study." In *Australian Aboriginal Anthropology*, Ronald W. Berndt, ed., pp. 92–140. Nedlands: The University of Western Australia Press.

Tonkinson, R. 1974. *The Jigalong Mob: Aboriginal Victors of the Desert Crusade*. Menlo Park: Cummings.

———. 1988. "Reflections on a Failed Crusade." In *Aboriginal Australians and Christian Missions*, Tony Swain and Deborah B. Rose, eds., pp. 60–73. Bedford Park, South Australia: Australian Association for the Study of Religions.

Weber, Max. 1956. *The Sociology of Religion*. Boston: Beacon Press.

Yengoyan, Aram A. 1979. "Economy, Society, and Myth in Aboriginal Australia." *Annual Review of Anthropology* 8:393–415.

———. 1980. "Myth and Ontology in Aboriginal Australian Society." *American Anthropologist* 82:839–43.

———. 1986. "Theory in Anthropology: On the Demise of the Concept of Culture." *Comparative Studies in Society and History* 28:368–74.

———. 1989. "Language and Conceptual Dualism: Sacred and Secular Concepts in Aboriginal Cosmology and Myth." In *The Attraction of Opposites: Thought and Society in a Dualistic Mode*, David Maybury-Lewis and Uri Almagor, eds., pp. 171–90. Ann Arbor: University of Michigan Press.

———. 1990. "Cloths of Heaven: Freud, Language, and the Negation in Pitjantjatjara Dreams." In *Personality and the Cultural Construction of Society: Papers in Honor of Melford E. Spiro*, David K. Jordan and Marc J. Swartz, eds., pp. 201–21. Tuscaloosa: University of Alabama Press.

———. In press. "Culture and Ideology in Contemporary Southeast Asian Societies: The Development of Traditions." Working Paper, Environment and Policy Institute, East-West Center, Honolulu, Hawaii.

CHAPTER NINE

Why the Thai Are Not Christians: Buddhist and Christian Conversion in Thailand

Charles F. Keyes

In this chapter I seek to answer the question: "Why have Thai *not* converted to Christianity?" Although I am posing a negative question, I believe an attempt to answer it will contribute to an understanding of the process of religious conversion. I should immediately qualify my question, because it is not precisely true that Thai have not converted to Christianity. Out of a total population in Thailand of 47.8 million in 1980, there were somewhat more than 250,000 Christians.[1] This number, however, seems almost insignificant given that Christian missionaries first came to Siam, as Thailand was formerly known, more than four hundred years ago. Moreover, most converts to Christianity in Thailand have not been Thai but immigrant Chinese or Vietnamese or previously animistic tribal peoples. Islam has enjoyed far greater success among Thai: there were at least three-quarters of a million Thai-Muslims (as contrasted with Malay-Muslims) out of a total of 1.8 million adherents in Thailand in 1980. But that is another story. Here, I want to confine myself to the confrontation between Christianity and Buddhism in Thailand and to the ways in which these two world religions approach conversion.

CHRISTIAN-BUDDHIST CONFRONTATION IN NORTHERN THAILAND

Let me begin with a Christian-Buddhist confrontation that I myself recorded. In 1967–1968 I carried out fieldwork in Mae Sariang district in the far northwestern Thai province of Mae Hong Son.[2] The town of Mae Sariang, of approximately two thousand people, and the larger district of some thirty-eight thousand that it served are typical of frontier areas in mainland Southeast Asia in being markedly complex ethnically and religiously. Although Buddhist Northern Thai constituted the dominant population of the lowland town and neighboring villages, there were also significant communities of peoples whose ancestors had come from Burma and smaller numbers of Indians and Chinese. Moreover, Central Thai or Siamese occupied most of the high official positions—district officer, provincial judge, provincial forestry office supervisor, and so on. The upland population—and most of the district's peoples lived in the uplands—was predominantly Karen of two distinctive types, Sgaw and Pwo. Other ethnic groups were represented, notably the Lawa (or Lua'), whose ancestors had lived in the area for longer than any other peoples, and a small number of Hmong who had recently settled in the district. Some Sgaw Karen had also settled in the lowland.

The majority of the lowland peoples identified as Buddhist, but they were affiliated with several different variants of Buddhism. Of the eleven Buddhist temple-monasteries in the town, one was Mon-Burman, two were Shan, a fourth Karen, and the remainder Northern Thai. There were also several other Karen Buddhist communities in the vicinity of the town. A small Muslim enclave in Mae Sariang of people whose forebears had come from Chittagong supported a mosque for their own community, but they did not seek to spread their religion beyond their numbers. Five different Christian groups, however, had established missions in the town with the explicit purpose of winning converts.

The most significant of the Christian missions was the American Baptist Mission (ABM), working in conjunction with the Church of Christ in Thailand. The ABM missionaries, who maintained both a mission and a hospital, worked primarily among Sgaw Karen. The New Tribes Mission, a "faith" mission that depends not on the regular support of a church mission board but on the irregular contributions of one or two congregations, was represented by a family and a bachelor missionary, all of whom were, like the ABM missionaries, from the United States. They worked almost exclusively among the Lawa. A French Catholic order was represented by an Italian priest who worked among both Sgaw and Pwo Karen. The Overseas Missionary Fellowship (OMF), which had before 1949 been known as the China Inland Mission, supported an American missionary family in Mae Sariang who worked among the Pwo Karen. Finally, while I was there, an American Presbyterian missionary, also affiliated with the Church of Christ in Thailand, came to Mae Sariang to set up a mission to work among the Northern Thai. From time to time Seventh-Day Adventist missionaries came to town, mainly to poach (at least in the perception of the other missionaries) in fields of the already converted, but the Seventh-Day Adventists were not then a permanent presence in the town.

My research in Mae Sariang—to study relationships between the Northern Thai and the tribal peoples and to study the culture of the dominant people of the town—led me to work with Buddhist monks, some of whom were also designated as missionaries to the tribal peoples. I also interviewed Christian missionaries and some (mainly Sgaw Karen) local Christians living in Mae Sariang about the role of the several churches in Thai-tribal relations. I was particularly interested in the hostels that the Baptists, Catholics, and New Tribes Mission had established to enable Karen and Lawa to attend government schools in the town.

Shortly after arriving in Mae Sariang I heard that the Christian community was upset that Christian children were being made to participate in Buddhist rituals at the government schools. The New Tribes missionary had sought the help of the assistant district officer in persuading the heads of the schools to refrain from making Christians go against their faith by participating in such rituals. The assistant district officer was unsympathetic, however, because he viewed the requirement to attend the rituals not as a religious issue but as one relating to national identity. I wrote in my field notes (Field notes, 15 October 1967) that the assistant district officer "thinks that all Thai must show respect to [Buddhist] priests and must *wai phra* [show reverence to Buddha images] as well as *wai khrū* [show ritualized respect for teachers]." When the schools did not move to change the requirement, the Baptist missionary called on the assistant district officer, who in no uncertain terms told the missionary "that a person cannot be Thai unless he is a Buddhist" (Field notes, 19 October 1967).

Several months later an incident at the government secondary school inflamed the issue. I quote from my field notes from an interview with the Baptist missionary: "It seems that the headmaster insisted that the Christian (and Moslem) students *wai* [show reverence toward] the Buddha in the morning ceremonies, although he explained that they could be worshiping their own god. One Karen adamantly refused to do so, saying that it would be against his religion. The headmaster pinched his hands very hard, but the student still refused." The student then related this incident to the Karen director of the Christian hostel, and the director in turn told the Baptist and New Tribes missionaries. The missionaries this time persuaded the assistant district officer to intervene, and he went to see the headmaster. "Apparently this infuriated the headmaster, who called a school assembly and had the Christians get up front and tell why they were Christians and what was wrong with the Buddha. Students and faculty jeered at the students" (Field notes, 3 June 1968). The missionaries found themselves frustrated in their efforts to change the requirement, but although some of the Christians talked of removing their children from school, none did. Rather, the students found themselves compelled to accept the requirement to show respect to the Buddhist religion if they were to attend government schools.[3]

Despite what the Christians and the missionaries said, the right to one's personal religious convictions was not really the issue. Rather, it was a question of one's relationship to religious authority. The missionaries pressed their case on the basis of Christian acceptance of the authority of a universal church, an authority that transcends state and ethnic boundaries. The assistant district officer and the heads of the schools, however, viewed the unwillingness of students to participate in a ritual act not as an expression of personal conviction—the secondary school headmaster even said that the students could worship God during Buddhist rites—but as an act of defiance of the authority of the state. The point can be generalized. Religious affiliation is never simply a matter of how one views oneself with reference to the ultimate conditions of one's existence; it always entails a commitment to a particular form of authority. Christian missionaries have failed to pose a serious challenge to the authority of Buddhism in Thailand. To understand the failure of Christian missionaries in Thailand is to understand the earlier success of Buddhist missionaries, because the conversion of Thai to Buddhism invested the religion with an authority that has made most Buddhists immune or resistant to the appeal of universalistic Christianity.

To recognize that converting from one religion to another means accepting the authority backing the new religion over that which has stood behind the old one leads to a new formulation of the question I have posed: namely, why have Buddhists in Thailand been unimpressed by the authoritativeness of the Christian message offered to them? To answer this question, we need first to consider how Buddhism gained acceptance in Thailand and then look at the efforts of Christian missionaries. Understanding the differences between Buddhist and Christian conversion can, I believe, help us to reflect on conversion more generally.

TO BE THAI IS TO BE BUDDHIST

The Tai-speaking peoples, who today as Siamese or Central Thai, Lao or Northeastern Thai, Yuan or Northern Thai, and Southern Thai make up the vast majority of Thailand's population, are descendants of peoples who until about the eleventh century were animists.[4] When the Tai began settling in what is today Thailand some time before the eleventh century, they encountered Mon (and perhaps other related peoples), who were already adherents of Buddhism. By the thirteenth century many of the formerly animistic Tai had "become" Buddhists, at least to the extent that several Tai chiefs were able to establish independent kingdoms that were structured around Buddhist monuments and supported by Buddhist monasteries. Between the thirteenth and fifteenth centuries Tai Buddhist missionaries, who had been trained in Sri Lanka, and their disciples traveled extensively throughout the region, carrying the Buddhist message not only to the elite of the cities but also eventually to the general populace in the villages. By the end of the fifteenth century most Tai-speaking peoples of what is today Thailand were Buddhists.

Thailand, or its premodern predecessor, Siam, was never populated only by Tai-speaking Buddhists. Some non-Tai, like the Mon, Khmer, and related Mon-Khmer peoples, were also converted to Theravāda Buddhism along with the Tai. Other peoples, however, living on the peripheries of premodern Siam, remained adherents of distinct localized animistic religions. Some Karen, Hmong, Mien, Akha, Lahu, Lisu, Lawa, and other tribal peoples living within the confines of present-day Thailand continue to follow animistic religions, although others have also converted to Christianity or Buddhism. Siam had also brought under its control principalities on the Malay peninsula whose populations were made up primarily of Malay-speaking Muslims. The drawing of the modern boundaries of Thailand left many Malay-Muslims within the country, and today they constitute the largest indigenous minority.

Chinese began to settle in Siam in increasing numbers throughout the nineteenth century and into the twentieth century prior to World War II. By the turn of the century, they constituted by far the largest minority population in Thailand and remain so to this day. The Chinese came with their own cultural traditions, which included some elements derived from Mahāyāna Buddhism as well as from Confucianism and Taoism. Such elements notwithstanding, Chinese religious syncretism, with its emphasis on ancestor worship, makes it very different from Theravāda Buddhism. Other non-Buddhist groups in Thailand are made up of migrants and the descendants of migrants from India and Vietnam. Both Hindus and Muslims are found among the Indians in Thailand. Some of the Vietnamese in Thailand follow a religious tradition similar to that of the Chinese, but many, if not most, are Catholics.

Most of the immigrant Chinese who remained in Thailand and their descendants became Theravāda Buddhist, although little is known about their conversion.[5] Other migrants and their descendants, unlike the Chinese, have tended to remain members of clearly recognizable stranger communities. Of the indigenous peoples, Thai-Malays have been the most resistant to Buddhist influences. Because they live in relatively remote areas, far from the center of Thai power, confrontation seldom occurred between (Thai) Buddhists and (Malay) Muslims until quite recently.[6] Although tribal peoples were more or less ignored until World War II, they assumed increasing relevance to the Thai state from the 1950s on because of concern about security on the national borders. This concern lies at the bottom of the recent government-supported efforts to convert tribal peoples to Buddhism. Throughout northern Thailand today, Buddhist missionaries now compete with Christian missionaries to persuade tribal peoples to adopt their religion.

By observing the conversion of tribal peoples to Buddhism, it is possible to gain some understanding of how Buddhism spread to other peoples, including Tai, in earlier times. In the 1960s, Buddhist monks, acting under a program created by the Thai Sangha and supported by the government, began to seek out tribal peoples in their home communities to "spread the religion" (*phoei phǣ sātasanā*) to them.[7] While engaged in fieldwork in Mae Sariang in 1967–1968, I witnessed efforts at Buddhist missionization, and I also saw a number of events in which tribal people who had previously been followers of local animistic religions publicly demonstrated their adherence to Buddhism. Although many tribal people have seen monks and temple-monasteries, and have even observed Buddhist rituals when visiting lowland communities, most have continued to follow religious practices centered on propitiating ancestral and locality spirits and on securing the vital essence or soul possessed by rice, humans, and certain animals such as elephants.

I accompanied one missionary, or *thammacārik* (Pāli, *dhammacārika*), "wandering *dhamma*," monk on a number of trips to tribal villages to observe how he was received and how he presented the message. The monk with whom I traveled was also the district abbot (*caokhana amphoe*), was locally born, and unlike many of the missionary monks sent from Bangkok in the early phases of the thammacārik program, had a long-term interest in the peoples living in the district, whatever their ethnic group. Although the thammacārik program was new and was tied specifically to political objectives, the role of the monk-missionary is an ancient one in Theravāda Buddhism. In the fifteenth and sixteenth centuries, monks belonging to a new Sinhala order (they had been reordained by monks in Sri Lanka or by other monks who followed the Sinhalese ordination tradition) had established "forest monasteries" (*wat pā*) throughout much of present-day Thailand. In doing so, they converted many villagers who had previously been animists.

The arrival of a monk in a tribal community today, as it must have done in Tai villages in early medieval times, disrupts social life, even if only temporarily. When we arrived in a tribal village, I was struck by how villagers, especially children, were fascinated by the district abbot's yellow robes and his shaven head and face. Although other monks might wear somewhat different colored robes—in Burma, for example, monks wear robes that are almost red, and most do not shave their eyebrows—they would still be as conspicuous as was the monk with whom I traveled. Villagers were always quick to offer hospitality but were then surprised when the monk spurned their usual gifts of liquor or refused to take an evening meal with them. These were some of the outward signs of his commitment to a "discipline" that sets monks apart from other humans. In one village we visited the Karen headman kidded about marrying off a village girl to the district abbot. The monk first responded in kind by asking whether the girl was beautiful but then explained that he was not allowed, because of his vow of celibacy, to marry or have any physical contact with a woman. Even with only their limited impressions and knowledge of the district abbot's life, villagers thought him an extraordinary person.

The Buddhist monk is more than extraordinary; he is a "man of prowess," to use a term suggested by Oliver Wolters (1982:6ff.). Such prowess is most apparent in the monk's encounters with secular authority. In one Lawa village I visited with the district abbot, the Border Patrol Police had established a school. Even though the three Border Patrol policemen who staffed the school were young, and were more teachers than policemen, they nonetheless carried guns and were perceived by the villagers as powerful representatives of the state. After we had settled in the village, these police-teachers came to visit. As villagers watched, they prostrated themselves before the monk, a man without any of the trappings of secular power. Tai villagers must have been similarly impressed in the fifteenth and sixteenth centuries when lords and high officials made their ways to monasteries located in the forests near their communities to make similar acts of obeisance.

Some monks have been tempted from time to time to translate their prowess into political power. Several monks in modern Thailand have not only won converts among tribal peoples but have, like the famous Northern Thai monk Khrūbā Srivijaya in the 1920s and 1930s, and his disciples Khrūbā Phlī (also known as Khrūbā Khao, the white-robed venerable) and Khrūbā Wong in the 1950s and 1960s, gained followings perceived by the government as threatening (cf. Keyes 1971). The government, in sponsoring a Buddhist missionary program, found that it could also stimulate the development of movements that are beyond government control. For the most part, however, monks rarely use their prowess to challenge existing authority; they are more likely to draw on that authority to assert a new understanding of the world.

The district abbot linked his prowess with the Buddha by publicly making obeisance before an image that he carried with him. He also told villagers that the Buddha was represented not only in images but also in stupas, or what in Thai are called *cēdī* (from Pāli, *cetiya*), and referred to the numerous stupas found throughout the district as well as elsewhere in northern Thailand. The Buddhist message that the district abbot sought to communicate was that the teachings of the Buddha—the dhamma—provide a better way of confronting fundamental problems than do beliefs in spirits and souls. The district abbot always began, however, by telling villagers that Buddhism was not against belief in spirits. He pointed out that Northern Thai believed in spirits as well, and when we were in Lawa villages he observed that the Lawa term for spirit was the same as the Northern Thai (*phī*). Rather, he taught, all spirits, like all humans, are subject to the law of *kamma*.[8] Although he attempted to explain this law, it was clear that he could not do so adequately given the time available to him and the absence of a common language. He usually ended by commenting that the teachings of the Buddha could best be understood with reference to written texts that monks could interpret.

As most of his visits to tribal villages were brief, all the district abbot could hope to do was to introduce the villagers to the foundations of Buddhism—the Buddha, as manifest in images and stupas; the dhamma, as contained in the written scriptures; and the Sangha, as represented by monks. And he could also impress them with his own charisma and with the way in which the authority of his religion was both respected and backed by the state. For villagers to "become" Buddhist, they had to have more sustained contacts with monks and to accept that their lives could be made more meaningful by adopting a Buddhist worldview. That the abbot was permanently based in a temple-monastery in town made it possible for him to promote long-term contacts, and he encouraged tribal people to participate in Buddhist rituals held at his and other temple-monasteries.

During my time in Mae Sariang, Sgaw Karen in the lowland village of Mǣ Tǫp Nụa, a community some few kilometers north of the town of Mae Sariang, took steps toward becoming Buddhists under the guidance of the district abbot. The village had been founded two generations earlier by migrants from upland areas. Although they continued to practice their indigenous religion, by living in the lowlands, cultivating wet rice with methods taught to them by the Northern Thai, and becoming increasingly involved, mainly through the teak trade, in the Thai-dominated economy, these villagers had developed close relationships with Thai Buddhists.

For at least a generation the Karen of Māē Tǫp Nụa had participated from time to time in Buddhist rituals in the temple-monastery of a nearby Northern Thai village. In doing so, however, they felt themselves to be, and were considered, "guests" or "strangers" (the word is the same in Northern Thai, *khāēk*) at the rituals of another community. On several occasions, I was told, elders in Māē Tǫp Nụa attempted to persuade their fellow villagers to donate sufficient money for the construction of a stupa in their own community. In this these elders were seeking to emulate a pattern already established in five other Karen villages in the plain near Mae Sariang. But for a long time these elders were unable to gather enough money to pay for the costs of the stupa, and particularly for the costs of the crown (called *hti* in Karen, from the Burmese). Finally, enough money was raised, most of it donated by six men. Each of these men thus acquired a distinctive title, *khō taka* (again, the word is borrowed from Burmese), "donor of a stupa."[9]

The district abbot persuaded villagers of Māē Tǫp Nụa to sponsor the ordination of several village boys as novices in connection with the stupa dedication. This ordination did not, however, lead to a continuing presence of the Sangha in the village because the boys remained novices for a few days at most. For the foreseeable future the stupa would provide the focus for the Buddhism that would be practiced by the Karen villagers of Māē Tǫp Nụa. The dedication of the stupa inaugurated a rite that villagers would repeat, I was told, at the traditional New Year and at an annual feast held on the same day as the first dedication. This rite entailed circumambulating the stupa and putting an offering of flowers, incense, and candles at its base. In this rite, villagers believed themselves to be "taking refuge" in the Buddha. More significantly, because the stupa was a visible presence in the village even when no ritual event was taking place, the stupa signified that the village had placed itself within the domain of the Buddha.

The villagers of Māē Tǫp Nụa did not abandon their animistic rites when they "became" Buddhist. But if the experience of the five other Karen villages in the lowlands that had already established stupas was any precedent, the stupa cult would eventually become far more important than the cult of the local lord of the land. The first stage in becoming Buddhist is situating oneself within a moral realm in which the Buddha is supreme, transcending in power any local spirit. In the next stage one must follow the teachings of the Buddha, the dhamma, as they are exemplified and interpreted by the Sangha. The Tai who became Buddhists some centuries earlier must have gone through a similar process of conversion.

Conversion to Buddhism does not require that people radically reject their previous beliefs.[10] Even when they come to understand the law of kamma through the moral stories and didactic teachings that monks draw from the scriptures, they can still retain their beliefs in spirits.[11] Spirits are merely one of many types of beings whose place in the cosmic hierarchy is a consequence of previous kamma. As people come to understand the dhamma they also learn to conceive of "suffering" (Pāli, *dukkha*) not as the consequence of the malevolence of spirits, although those may still be the immediate agents, but as the result of a more general "law," namely, that of kamma.

The root meaning of kamma is "action," and in Buddhist (as well as Hindu) thought the concept refers to the moral consequences of human acts. The Buddhist doctrine of kamma at once explains how certain aspects of one's present experience are consequences of previous acts, including acts in former existences, and provides an incentive to perform certain acts that will ensure greater freedom from suffering in this life or future ones (cf. Keyes 1983:13). In the process of making the Theravāda Buddhist version of the doctrine of kamma relevant to their worlds, Tai-speaking peoples adopted a Hindu-Buddhist cosmology that provided a way to conceive of the effects of previous kamma. Within this cosmology, which is concretely symbolized in the stupa and elaborated in many texts, spirits, gods, demons, and animals all have a place, as do humans in their various states—male and female, royalty and commoner, physically whole and physically impaired.

Previous kamma constrains but does not determine one's situation in this life; one also has considerable freedom to act, and depending on the way in which one chooses to act one will generate "merit" (Thai, *bun*, from Pāli, *puñña*) or "demerit" (Thai, *bāp*, from Pāli, *pāppa*). The greater one's merit, the less one will experience suffering in the future; contrariwise, the greater one's demerit, the greater the suffering. In practice, most Buddhists in Thailand, as in other Theravādin countries, exercise this freedom through rituals deemed to "make merit" (Thai, *tham bun*); the most significant are those involving offerings to the Sangha.

Those who have had any prolonged exposure to Buddhist teachings are aware that the Buddha's way, his dhamma, if fully understood and followed, leads ultimately to final release from the world of dukkha. Such a goal is remote, however. In traditional Buddhist thought as found in Thai popular practice, one can at best hope that one's merit leads to rebirth at the time of the future Buddha, Ariya Maitreya (Thai, Phra Sī An). In his presence, Nibbāna (Thai, *niphān*) will be attainable. For everyday Buddhist practice the doctrine of kamma is central. Against a worldview comprehended with reference to an immanent force that attaches a moral consequence to any significant action, Christian missionaries offered one that required acceptance of a personal God who passes judgment on one's actions.

CHRISTIAN MISSIONS IN THAILAND

Christian missionaries first came to the medieval Siamese kingdom of Ayutthaya in the mid-sixteenth century, but the church did not make a concerted effort to convert Siamese to Catholicism until the seventeenth century.[12] Even though the Catholic missionaries of the late seventeenth century had backing from the French court and a powerful voice in the Siamese court (in the guise of a Greek adventurer, Constance Phaulkon, who had risen to be the equivalent of chief minister to King Narai [1656–1688]), they failed utterly in their drive to win converts. In 1688 a palace coup resulted in the killing of Phaulkon and many of his supporters, the expulsion of the French, and the confining of Christianity to foreign enclaves.[13]

There were, I believe, two major reasons for the early failure of Catholic missionaries in Thailand. The missionaries correctly perceived that they had to have at least the partial sanction of the king if they were to be successful. There was not, however, a crisis of power in seventeenth-century Siam to provide the impetus for the conversion of Narai, as had occurred in late sixteenth-century Cambodia, where a Khmer ruler had indicated his willingness to convert to Catholicism if the Spanish in the Philippines would come to his aid (Chandler 1983:83). On the contrary, the legitimacy of the Siamese state was very much tied to the relationship between king and Sangha. At best, the Catholic missionaries were able only to provoke philosophical discussion among Narai and some monks and scholars at his court (Wyatt 1984:113). The degree of prominence that some Christians were able to achieve in Narai's court, however, was a major factor in stimulating attacks against the French in the country as Narai lay on his deathbed (Wyatt 1984:116–17). Although Phētrācha, after his accession to the throne during what the French have termed the "revolution" of 1688, allowed some missionaries to resume their efforts, these were subsequently limited almost exclusively to the foreign enclaves in the capital.

The early Catholic missionaries also failed because their message was inadequately translated. Instead of borrowing terms derived from Pāli and Sanskrit that would be recognizable to Thai as religious because of their usage in conjunction with Buddhism, the Catholics used terms for

Christian concepts that were derived mainly from Portuguese. Because of the failure to give Catholicism indigenous trappings, "Christianity," as one Thai Catholic scholar has observed, "was considered totally foreign by all the Thai people" (Kirti Bunchua 1986:3).

Christian missionaries were not to try seriously to convert the Thai again until the nineteenth century, after the capital of Siam had been shifted from Ayutthaya to Bangkok and a new dynasty had taken power. The new wave of missionaries who came in the nineteenth century also recognized they must at least gain the permission of the court to proceed. King Rama III (1824–1851) and Mongkut (1851–1869) allowed the Protestants to move beyond providing ministry to foreign enclaves and to proselytize among non-Christians. Beginning in 1828, Protestant missionaries were allowed into the kingdom, and their numbers steadily increased as the country began to be opened to the West. Catholic missionaries also returned in the nineteenth century, but they continued to confine their attention primarily to foreign populations, especially Vietnamese and Chinese. Protestant missionaries, in contrast, directed their attention primarily toward the Siamese (and later Northern Thai), who were at least (in Protestant eyes) nominally Buddhist. Many of the missionaries of the period, like their Catholic predecessors, also attempted to win converts at the court. They found some of the princes and nobles, including Mongkut himself during the period from 1824 to 1851 when he was a monk, to be very interested in learning about Western science, civilization, and religion. But this interest was not transformed into a willingness to convert.

The missionaries also had little success in gaining converts in Bangkok or among Central Thai. By the end of the century they had begun to focus more attention on the Northern Thai, and here they were to win some followers; only in northern Thailand is there a significant community of Christians who can trace their origins to indigenous Tai peoples. Initially, the missionaries in northern Thailand met with indifference and then open hostility on the part of the semi-independent ruler of Chiang Mai. In 1869 the prince of Chiang Mai had two Christian converts killed. The missionaries appealed to the king in Bangkok for support, and the Siamese court took the opportunity to assert its authority over the region by sending a commissioner to the prince with an order to allow the missionaries to pursue their proselytizing. The prince refused and warned that he would kill anyone who converted. "He considered that leaving the religion of the country was rebellion against him, and he would treat it as such" (Hughes 1982:4). Fortunately for the missionaries, the prince died returning from a journey to Bangkok to confront the king on the court's challenge to the prince's authority. The next prince was more tolerant and more under the control of the Siamese court. In 1878 the missionaries were able to obtain from King Chulalongkorn (1868–1910) a proclamation that granted them the right to seek converts. The proclamation stated that "whoever wishes to embrace any religion after seeing that it is true and proper to be embraced, is allowed to do so without any restriction" (quoted in Hughes 1982:4).

By challenging the prince of Chiang Mai and by gaining the proclamation of religious freedom from King Chulalongkorn, the missionaries undoubtedly acquired an aura of authority in northern Thailand that they had nowhere else. The missionaries in northern Thailand also were the first to introduce modern forms of medical care, and their successes in curing contributed to their image as men of prowess. Still, they won only relatively few converts. By 1915 there were about four thousand members of the church in Chiang Mai, and this figure accounted for at least half of the total number of Protestants in the kingdom at the time.[14]

Hughes, a student of the Protestant church in Thailand, has argued that the Northern Thai who converted to Buddhism were most likely to be those facing extreme personal crises, especially ill health, or who were marginal members of society. Moreover, the appeal of Christianity was greatest among those who thought fundamental problems of health and marginal social status derived from the actions of spirits. Hughes writes, "it seems that most of the people who turned to Christianity did so because they saw God as having great power, greater power than that of the local spirits" (Hughes 1984a:327–28; also see Hughes 1982:14 and Hughes 1984b, 1985). Most Northern Thai, however, see all spiritual beings, including God, as being subordinate to the law of kamma; thus, the Christian message appealed only to a very few.[15]

The second generation of Protestant missionaries in northern Thailand did not, apparently, have the charisma of the pioneers. The church in Chiang Mai actually lost members in the period prior to World War II, declining to a scant 3,300 in 1940. Even nationwide, membership in the Church of Christ in Siam had grown only 22 percent between 1920 and 1940, even though the population of the country as a whole had grown 57 percent. Missionary efforts came to a total halt during World War II but were resumed again in 1946 and intensified after 1949 when a number of missionaries who had been in China moved to Thailand. Since the war, missionaries and native evangelists have been subject to few governmental constraints. Despite this freedom, Protestant missionaries have converted only a small number of Thai, and most of those converts have come mainly from minority communities.

The tribal peoples of northern and western Thailand have been the main targets of Protestant missionization.[16] As with the Northern Thai who earlier converted to Protestant Christianity, tribal people have sometimes found in the Christian God a spiritual being whose power is greater than any local spirit and one whose domain encompasses a world far beyond the hills and valleys in which they live. A missionary from the Overseas Missionary Fellowship in Mae Sariang told me that the spirits of the Pwo Karen among whom he worked were as real to him as they were to those he sought to convert. For him, however, they were demons sent by the Devil, and he sought to demonstrate the greater power of God by showing the Pwo that if they believed in God they could abandon their rites for the spirits with impunity. He coupled his message with provision of modern medicines, which were often more potent than sacrifices made to the spirits in effecting cures for certain types of ailments. Tribal people have sometimes converted to Christianity because they find being a Christian less expensive than following the traditional religion (see, for example, Kammerer 1990, in press).

The percentage of Christians among tribal peoples in Thailand has increased rapidly, especially since the mid-1960s, when a number of missionaries who had previously been in Burma moved to work with similar groups in Thailand. Although precise data are not available, between one-third and one-half of tribal peoples in Thailand are today adherents to Christianity. Because the tribal peoples constitute such a small part of the total population of Thailand—less than 1 percent—the success rate of Christian missionaries among tribal peoples has not produced a significant expansion of Christians within the population of the country as a whole. Conversion to Christianity has, however, permitted some tribal peoples to reformulate their ethnic distinctiveness in Thailand in other than purely local terms. As the Thai state has extended its authority into the uplands of northern and western Thailand, tribal peoples have been forced to see themselves as part of a larger world. Although some, most notably among the Karen, have converted to Buddhism and have thus assimilated to some degree to Thai culture, more have turned to Christianity. As Kammerer has observed, "conversion to Christianity by Southeast Asian mountain minorities is simultaneously a claim to difference from and a claim to equality with valley-dwelling Buddhists" (Kammerer 1990:285; also cf. Tapp 1989).

Like Protestant missionaries, Catholic missionaries have encountered little interest in their message except among members of minority communities. Although a few Catholic missionaries have worked among tribal peoples, the majority of Catholics in Thailand are Chinese and Vietnamese immigrants or the descendants of such immigrants.[17] The church remained foreign to Thai society in another way as well. World War II and the end of colonial rule in much of the Third World prompted many mission boards to undertake a process of "indigenization" by accelerating the transfer of local churches to native clergy and organization. The Catholic church in Thailand went markedly against this trend. A church publication found it remarkable "that between 1950 and 1970 the percentage of foreign clergy . . . increased in Thailand. There were 101 of them in a total of 186, or 54.3%, in 1950; in 1970 they numbered 175 out of a total of 299, or 58.3%" (Pro Mundi Vita Centrum Informationis 1973:25). The publication goes on to provide an analysis of why this had occurred:

> The main reason for this increase was the influx of missionaries who had fled from mainland China when the Communists took over. Moreover, while little attention was paid to Thailand for a long time, the events in Southeast Asia during the last decades and the fact that China was closed to missionaries have attracted a number of these foreign priests to Thailand. (Pro Mundi Vita Centrum Informationis 1973:25)

The pressures to transform a mission church into one rooted in the society in which it has been implanted have been felt, nonetheless, by the Catholic church in Thailand, especially following Vatican Council II (1962–1965). In addition, an increasing number of Catholics in Thailand, even though of Chinese or Vietnamese descent, because they had assimilated to Thai culture to a significant extent also began to feel uneasy about the foreignness of their church.

Indigenization of the Catholic church has entailed adapting the Christian message to local cultures, including to existing religious traditions insofar as this is possible without compromising fundamental Christian dogmas. In Thailand the church has adopted many Thai Buddhist terms for Christian concepts and has adapted Buddhist temple architecture for Catholic churches. From the early 1970s on, foreign missionaries have been replaced by locally trained clergy.

Indigenization of the Catholic church in Thailand prompted a reaction by some conservative Buddhists who perceived a threat from a Christianity that was no longer clearly "foreign." In 1959, even before Vatican II, Colonel Pin Muthukan, the director-general of the department of ecclesiastical affairs, launched a virulent attack on the republication of a mid-nineteenth century catechism written in Thai. The attack on the new edition was prompted by the wider availability of the tract, made possible by modern means of publication and dissemination, which could thus lead to "misunderstandings" because of the unfavorable comparisons the tract drew between Buddhism and Christianity (Pin Muthukan 1963; n.d.). Colonel Pin saw this effort as distorting Buddhism and thus endangering it. He concluded with words that reflected the same view of Buddhism that I found among officials and teachers in Mae Sariang: "[As] our religion is one of the four guarantees of our national security, it means to destroy the religion is indirectly to destroy the national security" (Pin n.d.:103). The Thai government banned the catechism, confiscated existing copies and closed temporarily the press that had published it, and "invited the Reverend Brother [the priest who was responsible] to be investigated" (Pin n.d.:13)

Nearly two decades later the more sophisticated efforts of Catholics to clothe their religion in an acceptable Thai garb once again prompted a bitter attack, this time by a ranking Buddhist monk, Phra Sobhan-Ganabhorn (1984). This monk's diatribe against Thai Catholicism incorporated criticisms similar to those of Colonel Pin but added many specific attacks on leading Thai Catholic writers, who he claimed sought to subvert Buddhism, or to absorb it into Catholicism, through a misleading method called "dialogue." This time, some conservative Catholics echoed the criticisms and argued that the church should return to its more universal (i.e., "foreign") forms. Other Catholic leaders, like Professor Kirti Bunchua of the philosophy department at Chulalongkorn University, insisted, however, that they truly were interested in dialogue, that is, in seeking common ground to face common problems—such as peace and social justice—rather than in conversion (see Kirti Bunchua 1986; cf. Sērī Phongphit 1985). The turn to dialogue has, however, not yet helped the Thai Catholic church succeed in shedding the aura of foreignness that has for so long undermined any claim to authoritativeness within the Thai context.

The problems faced by the Thai Catholic church in acquiring a distinctive Thai identity have not beset the Protestant churches to the same extent. In 1934, even before World War II, the major Protestant denominations with missions in Thailand—most notably, Presbyterian, American Baptist, and Christian and Missionary Alliance—combined to create the Church of Christ in Thailand. Although there are still many Western missionaries from these denominations in Thailand, the leadership of the Church of Christ has for several decades been in the hands of Thai citizens. Still, the Christian message offered by the Church of Christ in Thailand has found little positive reception among Thai.

In the 1980s, Pentecostal and charismatic Protestant churches were much more successful than the Church of Christ in Thailand in gaining converts among Thai. Zehner maintains that the increase in Protestants of 150 percent from 1978 to 1988 can be credited primarily to the growth in Pentecostal and charismatic churches. It should be noted that the absolute growth in numbers of Protestants (147,000 in 1988 as compared with 59,000 in 1978) still leaves the Protestant population quite small relative to the total population of Thailand (Zehner, in press).[18] Zehner credits the success of the Pentecostal churches in Bangkok to their having independent leaders who have adapted for their church structures traditional Thai ideas of hierarchy based on the Buddhist notion of differential merit (Zehner n.d.). By 1990 the membership of Pentecostal and charismatic Christian churches accounted for a quarter to a third of all Thai Protestants (Zehner, in press).[19]

The relative success of Pentecostal churches in gaining converts may be seen as part of a more general pattern of religious dynamism, involving Islamic as well as new Buddhist movements, that has emerged in Thailand since the early 1970s. As I have argued elsewhere, I believe this dynamism can be traced to a crisis of political authority, a crisis that was particularly intense in the mid-1970s but which has persisted throughout the 1980s (Keyes 1978, 1989). At one level the crisis turns on how to interpret the official ideology that makes "religion" (*sātsānā*) a pillar of national identity. At another level the crisis has its roots in the social dislocations caused by the rapid economic growth in the Thai economy over the past three decades and by the associated widening of the gap between rich and poor in Thai society. Although Christian churches—and especially Pentecostal and charismatic Protestant churches—have gained some converts during this crisis, it still remains overwhelmingly true that Thai have not been attracted in significant numbers by any of the purveyors of the Christian message.

TRUTH AND AUTHORITY IN THE CONVERSION PROCESS

Missionaries offer their potential converts a vision of a new moral community. For this vision to be accepted by the evangelized, it must offer a better way than the existing one to confront the world as it is actually known. Following Max Weber, I believe that some religions offer more comprehensive and more rationalized views of the world than do others. I disagree, then, with Horton (1971; also see 1975a, 1975b), who challenges the Weberian approach as employed by J. D. Y. Peel (1968) in his study of a religious movement among the Yoruba. Horton observes that "for Peel, following Weber, to rationalize is 'to reorder one's religious belief in a new and more coherent way to be more in line with what one knows and experiences.'" He then continues:

> As regards the rationality of Yoruba and other traditional religions, I think Peel inherits two questionable views from Weber and other predecessors. One is the view that ideas about the pre-Christian gods make little reference to regularity or predictability—a view which shows itself briefly in his statement [Peel 1968:138] that in pre-christian as opposed to Aladura

> religion power was not inhibited by doctrine. Another is the tendency to confound a multiplicity of gods with incoherence. (Horton 1971:97–98)

I think Horton misunderstands Weber's argument about rationalization here. It is not that premodern religions lack coherence but that historic religions derive their coherence from a belief in an abstract being or principle to which all other supernatural powers as well as humans are subject. Although Christian missionaries may have equated indigenous "African beliefs in supreme beings with a belief in the Christian god, African converts accepted change and *development* in [their] concept[s] of the supreme being," as Horton himself recognizes (Horton 1971:100; emphasis added). If one comes to understand all supernatural beings in terms of the ultimate power of God—or the law of kamma—then I believe one can say rationalization has taken place.

Both Buddhism and Christianity have offered to adherents of animistic religions not only a more rationalized view of the world but also a more universalistic one. Animistic religions depend on practitioners making religious ideas passed on through oral tradition relevant to worlds known in the hills, the rivers, the fields, and the people one sees every day. Historic religions like Christianity and Buddhism can transcend the limitations of local place and time because they employ written scriptures that remain at least partially constant wherever and whenever they are found (cf. Fisher 1973:29). Although a scriptural tradition can lead to freezing of beliefs, it can also open up the possibility of a dialogue with tradition, which is far more difficult in a society in which religious ideas are transmitted orally.

Buddhism preceded Christianity in what is today Thailand, and Buddhist missionaries succeeded in converting most of the populace to a vision of a moral community ordered around the Buddha, his teachings (dhamma) as contained in written scriptures, and the order of monks, the Sangha, which had responsibility for studying, teaching, and exemplifying the dhamma. In time, most who had "become" Buddhists acquired a more rationalized view of the world than their animistic forebears had held because of their belief in the law of kamma, but they also continued many animistic practices because these could be encompassed within the new "total field" of religion based on Buddhism (see Tambiah 1970). Although the potential existed to define a moral community that included all Buddhists, in practice Buddhists were divided into distinctive moral communities, centering in some cases on particular representations of the Buddha, such as famous stupas (see Keyes 1975) or images, or on rulers who assumed the responsibility to maintain the shrines, support the Sangha, and order their realms according to the dhamma.

Christian missionaries have been unable to persuade many people in Thailand that their religion offers greater insight into ultimate Truth than does Buddhism. The nineteenth-century Protestant missionaries brought with them a postreformation idea that knowledge of the natural world could be separated from knowledge of the cosmos. This was a novel and unsettling idea to Buddhists of the time, but it did not open the way to the conversion of Thai Buddhists to Christianity. Rather, intellectual Buddhists, and most notably Mongkut before he became king and while he was still a monk in the 1820s, 1830s, and 1840s, turned from their encounters with missionaries to engage their own tradition, that is, Buddhist scriptures as well as religious practice, and ended by instituting a reformation of the religion such that Buddhists could also accept scientific knowledge without threat to their religious assumptions (see Reynolds 1976). Christianity has failed in Thailand, in part then, because it has not offered a more rationalized worldview to those who are already Buddhists.

It has also failed for another and certainly equally compelling reason. As Hefner (1987) shows well in his study of the Tengger of East Java, conversion entails not only envisioning oneself within a moral community but also situating oneself within a world shaped by politico-economic forces. Those who convert to Christianity in Thailand set themselves apart from the dominant religion of the society and also place themselves in an ambiguous, at best, relationship to a state that rules in the name of a Buddhist nation. But it is not simply that the state has backed Buddhism that led to this failure. After all, the Roman state not only stood behind the established cults of the time but through persecution also actively sought to prevent the spread of Christianity. Far from being stamped out, early Christianity drew strength from martyrdom and eventually grew strong enough to replace the Roman cults as the state religion. Closer to Thailand, Catholic missionaries who began their efforts in Vietnam at the same time they did in Siam were also successful in winning significant numbers of followers in the face of opposition and persecution by the Vietnamese state (Lange 1980; Yarr 1986). As Nock noted in his influential work on conversion, "that which is socially condemned very often exercises a certain power of fascination, and subterranean movements have an intrinsic attraction" (Nock 1933:212). Christianity never acquired such potency in Thailand, I maintain, because, at least until quite recently, it has never been able to shed its mantle of "foreignness." Until the recent efforts to "indigenize" Christianity, even those Thai who have faced profound crises of power have not found in Christianity a vision of a moral community that could be Thai.

Today some Christians feel they have as much to learn from Buddhists as they have to teach them. They, and a few Buddhists on the other side, have begun to promote a Buddhist-Christian dialogue, one that seeks to draw on both traditions to formulate an understanding of ultimate meaning for a world that has been radically changed by new means of transport and communication and by massive exchanges of peoples through migration and tourism (see Buddhadāsa 1984; Kirti Bunchua 1984; Swearer 1973; Wells 1963). In other words, Buddhists and Christians have a common quest for a moral community that will encompass them all. Their efforts are still tentative and as yet unfulfilled, but they may lead to a new mode of conversion.

NOTES

Acknowledgments. This paper has its genesis in a conference on "Christianity as an Indigenous Religion in Southeast Asia," which I organized together with Professor Jean-Paul Dumont in 1986 (see Keyes [1991] for a report on this conference). I am grateful to the Joint Social Science Research Council and American Council of Learned Society's Committee on Southeast Asia for sponsorship of that conference. I also want to thank Robert Hefner and Jane Keyes for comments on previous versions of this paper.

1. McBeth gives a figure for the early 1980s of 263,000 Christians, of which 75 percent were Catholic (McBeth 1983:34). Zehner (1990:4–5), drawing on figures from Smith (1982:265), puts the number of Protestants in 1978 at 59,000.

2. I am indebted to the National Science Foundation and the University of Washington for support of this research.

3. This issue was raised many years later in a way that forced the government to listen. In the mid-1980s Muslims in southern Thailand finally succeeded after many protests in getting the government to change the requirement imposed on all government-school students to show reverence to the Buddha. Although in this regard Muslims were to prove to have far more influence on the Thai government than were Christians, many have still felt themselves discriminated against because of their religion. This is especially evident in the controversy in the late 1980s centering on whether Muslim female students could wear Muslim dress to school. See Chaiwat Satha-Anand (in press).

4. I follow convention in using the term "Tai" to refer to any people speaking a Tai (or Daic) language and the term "Thai" to refer to citizens of the modern country of Thailand. Outside Thailand, Tai peoples include the Lao of Laos, the Shan of Burma, and the Lue of Laos and southern China.

5. Tobias (1977) has provided the only good description of how Sino-Thai practice Theravāda Buddhism. His work gives us an understanding of the results but not, unfortunately, much insight into the process of religious change. The small number of Chinese who were Muslim before coming to Thailand retained, as have their descendants, their adherence to Islam.

6. Confrontation has, however, increased as the Thai state has intensified its

control in southern Thailand, as the influence of the Malay *dakwah*, or Islamic missionizing movement, has been extended into the region, and as some Thai-Muslims have achieved national visibility. See Chaiwat Satha-Anand (1987, in press), McVey (1984), Surin Pitsuwan (1985), and Uthai Dulyakasem (1984, 1991).

7. In another paper (Keyes 1971) I have described the state-sponsored Buddhist mission program in its early phase. For a more recent, and quite uncritical, appraisal of the program, see Sanit Wongprasert (1988).

8. Since Thai follow Theravāda Buddhism for which Pāli is the sacred language, I will use the Pāli term "kamma" rather than the Sanskrit "karma"; similarly, I have used "dhamma" instead of "dharma" and "Nibbāna" instead of "Nirvāṇa."

9. Although most Sgaw Karen in Mae Sariang have become Buddhists as a consequence of contacts with Northern Thai, they still look to Burma for models on how to be Buddhist because many Karen in Burma have long been Buddhists and the Sgaw Karen language for Buddhism has been derived from Burmese.

10. Hayami (in press) makes a similar point about the Sgaw Karen Buddhist converts that she worked among in Mae Chaem District, Chiang Mai Province, in the late 1980s.

11. In about the fifteenth century, monks in northern Thailand composed a number of texts in the vernacular to make the dhamma better understood by the populace. The most widely known of such texts, called *ānisong* (from the Pāli word *ānisamsa*, meaning "blessings"), were associated with major rituals. These texts often provide a Buddhist reinterpretation of animistic practices, providing, thus, the rationale for retention of such practices. See Keyes (1969, 1983) and Anusaranaśasanakiarti and Keyes (1980).

12. On the history of the Catholic mission in the seventeenth to nineteenth century, see Launay (1920; translated into Thai by Prathumrat Wongdontrī 1985), Hutchinson (1933), Sērī Phongphit (1982, chs. 1–8), and Dụ̄an Khamdī (1986, ch. 3), Kirti Bunchua (1986), and Forest (1986).

13. An official Catholic publication gives the total number of Catholics in Siam in 1662 as 2,000, of which at least two-thirds had some Portuguese ancestry (413 Siamese-Portuguese and 379 Cambodian-Portuguese) or were Vietnamese (580). The number of Catholics declined to 1,372 in 1785, then in the nineteenth century increased slightly, reaching 2,500 in 1802 and 3,000 in 1881 (Pro Mundi Vita Centrum Informationis 1973:22).

14. Hughes gives the 1915 figure; he also reports that the total membership of the Church of Christ in Siam (that is, the Protestant church) in 1920 was 7,967 (Hughes 1982:22).

15. Koyama Kosuke, a Japanese Protestant theologian who spent many years teaching at the Thailand Theological Seminary in Chiang Mai, found it difficult to understand how the early Protestant missionaries made their message comprehensible to Buddhist Northern Thai. Writing about the way in which the message had been presented by the most famous of missionaries, Daniel McGilvary (1912), Koyama (1978:110) concluded: "I am forced to see how thoroughly

strange and unrealistic—how 'western'—is the Christian vocabulary to the ears of my Thai neighbors!"

16. The best studies of conversion to Christianity among tribal peoples in Thailand are those by Kammerer (1990, in press) on the Akha, Hovemyr (1989) and Hayami (1990) on the Karen, and Tapp (1989) on the Hmong.

17. According to a church publication, the number of Catholics in 1970 totaled 152,112, of whom most were Chinese (which would also include Sino-Thai) living in Bangkok and central Thailand, with a few in southern Thailand (in tin-mining areas), or Vietnamese, mostly living in northeastern Thailand. Catholic missionaries had also attracted a small number of Thai-Lao converts in northeastern Thailand (Pro Mundi Vita Centrum Informationis 1973:22).

18. Zehner warns that the figures may be overestimates. He has taken the statistics from Rick Clark, "Church Growth in Bangkok," *Update Christian Directory*, 1989–1990, p. 2.

19. Missionaries from the Church of Jesus Christ of Latter-Day Saints (the Mormon church) have gone to Thailand in increasing numbers since the 1970s. In late 1990 and early 1991 the Thai government moved to limit the activities of the Mormons after the president of Thailand's Mormon organization was arrested for writing articles in the church newsletter that allegedly "blasphemed Buddhism and insulted Thai culture" (*The Nation*, 7 January 1991). At the time, there were reportedly sixteen Mormon centers throughout the country.

REFERENCES

Anusaranaśasanakiarti, Phra Khru, and Charles F. Keyes. 1980. "Funerary Rites and the Buddhist Meaning of Death: An Interpretative Text from Northern Thailand." *Journal of the Siam Society* 68, 1:1–28.

Buddhadāsa Bhikkhu. 1984. *Phut-Khrit nai thatsana than Phutthathat* (Buddhism-Christianity in the Thought of Buddhadasa). Bangkok: Thian Wan.

Chaiwat Satha-Anand. 1987. *Islam and Violence: A Case Study of Violent Events in the Four Southern Provinces, Thailand, 1976–1981*. Tampa: University of South Florida, Religion and Public Policy Series, 2.

———. In press. "*Hijab* and Moments of Legitimation: Islamic Resurgence in Thai Society." In *Asian Visions of Authority: Religion and the Modern States of East and Southeast Asia*, Charles F. Keyes, Laurel Kendall, and Helen Hardacre, eds. Honolulu: University of Hawaii Press.

Chandler, David. 1983. *A History of Cambodia*. Boulder, Colo.: Westview Press.

Dụan Khamdī. 1986. *Kānphoeiphrāe sātsanā khrit nai prathēt Thai* (Spread of Christianity in Thailand). Bangkok: Odeon Store.

Fisher, Humphrey J. 1973. "Conversion Reconsidered: Some Historical Aspects of Religious Conversion in Black Africa." *Africa* 43, 1:27–40.

Forest, Alain. 1986. "But God Wasn't Siamese." Paper presented at conference, Christianity as an Indigenous Religion in Southeast Asia, sponsored by the Joint American Council of Learned Societies and Social Science Research Council Committee on Southeast Asia, Cebu City, the Philippines.

Hayami, Yoko. In press. "Karen Tradition According to Christ or Buddha: The Implications of Multiple Reinterpretations for a Minority Ethnic Group in a Buddhist State." *Journal of Southeast Asian Studies*.

Hefner, Robert W. 1987. "The Political Economy of Islamic Conversion in Modern East Java." In *Islam and the Political Economy of Meaning: Comparative Studies of Muslim Discourse*, William R. Roff, ed., pp. 53–78. London and Sydney: Croom Helm; Berkeley and Los Angeles: University of California Press.

Horton, Robin. 1971. "African Conversion." *Africa* 41, 2:85–108.

———. 1975a. "On the Rationality of Conversion." *Africa* 45, 3:219–35.

———. 1975b. "On the Rationality of Conversion, Part II." *Africa* 45, 4:73–99.

Hovemyr, Anders P. 1989. *In Search of the Karen King: A Study in Karen Identity with Special Reference to Nineteenth-Century Karen Evangelism in Northern Thailand.* Uppsala, Studia Missionalia Upsaliensia XLIX.

Hughes, Philip J. 1982. *Proclamation and Response: A Study of the History of the Christian Faith in Northern Thailand.* Chiang Mai: Payap College, Manuscript Division.

———. 1984a. "The Assimilation of Christianity in the Thai Culture." *Religion* 14:313–36.

———. 1984b. "Values of Thai Buddhists and Thai Christians." *Journal of the Siam Society* 72, 1–2:212–27.

———. 1985. "Christianity and Buddhism in Thailand." *Journal of the Siam Society* 73, 1–2:23–41.

Hutchinson, E. W. 1933. "The French Foreign Mission in Siam during the Seventeenth Century." *Journal of the Siam Society* 26, 1:1–72.

Kammerer, Cornelia Ann. 1990. "Customs and Christian Conversion among Akha Highlanders of Burma and Thailand." *American Ethnologist* 17, 2:277–91.

———. In press. "Discarding the Basket: The Reinterpretation of Tradition by Akha Christian of Northern Thailand." *Journal of Southeast Asian Studies*.

Keyes, Charles F. 1967–78. Field notes.

———. 1969. "New Evidence on Northern Thai Frontier History." In *In Memoriam Phya Anuman Rajadhon*, Tej Bunnag and Michael Smithies, eds., pp. 221–50. Bangkok: Siam Society.

———. 1971. "Buddhism and National Integration in Thailand." *Journal of Asian Studies* 30, 3:551–68.

———. 1975. "Buddhist Pilgrimage Centers and the Twelve-Year Cycle: Northern Thai Moral Orders in Space and Time." *History of Religions* 15, 1:17–89.

———. 1978. "Political Crisis and Militant Buddhism in Contemporary Thailand." In *Religion and Legitimation of Power in Thailand, Burma, and Laos*, Bardwell Smith, ed., pp. 147–64. Chambersburg, Pa.: Anima Books.

———. 1983. "Merit Transference in the Kammic Theory of Popular Theravāda Buddhism." In *Karma: An Anthropological Inquiry*, Charles F. Keyes and E. Valentine Daniel, eds., pp. 261–86. Berkeley and Los Angeles: University of California Press.

———. 1989. "Buddhist Politics and Their Revolutionary Origins in Thailand." *International Political Science Review* 10, 2:121–42 (special issue, *Structure and History*, S. N. Eisenstadt, ed.).

———. 1991. "Christianity as an Indigenous Religion in Southeast Asia: Report on a Conference Held in Cebu, the Philippines, 1–5 September 1986." *Social Compass* 38, 2:177–85.

Kirti Bunchua. 1984. "Social Change and Cooperation among Various Faiths in Thailand." In *Development Issues in Thailand* (Papers Presented at the First International Conference on Thai Studies, 1981, New Delhi), B. J. Terwiel, ed., pp. 227–36. Gaya: Centre for South-East Asian Studies.

———. 1986. "Indigenization of Christianity in Thailand." Paper presented at conference, Christianity as an Indigenous Religion in Southeast Asia, sponsored by the Joint American Council of Learned Societies and Social Science Research Council Committee on Southeast Asia, Cebu City, the Philippines.

Koyama Kosuke. 1978. "Aristotelian Pepper and Buddhist Salt." In *Readings in Missionary Anthropology II*, William A. Smalley, ed., pp. 109–14. South Pasadena, Calif.: William Carey Library.

Lange, Claude. 1980. "L'église catholique et la Société des Missions Etrangères au Vietnam (Vicariat Apostolique de Cochinchine au VIIème siècle)." Dissertation, Doctorat du Troisième Cycle, Université de Paris-Sorbonne.

Launay, Adrien. 1920. *Histoire de la Mission de Siam.* Paris. 1985. Translated by Prathumrat Wongdontrī into Thai as *Sayām lae khana mitchannārī Farangsēt* (Siam and the French Missionaries). Bangkok: Fine Arts Department.

McBeth, John. 1983. "The Church Clandestine." *Far Eastern Economic Review* (14 July): pp. 34–35.

McGilvary, Daniel. 1912. *A Half Century among the Siamese and the Lao.* New York: Fleming H. Revell.

McVey, Ruth. 1984. "Separatism and the Paradoxes of the Nation-State in Perspective. "In *Armed Separatism in Southeast Asia*, Lim Joo-Jock and Vani S., eds., pp. 3–29. Singapore: Institute of Southeast Asian Studies.

Nock, A. D. 1933. *Conversion: The Old and the New in Religion from Alexander the Great to Augustine of Hippo.* Oxford: Oxford University Press.

Peel, J. D. Y. 1968. *Aladura: A Religious Movement among the Yoruba.* London: Oxford University Press for International African Institute.

Pin Muthukan (Pin Muthukanta), Colonel. 1963. *Tǭp bāt luang* (Retort to Reverend Brother). Bangkok: Khlangwitthayā.

———. n.d. *The Retort to Reverend Brother.* [Bangkok?]: n.p.

Pro Mundi Vita Centrum Informationis. 1973. *Thailand in Transition: The Church in a Buddhist Country.* Brussels: Pro Mundi Vita International Research and Information Center.

Reynolds, Craig. 1976. "Buddhist Cosmography in Thai History, with Special Reference to Nineteenth-Century Culture Change." *Journal of Asian Studies* 35, 2:203–20.

Sanit Wongprasert. 1988. "Impact of the Dhammacarik Bhikkhus' Programme on the Hill Tribes of Thailand." In *Ethnic Conflict in Buddhist Societies: Sri Lanka, Thailand, and Burma*, K. M. de Silva et al., eds., pp. 126–37. London: Pinter Publishers; Boulder, Colo.: Westview Press.

Sērī Phongphit. 1982. *Kāthōlik kap sangkhom Thai: Sī sattawat hāeng khunkhā lae botrian* (Catholics and Thai Society: The Values and Lessons of Four Centuries). Bangkok: Mūnnithi Kamon Khīmthǫng.

———. 1985. "Church in Asia: Past, Present, and Future." *Seeds of Peace* 1, 1:8–11.

Smith, Alexander G. 1982. *Siamese Gold: A History of Church Growth in Thailand—An Interpretive Analysis, 1816–1982.* Bangkok: Kanok Bannasan (OMF Press).

Sobhan-Ganabhorn, Phra. 1984. *A Plot to Undermine Buddhism.* Bangkok: Siva Phorn.

Surin Pitsuwan. 1985. *Islam and Malay Nationalism: A Case Study of the Malay-Muslims of Southern Thailand.* Bangkok: Thammasat University, Thai Khadi Research Institute.

Swearer, Donald K. 1973. *A Theology of Dialogue.* Bangkok: Department of Christian Education and Literature, Church of Christ in Thailand (Sinclair Thompson Memorial Lectures, Series no. 8).

Tambiah, S. J. 1970. *Buddhism and the Spirit Cults in Northeast Thailand.* Cambridge: Cambridge University Press, Cambridge Studies in Social Anthropology, 2.

Tapp, Nicholas. 1989. "The Impact of Missionary Christianity upon Marginalized Ethnic Minorities: The Case of the Hmong." *Journal of Southeast Asian Studies* 27:70–95.

Tobias, Stephen F. 1977. "Buddhism, Belonging, and Detachment—Some Paradoxes of Chinese Ethnicity in Thailand." *Journal of Asian Studies* 36, 2:303–26.

Uthai Dulyakasem. 1984. "Muslim-Malay Separatism in Southern Thailand: Factors Underlying the Political Revolt." In *Armed Separatism in Southeast Asia.* Lim Joo-Jock and Vani S., eds., pp. 217–33. Singapore: Institute of Southeast Asian Studies.

———. 1991. "Education and Ethnic Nationalism: The Case of the Muslim-Malays in Southern Thailand." In *Reshaping Local Worlds: Education and Cultural Change in Rural Southeast Asia,* Charles F. Keyes, ed., pp. 131–52. New Haven: Yale University, Southeast Asian Studies.

Wells, K. E. 1963. *Theravada Buddhism and Protestant Christianity.* Chiang Mai: Thailand Theological Seminary (Sinclair Thompson Memorial Lectures, Second Series).

Wolters, O. W. 1982. *History, Culture, and Region in Southeast Asian Perspectives.* Singapore: Institute of Southeast Asian Studies.

Wyatt, David K. 1984. *Thailand: A Short History.* New Haven: Yale University Press.

Yarr, Linda. 1986. "The Indigenization of Christianity in Pre-Colonial Vietnam." Paper presented at conference, Christianity as an Indigenous Religion in Southeast Asia, sponsored by the Joint American Council of Learned Societies and Social Science Research Council Committee on Southeast Asia, Cebu City, the Philippines.

Zehner, Edwin. In press. "Thai Converts and Supernaturalism: Changing Configurations." *Journal of Southeast Asian Studies.*

———. n.d. "Merit, Man, and Ministry: Speaking Christian with a Thai Accent." Manuscript.

CHAPTER TEN

The Glyphomancy Factor: Observations on Chinese Conversion

David K. Jordan

CONVERSION AND THE NURTURANCE OF FAITH

This chapter is about voluntary religious conversion as I understand it to occur among Chinese in Taiwan.[1] I doubt that much of what I have to say applies only to Chinese from Taiwan, but they are my data base.

The social science literature on voluntary religious conversion—I exclude constrained conversion—impressive as it is in considering the cultural and political context and effects of conversion, seems to me often to make simplistic assumptions about how converts themselves understand the process. My goal here is to introduce a note of caution in this regard by examining what individual converts have told me about how they have come to believe (and to keep believing) what they believe. Typically their stated reasons have little to do with the issues we model in our analyses. I label this badness of fit "the glyphomancy factor," after the specimen case with which I begin.

I conceive of "conversion" here as being a self-conscious change in more or less enduring religious belief and affiliation from one religious system to another.[2] "Religious system" includes both a system of belief and a social structure of believers. Conversion is principally an individual activity, at least analytically, and our ideal type is the conversion of an individual, although of course when large numbers of people are involved we can also speak historically of conversion, as in the conversion of Latin America to Iberian Catholicism.

The definition in itself says nothing about the motivations for the change—it is a change, no matter how motivated. And it says nothing about the extent of the change; the switch from Baptist to Presbyterian, because both belief and group are involved, constitutes conversion under this definition just as much as switching from Hinduism to Islam. The definition also does not build in any evaluation of the religions to or from which conversion occurs. It is not necessary to become a believer in a "world religion" to be a convert.[3]

Because conversion involves beliefs and believers, it is related to the general problem of creating and sustaining religious faith, that is, to creating and sustaining the salience both of religious belief and of membership in a community of believers. Thus our analysis of conversion involves us necessarily in the mechanisms of faith maintenance: emotions, routines, and rhetorics.

In this chapter I examine three characteristic (but not exclusive) features of Chinese conversion: conditionality of belief upon other beliefs, the additive character of conversion, and the tendency to equate new beliefs isomorphically with earlier ones (what I call "pantheon interchangeability"). These admittedly cover only part of the general problem of Chinese faith maintenance and hence of Chinese conversion, but a broader discussion is beyond the scope of this chapter. I begin by illustrating them with the striking if peripheral custom of glyphomancy. I do so not because glyphomancy is at all central to most Chinese faith maintenance or conversion, but rather because it illustrates these features simultaneously and constitutes a vivid example through which we can keep the issue of faith maintenance before us as we think about conversion more generally.

By speaking of "the glyphomancy factor," I mean to stress the significance of the kinds of logics and experiences that believers themselves find compelling, and to suggest that we must incorporate those experiences into our higher-level "explanations" of changes in religious belief and affiliation. The expression "glyphomancy factor," then, is intended to be provocative.

GLYPHOMANCY FOR CHRISTIANS

Most Chinese characters consist of more than one graphic element, and the segregation of the elements is sometimes used in school to help students remember them, or in speech to disambiguate homophones. For example, the common surname Lǐ 李 can be described as made up of the two characters *mù* 木 and *zǐ* 子, and accordingly if I ask Mr. Lǐ how to write his name, he may tell me that he is named *mùzǐ Lǐ*, by which he means that his name is written with that Lǐ character which can be segregated into elements *mù* and *zǐ*. In some, perhaps even most, cases the division in fact corresponds with the etymology of the character. In others, it is merely a matter of convenience. In cases like that of Mr. Lǐ, the division has become entirely conventional, whether originally etymological or not.

If Mr. Lǐ visits a fortune-teller to learn about his destiny, however, the fortune-teller may choose to look more closely at his name and to seek "hidden" characters in it, ones that are not conventionally construed as part of its etymology. The fortune-teller may tell him, for example, that Lǐ actually includes the (overlapping) elements "ten" 十, "eight" 八, and "son" 子, thus meaning "eighteen sons," or (depending upon other parts of the name) that he is destined to have many progeny. (The fortune-teller may then confirm this prediction by pointing out how many Lǐs there are in the world, for example.) The art of segregating the parts of a Chinese character to discover an esoteric meaning in them is referred to by the neogrecism "glyphomancy" (Mandarin: *chèzì*), and Chinese glyphomancy has been well described in a fascinating article by Wolfgang Bauer (1979), from whom I have borrowed the example of Mr. Lǐ.

Glyphomancy has long been the stock in trade of the lesser sort of Christian missionary in China or, among foreign missionaries, of the missionary's lesser sort of native assistant. Chinese Christian glyphomancy seeks to demonstrate that Chinese characters contain Christian symbolism and that Christianity is therefore a public manifestation of the same cosmological view esoterically enshrined in Chinese characters by the sages of antiquity.[4] A Chinese word that Christians translate as "devil," for example, is *gǔi* 鬼 (ghost, demon). Christian glyphomancy sees this as a combination of "field" 田 (understood esoterically as the Garden of Eden), "man" 儿 (that is, the human voice of the Devil in Eden), and "private" 厶 (the clandestine approach to Eve). The related Chinese word *mó* 魔 (demon, devil) is etymologically made up of *gǔi* 鬼 and the simpler character *má* 麻 (hemp), borrowed for its sound. *Mó* 魔 is construed in Christian glyphomancy as placing the devil into the forbidden tree 木, located next to the tree of life—hence two trees 林—the whole being under a cover 广, referring, "of course," to secrecy. Thus a Christian interpretation allows us to understand that the ancient Chinese *mó* demon is none other than the Christian "tempter," just as a *gǔi* is. It also asserts that ancient Chinese inventors and users of the written language were perfectly well aware of this equivalence, and built the language in a way that would convey Christian truths to him who would but see.[5]

The use of Chinese analogies to Christian traditions (glyphomancy *sensū latō*) by no means occurred only early in the development of Christian missions in China. Consider the following conversation that I had in Taipei in 1985 with a college-educated Methodist whom I shall call Mr. Wáng:[6] "Jesus' miracle of the five cakes and two fish," Mr. Wáng explained, "was something often done by ancient miracle workers in China, which is how we know that it really happened. It shows the connection between the Bible and Chinese tradition, for the two fish, pressed into a circle, are none other than the *Yīn-Yáng* symbol, and the five cakes are five because that corresponds with the five elements."

"In the West," I objected, "it is the small number of loaves and fishes rather than the numerology that impresses people."

"If you told Chinese that Jesus had performed the miracle with six or four cakes, they would never believe it," he answered, "for everyone knows that is impossible. Because he used five, people believe in his miracles, for everyone knows that great Taoists could multiply fives. They did it all the time."

"Do they still do it?"

"No, no; they did it in ancient times."

He proceeded with other examples of his analysis of the Christian tradition and rapidly moved into glyphomancy proper. "The Chinese character 羊 for 'goat' or 'sheep' occurs as part of various other characters, all with particularly positive meanings, such as 'beauty' 美, 'virtue' 善, and 'devotion to duty' 義. The reason is that 'goat/sheep' when occurring as part of another character actually means 'Lamb of God.' For example, the character 義 for 'loyal devotion to duty' is made up of 'sheep' 羊 plus 'myself' 我, because a person can acquire this virtue only as a result of his ego acting with the Lamb of God.[7]

"Further, the word *chuán* 船 means 'ship' and is written with the character *zhōu* 舟, also meaning 'boat', plus various clutter added at the right side. The clutter can be read as the characters meaning 'eight' 八 and 'mouth' 口," Mr. Wáng maintained. "Thus it is clear that the arc (*zhōu*) of Noah, being a kind of *chuán* 船, contained eight mouths, namely, Noah's, his wife's, and those of his three sons and their wives. From this we see not only that Gospel truths are embedded in Chinese characters but also that we can't fully understand Christianity without proper attention to the esoteric meanings of Chinese script."

Religious interest in glyphomancy and related logics is not limited to Christians. Chinese sectarians (believers in the Unborn Mother, who dispatched the buddhas to save erring humanity) also make use of glyphomancy (and other linguistic esoterica) to legitimate sectarian views by finding them to be implicit in Chinese characters, the Chinese calendar, the five-elements theory, and the like.[8]

This excursion into Christian glyphomancy is intrinsically interesting (or perhaps depressing), but it is also an introduction both to a logic of belief and conversion and to a strategy of evangelization.[9] It is improbable that a social scientist would impute the conversion of Chinese to glyphomantic demonstrations or would describe Chinese Christian believing as belief in glyphomancy. This is not the sort of explanation we are used to, and it stands ignobly beside "relative deprivation," "the strains of modernization," "class oppression," and "anomie," or, for that matter, "rationalization," "hegemonism," and "the Protestant Ethic." Yet it is clear that Mr. Wáng finds glyphomancy a compelling demonstration of Christian truth: a reason to become a Christian and a reason to remain one. And it is clear that he is not alone in following this kind of logic. If, because of glyphomancy, some believers either convert to Christianity (or sectarianism) or sustain a belief in it, then a model of conversion, evangelization, or believing ought to make space for such a logic. In choosing the expression "the glyphomancy factor," I hope to underline the problem of including glyphomancy and other similar phenonema in our understanding of conversion.

THE GLYPHOMANCY FACTOR AND THE LOGIC OF CONVERSION

The glyphomancy factor has three distinct qualities. None of them is found exclusively in glyphomancy; on the contrary, I suspect each has much wider application than just to Taiwan or China. But each of them is present where glyphomancy occurs, and for the Chinese case it is convenient to link them under that rubric.

First, glyphomancy asserts theological, philosophical, and sometimes historical priority of Chinese characters (or Chinese tradition) over what are perceived as "modern," "latter-day," or "foreign" doctrines. Thus sectarian (including Christian) "truth" is demonstrated by the congruence of sectarian teaching with the already established wisdom of Chinese tradition. An important implication of this is that there is a hierarchy of philosophical truth, in which the familiar is prior and superior to the unfamiliar, which is evaluated in its terms. I shall refer to this as the "conditional" quality of conversion.

Note that Mr. Wáng is making *Chinese* tradition the yardstick against which a *foreign* religion is evaluated. The distinction is by no means lost on him, and appealing to nativist tradition to justify exotic beliefs by domesticating them may resolve ambivalence about Christian foreignness. (There are other ways, such as joining a Taiwan denomination without foreign contacts.) Robert Hefner (personal communication) has suggested that the strength of the Chinese sense of ethnicity permits a lack of concern with the implications of potential institutional authority in one rather than another religion. This ingenious suggestion would account for cases like Mr. Wáng. Ethnicity probably was not an issue in conversion at all periods of Chinese history, however, whereas the glyphomancy factor seems to have operated continuously. The familiar and already legitimate seem to be used to justify the novel and not universally believed; ethnic identity would have become a factor only later.

Second, religious belief or practice to which an individual is converted is, in China, added to existing belief, without necessarily implying to the believer the subtraction of anything. Believing in the authority of a sectarian scripture does not have to diminish the believer's belief in the authority of another scripture. The assimilation of Christian cosmological understandings need not diminish belief in traditional Chinese understandings. I shall refer to this as the "additive" quality of conversion. It is by no means exclusive to China.[10]

Third, glyphomantic logic has a tendency to assert the equivalences of religious elements. Thus, the Hebrew god may be equated with the sectarian societies' Unborn Mother, and Gautama Buddha of Buddhism is equated with Mohammed in Islam, Lǎozǐ in Taoism, and so forth. In a less institutionalized sphere the patronage of one healing god may be substituted for the patronage of another; participation in one shrine festival is interchangeable with participation in another. I shall refer to this quality of conversion as "pantheon interchangeability," although of course not only the pantheon may be so treated.

It seems to me that conditionality, additivity, and pantheon interchangeability are all important aspects of Chinese conversion and probably always have been. I concluded the introductory discussion of glyphomancy by suggesting that it was not peculiar to Chinese Christians, but that it has been a logic of Chinese philosophical persuasion for many centuries and in many contexts. The same, I believe, is true of conversion, and it would be shortsighted to build a model that does not cover the many cases in which conversion is *not* to Christianity or even Buddhism,[11] for the "tradition" of conversion in China is part of the cultural background of the latter-day converts and colors the ways in which they convert and in which they believe.

Conversion is not a new phenomenon in China, which has always been a country of religious sectarianism. Within different traditions the disciples of different masters have constituted themselves competing sects. The state has always encouraged a ritualistic and supernaturalistic element in all social life. And adherents of one or another cult have always competed with each other in claims of efficacy.[12] Conversion in traditional China was not a matter of moving from belief in a community-based "traditional" religion to a universalistic, rationalized "world" religion. Conversion instead (or in addition) might include moving from seeking to cure one's arthritis by praying to Māzǔ to seeking to cure one's arthritis by buying a charm from a newly arrived "Taoist" worshiping an unknown jinn. It might include largely abandoning the worship of one's village gods and becoming a Buddhist cleric, actively worshiping only a subset of the pantheon one worshiped before. It might include joining a millenarian sect that redefined an otherwise obscure member of the pantheon as a supreme ruler of the universe. It might include becoming a perfervid follower of a spirit medium possessed by a deceased fellow villager, a local divinity, or an unknown supernatural. In some cases it might include joining a sect that included foreigners: Christianity, or in earlier times Buddhism itself, or more recently Baha'i or Tenrikyō.[13]

It is a useful simplifying assumption in generating theories of conversion, when applied to the non-Western world, to assume conversion from a unitary "traditional" religion to an intrusive "world" religion, with attendant "abandonment" of old religious beliefs (or with their residual continuation resulting in "syncretism"). But if it is appropriate to speak of someone in Albuquerque or Amsterdam "converting" from being a Catholic to being a Lutheran or from being a Lutheran to being a Unitarian, then I submit that it is equally appropriate to speak of conversion when a Chinese devotee of Guān Gōng joins a sect devoted to chanting Buddhist scriptures, for the commitment, the belief, the fervor, and the balance of participation in religious activities need not be any less or greater.[14]

Conversion is Conditional

Glyphomancy is a logic of persuasion, a rhetoric. It is not the only rhetoric that figures in the establishment and sustenance of Chinese religious belief. For example, one might stress the role of divination and miracle making in this connection (e.g., Jordan 1990) as well as the combination of traditionalism and "goodness of fit" with village life in a rural context (Jordan 1972). But persuasion, like nagging doubt, is a constant and inevitable process for a believer in a society in which there is variation in belief (or in intensity of belief), and persuasion necessarily proceeds with at least some reference to evaluative criteria external to the religious system being defended. (This is not to say that such criteria are or need to be "fairly" or "objectively" applied, only that they are normally believed to be.) This makes something like conditionality more or less inevitable, at least in China.

The underlying logic of conditional conversion is that a proposed new religious belief or activity is evaluated against a belief that one already holds and that the innovation can be rejected if it is regarded as incompatible. I spent 1976 living in one of Taiwan's oldest Buddhist monasteries.[15] Eventually I was treated to the assistant abbot's account of how he came to be a Buddhist monk. He had been something of a playboy in high school and had failed to gain admission to a university, but he had hoped to defer military service by becoming a student anyway. He was eventually admitted to a Christian theological seminary, where he studied for a couple of years. When he finished there, he did his military service, during which he became disillusioned with Christianity. After his time in the army he entered a Buddhist monastery for brief religious training, then took vows and became a monk. This move involved withdrawal from the social world of his former army buddies, only one of whom would tolerate his presence thereafter, because monks have very little prestige in Taiwan.

The compelling logic by which he rejected Christianity and embraced Buddhism, he told me, was represented in one inescapable fact: In Christianity there can be but one Christ, but in Buddhism we can all become buddhas. Thus Christianity is inherently inegalitarian (and wrong), whereas Buddhism is inherently egalitarian (and right).

Of course, there are many other differences between Buddhism and Christianity, and one could imagine the committed believer of either faith finding any of them an obstacle to conversion to the other. Yet the assistant abbot had no such compunctions. The overwhelming difference was that of egalitarianism; all else was so much detail in faith and practice. I do not know how the assistant abbot developed such a conviction about the importance of human equality (although it is much stressed in Taiwan's schools), but it was for him the logic by which the would-be ultimate moral authority of Buddhism and Christianity could be weighed against each other. His belief in Buddhism was, in other words, "conditional" in the sense that its ultimacy was subordinate to the ultimacy of his belief in egalitarianism.

Not all conditions need be so cerebral. Max Heirich (1977) has shown the force of one's social milieu in making conversion a viable course of action, and this is surely as true of Chinese populations as of others. Thus college students in Taipei are overrepresented among new converts to Christianity. Although there are a number of possible reasons for this, surely once Christian conversion is an established phenomenon, the world of the college student provides a social structure within which it is more probable than do groups where Christians are less well represented.

Healing and Conditionality

Beyond overarching logics and social pressures, responsiveness to healing may be a condition of conversion. Physical healing is an important aspect of Chinese religion, as of nearly all religion through nearly all of human history. Chinese temples are repositories of oracles and charms relating to health, and the Chinese pantheon is replete with senders of plagues on the one hand and with healers and controllers of plagues on the other. Further, Chinese medicine is informed by cosmological imagery and by vocabulary intimately related to the cosmological elaborations of fortune-telling, "astrology," and Taoist liturgy (see, for example, Saso 1972).

The success or failure of a therapeutic method, particularly a medical therapy, is an important logic both for conversion and for sustained loyalty to a particular cult, sect, or system of practice.[16] Because no single therapeutic system could be consistently effective, most Chinese used a variety of kinds of medical and religious treatments. For any given experience of illness, the means of healing available were arranged in a hierarchy of resort determined by the patient's beliefs about available therapies, their costs in time, energy, or social status; and by the patient's understanding of the illness or other disorder requiring attention. Specialists were consulted both because of their known expertise and because of an estimated probability of the kind of diagnosis that they would make.[17]

Traditional Chinese religion always provided a wide variety of means of healing, luck changing, and the like, and individuals moved from one to another as success or rumors of success seemed persuasive. Since few systems of healing were repudiated entirely, "conversion" was often a matter of a shifting hierarchy of resort, placing the therapeutic system of one's new religious affiliation above that of old ones. This attitude probably still holds. In the 1960s, Christian missions were enjoying a success in Taiwan that they have had neither before nor since. I took to asking (non-Christian) informants why people converted to Christianity. The most common reply was that conversion was associated with the use of Christian hospitals. In some cases the hospitals were perceived as more accessible to "insiders." In others the conversion was regarded as the natural result of successful healing at a Christian hospital. (Compare the lifelong devotion of some healed patients to the cult of one or another traditional god credited with the healing.) Conversion, in other words, was "conditional" upon the effectiveness of the therapeutic system associated with the religion.[18]

Other benefits of conversion to Christianity were probably also part of a hierarchy of resort, although less directly medical, and therefore perhaps less well described by that term. James A. Collignon (1981) reflects on the stagnation and slight decline of the Catholic church's success in evangelization in Taiwan after it discontinued its postwar program of distributing relief goods. He speaks of "rice Christians," who left the church when it no longer offered any material benefit.[19] Although in retrospect their conversions may be dismissed as somehow not genuine, there was little doubt at the time of the success of missionary efforts. I would submit that what was involved was simply conditional conversion, the condition being the success of the system of solving problems and its elevation in a hierarchy of resort.[20] The conversion may also have been additive (and hence reversible), and the effective mechanism may have been pantheon interchangeability, subjects to which we now turn.

Conversion Is Additive

By conversion being additive, I mean simply that much Chinese conversion has involved the addition of beliefs and practices, not their replacement. To the extent that religion intergrades with other aspects of life and therefore has uncertain boundaries, this is probably true of all religious conversion. And in any case, there is almost certainly a continuum in the extent to which converts do or do not abandon old beliefs, particularly if they are not seen as significantly competing with "equivalent" new ones. It is not unusual for Chinese sectarian societies to encourage members to prefer a society's oracles to outside ones (or actively discourage the use of outside ones) and to claim peculiar importance for the society's cult objects. But at least in Taiwan, a sectarian society rarely prohibits all participation in nonsectarian religious activities.

The Compassion Society (described in Jordan and Overmyer 1986, chs. 6–8) is a case in point. The society centers on the nonexclusive worship of a deity referred to as the "Golden Mother of the Jade Pool" (Yáochí Jīnmǔ), and members are encouraged to refer to her simply as "Mother." My notes are full of touching tales of her nurturing her followers, and association with her cult has undoubtedly transformed the worldviews of at least some of the sect's converts. But this sect celebrates popular Taoist rites and performs Buddhist chants as acts of merit, and the sectarian temples not only include the statues of other popular deities but are also proud to carry their goddess in a palanquin in local community festivals in the same way that other deities are carried. Although membership in the Compassion Society inhibits individual participation in some other religious institutions, the limitation is by no means absolute. And although the society claims that the Golden Mother is prior to other gods, the rest of the pantheon is not displaced by her position, nor is its worship prohibited.

My monastery, being an orthodox Chán ("Zen") establishment, might also have been expected to purge its believers of attachment to competing popular forms of worship. On the contrary, it housed certain venerable local josses that had no connection with Buddhism but who had been deprived of their proper temple during Japanese rule in Taiwan, when one of the statues was also repainted to look like a different god to avoid Japanese persecution. The god, still incognito, occupies a prominent side altar in the monastery, where he entertains yearly visits from emissaries of subordinate temples founded from his original temple. The abbot found it embarrassing to explain to a foreigner why this "un-Buddhist" deity was enshrined in the temple and its "un-Buddhist" devotees tolerated. At the same time, his presence was clearly not regarded as threatening, but merely deviant. Monastic Buddhism does normally maintain a certain distance from other manifestations of Chinese belief. But it is a rare lay Buddhist, in my experience, who is not also at least in part a believer and participant in non-Buddhist Chinese religious traditions as well. Even becoming a Buddhist nun, while it may commit one enough to Buddhism to make non-Buddhist practice unnecessary or undignified, does not require that one regard non-Buddhist religious belief or practice as invalid.

Despite the intention of foreign missionaries of Christianity, Chinese Christians have always tended to regard it too as additive rather than substitutive and to expect a continuity that purists avoid. Gwo Yun-han, pastor of Grace Baptist Church in Taipei, sees this as an evangelical problem: "In the [Protestant] Christian churches no icon is provided for people's eyes to see, nor is there anything similar to what is found in the temples or shrines. Therefore when a Chinese person happens to go into a Christian church, a certain kind of negative reaction automatically occurs. Sometimes the walls of a church building can literally fence the people away from Christianity" (Gwo 1988:34). The concept of a supreme god has not been problematic, because the pervasive bureaucratic metaphor of Chinese religion easily admits of a top figure (whose names are many). Historically, problems arose instead when Christian practice struck Chinese as orthogonal to highly cathected Chinese rites (hence unable to displace them) and seemed to missionaries to conflict with them. The prime example, of course, is the practice of ancestor worship, and the famous "rites controversy" that ended in the collapse of the Jesuit enterprise in China in the early eighteenth century when Clement XI, having established that Chinese ancestor worship constituted "worship," prohibited it to Chinese Christians.[21]

With the new flexibility of Vatican II, Taiwan Catholics by the middle 1960s had churches modeled on temples, incense sticks interchangeable with those of temples, and ancestral tablets both for congregations and for families (albeit worded slightly differently from the non-Christian equivalents). One foreign priest enthusiastically told me in 1968 that he was encouraging people in his parish to refer to the church as the "God temple" (*Tiānzhǔ miào*) rather than by the usual Chinese Christian expression "God hall" (*Tiānzhǔ táng*) because it would grant the local church the legitimacy of being a real temple.

That this may represent a degree of syncretism is trivially true. To the extent that Chinese forms of architecture and liturgy were superficially wedded to Catholic ones, it was syncretic.[22] More subtly, however, the enthusiasm with which Chinese Catholics erected home altars and set up ancestral tablets suggests that official Catholicism had long been overlooking or resisting the additive quality of the Chinese conversion process, by which the logic and appeal of the cult of ancestors had by no means been superseded in pious Catholics, even when it had been successfully suppressed, or by which would-be converts were repelled by the inscrutable need to replace ancestral rites.

Some aspects of traditional religion had been displaced by Catholicism. But I would argue that the process had also been additive and that the resultant syncretism is in fact a realistic recognition of conversion's additive character. I do not know whether Catholics, like our Methodist informant Mr. Wáng, practice glyphomancy. But it is clear that the glyphomancy factor remains relevant.

Conversion Involves Pantheon Interchangeability

Reference has already been made to the substitution of one deity for another. So adherents of the Golden Mother claim a parallelism among Lǎozǐ in Taoism, Jesus in Christianity, Confucius in Confucianism, and so forth. Similarly, changes can be made in what Roberts, Chiao, and Pandey (1975) have referred to as a believer's "personal pantheon." I isolate this phenomenon for particular discussion because most Chinese conversion probably fits this model most closely.

As a typical case, let us imagine a believer who is a special devotee of a certain god. He petitions the deity for assistance with something and does not receive an obvious response. At the urging of friends or relatives, he takes his petition to a different shrine. (Or he happens to visit another shrine and simply offers a prayer.) This time he receives a response and then shifts his allegiance to the newly discovered shrine or deity. Some of Taiwan's proudest temple buildings were constructed with money contributed by the beneficiaries of such abrupt changes of fortune. We can appropriately describe this as conversion, because the believer has shifted to a new temple such institutional affiliation as Chinese popular religion provides and has changed the name of the god whom he believes to be his benefactor. If the shrine happens to be a sectarian one, he may take on a few sectarian terms, behaviors, or doctrines.

A Methodist probably makes fewer adjustments in converting to Christian Science. Yet in the Euro-American arena we speak of such a change easily enough as conversion, while in Chinese cases of the kind just described we hesitate over our suspicion that the underlying intellectual and emotional system of the believer is too little changed to merit the term. In many cases the doctrinal system (to the extent that it matters to him) is also little changed. This kind of substitution of one deity for another (or one shrine for another or one undercathected dogma for another) is an everyday occurrence among my Chinese informants, many of whom tell of miraculous changes of luck associated with one or another shrine or divinity, but few of whom speak of transformations in their view of the cosmic order of things.[23]

CONCLUSION

Conversion is nothing new in China. Conversion back and forth among competing religious alternatives at all levels has been a constant option through most of Chinese history. Perhaps as a long-term adaptation, conversion has itself become part of the popular religious system, which has expanded to "contain" the notion of alternative standards of faith and practice among which conversion occurs. Traditionally, most Chinese conversion was probably "additive" (it did not require abandonment of old beliefs, merely their subordination to new ones); it was "conditional" (adherence to a religious regimen was conditioned by external standards of evaluation, such that the new religious system was not, at least initially, ultimate but was accepted only if congruent with an outside standard); and it probably normally involved "pantheon interchangeability" (loyalties were shifted from one cult or sect to another with little dramatic change in cosmology or values).

China, said to have domesticated Buddhism and largely to have resisted Christianity, has tamed conversion as well. If this puzzles us, it is because we so rarely allow for the glyphomancy factor. The term "glyphomancy factor" is intended to underline that traditional Chinese conversion (which provides the model for much modern Chinese conversion) rarely involved the exclusivity that seems implicit in the word "conversion" as used in colloquial English. As a result the constant Chinese shifts of emphasis and balance among religious alternatives are readily ignored, and "real" conversion is sought in switch of allegiance to a "world religion" outside the sphere of traditional Chinese belief altogether. Conversion is then seen as a shift from "traditionalism" to "rationalism" or the like. Such a change may be a sign of profound societal alienation and possibly psychopathology, but at least it is "real" conversion.

In Taiwan (and China more broadly), however, conversion to so-called world religions does not always give evidence of being qualitatively different from conversion among traditional alternatives. This is not to say that modern Chinese Christians or Muslims have the minds of Míng dynasty Taoists; they do not. Neither, however, do modern Taoists. China in general and Taiwan in particular are hardly immune from the currents of thought and practice that blow over the modern world, and Taiwan is indeed a major center for the scientific and technological revolution that was once imagined to be "Western science" and is still sometimes so described. But the changes that sweep the Chinese worldview do not seem to be closely associated with Chinese religious conversion so much as with the subtler transformations brought upon us all by technological change on the one hand and political change on the other.

How Chinese is all this? Does the glyphomancy factor turn up elsewhere? Clearly it does. A wide range of papers on contemporary religious conversion, from Indonesia (Geertz 1964, Hefner 1987) to Africa (Horton 1971, Ranger 1978) stress that "traditional" religion in these areas is hardly inflexible, nor are "world" religions more "modern," "rational," or "worldly" than traditional religions would probably have evolved to be in the context of "modern" circumstances.

If the glyphomancy factor can be suspected behind most voluntary religious conversion, is there anything special (besides glyphs) in its Chinese manifestation? I doubt it. Rather, our models of voluntary conversion have been social rather than psychocultural, focused on such variables as political power and ethnicity (and hence the "strategies" of conversion) rather than on the converting individual's sense of well-being or of place in the cosmos. Politics and ethnicity have their roles in Taiwan conversion, too, especially in modern non-Chinese sects like Tenrikyō and various non-native Christian denominations. Indeed, a certain social éclat comes with being a Baptist college student. But the glyphomancy factor emerges in the process of coming and continuing to believe rather than in the process of affiliation. As we seek this process elsewhere, the glyphomancy factor will undoubtedly raise its head and peer back at us.

Is the expression "world religion" then useful at all? From the perspective of individual motivation, probably not. Buddhism, a "world religion," is entirely traditional in China, despite widespread historical knowledge that it is not of Chinese origin. Are Taiwan Buddhists more "worldly" than followers of local syncretistic sectarian societies? Is a conversion from Buddhism to Tenrikyō different by definition from a conversion from Golden Mother worship to Tenrikyō or a conversion from Tenrikyō to Buddhism? I think not. The more important issue by far is what is changed in the conversion, how much, for whom, and with what effect. I suspect that for the believer most conversion most of the time is glyphomantic. If so, the faiths to and from which the individual moves are analytically interchangeable. If we are concerned with believing, then our analytical concern needs to be with the character of the conversion experience, not with the beginning or end faiths.

EPILOGUE

"Some people think it is curious that Jesus was not Chinese," Mr. Wáng told me. "That the Christian message was late coming to China is Cain's fault. When Cain, the agriculturalist elder brother, killed Abel, the pastoralist younger brother, he fled to China, where he taught people agriculture. That was good. But he was unable to communicate the true doctrine because he was wicked. (Agriculture was later wrongly credited to [the culture hero] Shénnóng. It remained for missionaries from the lands of pastoralists to sort out the true history.) This left Chinese to wallow in superstition and Satan worship. Most Chinese do not even know that they are worshiping Satan. However, this is clear from the Book of Revelation, which speaks of Satan as an 'ancient snake' (*gǔshé*), which is clearly a reference to the dragons that Chinese portray everywhere. Chinese fondness for dragons (inadvertent Satan worship) is responsible for Chinese history being plagued by millennia of war, while the Christian lands of the West have had centuries of peace."

NOTES

Acknowledgments. I am indebted to Kevin Birth, Stanley Tambiah, and especially Robert Hefner for their comments and advice about earlier drafts of this paper. Most of the research on which this paper is based was conducted in Taiwan in 1966–1968 under a grant from the National Institute for Mental Health, in 1976 with the financial assistance of the Chinese Cultural Center of New York, and in 1984–1985, when I was a Language and Research Fellow of the Committee on Scientific and Scholarly Cooperation with the United States, Academia Sinica, Republic of China. I am most grateful for this financial assistance.

1. Secondary reference is to the much greater cultural tradition of which Taiwan Chinese are only a small part, for, depending upon how "conversion" is defined, it seems to me that one can see it going back to the Neolithic.

2. One loose end in this definition is the word "from," because I shall argue that conversion is often additive. I justify leaving in the "from," however, on the assumption that additive conversion precipitates a new integration of religious belief and affiliation for the believer. But I admit to being nervous about it.

3. That difference, if it exists, is to be sought largely in long-term historical developments, I suspect, rather than in the experience of the individual convert.

4. The mythical creator of Chinese script is one Cãngjié, commemorated today primarily by the widespread use of a computer coding system for Chinese characters named after him.

5. The example comes from Kang and Nelson (1979:3–4). The authors explain: "It is the purpose of this book to propose, therefore, that the ancient Chinese people were quite familiar with the same record which the Hebrew Moses is popularly given credit for writing some 700–1,000 years later" (Kang and Nelson 1979:5). They argue that evidence of this kind demonstrates that ancient Chinese were monotheists, but that their proto-Hebraic religious system was destroyed in the Qín dynasty under the influence of Taoism and, later, Buddhism. I am grateful to Christian Jochim for bringing this book to my attention.

6. Mr. Wáng (a pseudonym) has a bachelor's degree in history from one of Taiwan's best universities and received his Christian education as an adult convert. He has been exposed to the non-Chinese world principally through his study of English, through contact with foreigners in the Methodist church or as a Chinese teacher at various times, and through a stay of a couple of years in Arabia. The "quotations" here are close paraphrases, from notes that I wrote from memory immediately after my conversation with him. Summaries of his logic that do not closely follow his words are not in quotation marks.

7. Of course, "sheep" 羊 is also an element in "rank smell" 羶, "envy" 羨, "itch" 痒, "dried fish" 鯗, and "meat soup" 羹.

8. An example of glyphomancy in a sectarian context from a Unity Sect postinitiation instructional session may be found in Jordan and Overmyer (1986:229–33).

9. For present purposes, and somewhat contrary to its etymology, I use "evangelization" to name the process of inspiring someone else to change his religious belief or affiliation, regardless of the belief or affiliation being taken on or abandoned, reserving "conversion" and "converting" for what the new believer does. In this usage, Buddhist, Taoist, or sectarian recruitment is just as "evangelical" as Christian recruitment. I shall use the term "sect" to refer to a religious social group, including Christian churches when they are not explicitly contrasted with sectarian societies. By "sectarian societies" I refer to various Chinese "new religions" of the kind described by, among others, Jordan and Overmyer (1986) or those often tagged with the "genericized" name "White Lotus," originally the name of a famous pseudo-Buddhist sect.

10. See Ranger (1978:487) for a Shona Catholic example.

11. It is my understanding that although there are many Muslims in China, they are, when ethnically Chinese, usually descendants of marriages with Central Asian immigrants, known collectively as the Húi "ethnicity"; they are not the products of evangelization (Dru C. Gladney, personal communication).

12. "Cult" here refers not to a social group but to the system of belief and ritual centering upon a particular divinity. This is the same as English usage in such phrases as "the cult of the Virgin" but contrasts with such usage as "she joined a cult and had to be deprogrammed."

13. Tenrikyō is a Japanese "new religion," based on a revelation in 1838. It has had missionary activity in Taiwan through much of this century. The present mission headquarters in Taipei was chartered by the Ministry of Interior in 1973. See Chang (1988) for a brief overview of this neglected movement in Taiwan religiosity. Islam, although most sinologists globally include it when speaking of "foreign" religions in China, does not seem to have been a proselytizing religion.

14. For exactly this kind of reason Travisano (1970) distinguishes between conversion and what he calls "alternation," a distinction that has, unfortunately, not become general in the literature on conversion.

15. Residence in the monastery was more or less accidental. It afforded the possibility of incidental observation of monastic routines and informal interaction with resident clerics, but my research program did not focus on monastic Buddhism.

16. Traditional Chinese illness and healing are not necessarily medical. In the religious sphere of healing, anyway, they include a range of individual and family "inharmonies" that may or may not be medical. Financial reverses are a conspicuous example. Traditional religious healing was often directed toward the correction of both medical and nonmedical "inharmonies" simultaneously.

17. The concept of a hierarchy of resort originates with Lola Romanucci Schwartz (1969), using data from the Admiralty Islands. Although Schwartz is particularly concerned with shifts in hierarchies of resort in connection with modernization, the concept is far more widely applicable and provides one of our most effective conceptual tools for describing the hierarchical decision tree governing selection among alternative available therapies.

18. The therapeutic system did not, apparently, need to be regarded as doctrinally or philosophically related to the sponsoring religion. Most of my Taiwan informants were aware that "Western" medicine was not necessarily "Christian" medicine, even when it came from a mission hospital. But, one informant explained, "If you want to use their hospital, it is embarrassing not to be a Christian." Today the association of modern style hospitals with Christian missions is much weaker.

19. Joseph Huang (1988:28–29) writes: "A wave of conversions in the 1950's brought the number [of believers] to approximately 300,000 by 1970. . . . membership currently stands at 292,000." Gwo (1980:32) provides the following membership figures for major Taiwan Protestant churches: Presbyterian, 210,000; Assembly Hall (a Taiwan-based denomination), 50,000; True Jesus (a Taiwan-based denomination), 25,000; China Baptist Convention, 15,000; Seventh-Day Adventists, 5,500. In 1980 the total number of denominations was 57; the total number of believers, (approximately) 310,000 (or 1.6 percent of the Taiwan population).

20. Today many Protestant missionary denominations in Taiwan offer free or cheap English lessons taught by American volunteers. In view of the high material level that Taiwan has achieved, English lessons (associated with high-paying jobs) are clearly more valuable than relief goods. Were the supply of native English speakers to be cut off or were mission or government policy to

prohibit this instruction, a good many "English-class Christians" might appear, and once again religious conversion would be found to be conditional, based on a system of religious—in this case religious-institutional—remedies for the "inharmonies" of life. To the best of my knowledge, this possibility has not been studied, however.

21. Clement XI also prohibited use of the old Chinese titles Tiān (Heaven) and Shàngtì (Supreme Emperor) as translations of *Deus* to avoid assimilation of the two "different" concepts of ultimate divinity. A Vatican decree in 1939 finally permitted Chinese Christians to take part in ancestral rites and in state rites for Confucius. This was reinforced by the Second Vatican Council (1962–1965), which actively encouraged the nativization of liturgy where possible.

22. Advocates of Catholic sinification insisted that no compromise was being made with Catholic dogma, but that only the superficial trappings that represented the Universal Church in its parochially European manifestation were being modified. In contrast, an American Protestant missionary told me that he found the Catholic changes deceptive. "Conversion must be a change in the very core of one's being," he argued. "Outward differences can be a symbol of this. It is not doing anyone any good to pretend that being a Christian does not involve change. Yet these sinified churches suggest exactly that." (Perhaps only inadvertently in concert with this logic, his wife taught converts American English and gave occasional lessons in American cooking.)

23. It is unclear to me the extent to which we can regard the followers of the Golden Mother (and similar sectarian developments) as internalizing a cosmological understanding different from that of non–Golden-Mother religious Chinese. The Golden Mother belief certainly entails an apocalyptic vision and a cosmic myth of great distinctiveness. At the same time, the ordinary pantheon remains relatively intact, merely being subordinated to the historically and bureaucratically superior Golden Mother. Priestly Taoism has always taught that the popular pantheon was subordinate to esoteric Taoist figures, so the idea is hardly unfamiliar. And the theme of changes of kalpas is already familiar from popular Buddhism, even though it is not similarly stressed. For some sectarians a distinctive change of cosmology has apparently occurred. For others only pantheon interchange seems to have gone on. Some converts, it would seem, are more converted than others.

REFERENCES

Bauer, Wolfgang. 1979. "Chinese Glyphomancy (Ch'ai-tzu) and Its Uses in Present-day Taiwan." In *Legend, Lore, and Religion in China: Essays in Honor of Wolfram Eberhard on His Seventieth Birthday*, Sarah Allan and Alvin P. Cohen, eds., pp. 71–96. San Francisco: Chinese Materials Center.

Chang Chiao-hao. 1988. "Religious Strength in Diversity." *Free China Review* 38 (1):40–45.

Collignon, James A. 1981. "The Catholic Church in Taiwan: An Interpretive Essay." Appendix to Allen J. Swanson, *The Church in Taiwan, Profile 1980: A*

Review of the Past, a Projection for the Future, pp. 399–406. Pasadena: William Carey Library.

Geertz, Clifford. [1964] 1973. "'Internal Conversion' in Contemporary Bali." Reprinted in *The Interpretation of Cultures: Selected Essays by Clifford Geertz*, pp. 170–89. New York: Basic Books.

Gwo Yun-han. 1988. "Protestants Spread the Good News." *Free China Review* 38 (1):32–35.

Hefner, Robert W. 1987. "The Political Economy of Islamic Conversion in Modern East Java." In *Islam and the Political Economy of Meaning*, William R. Roff, ed., pp. 53–78. London: Croom Helm.

Heirich, Max. 1977. "Change of Heart: A Test of Some Widely Held Theories about Religious Conversion." *American Journal of Sociology* 83:653–80.

Horton, Robin. 1971. "African Conversion." *Africa* 41:85–108.

Huang, Joseph. 1988. "Catholicism Seeks Evangelical Revival." *Free China Review* 38 (1):28–31.

Jordan, David K. 1990. "Eufunctions, Dysfunctions, and Oracles: Literary Miracle-Making in Taiwan." In *Personality and the Cultural Construction of Society: Papers in Honor of Melford E. Spiro*, David K. Jordan and Marc J. Swartz, eds., pp. 98–115. Tuscaloosa: University of Alabama Press.

———. 1987. "'Sacrifice' and 'Exchange': Misgivings about the Logic of Folk Liturgy." (Paper prepared for the annual meeting of the American Anthropological Association, November 1987.)

Jordan, David K., and Daniel L. Overmyer. 1986. *The Flying Phoenix: Aspects of Chinese Sectarianism in Taiwan*. Princeton, N.J.: Princeton University Press.

Kang, C. H., and Ethel R. Nelson. 1979. *The Discovery of Genesis: How the Truths of Genesis Were Found Hidden in the Chinese Language*. St. Louis: Concordia Publishing House.

Ranger, Terence. 1978. "The Churches, the Nationalist State, and African Religion." In *Christianity in Independent Africa*, Edward Fasholé-Luke et al., eds., pp. 478–502. London: Rex Collings.

Roberts, John M., Chien Chiao, and Triloki N. Pandey. 1975. "Meaningful God Sets from a Chinese Personal Pantheon and a Hindu Personal Pantheon." *Ethnology* 14:121–48.

Saso, Michael R. 1972. *Taoism and the Rite of Cosmic Renewal*. Pullman: Washington State University Press.

Schwartz, Lola Romanucci. 1969. "The Hierarchy of Resort in Curative Practices: The Admiralty Islands, Melanesia." *Journal of Health and Social Behavior* 10:201–9.

Travisano, R. V. 1970. "Alternation and Conversion as Qualitatively Different Transformations." In *Social Psychology through Symbolic Interaction*, G. P. Stone and H. A. Farberman, eds., pp. 494–606. Waldham, Mass.: Ginn-Blaisdell.

CHAPTER ELEVEN

Afterword: Boundaries and Horizons

Peter Wood

Conversion to Christianity means different things to different peoples and entails divergent social consequences. The essays in this volume clarify some of the variables, such as the social position of those who embrace the new religion, their motives, the receptivity of their communities to intellectual innovation and other forms of change, and—what is not quite the same thing—the mutability of their cultures. These essays, moreover, make a strong case that these variables combine to create even more variability. On the evidence at hand, the variations do not offset each other. Differences in the *process* of conversion seem, to the contrary, to lead to differences in the *results*. The Christianity that conversion produces in different human communities is complexly diverse.

That fact, however, does not necessarily support the conclusion that conversion to Christianity is whatever an indigenous people make of it. If, taken singly, these ethnographic studies suggest a tremendous latitude in turning an imported religion into a locally useful set of beliefs and practices, these same studies when taken together suggest some constraints on the possible variations and some emergent transcultural patterns. The attempt to identify such patterns is a serious departure from the orthodoxies of contemporary anthropology and of much of contemporary theology. The prevailing view in these disciplines is a radical skepticism about the possibility of Christianity having intellectual content or social consequences that transcend cultural differences. Writings on the subject usually are informed by strong doubts that the ethnographic record can support any unitary phenomenological or sociological account of "conversion" to Christianity.

The contributors to this volume do not offer a decisive break with this pervasive relativism. But, especially in their critical reflections on work by Robin Horton and by Robert Hefner, several of the contributors pursue lines of inquiry that point to a more synthetic and more integrated view of Christian conversion. To be sure, the progress in this direction is tentative. All of the contributors seem to accept without cavil the propositions that, in accounting for religious developments, the local perspective is the primary reality; that religious meaning is to be found first of all in the exegetical accounts of religious participants; and that, in evaluating any claim that a religion has transcended a cultural boundary, the burden of proof remains on those who say it is so, rather than on those who say it is not. In brief, for these essayists "culture" and cultural boundaries retain privileged positions. The novelty—and the importance—of this volume is that those privileges are not absolute. Most of the contributors entertain the possibility that there may indeed be important aspects of conversion to Christianity (and, more generally, to world religions) that are better understood as generalized or generalizable social processes.

The essays by Aram Yengoyan and David Jordan do not share this inquisitiveness. They remain well within the radically relativist perspective that dominates most anthropological discussions of religion. The essays by Donald Pollock and William Merrill step away from that perspective only momentarily and with a very deliberated ambiguity. The remaining five essayists tug more forthrightly against the current, but with a still considerable circumspection.

A reader who is familiar with the general outline of world history but who is a stranger to contemporary academic discussions in anthropology and in theology might have genuine difficulty in figuring out the intellectual orientation of these essays. The views expressed by most of the contributors appear to be at odds not only with the prevailing traditions of church history but also with what many informed readers would see as the plain facts. Christianity, after all, arose as an obscure Jewish sect to become the official religion of the Roman Empire, the dominant faith in nearly all of Europe for close to fifteen hundred years, and the self-declared affiliation of millions of individuals in Asia, Africa, and the Americas. In that light, it is difficult to deny that Christianity has proved capable of overcoming a great variety of cultural barriers and of flourishing in diverse social circumstances.

The nine essays in this volume (and the many other recent works of anthropological scholarship on this subject) do not, despite what may sometimes seem an inclination in that direction, commit this historical solecism. The general point is not that conversions to Christianity have not occurred, nor is it that Christianity is nothing more than an empty container that different peoples proceeding from dissimilar principles have from time to time filled up with their own infusions. Rather, these essays contribute to a fine-tuning of our understanding of how and why Christianity takes hold in some contexts and fails to take hold in others.

To achieve that fine-tuning, the contributors venture some distinctions: not all alleged conversions of communities of Indians, Australians, Africans, or other peoples are of equal *depth*; some conversions are motivated by political or by economic expediency that may or may not be followed by deep intellectual commitment; and in other cases Christianity has, in effect, been outmaneuvered or coopted by local traditions.

These distinctions amount to an important qualification on what might be called the metropolitan view of Christianity. They would seem to add up to an argument that Christianity is not a coherent "world religion" with many different manifestations and local variants, but a congeries of mythic, doctrinal, ritual, epistemological, and sociological elements that have had separate and uneven influences in different cultural contexts.

And this, in turn, is an argument about a fundamental matter. Either Christianity is, as most Christians and many other observers believe it to be, a coherent whole (albeit one that is imperfectly realized in this world), or it is, as these anthropological studies tend to show, a massing of historically and culturally contingent elements (albeit one that frequently aspires to the illusion of internal coherence). To phrase it thus is perhaps to overstate or make too controversial what is really more of an underlying tension between two views.[1] For the most part, scholars of religion and anthropologists ignore one another rather than brace the radically different implications of each other's studies.

Moreover, the issue of whether Christianity is one thing or many touches on other contentious intellectual and cultural matters that are more often alluded to in academic studies than openly discussed. The view that Christianity is some kind of integral whole readily connects with the view that, on balance, Christianity has worked to the moral improvement of our own and other civilizations. In contrast, the view that Christianity is an admixture of elements that readily dissociate outside the special conditions of Western society and culture more easily connects with views that are unsympathetic with both Christianity and Western civilization. There are exceptions to both of these rules of thumb, but the affinities are nonetheless real and affect the way many scholars approach the substantive issues.

In this volume these large but largely unspoken tensions between the metropolitan and the culturally particularist views of Christian conversion are reflected in the contributors' frequent observations of historical ironies. When the authors come to terms with the variables that either encourage or inhibit conversion, they often find the missionaries' suppositions to have been askew. But the missionaries' conceptual failures nonetheless turn out to offer valuable clues to what makes a culture susceptible to Christian conversion.

But the antimetropolitan view of Christianity is balanced in most of these essays by an awareness that Christianity (and other world religions), despite the diversity of its local manifestations, is a means of entry to some kind of "macrocosm." The definition of that word remains elusive. For some of the contributors it suggests access to and participation in global markets and international institutions; for others it is synonymous with any movement toward a more geographically inclusive or regional integration; for some it marks a change in emphasis from a religion focused on local affairs to more encompassing realities; and for others the term conveys a shifting combination of all of these meanings. The lack of precision is perhaps excusable in so exploratory a quest, but it nonethless complicates the task of sorting out the points on which the contributors agree from those on which they only apparently agree.

Robert Hefner's introduction stands by itself as a sophisticated and theoretically informed model of the social processes implicated in conversion to world religions. The nine ethnographic essays touch on some of Hefner's themes, but they also present their own independent stories of transcultural patterns in Christian conversion. It may be useful to recapitulate those stories.

• • •

In Donald Pollock's view, the hallmark of conversion to Christianity among Amazonian Indians is that four hundred years of missionizing have produced so few converts. In his intriguing analysis of this limiting case, he suggests that Amazonian Indians understand perfectly well that Christianity offers them an identity in the macrocosm and a way to increase their participation in Brazilian society; but they have, in effect, preferred their own company. When communities such as the Siriono do convert, they do so in a manner that seems to strengthen "social and conceptual boundaries" and thus implicitly thwart the universalistic burden of the Christian message. In contrast, when (Catholic) missionaries among the Culina get the idea that, instead of attempting to persuade Indians to relinquish their traditional way of life, they will convert the Indians by working within their culture, they proceed with an inaccurate and awkwardly idealized understanding of Culina culture. In Pollock's account the Amazonian Indians retain the conceptual upper hand. They resist conversion, convert, or apostatize as suits their own convenience, which seems to be defined by cultural rewards that the agents of Christianity cannot comprehend and that Christianity itself cannot measure.

This kind of incommensurability appears even more strongly in Aram Yengoyan's account of why the Pitjantjatjara and other Australian Aboriginal communities have not converted. In Yengoyan's view various Pitjantjatjara presuppositions make Christian conversion "a virtual impossibility." Among the presuppositions are the understanding of mythic realities as essentially timeless and instantiated in the physical environment, an ethic that important knowledge is shared among (and only among) similarly situated members of the community, and a discounting of the importance of individuals who act alone. Yengoyan also suggests that so long as the Pitjantjatjara can maintain their social system based on complex marriage rules and so long as they can keep free from an entangling dependence on the cash economy they will continue to adhere to their traditional religion.

As in Pollock's analysis much of the immunity to Christianization seems to be conferred by a mismatch between the highly individuated person posited by Christianity and indigenous alternatives to defining human identity and worth. For the Pitjantjatjara the embedding of the individual in a "complex mesh of cross-cutting groups" seems to leave little room for either the kind of spiritual malaise that Christian doctrine suggests is intrinsic to the human condition or the egocentric search for salvation that it usually attempts to prescribe in an effort to relieve that malaise.

One of Yengoyan's most striking points about Pitjantjatjara indifference to missionizing is his contrast of Aboriginal and Melanesian temporalities. Societies in both areas would appear to be vulnerable to missionaries who appeal to the resentments of uninitiated males and women who are excluded from the religious mysteries controlled by senior men. But Aboriginal societies have withstood this pressure far better than Melanesian societies. Yengoyan, citing the work of Schieffelin, Jorgensen, and Stephen, accounts for this difference by suggesting that the well-known tendency of Melanesian societies to emphasize individual initiative and entrepreneurship provides a practical ground for challenges to traditional religious authority that is further licensed by the cosmological presupposition that the ancestors are still actively involved in shaping the contingencies of contemporary social life.

Where the Pitjantjatjara posit an unchanging dreamtime fixed in supposedly unchanging myths and thus remain relatively unreceptive to theological novelty, many Melanesian societies are predisposed to religious enthusiasms based on innovations that claim to provide more up-to-date arrangements with the suprahuman world. Melanesian cosmologies, in effect, embody a sort of process theology that, in the right circumstances, provides an opening for Christian proselytizing.

John Barker's account of one Melanesian community that seemingly cast its lot with Christianity early in this century provides mixed support for Yengoyan's thesis. The Maisin appear to have mastered Christian ideology and turned Christian (Episcopalian) affiliation to their practical advantage in external relations for several generations. But Barker shows that the results of this enthusiastic conversion are peculiarly contextualized. After seventy years the Uiaku mission station remains both physically and symbolically separate from the village it serves, and most of Maisin life continues to be more deeply informed by traditional Maisin culture than by Christian precepts.

Barker's analysis, however, goes further. He suggests that even though the Christian domain in Maisin culture remains distinct it has provided the Maisin a means to reformulate various aspects of traditional Maisin society. The mission church and school provided a social basis for "wider community unity" than was possible under the previous system of shifting alliances. And Christianity has become the preferred idiom through which the Maisin advocate changes in their own customs, such as the streamlining of the mortuary exchanges proposed by mourners in 1982.

Part of what the Maisin have acquired from Christianity is what Barker calls a "rhetoric of conversion," which really seems a tendency to recast problems and complaints as moral lamentations. Barker says Christianity contrasts with what the Maisin now understand to be their traditional culture in its more explicit set of ideal social relations, the failure to achieve which is perhaps perceived with a heightened sense of frustration and guilt.

If the Maisin conversion to Christianity is ambiguous, at least it has not, according to Barker's analysis, impelled the Maisin to do anything they were not already disposed to. By contrast, the conversions in a village in the Tengger highlands of East Java described by Robert Hefner seem fraught with unintended consequences.

In Hefner's view the Javanese who converted under the tutelage of the missionary Paulus experienced a kind of progressive and irreversible sociocultural change. They turned to Christianity with expectations that it would help them articulate some of their Javanist cultural concerns and legitimate their identity as non-Muslim and non-Hindu conservators of Javanese tradition. But when, after developing deeper knowledge of Christian doctrines, these converts began to see that Christianity was incompatible with many of these concerns, they found the possibility of turning back to have been intellectually and emotionally foreclosed.

Hefner's analysis suggests that beyond a certain level of involvement in Christianity (he implies the same is true of other world religions) cultural horizons are irreversibly altered.

According to this account, conversion to Christianity can proceed successfully even if the converts have only a vague grasp of the symbolic and cosmological content of their new religion. But Hefner also makes it clear that Javanese society in general and historical circumstances in the Tengger highlands in particular supplied a very special set of preconditions quite unlike those of Amazonia, Australia, or New Guinea. The Javanese have had many centuries of experience with religions that make universalistic claims; Christianity has had a Javanese history of being more often withheld than forcefully advocated, and in context therefore remains exotic. Moreover, because it is remembered as a "Dutch" religion, Christianity is associated with exclusive elites, which in turn makes it homologous to traditional Javanist religion, the province of the erstwhile Javanese aristocracy, whose dispossessed members made up an important segment of the nineteenth-century non-Muslim settlers in East Java.

To these factors Hefner adds the tortuous politics of religious competition in Java. Muslim pressure on non-Muslims has virtually eliminated the possibility of communities evolving relaxed and workable syntheses of religious elements from their diverse traditions or, like the Maisin, developing a two-tier model of indigenous and exogenous religious domains. Individuals who lack a strong personal commitment to a single faith recognized by the Indonesian government are under a legal obligation—and considerable practical coercion—to make a public choice of affiliation, regardless of their knowledge of or concern for the intellectual content of their choices. In such circumstances individuals who are predisposed (perhaps by prior involvement in Javanist traditions) to esoteric study and to personal exploration of spiritual matters may, like Paulus's converts, find Christianity an attractive option.

Hefner observes that the cultural knowledge embodied in a complex missionizing faith exceeds the knowledge of the individual participants. To the extent that neophyte converts accept the logic of exploring the faith in its own terms, they find themselves in the midst of ever more elaborate, more philosophically sophisticated, and more intellectually self-justifying religious views. They encounter not only the formal "institutions for the controlled dissemination and defense of knowledge" operating on a world scale but also the radical disproportion between those institutions and their own attempts to comprehend religious truths.

David Jordan's account of Christian conversions among Chinese in Taiwan provides a succinct counterpoint to this theme, for the Chinese converts, coming from a cultural background even richer in the diversity of possible religious affiliations than the Javanese, are strongly disinclined to explore Christianity on its own terms.

Jordan outlines several intellectual mechanisms that together serve as a cultural prophylactic against taking exclusivistic religious claims very seriously or pursuing their epistemological implications very far. In his view Chinese conversions are, first of all, highly provisional. Converts are made and unmade on the basis of the religion's therapeutic performance, ability to confer luck, or other seemingly extrinsic criteria. In Jordan's analysis this kind of provisionality is a symptom of a deeper process in which all basic questions about the validity of religious claims are judged by principles that gain their persuasive force from Chinese history and culture. The "lesser sort of Christian missionary" and the ordinary adherent who discover ad hoc etymologies that purport to show ancient links between China and the Old Testament and the Buddhist monk who rejected Christianity because, unlike Buddhism, it unfairly limited the number of individuals who could aspire to cosmological supremacy are alike in appealing to external, and, from the point of view of Christian doctrine, irrelevant criteria.

In Jordan's view Chinese culture gains further immunity from Christianity's deeper claims by tolerating (and perhaps encouraging) multiple religious affiliations and by a tendency to map initially unfamiliar religious positions onto familiar orthodoxies. In this context, individuals may find it relatively easy to convert in a superficial sense, but they are unlikely to be drawn into or experience a transformation of their "underlying intellectual or emotional system." The shifts in affiliation are nonparadigmatic.

Jordan suggests that "conversion" in this sense of sect swapping (he cites Travisano's term "alternation") and accretion of new religious affinities without relinquishing old ones is part of the popular Chinese religious system. It would appear to be a system as resistant to genuine displacement as that of the Pitjantjatjara, but Jordan offers an important qualification: Chinese culture and the Chinese worldview may be able to absorb and disarm religious challenges, but they are open to far-reaching and deep transformations *outside* the domain of religion.

If Jordan is correct, Chinese society has narrowed the domain of religion (or at least of religious doctrine and worship) to an arena of competing rhetorical claims. The truly ultimate matters, the epistemological and cosmological horizons and the ontological realities of human life, are seemingly situated in cultural certainties to which religious discourse has no access. Jordan is ready to see analogous processes in other parts of the world, including Africa, but Terence Ranger's account of the extralocal context of religious affiliation in central and southern Africa suggests something else.

Ranger argues that many African societies in those regions drew in precolonial times and continue to draw today on two somewhat antagonistic organizing principles. On one hand, African religions can be intensely attentive to the local and internal affairs of the kingdom (or other political unit) and can concentrate to the seeming exclusion of all else on the microcosm of village life. On the other hand, in Ranger's view, these societies are susceptible to religious movements that dramatically cut across political boundaries and that often establish enduring associations among people in widely separate and culturally dissimilar communities. Ranger suggests that to some extent the microcosmic and macrocosmic components in African religion subsist in ordinary circumstances side by side without obvious conflict. Participation in a local ancestor cult need not preclude initiation into a spirit possession cult or attendance at a regional shrine.

But Ranger also argues that the underlying tension between the microcosmic and macrocosmic components can erupt. This disjoining of conceptual forces is in evidence in the historical record of chiefs and kings who attempted to take control of regional cults as well as in the resistance and occasional escape of cults from political control. The principles that inform this conflict are even more evident in the periodic rise of witchcraft eradication movements and prophets who attack the moral backsliding of parochial communities and whose renown and appeal often extend across ethnic and linguistic, as well as political, boundaries.

Ranger hypothesizes that African religion embodies an internal "regular oscillation" between the poles of microcosmic and macrocosmic conceptual focus and between local and panregional organizations. He suggests, moreover, that Christianity has been successfully assimilated to this model. Like the Chinese, and unlike Australian Aborigines, southern and central Africans, by this account, have ready reference points to comprehend the process of acquiring new religious affiliations. But unlike the Chinese model (i.e., "ethnomodel") of conversion, the African model appears to be epistemologically open-ended. It does not treat all religions as functionally equivalent, and it does not reduce religious claims to propositions judged by the degree to which they approximate preestablished axioms. Rather, it seems to treat religious claims as experiential constructions, the validity of which is judged, depending on context, by shifting criteria of coherence and efficacy.

These are perhaps unstable grounds on which to build rigid theological structures. Missionaries in the nineteenth century were relatively successful in attracting initial converts and establishing new congregations. But African Christianity later proved to be doctrinally and administratively volatile, as was evidenced in the rise of native Christian churches, the prominence of prophets offering syncretistic visions of reassembled Christian elements, and the success of anti-Christian movements, such as the Church of the Black Ancestors, that pointedly attack Christian symbols while appropriating other aspects of mission Christianity. It is hard to imagine African Christian converts faced with the situation of the Javanese converts described by Hefner, who felt themselves moved to a point of intellectual involvement that precluded temporizing adjustments or attempts at a religious synthesis more accommodating to exogenous cultural concerns. The cultural preconditions of conversion in this region of Africa favor intellectually deep and existentially far-reaching involvement, but it is an involvement also subject to ongoing revision and sometimes radical reinterpretation.

Ranger's account shows that Christianity in this region has conformed to a traditional pattern whereby diverse and competing religious claims are subject to complex contextualization. In describing the New Guinea Maisin's two-tier manner of contextualizing Christianity and local tradition, Barker refers to some African examples. The similarity is indeed striking, but so is the absence among the Maisin of any significant tendency to elaborate and exploit differences between traditions. The Maisin seem to extend Christian idioms and adapt local customs at relatively low intellectual cost. At least in the broad perspective offered by Ranger, most African societies seem distinctly less inclined than the Maisin to settle once and for all on the terms by which Christianity and local customs will get along.

Yengoyan's suggestion that belief in the continuing creative involvement of the ancestors in social life eased the reception of Christianity in New Guinea might be extended. In African cosmologies the ancestors generally help steer the world back on course. Their participation is active but usually motivated by the need to correct the failings and deviations of the living. The underlying expectation is that, over time, right order will be restored. Melanesian cosmologies, by contrast, are more linear. Even in cargo cults and other prophetic movements, the ideal is not restoration of a past order but the revelation of something vastly better.

The reception of Christianity in Africa and in Melanesia reflects this difference. In Africa, Christianity was taken into a religious domain dominated by an equilibrating concern with contemporary moral failings and by the ongoing search for ways to restore the integrity of the community. Accordingly, African Christianities have been employed like other religious cults and have been modified or dispensed with as suggested by circumstances. In New Guinea, by contrast, Christianity has been characteristically brought into the symbolic realm of outward-looking social contexts connected with a prospective view of opportunities for the community. In these societies the external world is a rich field of opportunities to elaborate both wealth and identity, a symbolic complex that meshes easily with access to the Christian macrocosm.

Charles Keyes's analysis of the factors that have inhibited conversion to Christianity in Thailand emphasizes the Christian missionaries' lack of "authority." He points out that Christian missionaries have always been foreigners purveying what is seen as a foreign religion in competition with state-sponsored Buddhism, which was engaged in missionary activities of its own.

The close association of Buddhism with the Thai national identity would seem to present few conceptual openings for Christianity except among those marginal populations that have little invested in the Thai polity. Keyes cites several factors that contribute to the relative failure of Christianity to appeal to members of these groups. First, the Christian missionaries have generally required converts to abandon religious activities involving non-Christian spirits. Buddhist missionaries, by contrast, offer assurances that adherence to Buddhism and participation in local cults are fully compatible. Second, missionary Buddhist monks display a religious virtuosity more impressive to tribal villagers than the personal qualities of Christian missionaries. Third, the villagers recognize that the Buddhist monks are held in esteem by agents of the state, but Christians are, at best, tolerated and are occasionally the objects of scorn. And, fourth, the doctrine of karma and other components of Buddhist cosmology appear to hold for many Thai intellectual attractions not comprehended by Christian doctrines.

Thai peoples, like the Chinese, appear to have no predisposition against adding to their religious repertoire, so long as the additions do not attempt to claim intellectual exclusivity. Unlike the Chinese, however, Thai appear distinctly reluctant to reconstruct Christianity into a more endogenous form. They may, for the most part, reject the religion, but they seem to respect its intellectual boundaries.

Keyes's account gives little information about the grounds of conversion for the approximately two hundred thousand Thai (0.4 percent of the population) who, in 1980, were in fact professed Christians. But it is clear that the religious domain for the Thai, like that of the Javanese, is closely articulated with issues of historic migration and national identity; and that the endemic model of conversion involves establishing reliable relationships with powerful and authoritative religious agents.

William Merrill's analysis of the Jesuit mission to the Tarahumara in northern Mexico in the seventeenth and eighteenth centuries presents yet another case in which Christian doctrines held little appeal and were generally not absorbed into the native culture—even though that culture was open to other colonial influences. Merrill observes that the Tarahumara quickly appropriated Catholic rituals and religious ceremonies. Even Indians who were not affiliated with the missions (*gentiles*) imitated the paraphernalia of Catholic ritual and "created their own sacraments." But neither imitation of nor participation in Christian rituals appeared to precipitate interest in Christian beliefs.

Like Jordan in his analysis of Chinese conversions, Merrill suggests that the acceptance by many Tarahumara of a formal affiliation with the church (through baptism) ought, in some sense, to count as conversion. Merrill argues, moreover, that the Tarahumara use of Catholic ritual is a transformation of Tarahumara culture conceivably as profound as a more explicitly intellectual conversion might be. For comparative purposes, however, the essential point is that the Jesuit missionaries, though able to engage the Tarahumara in (ostensibly) Catholic ritual and though able to attract many Tarahumara to new settlement patterns and new forms of production, were unable to make Christian doctrines even minimally persuasive.

Among the factors that inhibited intellectual change, according to Merrill, were conflicts between the mission program and other components of the Spanish colonial system. The missions aimed, ideally, at establishing stable, "economically self-sufficient" communities, but they were also expected to supply Indian labor for Spanish plantations, mines, and other enterprises. The missions also competed with other opportunities that were available to Indians in the colonial labor market; and mission attempts to reform Indian customs were countered by settlers who encouraged those customs. The mission conception of a long-term educative process grounded in intergenerational loyalty to stable communities was never realized. In fact, even competent short-term instruction in Christian precepts appears to have been exceptional.

The rigidities of the colonial mission system were not, however, the only obstacles to the successful insinuation of Christian concepts into Tarahumara culture. The Tarahumara were able to incorporate selectively many elements of what the missionaries and other representatives of Spanish colonialism had to offer. Had the Tarahumara a positive reason to investigate the Christian message, they no doubt would have overcome the awkwardnesses in the Jesuit missions' manner of purveying that message. Instead, they remained (and still remain) conspicuously indifferent to that fund of possible meaning.

Merrill suggests some of the grounds of this resistance. The priests were occasionally depicted as sorcerers; conversion "rendered the land sterile"; the missions had already provoked a larger sense of community and "a higher level of community integration" than the Tarahumara had known before, and this in turn created a "new identity" that the missionized Tarahumara (the "baptized") sought to protect from dissolution in the wider colonial system. Merrill also suggests the Catholic teachings were filtered through a "continuingly vital" native "ideology" in which ritual actions "are complete unto themselves and to a large degree intrinsically efficacious."

Such a presupposition about the nature of ritual is indeed a strong barrier to the infiltration of new religious concepts. The possibility of symbolic reinterpretation or the opening up of new cosmological horizons is almost precluded when the realm of native discourse about religion is limited to the calculation of ritual effects. Tarahumara religion appears, in one sense, to be highly open to innovation and to be able to shift rapidly to accommodate external pressures and changes in other domains of Tarahumara society; but, intellectually, it is nearly a closed circuit.

In the case of the Tarahumara, as in several of the other ethnographic cases in this volume, Christian missions were closely associated with Western colonialism. Howard Kee's magisterial summary of the original emergence of the institutionalized Christian church is, among other things, a useful reminder that the missionizing impulse is more than an adaptation of Christianity to the circumstances of the colonial and postcolonial eras. An outward-looking, exocultural orientation is, as Kee shows, one of the distinguishing and sustaining conditions of Christianity from its beginnings in the religious ferment among Jews in first-century Palestine. This cross-cultural orientation was, moreover, aimed not merely at increasing the number of formal adherents or at exporting ritual practices but also at propagating a faith made up of a complex combination of emotional and intellectual claims.

In Kee's account Christianity's attempt to transcend cultural boundaries can be traced to the "crisis of social identity" among Jews in the increasingly secular Maccabean state. Jewish leaders who remained committed to the scriptural tradition of Jews as a covenanted people with a divinely ordained historical purpose sought ways to resist the growing cultural and religious assimilation of the Jewish people to Greco-Roman culture. Some sought a politically autonomous Jewish state; others, such as the Sadducees, sought to reemphasize the importance of the temple and of priestly Judaism; others, such as the Essenes, propounded a millenarian faith that looked forward to the establishment of strict boundaries and exclusive membership in a purified theocratic regime; and others, such as the Pharisees, turned toward voluntary community gatherings for the study of sacred texts and the elaboration of pietistic regimens.

The "Jesus movement," as Kee calls it, was conditioned by these alternative ways of rehistoricizing the Jewish people. It shared some of their themes, borrowed some of their innovations, and emphatically rejected other features. Like the nationalists and the Essenes, the Jesus movement drew on Jewish prophetic tradition. Like the Essenes, the early Christians created a key ritual involving "a meal of bread and wine." Like the Pharisees, they evolved a form of worship centered on a private gathering of adherents. But in sharp contrast to all of these attempts to reformulate Judaism, the Jesus movement appears to have broken decisively with traditional barriers to religious participation and with the conception of the proper boundaries of the community of the faithful. The movement welcomed outsiders and "socially, physically, and ritually marginal types," and it set aside "the basic patriarchal, hereditary structure of social identity in the Jewish tradition."

In its earliest stages the Jesus movement expected an imminent end to the existing world order. Participants, therefore, attempted to propagate their message as quickly and over as wide an area as they could and did not attempt to institutionalize their arrangements. Kee notes that one aspect of this initial fluidity was a procedurally unconstrained approach to spreading the faith. Kee cites, for example, Paul's instructions (1 Cor 9:19–23) to the effect that he adopts the approach most appropriate for the local situation.

The church that succeeded these early developments inevitably became more systematized and rule bound. The contrasts with other Jewish movements hardened into doctrinaire controversy with the Pharisaic community, and the intuitions about prophetic tradition became more elaborate and fixed as scriptural interpretations. The ideal of a community founded on the abolition of human difference in profound commonality gave way to more durable arrangements.

Yet despite these developments, Christianity retained its sense of itself as a faith of universal validity founded on truths that are accessible and of urgent value to people everywhere. An important part of the meaning of Christianity has, for most of its history, been in its insistence on the applicability of its spiritual message to all peoples. It is a faith that is intellectually adapted by its own teleology to the attempt to win converts in diverse cultural contexts.

Its success in some cases and failure in others should not, on the evidence in this book, be understood simply as an issue of whether a culture was predisposed to find Christianity compatible with or adaptable to preexisting standards. Such barriers are, to some extent, comprehended in Christianity's deeper message, so that there is at least the possibility that local standards will be modified in the encounter to the degree that a still more radical transformation may ensue. In this sense the ability of Christianity to realize its missionary aim may depend as much on its indifference (and self-proclaimed superiority) to certain aspects of culture as on its attentiveness to others.

• • •

The process of conversion in all times and places involves both epistemological and pragmatic challenges to the existing cultural order. Christian belief makes little or no headway in circumstances, such as appear to be widespread among Amazonian and some Mexican Indians and among Australian Aborigines, where the universe is conceived as fundamentally fixed. The native religions in such cultures emphasize conceptual and ritual congruity. They tend to treat discrepancies in the cosmically validated ideal patterns as problems to be overcome ritually. And, from a point of view conditioned by such religions, religious theories that postulate and attempt to build on human dissatisfactions, such as those that lie close to the heart of Christianity, appear beside the point.

Christian belief may find a considerably greater degree of acceptance where there are vigorous traditions that encompass the addition to or alteration of religious affiliation, such as appear to be common in China and Africa. These traditions themselves, however, may pose an intellectually complex and sometimes sophisticated obstacle to a deeper comprehension of Christian teachings. A conversion tradition like that described by Jordan for Chinese in Taiwan greatly reduces the exogenous content of new religious messages by translating them into familiar and frequently banal terms. A conversion process such as Ranger hypothesizes for large parts of sub-Saharan Africa is more capable of absorbing new religious content, but it is also disposed to rearrange and reformulate that content with little regard for its claim to ultimacy.

In all these situations the possibilities of conversion are tempered by people's concepts of religious knowledge—whether such knowledge is or should be open to critical reflection; whether it is experienced as pervading life or is, alternatively, mostly contextualized; and whether it is a repository of timeless realities, or a conditional stage of understanding. None of these cultural variations in epistemological predispositions can *preclude* the possibility of conversion to Christianity, but they can militate against conversion, at least conversion in the sense of informed conviction of the validity of Christian teachings.

Conversion can, of course, mean other things. Affiliation to a Christian church, an explicit claim to Christian identity, or merely a borrowing of religious elements associated with Christian tradition can be construed as indices of conversion. The Christian missions conducted during periods of colonial rule and the continuing association of Christianity with Western goods, with the "macrocosm" of the world economy, and, to a lesser extent, with Western culture provide Christianity with surplus but very powerful meanings. Peoples in many parts of the world who encounter Christian missions do not have particularly clear grounds to disentangle the underlying religious message from these other symbolic implications, and they may, like the Maisin in New Guinea, be motivated to "convert" as much by the contextual accretions to the Christian message as by the message itself.

In all actual circumstances the epistemological and the pragmatic considerations are virtually inseparable. The social situations in which conversion is presented as an opportunity (or a threat) force a response conditioned partly by people's religious assumptions and partly by their calculations of what good or harm might come from the choices at hand. In some cases factors such as Pitjantjatjara cosmology or Thai national identity may appear to make the process relatively one-sided, but an enlarged analysis restores the complexity. As Yengoyan notes, some Australian Aboriginal individuals and some tribes have converted in response to "economic need or social deprivation or both." And as Keyes notes, the Thai perception of Christianity as a "foreign" religion has not prevented several hundred thousand Thai from becoming Christians. The epistemological interplay between Christianity and other religions and the practical adjustments between local traditions and the world system with which Christianity is linked make up a fundamental complexity that cannot be resolved into either a purely intellectualist account or an account focusing on Western hegemony and native resistance.

Christianity remains an intellectual horizon that may make the human macrocosm more visible and more accessible to people who seek to join it. But it is not only an intellectual horizon. It is also a religion with a substantive content, the espousal of which genuinely and frequently disrupts and transforms peoples' lives.

One influential strain of contemporary theology (see, for example, Shorter 1988) argues that Christianity has no legitimate meaning apart from the cultural forms in which it is always embedded and that the church should recognize, learn from, and celebrate this cultural multiplicity. "Inculturation" theology, whatever else may be said about its claims, appears to misconstrue the ethnographic realities. The instances of Christian conversion (and nonconversion) presented in this volume are evidence of an intellectually and socially complex process in which contemporary people in non-Western societies are struggling with new religious possibilities. Their cultural identities and their traditions affect that struggle but are not the whole of it. If Christianity has any single meaning in this welter of cultural contexts, it lies in the promise of a truth that transcends them all.

NOTES

1. A more explicit controversy arises from the recent tendency by many mainstream Protestant churches and by important segments of the Catholic church to morally condemn the motives, the process, and the outcome of the whole missionary enterprise in Christianity. The National Council of Churches, for example, issued a statement in May 1990, *A Faithful Response to the 500th Anniversary of the Arrival of Christopher Columbus*, which attacks the "complicities" of Christian missionaries in "forcing conversion to European forms of Christianity," and in participating in "the desecration of religious sites, and other crimes against the spirituality of indigenous peoples." An editorial in the journal *First Things* (October 1990) responded to the NCC, saying that "as a historical generalization," its statement is "quite inaccurate," and that "despite the sin that mars every human endeavor, the history of the West in the New World has been, on balance, one of achievement and blessing for humankind."

Castigation and ideological abandonment of what has been, until recently, a central focus of Christian commitment has divided the broader Christian community. The missions sent out by many churches persist in seeking conversions, but others seek "dialogue" with native traditions or reformulation of their own doctrines. The moral charges and countercharges in this debate heighten the significance—and deepen the pitfalls—of the attempt to engage in objective, anthropological study of Christian conversion.

REFERENCES

National Council of Churches of Christ in the USA. 1990. *A Faithful Response to the 500th Anniversary of the Arrival of Christopher Columbus: As Adopted by the Governing Board, May 17, 1990; A Resolution of the National Council of the Churches of Christ in the USA*. New York: NCC News Services.

"Repenting of America, 1492–1992." 1990. *First Things* 1(6):5–7.

Shorter, Aylward. 1988. *Toward a Theology of Inculturation*. New York: Orbis Books.

INDEX

Compositor: Asco Trade Typesetting, Ltd.
Text: 10/12 Baskerville
Display: Baskerville
Printer and Binder: Edwards Bros., Inc.